THIS DOCUMENT IS THE PROPERTY OF HER BRITANNIC MAJESTY'S GOVERNMENT, and is issued for the information of such persons only as need to know its contents in the course of their official duties. Any person finding this document should hand it to a British forces unit or to a police station for its safe return to the MINISTRY OF DEFENCE, HQ Security, London SW1A 2HB, with particulars of how and where found. THE UNAUTHORISED RETENTION OR DESTRUCTION OF THE DOCUMENT IS AN OFFENCE UNDER THE OFFICIAL SECRETS ACTS OF 1911-1939 (When released to persons outside Government service, this document is issued on a personal basis and the recipient to whom it is entrusted in confidence, within the provisions of the Official Secrets Acts 1911-1939, is personally responsible for its safe custody and for seeing that its contents are disclosed only to authorised persons.)

PE(Sy) Form 14

THE SECOND WORLD WAR
1939—1945
ARMY

ARMY RADAR

COMPILED BY
BRIGADIER A. P. SAYER
C.B., D.S.O. (LATE R.E.)

RESTRICTED
The information given in this document is not to be communicated, either directly or indirectly, to the Press or to any person not authorized to receive it.

The Naval & Military Press Ltd

THE WAR OFFICE
1950

Published by

The Naval & Military Press Ltd
Unit 5 Riverside
Bellbrook Industrial Estate
Uckfield, East Sussex
TN22 1QQ England

Tel: +44 (0) 1825 749494
www.naval-military-press.com

Cover image: WAAF radar operator Denise Miley plotting aircraft on the cathode ray tube of an RF7 Receiver in the Receiver Room at Bawdse Chain Home radar station.

In reprinting in facsimile from the original, any imperfections are inevitably reproduced and the quality may fall short of modern type and cartographic standards.

FOREWORD

This book is one of a series of volumes, compiled by authority of the Army Council, the object of which is to preserve the experience gained during the Second World War, 1939–1945, in selected fields of military staff work and administration. The author has been given access to official sources of information, and every endeavour has been made to ensure the accuracy of the work as an historical record. Any views expressed and conclusions drawn are those of the author, and do not necessarily reflect those of the Army Council, which, so far as they relate to current training, are to be found in the official manuals, training memoranda, etc., issued from time to time by the War Office.

For the operational background, the reader is referred to the Official History of the War.

THE WAR OFFICE
February 1950.

CONTENTS

		PAGE
	ABBREVIATIONS	vi
	SYNOPSIS OF CHAPTERS	x
	GLOSSARY OF RADAR TECHNICAL TERMS . .	xvii
PART I.	INTRODUCTION TO RADAR	1
PART II.	ANTI-AIRCRAFT APPLICATIONS	39
PART III.	COASTAL DEFENCE RADAR	116
PART IV.	MISCELLANEOUS APPLICATIONS	159
PART V.	WAR OFFICE RADAR RESPONSIBILITIES . . .	188
PART VI.	THE MINISTRY OF SUPPLY	243
PART VII.	GENERAL COMMENTARY	272

APPENDICES

		PAGE
I.	Detail of W.D. Scientific and Technical Staff engaged on initial investigation and experiments.	299
II.	Note on early proposal by Butement and Pollard, of nature of Radar	301
III.	War Office Radar Staff	305
IV.	Samples of Specifications for Army Radar Equipment . . .	306
V.	Table of Major Equipment Provision.	318
VI.	Graph of Policy and Provision	322
VII.	ILLUSTRATIONS	323
	1. G.L. II—A.A. No. 1 Mark II—Receiver Unit . .	323
	2. G.L. III—A.A. No. 3 Mark II—Aerials . . .	324

3.	G.L. III—Operators in Action inside Cabin	325
4.	G.L. III—Range Tubes	326
5.	G.L. Auto—A.A. No. 3 Mark IV	327
6.	1½ m. S.L.C.—A.A. No. 2	328
7.	10 cm. Auto S.L.C.—A.A. No. 2 Mark VIII	329
8.	1½ m. Light Warning—A.A. No. 4	330
9.	Gorgonzola—10 cm. set—A.A. No. 4 Mark V	331
10.	Coastal Artillery Fire Direction—C.A. No. 1	332
11.	C.A. No. 1 Mark III on Tower	333
12.	C.A. No. 1—Internal	334
13.	L.A.A., G.R. set—A.A. No. 6	335
14.	P.P.I. Display	336
15.	Type A Display	337
16.	Echo Matching	338
17.	Window.	341

VIII. FIGURES 342

1.	Simple Wave Form	342
2.	Pulsed Transmissions	343
3.	Single Pulse Presentation	344
4.	C.R.T. Presentation Picture with Spiral (and Expanding) Time Base	345
5.	C.R.T. Presentation of Plan Position Indicator (P.P.I.) of which the Time Base is radial and rotates continuously	346
6.	Gridded Presentation of C.A. Fall of Shot	347
7.	Gridded Presentation for Field Artillery Use	348
8.	Diagram of an imaginary Strip of transmission showing the wave meeting a rotatable Aerial Frame with two vertical dipoles	349
9.	C.R.T. Range or Selector Tube Picture of Jamming	350
10.	An example of S.L.C. Selector Tube Picture of Jamming	351

IX. PLATE 352

    South Eastern Coastal Radar Chain 352

ABBREVIATIONS

A.4 and A.5.	Technical Artillery Branches concerned with Radar (M. of S.).
A.A.	Anti-Aircraft and class of Radar sets.
A.A.1.	Branch concerned with Radar (W.O.).
A.A. Command. } A.A.Cd. }	Anti-Aircraft Command.
A.A.S/L.	Anti-Aircraft Searchlight.
A.C.A.S.	Assistant Chief of Air Staff (A.M.).
A.D.E.E.	Air Defence Experimental Establishment.
A.D.G.B.	Air Defence of Great Britain.
A.D.R.D.E.	Air Defence Research and Development Establishment.
A.D.R.P.	Assistant Director Radio Production, attchd. to M.A.P.
A.F.	Auto-follow.
A.F.1.	Army Auto-follow experimental model.
A.I.	Air Interception (R.A.F.).
A.I.D.	Air Inspection Department (M.A.P.).
A.I.X.	Air Interception set (centimetric wave-length).
A/J.	Anti-Jamming.
A.M.	Air Ministry.
A.M.E.S.	R.A.F. Type Radar followed by the type number.
A.M.R.E.	Air Ministry Research Establishment—Bawdsey.
A.O.R.G.	Army Operational Research Group.
A.P.F.	Accurate Position Finder (Canadian).
A.S.E.	Admiralty Signals Establishment.
A.S.V.	Air Detection of Surface Vessel (R.N. and R.A.F.).
B.A.S.	British Army Staff, Washington.
B.J.C.B.	British Joint Communications Board—Technical link to United States.
Brig. H.D.	Special appointment for Home Defence (W.O.).
B.R.S.	Bawdsey Research Station (A.M.)
B.S.M.	British Supply Mission, Washington.
B.X. } B.Z. }	Station of Experimental C.A. sets at Dover.
C.A.	Coast Artillery, and class of Radar sets.
C.A.E.E.	Coast and Anti-Aircraft Experimental Establishment.
C.A.S.	Coast Artillery School.
C.A.T.C.	Coast Artillery Training Centre.
C.A.T.E.	Coast Artillery Training Establishment.
C.C.B.	Combined Communications Board, Washington.
C.D.	Coast Defence, and class of Radar Sets.
C.D./C.H.L.	Coast Defence and Low Flying Chain (Army type).
C.D.U.	Coast Defence U boat detection (Army/Navy).
C.G.M.P.	Controller General of Munitions Production (M. of S.).
C.G.R.S.D.	Controller General of Research and Scientific Development (M. of S.).
C.H.	Chain Home (R.A.F.).
C.H.L.	Chain Home Low (R.A.F.).
C.I.E.M.E.	Chief Inspector of Electrical and Mechanical Equipment.
C.I.E.S.E.	Chief Inspector of Engineer and Signal Stores.

C.I.G.S.	Chief of Imperial General Staff.
V.C.I.G.S.	Vice Chief of Imperial General Staff.
D.C.I.G.S.	Deputy Chief of Imperial General Staff. For Technical Policy and Organization.
A.C.I.G.S.	Assistant Chief of Imperial General Staff.
C.O.D.	R.A. Coast Observer Detachment.
C.O.L.	Chain Overseas Low (R.A.F.).
C.P.R.	Controller of Physical Research—ex-D.D.S.R. (M. of S.).
C.P.R.S.D.	C.P.R. and Scientific Development—ex-C.P.R. (M. of S.).
C.R.	Cathode Ray.
C.R.T.	Cathode Ray Tube.
D.A.A. and C.D.	Director of Anti-Aircraft and Coast Defence (W.O.).
D.D.A.A. and C.D.	Deputy Director of Anti-Aircraft and Coast Defence (W.O.).
D.C.D.	Director Communication Development (A.M.).
D.D. of A.	Deputy to D.G. of A. (M. of S.).
D.D.G.S.E.	Deputy Director General of Signals Equipment (M. of S.).
D.D.S.E.	Deputy Director of Signals Equipment (Production) (M. of S.).
D.D.S.R.D.	Deputy to C.P.R.S.D. (M. of S.).
D.E.S.E.	Director of Engineer and Signals Equipment (M. of S.).
D.F.	Direction Finding.
D.F.W.	Director of Fortifications and Works (W.O.).
D.G.A.R.	Director General of Army Requirements (W.O.).
D.G.Mech.E.	Director General of Mechanical Engineering (M. of S.).
D.G.M.P.	Director General of Munitions Production (W.O.).
D.G. of A.	Director General of Artillery (M. of S.).
D.G.S.R.D.	Director General of Scientific Research and Development (M. of S.).
D.M.E.	Director of Mechanical Engineering (W.O.).
D.M.G.O.	Deputy Master General of Ordnance (W.O.).
D.M.O. and I.	Director of Military Operations and Intelligence (W.O.).
D.M.T.	Director of Military Training (W.O.).
D.D.M.T.	Deputy Director of Military Training (W.O.).
D. of A.	Director of Artillery (M. of S.) (ex-W.O.).
D. of M.	Director of Mechanization.
D.D. of M.	Deputy Director of Mechanization (M. of S.) (ex-W.O.).
D.O.S.	Director of Ordnance Services (W.O.).
D.R.A.	Director Royal Artillery (W.O.).
D. Radar	Director of Radar (W.O.).
D.R.P.	Director of Radio Production (M.A.P.).
D.S.D.	{ Director of Staff Duties (W.O.). { Director Signals Division (Admiralty).
D.D.S.D.	Deputy Director of Staff Duties (W.O.).
D.S.E.	Director of Signals Equipment (M. of S.).
D.Sigs.	Director of Signals (W.O.).
D.Sigs.E.	Director of Signals Equipment (ex-D.E.S.E.) (M. of S.).
D.S.I.R.	Department of Scientific and Industrial Research.
D.S.R.	Director of Scientific Research (M. of S.) (ex-W.O.).
D.D.S.R.	Deputy Director of Scientific Research (M. of S.) (ex-W.O.).
D.S.R.D.	Director of Scientific Research and Development (ex-D.D) (M. of S.).
D.D.S.R.D.	Deputy Director of Scientific Research and Development (M. of S.).
D.W.S.	Director of Warlike Stores (W.O.).
E.B.E.	Experimental Bridging Establishment.
E./F.	Elevation Finding.

E.F.C.	Electrician Fire Control (R.A.)
E.S. 3 a 3 (T).	Radar Production and Technical Development Branches (M. of S.).
F.A.	Field Artillery and class of Radar sets.
F.C.	{ Fire Commander in Coast Artillery. { Fire Control in A.A. Artillery.
G.C.I.	Ground Control Interception (R.A.F.)
G.D.A.	Gun Defended Area (A.A.).
G.L.	A.A. Gun Laying Set, followed by type number.
G.O.R.	Gun Operations Room for A.A.
G.R.	Gun Range only (Army)
G.S.	General Staff (W.O.).
g.	Force of Gravity.
H.A.A.	Heavy Anti-Aircraft Artillery.
H_2S.	Bombing Target Recognition (R.A.F.).
I.E.M.E.	Inspector Electrical and Mechanical Equipment.
I.E.S.S.	Inspector of Engineer and Signals Stores.
I.F.C.	Instructor, Fire Control, R.A.
I.F.F.	Identification of Friend from Foe.
Light A.A. L.A.A.	} Light Anti-Aircraft Artillery.
L.W.	Light Warning Equipment.
M.A.P.	Ministry of Aircraft Production.
M.B.	Mobile Base.
M.C. of S.	Military College of Science.
M.G.O.	Master General of Ordnance (W.O.).
M.G.O. 11 and 13	Engineer and Signals Equipment Branches (W.O.).
M.G.O. 14.	Artillery Branch concerned with Fire Control (W.O.).
M.O. 2 and 3	Branches concerned with A.A. and C.D. (W.O.).
M. of S.	Ministry of Supply (often referred to as The Ministry).
M.R.	Medium Range.
M.R.U.	Mobile Radio Unit (R.A.F.).
M.Z.P.I.	Microwave Zone Position Indicator (Canadian).
N.T.	Naval Type Radar, followed by the type number.
O.P.T.E.C.	Operational and Technical Committee, Radio Board.
O.R.G.	Operational Research Group.
P.O.	Post Office.
P.P.I.	Plan Position Indicator.
P.P.P.Ctee.	Production Planning and Personnel Committee, Radio Board.
R.A. 2.	Branch concerned with Radar—ex A.A.I. (War Office).
R. and D.	Research and Development.
R.A.T.E.	Royal Artillery Training Establishment.
R.D.F.	Range and Direction Finding (now Radar).
R.E. and S. Bd.	Royal Engineer and Signals Board.
R.M.O.	Radio Maintenance Officer (Army).
R.O.C.	Royal Observer Corps (Under Air Ministry).
R.P.E.	Radio Production Executive.
R.P.U.	Radio Production Unit.

R.R.D.E.	Radar Research and Development Establishment; Ex-A.D.R.D.E.—often referred to as the Establishment.
S.A.A.A.	School of Anti-Aircraft Artillery.
SA/AC.	Scientific Adviser to Army Council (W.O.).
S.A.A.D.	School of Anti-Aircraft Defence.
S.A.C.	Scientific Advisory Council (M. of S.).
S.A.T.	Scientific Adviser on Telecommunications (A.M.).
S.E.A.C.	South-East Asia Command.
S.E.E.	Signals Experimental Establishment.
Sh.D.	Ship Detection Radar set (Australian).
S.L.C.	Searchlight Control Radar.
S.M.A.	Senior Military Adviser. Ex-D.M.G.O. (M. of S.).
S. of A.	School of Artillery.
S.R.D.E.	Signals Research and Development Establishment, ex-S.E.E.
S.R. 11	Scientific Research Branch for Radar (M. of S.).
S.T.C.O.	Senior Telecommunication Co-ordinating Officer (M. of S.).
T. and R.	Transmitting and Receiving.
T.C.O.	Tactical Control Officer (on A.A. Gun Position).
T.I.F.C.	Technical Instructor in Fire Control, R.A.
T.I.S.C.	Treasury Inter-Service Committee.
T.O.	Training and Operations Directorate in War Office later replaced by M.T.
T.R.E.	Telecommunications Research Establishment (M.A.P.).
U.N.B.	United Nations Beaconry.
U.H.F.	Ultra High Frequency.
V.H.F.	Very High Frequency.
W.D.	War Department.
W.O.	War Office.
W.S.	Ordnance Supply Branches (W.O.). Warlike Stores (Army).
W.S.W.	War Special Wireless Course.
W.T.S.F.F.	Weapons Technical Staff Field Force (Wheatsheaf).
Z.P.I.	Zone Position Indicator (Canadian).

RADIO FIRMS REFERRED TO IN THE TEXT

British Thompson Houston—B.T.H.
A. C. Cossor.
Metropolitan-Vickers—Metro-Vick.
Pye Radio.
General Electric—G.E.C.
Electrical and Musical Industries—E.M.I.

SYNOPSIS OF CHAPTERS

PART I
INTRODUCTION TO RADAR

CHAPTER I. RADAR 1
    Radar in general—Meaning of Radar and earlier titles—Achievements and uses—What it is and how it works—Origin.

CHAPTER II. PRE-RADAR ARMY DEFENCE MEASURES . . 7
    Long-range detection—R.E. and S. Board—Acoustic methods—Direct gun action based on Visual methods—Searchlights and Sound Locators—Fixed Azimuth—Coastal Artillery action dependent on visual methods—Existing W.D. Scientific staff investigate application of Radar to Army purposes.

CHAPTER III. CONTROL OF ARMY RADAR DEVELOPMENT . 12
    Primary aims—H.A.A. fire control—W.O. A.A. Standing Committee—R.D.F. (W.O.) Committee—Inter-Service Committee on R.D.F.—R.D.F. (Radar) Board—Low Cover Sub-Committee—R.D.F. (Radio) Policy Sub-Committee—Radio Board—R.P.E.—Radar links with U.S.A.—D.S.R.—Division of responsibility between W.O. and M. of S.—S.A.C.'s R.D.F. Applications Committee.

CHAPTER IV. INTRODUCTION TO ARMY RADAR 20
    First proposal—P.O. Research establishment—Tizard Committee—Radio Research Board's investigations—R.E.S. Board contact Watson-Watt—Report possible Army developments—W.D. Scientist attached Bawdsey establishment—Report result of investigations—Formation of Army cell at Bawdsey.

CHAPTER V. THE PERIOD OF INITIAL EXPERIMENT . . . 27
    Development of Medium-Range Warning equipment—Research and experiments on accurate short-range working—H.A.A. fire control and Searchlight direction—Need for G.S. guidance and priority requirements—H.A.A. fire control problems—Young's estimate of performance needed—Proposals to associate with Acoustic appliances—Progress Report, 1937—Proposal for ultra-short wave-length working—Forecast of future form—Application to C.D.—Trials progress in 1938—First complete specification by G.S.—Army Radar equipment needs approved by Treasury with Air Ministry needs—Treasury approval to new Army Development establishment.

CHAPTER VI. COMMENTARY 36

PART II
ANTI-AIRCRAFT APPLICATIONS

CHAPTER VII. ARMY A.A. RADAR 39
    Medium-Range Warning—H.A.A. fire control accuracy problems—Enemy Aircraft performance and tactics—Effects on Radar design—Other Radar Aids.

CHAPTER VIII. H.A.A. ARTILLERY RADAR—EARLY TYPES . . . 45

Experimental G.L. set—Delay in Elevation finding method—Continuous following in Bearing—Decision to produce G.L.I. as aid to Visual methods—Modifications and addition of E/F attachment—Start of Instructors' training—Operational effect—Progress on G.L. II for full fire control—Continuous following method for angular measurement—Improved elevation finding—Approved for production—Operational effect—Excellent design—Performance.

CHAPTER IX. H.A.A. ARTILLERY RADAR—CENTRIMETRIC TYPES . 56

Use of centimetric wave-lengths—New Magnetron produces remarkable advance—Revolution in technique and design—Full details given to U.S.A.—Nov. 1940, W.O. outline specification for set on 10 cm. wave-length—Experimental models demonstrated early summer 1941—G.L. III models available for trials at end of 1941—Slow proof of prototypes—Supply starts end of 1942—Form of G.L. III—Performance—Operational effect assessed. Canadian pattern—Unripe design—Lack of technical information—Insufficient co-operation—Z.P.I. inadequate—A.P.F. good—Different manual operation method—Delayed deliveries—Valuable equipment—Performance.

CHAPTER X. H.A.A. AUTOMATIC RADAR 68

Advances in technique—Reduction in mass of moving parts—Common T and R—Narrow beams—Experimental conversion of G.L. III to Auto—Improved smoothness of rates—Capacity for dealing with higher rates without loss of accuracy—Complete Auto-follow *v.* Auto-error correction—U.S. in advance of U.K.—S.C.R. 545 and 584—New design A.F.I. lightweight set—Development for G.L. IV and VII—High Performance—Delay in production—Attempted modification of G.L. III, both types—Auto-follow Radar *v.* Flying Bombs—Effect in use with electric predictors—Radar to shell burst as complete operational chain.

CHAPTER XI. ANTI-AIRCRAFT SEARCHLIGHT RADAR 78

Sound Locators defeated by high-speed targets and low-grade operators—Rush demand for Radar control—Immature design—Effective aid to night interception—Improvements—Large-scale production—Diversion to A.A. fire control for special sites—Maggie and Baby Maggie—Development of accurate range unit—Diversion to special light fire control set for Landing operations—Emergency use only—Centimetric type development—Development to Auto-follow—Improved discrimination and performance—Crash production of Mk. VIII—Main production of Mk. IX to follow—Operational effect.

CHAPTER XII. ANTI-AIRCRAFT AUXILIARY RADAR 92

Local gun-site warning—Early types combined warning with fire control—Higher speeds increase warning range—Later accurate fire control sets required separate means of warning—Auto-follow sets with auto-search and scan for warning—Separate Light Warning set—Inter-Service design—Limitation on performance and liability to Window—Special emergency provision of centimetric type—Gorgonzola—Improved range and discrimination—Limited supply—Good performance—M.Z.P.I.—U.S. types—Tactical Control—A.A. Command use of adapted G.C.I.—Canadian Z.P.I.—Need for large-scale displays—Remote displays—Area control—Intermediate and Light A.A.—Range only—Weapon could not justify individual Radar set—Emergency expedients—Anti Flying-bomb operations.

CHAPTER XIII. RADIO PROXIMITY FUZE 104
    Completion of H.A.A. chain of operation—Doppler effect—Delayed U.K. development—U.K. production failure—U.S. provision—Security aspect—Release for operational use by stages—Over land difficulty of self-destruction—H.A.A. use against Flying Bombs—Effect—F.A. use against ground targets—Effective air bursts.

CHAPTER XIV. COMMENTARY 111

PART III
COASTAL DEFENCE RADAR

CHAPTER XV. 1½ METRE COAST DEFENCE RADAR 116
    C.D. distinct from C.A.—Initial trials in May 1939—Early summer gives special results—Abnormal ranges—Detection of low flying aircraft—Observation of shell splashes—Butements Spiral Time base—Coastal watching and tracking shipping—Sept. 1938 Anti-Submarine trials—Cockcroft's party in Fair Isle and Shetlands—Improvised sets for R.N.—Low air cover sets for R.A.F.—Use as embryo of G.C.I.—Planning Anti-Invasion chain—Cover against small craft along S.-E. Coast—Gaps in cover—Duplication with R.A.F. low-flying cover.

CHAPTER XVI. CENTIMETRIC COAST DEFENCE RADAR . . . 126
    Introduction of N.T.271 centimetric type—Modification for shore use—Extension of effective cover—Protection of coastal convoys—Extension of chain along East and South coasts—Plotting and control—Liaison with Naval Authorities—Emergency provision for Gibraltar and Alexandria—Employment during escape of German heavy ships up Channel—E-boat Alley and low coastline difficulties—Tower stations—Transfer of responsibility of all C.D. stations to R.A.F.

CHAPTER XVII. COAST ARTILLERY RADAR 135
    C.A. set developed from 1½ m. C.D. type—Refinements for accurate range and bearing measurements—First model available early 1941—C.A.E.E. and C.A.S. trials—Advent of N.T.271 permitted conversion to centimetric working—Modification of design in production—1½ m. type cancelled—Pilot and Training models available early summer 1942—Experimental model installed at Dover for operational trials and use—Standard installations and special cases—Fire Direction duties—Fire Command Radar—Warning and tactical control—Original C.D. type installed—Replaced by 10 cm. as C.A. No. 2 equipment—Similar to centimetric C.D. types—Installed in or adjacent to Fire Command Post—Increased to Medium power—Addition of expanded range unit—Performance and Fall-of-Shot observation—Experimental development of 3 cm. set for accurate observation of Fall of Shot—Gridded display—Experimental model in operational use at Dover—Marked improvement—Additional sets built by R.R.D.E.—Employed operationally as complete Fire control and Fire correction sets—Special use in Normandy invasion—Development of special form for man-portage and air transport—Provision for S.E.A.C.—Need lapsed—Diversion for Naval use—Experimental trials for F.A. use against ground targets.

CHAPTER XVIII. RADAR EFFECT ON C.A. OPERATIONS . . . 145
    Advances in Radar reflected in operations—Extracts from Operational reports—Comments and assessments of value of Radar by Operational, Training and Scientific authorities.

CHAPTER XIX. COMMENTARY 155

PART IV

MISCELLANEOUS APPLICATIONS

CHAPTER XX. IDENTIFICATION 159

Essential need for long range—Positive identification of enemy craft impossible—Negative method by recognition of friendly craft—Essential features—Automatic response on interrogation—Security to prevent enemy simulation—Uniformity and universal use—Five development stages—Increasing security and improved performance and facilities—Separate wave-band—Coded responses—Different wave-lengths for Interrogation and for Response—Homing Beacon facilities.

CHAPTER XXI. INTERFERENCE 166

Natural causes—Clutter, birds, abnormal ranges, atmospheric—Different causes affect different wave-lengths—Stray transmissions—Screening of local echoes—Deliberate electrical jamming—Ground based and Air-borne—A./J. measures—Palliatives to reduce effects—Set design to provide reduced susceptibility—Narrow beam and High power—Character of different types of jamming—Very high power needed for jamming off beam—Jamming locator—Wave-length and pulse rate changes—Design of receiver—Form of display—Mutual interference—Frequency separation—Window—False reflection surfaces—Cluttering of display to cover target echoes—Minimum effort for optimum effect—Size and density of infection of area for effect—Excessive number of types of equipment about same frequency—Serious menace.

CHAPTER XXII. MINOR APPLICATIONS 174

Special Reflectors—Meteor determination—Survey uses—Injected signals—Trajectory tracking—V2 rockets—Observation of Shell bursts—Location of ground targets.

CHAPTER XXIII. FIELD ARMY APPLICATIONS 179

Use of 3 cm. C.A. set against ground targets—Clutter reduction and discrimination—Observation of ground shell bursts and air bursts—Detection of movement—Doppler effect—Warning not location—Trajectory tracking—Mortar bombs for location of mortar sites. All late in development—Delayed in production—Loss of practical experience of use against enemy.

CHAPTER XXIV. COMMENTARY 186

PART V

WAR OFFICE RADAR RESPONSIBILITIES

CHAPTER XXV. RADAR RELATIONS 188

Aids to and from the Dominions—Radar links with U.S.A.—Supply of Radar to U.S.S.R.—No reciprocation—Other belligerent allies and non-combatants.

CHAPTER XXVI. ARMY RADAR POLICY 193

G.S. responsibility for Policy and general direction of development of Radar—M. of S. responsible for advice, experiment and development—Early stage of Acceptance by G.S.—1941 saw start of G.S. Direction stage—Policy background—G.S. Policy Statements—Influence of limited production capacity—I.F.F. policy—Specifications of performance requirements to guide development—Co-operation between G.S. and Technical Artillery directorate in M. of S.—Approach to complete auto chain of control for H.A.A.

CHAPTER XXVII. SIDELIGHTS 203
U.K. and U.S. liaison—Inter-Service priorities—Production requirements—Time factor—Priority needs not carried through to production—Emergency provision—Modification Control—Enemy Radar.

CHAPTER XXVIII. RADAR TRAINING 210
Urgent problem of Training in 1938-39—Selected officers learn Radar for instructing volunteers to become Instructors for A.A. Radar—Wing of S.A.A.A. instituted at Landguard—Two courses for officers and other rank instructors before out-break of war—Lack of training equipment—Move to Watchet and further War courses—C.A.S. Wing established at Llandudo—Training equipment improvised—All students qualifying for Is. F.C. or for T.Is. F.C. for A.A. or for C.D./C.A.—Training of A.A. operators at R.A.T.C.—For C.D. at C.A.S. and later by C.A.T.C.—M.C. of S. courses on basic work—Later higher technical courses—M.C. of S. on conversion training of Electricians R.A. as R.E.M.E. mechanics—Wide variety of high-grade technical courses—Special inter-service and American officers' courses—Training at S. of A.—Delayed provision of trainers.

CHAPTER XXIX. A.A. COMMAND RADAR TRAINING 221
A.A. Cd. the primary source of operational experience—Majority of early trainees as Instructors allocated to the Command—Operators selected and trained at A.A. Divisional Schools—Later provided from R.A.T.C.—S.L.C. operators trained by Command until S/L wing of S.A.A.A. took over—Three Command schools for mechanics' training—Extended to meet needs outside the Command—Formation of Petersham Radio School—Radio officers and Scientific users—Conversion from A.A. Command concern to W.O. control—Link with O.R.G.

CHAPTER XXX. RADAR OPERATIONAL RESEARCH 227
Scientific observation of equipment in action—O.R.G. initiated by A.A. Command—Later a limb of A.D.R.D.E. under M. of S.—Radar and Fire Control problems—Extension to C.D. and C.A.—Jamming and J. watch—Anomalous propagation—Flying bomb and V2 rockets—Later scope of activities covered many other weapons and their aids.

CHAPTER XXXI. SUPPLY, MAINTENANCE AND REPAIR . . . 235
R.A.O.C. Supply and Technical sides—No personnel available with knowledge of Radar—Many problems to meet immediate and future needs—Engineering side most affected—Formation of R.E.M.E.—Maintenance and Repair organization developed—Effective results.

CHAPTER XXXII. COMMENTARY 239

PART VI

THE MINISTRY OF SUPPLY

CHAPTER XXXIII. HEADQUARTERS ORGANIZATION 243
Wide scope of activities—Not confined to Army needs—Different Supply arrangements for the three Services—W.O. linked to M. of S. but separated from it—Divided responsibility for Radar—Production divided between M. of S. and M.A.P.—No contact for W.O. for complete Radar picture—Handicap on forward planning—Changes within Ministry affecting control and direction of R. and D.—Experienced directorates transferred from W.O.—Eventual elimination of Military direction—Complete separation of

Production from Development—No single authority concerned with Radar equipment as a whole—Technical Artillery directorate concerned only with Fire Control applications of Radar—Not completely representative of G.S. —High level representation for Army Radar on Inter-Service bodies inadequate—Not solely concerned with Radio and Radar.

CHAPTER XXXIV. RADAR EXPERIMENTAL ESTABLISHMENT . . 249

Growth—Military control with Scientific aid—On Transfer to Ministry gradual replacement of Technical Military (user) direction by Scientific— Some competition between R. and D.—Unbalanced staff—Inadequate Engineering and Design side—Effect on major equipments put into production form—Excellent scientific advances—Lack of enforcement of decision in finalizing a design and control of alterations in production.

CHAPTER XXXV. EXPERIMENTAL AND TRIALS ARRANGEMENTS . 254

Responsibility for trials at different stages—A.D.R.D.E. the sole official technical authority for all Radar equipment design—Aid by C.A.E.E.— Separate C.A.E.E. trials—W.O. schools post-production trials for instructional purposes—A.A. Command trials in operations—A.A.Cd. special trials site—A.O.R.G. trials as basis for operational observation duties— Field observation by A.O.R.G. and Wheatsheaf.

CHAPTER XXXVI. RADAR PRODUCTION 259

Production responsibility divided—Separated from development—Engineering experience not made use of in early stages—Release for Production responsibility of Scientific and Technical Artillery departments—Production side not consulted early—Production link to M.A.P.—Difficulties and false forecasts—No access for accurate information—Inspection by A.I.D.— C.I.E.M.E. responsible for "after care" details—Much Engineer design and production effected by M. of S. production department—Methods of production—Time for supply materially affected by production period.

CHAPTER XXXVII. COMMENTARY 265

PART VII

GENERAL COMMENTARY

CHAPTER XXXVIII. ORGANIZATION FOR RADAR PROVISION . . 272

Guidance from experience—Different methods of control by each Service— Comparison of Service methods for Radar—Impression of effect of each —Summary of comparison—General impression in favour of direct Service control—Effect of research needs on control method—Centralization of research—Separate development.

CHAPTER XXXIX. THE WAR OFFICE AND THE MINISTRY OF SUPPLY 280

Suitability of relationship of M. of S. to the Services—Questions raised by Select Committee—General answer for Radar—Delays due to inadequate organization and control—Time factor—Inadequate information—Excessive requirements—Over optimism—Opportunity for reorganization missed— Needs of War and of Peace different—Change to peace conditions.

CHAPTER XL. SOLDIERS AND SCIENTISTS 285

Army's essential need for Scientific aid—Pre-war provision—War experience —Scientific advice—Direction and control of Scientific effort—Replacement of military by Scientific control—Experience of Scientist with military control—Views of military officer controlling Scientific work—Practical objective requires military control—Research—Military direction with Scientific advice necessary for war—Operational research—Wider association of Scientists with Services—Non-existent in peace—Association of soldiers and scientists at higher levels—American surprise at close link-up in United Kingdom.

CHAPTER XLI. GENERAL REVIEW 292

Disappointments and delays—Causes—Difficulties of decision on incomplete information—"Might-have-beens"—Electric predictor—Beam set—Elevation measurement—Duplication of effort—Security measures—Satisfactory results—Effect of restrictions on early Radar—Magnetron protection—Release for operational use—Window—Vulnerability of defence equipment—Radar as part of chain for H.A.A. control—Salient points of operational value—Outstanding technical advance—Appreciation of combined effort to provide Army Radar.

GLOSSARY OF RADAR TECHNICAL TERMS

The more important technical terms used in this book are briefly explained in the following Glossary for the benefit of the non-technical reader.

They are arranged under five headings: Radiation of Energy; Aerial Feed; Presentation; Echo Signals; and Devices—according to the aspect of Radar in which the particular term is used.

INDEX TO GLOSSARY

Aerial	I (a)	Goniometer	V (c)
Aerial Array	I (b)		
Aerial Feed	II	Interrogator	V (e)
Aerial Reflector	I (c)		
Anomalous Propagation	V (d)	Jamming—Noise	IV (j)
Automatic Aiming	V (b)	Joint—Rotating	II (c)
Automatic Following	V (b)	Lobe—Definition	I (d)
Automatic Gain Control	IV (i)	Lobe—Side	I (e)
Base Time	III (d)	Magnetron—Cavity or Resonator	V (a)
Beam	I (f)		
Beam Switching	I (h)	Meter Display	III (c)
Beam Width	I (g)		
Blip	IV (e)	Noise	IV (j)
Blob	IV (d)		
Break	IV (c)	Plan Position Indicator (P.P.I.)	III (g)
		Propagation Anomalous	V (d)
Cable Feeder (Wire)	II (a)	Putter-on	V (h)
Cathode Ray Tube	III (b)		
Cavity Magnetron	V (a)	Resonator Magnetron	V (a)
Clutter	IV (f)	Responsor	V (g)
		Rotating Joint	II (c)
Display—Definition	III (a)	Scan	I (k)
Meter Display	III (c)	Search	I (i)
Plan Position Indicator Display	III (g)	Side Lobe	I (e)
		Split	I (h)
Type A Display	III (e)	Strobe	IV (g)
Type B Display	III (f)	Strobe Marker	IV (h)
Doppler Effect	V (j)	Sweep	I (j)
Doppler Radar	V (i)	Switch—T-R	II (d)
Echo—Definition	IV (a)	Time Base	III (a)
Echo Permanent	IV (b)	Transponder	V (f)
		Type A Display	III (e)
Feeders. Wire or Cable	II (a)	Type B Display	III (f)
Gain Control, Automatic	IV (i)	Wave Guides	II (b)

I. RADIATION OF ENERGY.

(a) *Aerial*. The means through which transmission and/or reception of radiation of electro-magnetic energy—Radio or Radar—is effected. It may take the form of a single wire, a series of wires, a pair of connected metal rods—

di-poles—of a length appropriate to the wave-length used, or the orifice of a tube—wave guide—of particular cross sectional dimensions.

(b) *Aerial array.* A specially arranged series of aerial elements to concentrate the radiation in a particular direction.

(c) *Aerial Reflector.* An inactive element used in conjunction with an active aerial element to cause the maximum radiation by adding the reflected radiation from the rear to the forward radiation. The reflector may take the form of a rod for use with a rod aerial element, a metal or wire mesh sheet to back an aerial array or, in the case of ultra-short wave-lengths, a parabolic cylinder or a paraboloid, at the focus of which the active aerial element is situated.

(d) *Lobe.* The form of the radiation shown graphically—polar diagram—in a field-strength diagram which limits the boundaries of the effective radiation to a solid angle beyond which the field strength is reduced below a fixed proportion of the maximum radiation.

(e) *Side Lobe.* Radiated energy lost to the main lobe by stray emissions; they cause unwanted echoes from local objects which tend to clutter up the display or confuse it.

(f) *Beam.* A radiation restricted to a small solid angle in which the greater part of the radiated energy is concentrated.

(g) *Beam width.* The angular width of the beam measured between limits where the power intensity is reduced to one-half of the maximum.

(h) *Beam Switching.* Originally referred to as "Split."

The movement of the beam slightly to either side of the mean position and the comparison of the two signals from the two positions; when the two signals are equal the target lies between and equidistant from the two switched beam positions. This provides a means of more accurate determination, than is possible by direct single observation, of the true direction of the target in bearing and/or elevation.

Another method is to move the beam continuously in a narrow cone and to compare the signals at selected opposing points in the cycle. This gives both bearing and elevation readings continuously.

(i) *Search.* The term applied to the exploration of an area or region by moving the beam by manual control; suitable for the detection of the slower moving targets such as shipping.

(j) *Sweep.* The exploration of a region by continuous rotation mechanically, or of a limited arc by automatically reversing mechanical means; this is more suitable for the detection of the faster moving aircraft targets.

(k) *Scan.* The detailed examination of a small area by the rapid movement reciprocally of the beam.

II. AERIAL FEED.

(a) *Wire or Cable Feeders.* The aerial may be fed from the transmitter and may feed the receiver by special connections; bare wire feeders can be used in some static sets or specially insulated wire feeders may be employed. With the short-wave working—*e.g.* 5m. G.L. sets—the length of the feeders is critical for each spot wave-length used; slip rings are necessary for rotating aerials.

(b) *Wave Guides.* With ultra-short wave-lengths a metallic tube may be used instead of wire or cable. The tube has critical dimensions and for use with a rotational or traversing aerial it requires specially designed rotating joints to permit unmodified transmission and reception. As commonly used the guide is rectangular in section and of appropriate dimensions for the energy at the required frequency to be propagated.

(c) *Rotating joint.* This device permits one section of a wave guide to rotate relative to another while still permitting unchanged transmission of the energy.

(d) *T–R Switch.* When the same aerial is used for transmitting and for feeding the receiver with the echo signals in the intervals between the pulses, the receiver requires protection from the strong radiation energy emitted. This is provided by a device known as a T–R switch which isolates the receiver during the periods of transmission. It was sometimes referred to as the gas-filled switch.

III PRESENTATION.

(a) *Display.* The visual indication of the received echo signals; the more normal method is by means of glowing markings on the screen of a Cathode Ray Tube—a variety of forms of this marking may be used according to the particular needs of the set. (See Figs. 3 to 7.) The other form of visual indication sometimes used employs a form of meter of which the needle or pointer moves in accordance with the echo signal.

(b) *C.R.T. or Cathode Ray Tube.* This is a special type of large electronic valve or vacuum tube in which electrons are caused to move very rapidly in a narrow pencil beam to strike the screen formed at the head of the tube; this screen is covered by a material which glows when struck by electrons. By making the electron beam very fine the glow is confined to a point and if that beam is moved rapidly over or about the screen a glowing graph is produced.

For radar displays this movement of the internal beam is effected continuously by the minute differences in voltage of the received signals. Any particular event occurring to the pulsed transmission such as the intervention of an object that reflects back an echo signal, will be shown in the glowing graph on the screen. In fact, this graph shows everything that is happening to the radio waves and what they are doing, and it does so continuously. For general use the screen is coated with fluorescent material that only glows momentarily while under bombardment by the electrons; in some cases where a longer or continuing glow is required some phosphorescent material may be combined with the fluorescent coating.

For a normal radar transmission unaffected by any echo signal or other extraneous influence, the trace on the tube will be regular and of a length that is a specific function of Time; it therefore provides a Time Scale which can be simply translated in terms of distance or the travel of the radar pulses. By continuously causing the C.R.T. to accept and show succeeding pulses, a steady graph is produced on the screen and any variation in that steadiness can be recognized as an extraneous influence such as an echo signal. This regular and continuous line of the Time scale is referred to as the Time Base.

(c) *Meter Display.* In the meter form of display the minute variations in voltage between a pair of signals from an echo received by separate aerials—in beam switching—are applied to the needle so that it moves from the central position to one side and indicates the direction in which the aerial system should be turned to balance the signals; this balancing is necessary to determine the true direction of the source of the echo.

(d) *Time Base.* Referred to in (b) above—a Linear Time Base is the more general form used in which the "spot" moves at effectively constant speed in the direction of the Time Scale. Such Time base may be a horizontal straight line, a circular or spiral line, a straight radial line rotating in consonance with the aerial of a set, or other form in which the rate of movement of the "spot" along it is constant throughout its useful length.

(e) *Type A Display.* A Range-amplitude display in which the Time Base is a straight horizontal line; the normal display for Army Radar detection, selection and Range measurement—(see Fig. 3).

(f) *Type B Display.* A Display in which the echo signal appears as a bright spot on the screen and whose rectangular co-ordinates indicate the bearing and range of the target or object.

(g) *Plan Position Indicator—P.P.I.* A Display indicating as on a map the relative positions of all echo-producing objects within the range of the radar set. In its more usual form the Time Base rotates radially with the aerials—(see Fig. 5).

IV. ECHO SIGNALS.

(a) *Echo.* A reflection of the pulsed wave from a target or other object which causes a deflection or a change of intensity on a C.R.T. display.

(b) *Permanent Echo—P.E.* A radar echo at a fixed station, from any fixed object, structure or ground surface.

(c) *Break.* The effect of an echo signal which causes an interruption or gap in the Time Base of a Type A display. This is an alternative term to Echo and was used more generally than the latter; the term Blip was also frequently used though it now has a different official meaning.

(d) *Blob.* A term occasionally used for the Echo signal on a Type B display—unofficial.

(e) *Blip.* Officially the signal from a Responsor, on the C.R.T. display causing a deflection or change of intensity—often used unofficially instead of Break.

(f) *Clutter.* The term applied to interference on a display by unwanted echoes such as permanent echoes, wave clutter from the sea surface or induced clutter such as "Window".

(g) *Strobe.* A device associated with the display that makes it possible to select a particular part of the Time Base or a particular echo or break for special purposes. Such purpose may be to enlarge the scale of a portion of the Time Base for more accurate reading, to select a particular signal for transfer to another display for accurate angular measurement, to apply to an individual echo increased power or amplitude for easier reading, to apply automatic following to a selected target echo, and a wide variety of other purposes.

(h) *Strobe Marker.* A bright spot, a short gap or other mark that can be moved on or below the Time Base by the Strobe control so that it can indicate the echo or part of the Time Base that is being dealt with specially.

(i) *Automatic Gain Control—A.G.C.* A device actuated by the received echo which varies the amplitude of the signals to maintain them at a standard level; this simplified accurate reading and particularly so in the case of echo matching for angular determination as it eliminates much of the "fluttering" of the signals.

(j) *Noise.* Generally unwanted energy of a random character present in a transmission system; in a radio system noise properly so named appears as a background hum or disturbance, but in radar it tends to thicken the Time Base or cause furriness and in greater intensity to obscure the echo signals. Much magnified induced noise is a method of jamming a radar set.

V. OTHER RADAR DEVICES.

(a) *Cavity or Resonator Magnetron.* A Magnetron valve for ultra-short wavelengths, whose power output has been greatly increased by the provision of a number of cavities, acting as resonators, in one anode spaced around the cathode.

(b) *Automatic Following.* Ordinarily applied to any form of following a target without manual aid once the set has been put onto a selected target echo. Officially, now, the term should only be applied to equipment that follows automatically in Range, Bearing and Elevation.

For those sets that follow automatically in Bearing and Elevation only the correct term is Automatic Aiming.

For Army radar sets described in this publication A.A. No. 3 Mark VII should be described as Automatic Following while the Searchlight set, A.A. No. 2 Mark IX and the American set S.C.R. 584, should be described as Automatic Aiming.

Both classes are based upon a system in which a mechanism is actuated by the particular echo signal and automatically directs the radar beam so that it is always pointing at the moving target producing the echo; any variation in the accuracy of pointing immediately causes the set to correct it.

(c) *Goniometer.* An instrument which when coupled to a suitable aerial system enables the angle of arrival of the echo waves to be determined by the turning of a knob or handle.

In the case of Elevation finding for the Army G.L.II set it enabled the direct ray and the angle of the ground reflected ray from the target to be combined to provide the true target elevation angle.

(d) *Anomalous Propagation.* This term has been used throughout this record, but the official term now adopted is Super-Refraction.

This phenomenon is the bending or refraction of radio waves in the lower layers of the atmosphere in certain conditions. It gives rise to abnormally long ranges at times that may be roughly compared to visual mirages in some special atmospheric conditions. The conditions appear to vary with the wave-length of the transmissions.

(e) *Interrogator.* A pulse transmitter used specially to excite or actuate a transponder.

(f) *Transponder.* A combined receiver-transmitter unit which receives pulses from a radar set or an Interrogator as a result of which it transmits a pulse or series of pulses that can be recognized at the station from which interrogation was effected.

(g) *Responser.* A receiving unit designed to receive the signals from a transponder after it has been actuated.

Note.—All these three items (e), (f) and (g) are the primary components of the system of Identification of Friend from Foe—I.F.F.

(h) *Putter-on.* This term was applied to any Army radar set used for searching, detection and selection of targets and for indicating the position of that target to a narrow beam accurate set for directing or controlling fire against the selected target.

(i) *Doppler Radar.* This may be described as any form of radar which detects radial movement of a distant object relative to the set, by means of the change of frequency of the echo signal due to that motion.

It was adopted as a means of distinguishing between static echoes and those from a moving object. In embryo or experimental form it was applied to the detection of moving vehicles by the elimination of static echoes, and also employed in the Radio Proximity Fuze.

(j) *Doppler Effect.* This effect is observable with any form of wave transmission and is caused by the addition or subtraction of the speed of movement to or from the speed of travel of the waves. With an approaching source the waves have to travel a continuously reducing distance to arrive at the receiver and, therefore, the frequency of the received waves is higher than that at the source —with a receding source the distance continually growing the frequency is lower.

If the comparatively slow travel of sound is considered, a common example where the effect can be recognized by anyone may help to explain this Doppler effect.

Standing on a railway platform one may hear a whistle from a distant train halted by a signal—the train and the receiving car are still and the pitch of the whistle is the same to both. If the whistle were from a moving train approaching the station the pitch to the ear would be higher because of lesser distance the sound has to travel; as the train actually passes, still whistling, it must be noticed that the pitch immediately drops. This is accentuated if one is in a moving train and another train approaching from the opposite direction is whistling—here with the doubled movement of the two trains the sudden drop in pitch as they pass is very noticeable.

With both trains moving at steady speed the change in pitch is also steady, but if one of them is accelerating or increasing speed it can be noticed how the pitch of the whistle gets higher and higher till the passing point and then comes the sudden drop and a continuing lowering of pitch. It is the change of pitch *not* the volume or intensity of the sound that is the factor that counts.

The pitch of the whistle is the frequency of the sound wave and the effect can be noticed by anyone irrespective of his knowledge of sound waves and their habits.

Exactly the same thing happens with radio waves or radar pulsed waves. The Doppler radar set can be arranged to ignore all the static echoes and to make use only of the echoes from moving objects. The Radio Proximity Fuze operates simply on the movement of the shell relative to the target; the experimental "Watch-dog" set similarly operates on the changing distance between the set and a moving vehicle, and takes no notice of echoes from stationary objects.

RESTRICTED

PART I

INTRODUCTION TO RADAR

CHAPTER I. RADAR

Radar, like many other inventions, was the child of Necessity, and in this case the particular necessity was the vital need of this country—with its nerve centre and industrial areas within easy reach of air attack from the Continent—to close the widening gap between the increasing offensive possibilities of aircraft and the defensive measures to counter air attack.

Radar was born under the increasing menace of war and its growth was hastened by the actual stress of war and the urgent needs that war brought with it.

This country and America were not the only ones to develop and make use of Radar—both Germany and Japan produced and employed it. The latter, however, appears to have been surprisingly weak in its employment; but Germany, after her initial failure to appreciate the full possibilities of this new aid, did make large strides forward technically and operationally. For ranging their warships' guns the Germans were at least on a par with this country in those early days, as witness the equipment fitted in the *Graf Spee*. Later, their employment of Radar for anti-aircraft purposes was no mean effort, but they failed to make the advances in ultra-short-wave technique that marked our development and more than maintained our technical and operational lead. They never caught up with the continually improving performance produced by the United Kingdom and the United States. Our scientists kept us at least one jump ahead throughout the war.

What the name RADAR means and how it came into use must be made clear. For the sake of simplicity the term "radar" will be used throughout this record, though to many concerned with it in the early days the title R.D.F. by which it was first known may be more familiar. This system makes use of Radio waves but does so in a special manner, and it is this that distinguishes Radar from Radio as generally known in connexion with communications and broadcasting.

The name Radar is actually of late origin, as it came into official use only in 1943 when it was adopted universally by agreement with the United States of America. The word "RADAR" is an American palindrome formed from the initials of **RA**dio **D**irection **A**nd **R**ange; this is not, actually, entirely satisfactory in describing the system in that it places "direction" before "range," thereby reversing the primary features, at any rate in respect of the accuracy of measurement.

For a short period before the term "radar" was adopted, "Radio Location" had been the official title, and these words fairly, but briefly, represent the object of this method—actual location of an object in space.

In the earliest stages of development the British, as the first to initiate and apply this technique effectively, referred to it officially as "R.D.F." These initials implied Range and Direction Finding which more correctly emphasized the range aspect as the primary feature. R.D.F. was sometimes incorrectly interpreted as Radio Direction Finding, but that applies to more normal radio technique and not to what was to become Radar.

With the strict secrecy necessarily imposed on this method and its development, another name will be found in early reports that might well confuse a searcher among the old records. This is "CUCKOO," which was perhaps an unofficial code name or possibly even just a "pet" name, used by the small group of scientists and the equally limited number of service officers concerned in those early days. This name is really quite expressive in that it might almost be said to be onomatopoeic, or at least to represent, with its hard and short "CUC," the powerful short pulse transmission and its gentle "KOO," the small part reflected back from the target or other object.

A number of other names or titles were suggested at times, such as "E.R.A." of unrecorded significance, but need not be detailed here.

The answer to the question "What did Radar achieve?" is not easy to express briefly. It has been claimed by different high-level authorities that radar "changed warfare more than any other device since the aeroplane became an effective weapon"—that it "brought about the greatest revolution in Naval tactics since the introduction of steam"—that the effect of the development of radar "is on a par with that produced by the use of gunpowder." Let it suffice to add the statement made by Sir Stafford Cripps, formerly the Minister of Aircraft Production and President of the Radio Board, that "Radar contributed more than any other scientific factor to the victory over Germany."

Still in general terms, it can be said that Radar revolutionized Air Defence in the air and from the ground, and brought about radical changes in Naval operations by the elimination of surprise or the denial of it to the enemy. In all its operational aspects its independence of conditions of visibility was an enormous asset. It provided most accurate aids to navigation for surface vessels and aircraft, and enabled the latter to recognize their bombing targets through cloud; it enabled the Navy to guard and control convoy movements and to bring its light invasion craft accurately to individual selected landing-points on the enemy's coast. Local anti-aircraft fire from ships or from the ground became increasingly effective by the accuracy of its direction or control of fire. Long-range gunnery against surface vessels, from ships or from shore, in all conditions of visibility or obscurity, became with its aid a practical and profitable means of effective engagement.

To illustrate its achievements some of the outstanding actions of the war, to which radar contributed or which it made possible, may be recalled.

It was radar that made possible the winning of the Battle of Britain—it eliminated the waste of maintaining standing air patrols and made it possible to get the "famous few" into the air in time and at the right place to intercept the enemy raids.

Radar made it possible for the Navy, aided by the Air Force, to win the Battle of the Atlantic and to defeat the U-boat menace. A statement from German sources, from Admiral Donitz in fact, makes this clear. He is quoted as having said:

"The enemy deprived the U-boat of its essential feature, namely the element of surprise, by means of radar. With these methods he conquered the U-boat menace. The scientists who have operated radar have been called the saviours of the country. It was not superior strategy or tactics which gave him success in the U-boat war, but superiority in scientific research."

It was radar that put our night fighters on the tails of enemy bombers, and radar that made offensive bombing of communications and other targets an effective prelude to D. Day.

Radar enabled our cruisers to shadow the *Bismark* through days and nights of northern Atlantic conditions, until heavy ships were available to give the *coup de grâce* with the aid of radar. It was that aid, also, that reduced losses in the northern convoys to Russia and enabled the *Scharnhorst* to be sunk off North Cape; the Navy will also acknowledge the part played by radar in that remarkable night battle off Cape Matapan, and in actions supporting and maintaining Malta.

A glance back at the results of heavy air attack on surface vessels, in the earlier days of the war, will assist in assessing the value of the improved radar shown in actions of later date that gave our vessels in Eastern waters the power to deal effectively with Japanese "suicide" bomber attacks.

Radar provided the Army with the means of making its A.A. fire growingly effective, the climax being reached during the flying bomb attacks on this country. It also converted our modern Coastal guns into offensive weapons and made the passage of narrow waters, such as the Straits of Dover, a perilous and often costly operation for the enemy.

At the start of the war radar was mainly of a defensive character, but even while this country was still suffering under the air assault radar began to take on at least an offensive-defensive nature, and in some forms its use for truly offensive operations was prepared and tested operationally. This was of course particularly noticeable in Naval and Air Force employment, as they had the power of reaching and seeking out the enemy, while the Army was always dependent on the other Services to put them in contact with the enemy overseas before they could become effectively offensive. Equipment for offensive use in aid of the ground forces was developed but actually never got into the hands of the troops before the surrender in Europe.

In addition to its war uses and achievements radar has valuable possibilities for peace time. Navigational aids for air and sea movement have direct and immediate application to peace service, as have many other radar devices. There is here a wide field open to the scientists that may well occupy their brains and ingenuity. Indeed, already, new peace-time uses have been established.

Before embarking on this record of Army Radar and its development, it is desirable to have some idea of what radar actually is and how it works. In the second half of 1945, when the cloak of secrecy had been largely removed, descriptions and explanations were broadcast on the radio and appeared in the press; some were good, some misleading, and some, if not most, were little understood.

For the military readers for whom this history is primarily intended, the following description of radar is offered—of radar as a system—irrespective of the particular means of applying it and of the uses to which the Services put it to assist their operations of war. It assumes that the reader is not entirely unacquainted with radio broadcasting and its use of radio-waves, but it endeavours to avoid highly technical or scientific details. It is not claimed as a complete definition but it aims at providing a general answer to the question "What is Radar?" It should enable the reader to appreciate the difference between ordinary radio for broadcasting or communications and radar.

A suitably designed receiver, equipped with special aerials for the purpose, can pick up radio emissions from a distant station and can determine the direction or bearing of that station. Two such receivers separated from one another can locate the plan position of the distant station by plotting the bearings from each of them. Two-station working, however, does not lend itself to very rapid location and if there are several stations working on the same wave-length it is almost impossible to ensure that both receivers are observing on the same station at the same time. Mono-static or single-station working is essential if the distant station is moving rapidly as in the case of an airborne set. A single receiver requires means of measuring the range as well as the direction to locate the target on the ground or sea, and for complete location in space of an aircraft it also needs means of determining height or the angle of elevation.

The word "emission" has been used above to cover transmission from the distant station and also the reflection of radio waves transmitted from elsewhere. Some years ago it was found that short wave-length radio waves were reflected from any object in their path and that the reflections were particularly good from metallic or other conducting objects. This phenomenon was mentioned in 1922 by Marconi who attributed its discovery to Hertz; he suggested that use might be made of it for detecting ships and determining their bearing in relation to another ship or to a shore station. These reflections can be used in exactly the same way as original transmissions from the distant station if the receiver is sufficiently sensitive to pick up the smaller signals. Further, if a transmitter is associated with the receiving set, the one station can control the transmission causing reflections and can also correlate the outgoing wave with the received reflected wave.

This gives the chance of adding range measurement from the single station to the target, for it is possible to "mark" the transmitted waves by modulation. This enables a particular bit of the reflected or echo wave to be recognized as attributable to a particular bit of the transmission wave that caused it. As the speed of radio waves is known accurately—185,606 miles a second—the direct range along the line of sight can be measured if a "clock" capable of measuring or distinguishing extremely minute time intervals is used. Such a "clock" became available with the development of an electronic device known as a cathode ray tube; this gives a visual picture of the waves reflected back from any objects and, therefore, the distance of those objects from the radar receiver. The picture is shown on a time scale, but range measurements can be read since time and distance are directly related in the constant speed of movement of the waves.

Modulation may be applied either to the frequency or to the amplitude, both of which are functions of the wave form (Fig. 1); both are used, but the amplitude method is the more generally employed and produces a series of "pulses" with gaps between them (Fig. 2). This method was used in 1931 by Sir Edward Appleton and his associate Dr. Builder in their investigations of the ionospheric layers; they also employed the cathode ray tube for their measurements. Since that time the pulse technique and the cathode ray tube have been developed and improved, and form the basis on which radar has been developed. Some explanatory notes on the cathode ray tube, and the forms that its picture takes in different types of equipment, are included in the Glossary of Technical Terms.

Here then is radar in essence—the transmission of short-length radio waves broken up into a series of pulses of short duration, and the receiving or picking up of the reflected or echo pulses from a target at a distance, in the intervals between the pulses. This provides the means of complete location of a target in space from a single station; it gives accurate range along the "line of sight" and the means of angular measurement in elevation and in azimuth. The accuracy of its location in space, relative to the radar set, is dependent upon the accuracy of each of these measurements.

It should be appreciated that the achievement of detection and location in this way is entirely independent of any form of active co-operation, willing or unwilling, at or by the target, and that without special equipment the target is unaware of the fact that it is being located. Further, it is independent of visibility conditions and practically unaffected by darkness, fog, smoke, cloud or rain.

This pulse technique gets over the difficulty of the strong transmission possibly obliterating or swamping the weak return signal. By arranging for the intervals between the pulses to be sufficiently long and the duration of the pulse to be very short, the outward travel of the pulsed wave and the returning echo wave from the target are completed before the next transmitted pulse is sent out. The presentation of the signals on the screen of the cathode ray tube (see Fig. 3) with a linear "Time-Base" causes the small echo signal to appear at a distance from the large signal made by its parent pulse. That distance is in direct relation to the range of the target from the radar set and can be read by using a suitable scale.

This separate and clear echo signal, called the "break," also makes it possible to determine the bearing and elevation of the target in relation to the set. The special means or devices for getting the accurate readings continuously for Army equipment will be dealt with in the later chapters. Whatever devices are applied, however, they are all dependent on the original clear and separate break that appears on the screen of the C.R. Tube.

It is very doubtful if any one individual could fairly claim to be the sole inventor of radar as a practical operational system. A number of people have appreciated the possibilities of practical application of the basic idea; a number, also, have contributed in a greater or lesser degree to the development of radar in practical form by original suggestions for particular means or methods of applying its principle; and there are others who have "invented" particular devices, methods or technique for improving its accuracy of performance, ease of operation and extension of its utility. Mention of the names of some of these individuals will be found in the course of this record, but such references should not be taken as justifying any claim to authorship of an idea or invention. Nor must the omission of names be taken as denying claims of others or minimizing their share in the development.

The War Office is not concerned with such matters, nor has it any desire to usurp the functions and responsibilities of other Ministries. It can, however, support the claim that the inception of radar for practical war uses, and more particularly its effective application, lies with this country and that there can be no question of the fact that effective operational radar as such, and many of its key developments and advances, are of British origin.

This book aims at providing an historical record of the application of radar to Army uses and its development for those particular purposes. In view of the joint effort in the earliest days and also of the subsequent very close co-operation of the three Services and of the scientific staffs working for them, it is not possible to deal with Army radar without occasional reference to developments by and for the other Services.

Though it will concern itself here primarily with the Army aspect, it should be realized that the War Office recognizes fully the leading part that the Air Ministry took in the initial research and development and the willing and valuable aid given to the Army in the adapting of this new technique to its particular needs.

Though a number of persons gave much valuable assistance, mention of each, individually, cannot be made here. Acknowledgment, however, must be made of the great help, guidance and assistance given by Mr.—now Sir—Robert Watson-Watt, who was, if not the inventor, at least the foster-parent of radar. In addition, after the formation of the Ministry of Supply, and through its Scientific Advisory Council, the support and advice given by Sir Edward Appleton was particularly helpful; his constant interest and his assessment of new ideas were of material value. Professor—now Sir John—Cockroft also did most valuable work for the Army and, in fact, for all the Services, during his service in the Ministry of Supply.

CHAPTER II. PRE-RADAR ARMY DEFENCE MEASURES

During the war of 1914-18, the developments in aircraft converted the possibility of air attack into a reality, and from that time this new form of attack grew into a major menace. From the experiences in that war with the improvised and embryonic means for meeting the air menace, it was apparent that the problem of successful defence in future wars would not be easy of solution. Every country that could do so pressed on to the utmost the development of heavy bombers, as a counter-offensive measure rather than a specific means of defence, and fast fighters for interception of the enemy attack. Parallel with these air measures efforts were also concentrated on gun and searchlight ground defences for local resistance to this new terror.

The first and essential problem, however, for those countries whose vital centres had little land space between them and their frontiers or coast lines, was how to get early warning of approaching attack. In this country the very limited distance from London to the coast most immediately threatened from the Continent, made adequate early warning of approach impossible without some means of increasing the range of detection beyond that of the human eye and ear. For us, therefore, this problem was of first urgency and even of greater importance than the improvement of our ground weapons.

Many methods, possible and improbable, were considered and some were examined and tested on a small scale; only a very few, however, got as far as full-scale trials. The majority of suggestions centred round means of picking up some emanation from the aircraft itself, inherent in its structure, in its electrical and mechanical parts or in its travel through the air. The electric discharges from the magnetos of the engine were considered; the development of infra-red detectors to pick up the heat sources of the engines and exhausts was investigated; as was also the only other emanation available—the noise from the engines, propellers and the passage of the aircraft through the air.

The first possibility referred to was not pursued as it offered little likelihood of success for long-range detection and it was possible to screen these electric emanations without much difficulty. The Admiralty undertook infra-red research work on behalf of all three Services but held out little hope of success for long-range detection; it did, however, achieve a measure of successful development that produced some useful equipment for other purposes.

The War Office was allocated the acoustic method to tackle and the Air Ministry eventually initiated radar development.

From 1864 up to the late war the War Office had been kept in touch with developments and new advances in certain aspects of engineering, and some scientific matters, through the agency of a body known in recent years as the Royal Engineer and Signals Board.

This Board was responsible for investigating and bringing to notice new developments and inventions in the engineering and scientific worlds that might have useful application to military purposes. In addition it had the responsibility for development of new methods and for the design of certain classes of equipment for the Army. For these purposes it controlled a number of W.D. experimental establishments.

It maintained many external contacts, including sources abroad, with scientists and scientific establishments as well as with engineers and engineering bodies. Though not actually a part of the War Office, it was administered by one of the directorates in the M.G.O.'s department; it reported to the Director of Artillery until 1932, when it came under the Director of Mechanization, and in addition had access to the Staff Duties branches and to the Weapons Directorate with which its activities were concerned.

The Board was organized under a senior R.E. officer as President with a small headquarters staff and a number of sections for different classes of work. These were known by their old title of Committees, each being under a senior Engineer or Signals Officer. Those sections more immediately concerned with radar were B and C Committees. B Committee, concerned with air defence, searchlights, acoustics and similar matters, had its Air Defence Experimental Establishment with headquarters at Biggin Hill, subsequently moved, at the beginning of the war, to Somerford at Christchurch. C Committee, dealing with radio and communications, controlled the Signals Experimental Establishment at Woolwich. The Board provided for the initial investigation of radar for Army use, the scientific staff for the start of this special work, and facilities for construction of experimental equipment. A separate committee known as D Committee, with Colonel C. E. Colbeck, formerly the B member, in charge, was formed solely to deal with this important new subject.

The Board was taken over in 1939 by the newly-formed Ministry of Supply, at the same time as the M.G.O.'s department was transferred from the War Office. It continued to function as a corporate body, however, until late in 1940, when it was split up; B, C and D Committees then became branches in the Directorate of Scientific Research, while the other committees concerned with engineering and allied matters were absorbed into another department of the Ministry.

Research into the acoustic possibilities, pursued by the A.D.E.E. with Dr. W. S. Tucker as its acoustics expert and Director of Research, produced good results. Acoustic appliances were developed and by about 1932 practical trials had proved the value of this work. By these means the coastal detection frontier could be pushed outwards by some 30 to 40 miles in favourable meteorological conditions, though the average was more of the order of 20 to 25 miles, which was a considerable advance on that by the human eye and ear.

The trouble with sound, however, is its slow rate of travel, only some 1,100 ft. a second, and the lack of means of speeding it up to compete with the improved speeds of aircraft. In addition to the sound lag, there are conditions of the atmosphere that distort its path of travel, and, in occasional special cases, almost prevent it arriving at the ground surface at all. With the increasing speeds of aircraft it was realized that acoustic long-range detection could not have a very long effective life. This of course was amply demonstrated by the speed trial of a "jet" plane just after the Second World War, when over 600 miles an hour was recorded which meant that the aircraft itself was only some 70 yards a second behind its own sound.

No alternative to the acoustic method was then available or in sight, and warning schemes using large 200 ft. acoustic mirrors, as they were called (concrete strip walls 200 ft. long and 25 ft. high—segments of a sphere—equipped with sensitive microphones on the focal curve) were planned for this country and for certain overseas stations and territories. However, radar came into the picture just in time to obviate expenditure on their construction and to provide a more effective and lasting means of detection at considerably longer range.

Up to the time of the introduction of radar, all direct air defence measures were based upon visual information with, in some cases, aid from the ear; this latter was never available in an aircraft and seldom effectively in a ship.

With the growing power of aircraft to operate in darkness, visual methods were increasingly handicapped. For ground weapons, searchlights were provided to illuminate hostile aircraft to enable them to be engaged by visual methods at night by A.A. guns; but the possibility of engagement by our fighters with this illumination to help them was contemplated; the searchlight, however, could not give much assistance in cloud conditions.

For the purpose of accurately directing the searchlight to pick up and to keep the target illuminated, sound-locators were developed at the A.D.E.E. to improve upon the early patterns. The Mark IX sound-locator, with its "course finding" sight, was an achievement of Dr. Tucker and his team, and put our equipment ahead of that of any other country. It must be said, however, that in war conditions it did not produce the results of which it was instrumentally capable; this was due to the difficulties of training the grade of operator allocated to searchlight units. Some improvement was effected by the introduction at the beginning of the war of a device designed by the Marconi-E.M.I. Company, which became known as the Visual Indicating Equipment; this enabled operators to follow visually by means of a C.R. Tube indicator that showed the correctness or otherwise of their line and the direction in which to move it to correct inaccuracy. It was intended as an aid to the binaural effect in their ears, but was often employed as a direct visual means of directing the locator without reliance upon the ears. Even with this aid, however, the results were not up to the standard that they should have attained.

It may be noted that this instrument, the Mark IX sound-locator, in the hands of a well trained and intelligent crew, was capable of very good pick up and steady following. As far back as 1932 the possibility of employing this locator to provide the means of accurate control of A.A. fire against unseen targets was contemplated and some initial trials were carried out with a measure of success. It could not, by itself, provide the full information needed as it could not measure either range or height, and combined with visual range and height finders it was limited in its capacity, so this method was not pursued.

One other measure, based upon the use of these sound-locators, was being introduced for important centres such as London at the time of the outbreak of war. This was known as the "Fixed Azimuth" system which, by a network of fixed automatic communications from a ring of sound-locators outside the perimeter, provided information to the central control station which would give the necessary predicted point to the selected batteries, and the time at which to engage the target with a concentration of fire. This system was, of course, subject to the limitations of sound and did not prove of much value, though early radar (G.L.) sets later made use of the communications and display pillars at gun sites.

Apart from air defence measures the Army was responsible for the protection of important harbours, ports and anchorages against attack from the sea. Here, also, all fire control and warning of approach of hostile craft were based solely on visual information; for close defence by night the aid of searchlights was, of course, necessary. During the war and just before it sufficient advance had been made in infra-red appliances to contemplate their use, first as a form of "burglar alarm" across a narrow port approach, and later as sweeping beams of greater range to locate ships in bearing. They had not, however, reached the stage of being adopted as normal equipment by the time radar methods became available and were not comparable in performance with radar. Visual methods must be taken as the standard in use before the introduction of radar.

This short outline of the conditions existing in pre-radar days indicates the precarious defence arrangements that would have had to be relied upon to meet the growing power of air attack, and also the limited capacity of our coastal weapons to deal with serious surface vessel attack in bad visibility conditions. It may be said, however, that this condition was practically the same for all nations and this country was not lagging behind the others.

In the later chapters of this record it will be seen how the change from almost impotence to real effectiveness was made possible by the use of radar and its rapid development during the war.

When radar first made its appearance under the auspices of the Air Ministry it was the R.E. and S. Board and its Air Defence Experimental Establishment that were available to undertake the investigations of the possibility of applying this new technique to Army uses.

The initial investigation of the principles, and the experiments to prove this new method for the Army, were carried out solely by members of the War Department scientific and technical staffs of the experimental establishments under the R.E. and S. Board. It was these scientists, who had already gained practical experience of Army needs, of the limitations imposed by the class of operator likely to use Service equipment, and the conditions of use of such equipment in the field, who investigated and assessed the possibilities of this method for practical use. They had to consider if the special technique used for the long-range needs of the Air Force could be adapted and applied to meet the special short-range and high-accuracy requirements of the Army.

They carried out the initial research, experiment and development of equipment to prove the suitability of radar for the Army. They also forecast with considerably accuracy the future forms that development should take. These W.D. scientists were initiated into this new technique and very materially assisted by Mr. Watson-Watt and his research team with whom they were so intimately associated in the early days. On the other hand their experience of equipment design and conditions of use was also of value to that group working on development for the Air Ministry.

This point—that the initial work for the Army was done entirely by experienced W.D. scientists and technicians—is stressed here because so much of the publicity given on the subject of radar, after the end of the war, tended to give the credit for radar development to research scientists brought in specially from outside sources, and to firms producing radar equipment for the Services. It is only fair to those who really did put Army radar into practical equipment form that they should be given the credit for this early work. They do not belittle in any way the great help given by the Air Ministry team at Bawdsey or the excellent work done by those who came in and reinforced them when the war broke out. These latter, surely, do not forget what the body of W.D. scientists and technicians had achieved before they themselves were introduced to the subject, or how they were helped by this body's experience of the military aspects and by the practical, though elementary, equipment that was available to them on their arrival and which formed a basis on which to build the future improved equipment resulting from their combined efforts.

The Army owes a debt of gratitude to those scientists who came in to help, and their excellent work and co-operation are fully recognized; but the Army should also appreciate the work of those who served them for years, and the value of their initial development of Army radar. It is desirable, at least, that the Army should know of their existence and recognize their achievements in this new technique which proved of such great value.

It is appropriate that this War Office account of the development of Army radar and its effect as an aid to the efficient use of Army weapons, should record the names of those members of the W.D. scientific staffs who took part in the early investigations of this new technique and its development for Army use. It was not until August, 1939, when development had already reached a practical stage and the early type of equipment was in production, that this staff was transferred to the control of the Ministry of Supply and additional staff from external scientific sources was brought in to reinforce their efforts. During that early period, therefore, the War Office was entirely responsible for them—they were serving as its employees. A detail of the personnel concerned is given in Appendix I.

CHAPTER III. CONTROL OF ARMY RADAR DEVELOPMENT

Before starting on the record of the development of Army radar, it is desirable to give some idea of the arrangements and organizations that came into being for the direction and control of development, production and use of radar.

With the early work of the Air Ministry having already tackled the problems of long-range detection and early warning of approach of hostile aircraft, the highest priority of importance for the Army was assigned to the provision of means to make its anti-aircraft fire as effective as possible. This placed Army radar aids for that purpose among those items accorded first priority for development.

The R.E. and S. Board concentrated much of its available scientific staff on this work and the General Staff was kept closely in touch with progress, as was also the Artillery Directorate co-operating in that development.

In these early days the General Staff were hardly in a position to initiate policy in respect of radar in more than general terms; they had to rely upon the judgment of the Board and the Directorate of Artillery until practical proof of what radar could achieve could be provided by actual results of trials.

In 1938 trials results for H.A.A. use were becoming available and possibilities of other useful applications of radar were emerging from the experimental work. This pointed to the need for G.S. consideration of radar for the Army as a whole, and of the manning, training, repair and maintenance organization that would be necessary to employ this type of equipment.

It was evident that the War Office Anti-Aircraft Standing Committee was not appropriate for the wider aspects, though it provided useful G.S. support to the policy of the Board, and obtained essential information from the Air Ministry on their assessment of the performance to be expected of German aircraft and the nature of air attack to be met.

At the same time as this committee was holding its first meeting, the General Staff and the D. of A. were considering the proposed application of radar to Coast Defence purposes.

In addition there were matters of inter-Service responsibilities and the likely competition between the Services for the limited production capacity available. This suggested the need for consideration of radar as a whole and not only radar for each Service individually.

Steps towards this wider consideration of radar matters were taken by the setting up by D.G.M.P. of a War Office Committee called the "R.D.F. (W.O.) Committee" at the end of June, 1938. This committee included in its membership the D.S.R.s Admiralty and Air Ministry, and Mr. Watson-Watt, in addition to W.O. and other Army representatives. The first item of its Terms of Reference was: "To correlate Admiralty, War Office and Air Ministry requirements in R.D.F."

It had, therefore, in its composition and terms, quite an element of inter-Service working, at least on the scientific side. It was, perhaps, this that roused the Air Ministry, as the original "Father of Radar," to set up an "Inter-Service Committee on R.D.F." at the end of September; in consequence the W.O. Committee fell into abeyance.

That W.O. committee, however, had effected several useful and important actions: it helped the provision of additional staff for radar work, and approved the provision of a new Army establishment to be built at Christchurch for development of Army radar equipment and for the rest of the A.D.E.E. work. Perhaps most important of all was the agreement reached that the War Office should include its initial Army requirements for radar equipment with those of the Royal Air Force, in the submission to be made to the Treasury by the Air Ministry.

The Inter-Service Committee on R.D.F. was set up by the Air Ministry in September, 1938, and the War Office representatives nominated to serve upon it were: the Director of Mechanization—General Davidson; the Director of Scientific Research—Dr. Gough, and Brigadier Loch, then Brigadier Home Defence, but later to become Director of Anti-Aircraft and Coast Defence.

The Terms of Reference of this committee were:

(a) To examine the progress of research and development on R.D.F. from the point of view of strategic and tactical applications.
(b) To suggest relative priorities in R.D.F. research and development.
(c) To recommend on relative priorities in application and production.
(d) To recommend on scale of provision for research, development and production in R.D.F.
(e) To recommend action required to avoid or mitigate mutual interference between R.D.F. and other military organizations.
(f) To recommend on provision of facilities for large-scale tactical trials and operational research work involving one or more Services.
(g) To consider and recommend on submissions from Service R.D.F. panels.

The Terms of Reference of Panels were:

"To consider and to report to the Inter-Service R.D.F. Committee on matters, within the terms of reference of that body, predominantly affecting one Service."

The committee held its first meeting on 2nd November, 1938, with Air-Marshal W. Sholto Douglas, A.C.A.S., as chairman; it was decided that each Service department was to form a panel to deal with its own problems and to submit to the main committee matters for their consideration or guidance.

This committee did not meet very frequently—its second meeting was held at the beginning of February, 1939, and by the beginning of 1940 only six meetings had taken place.

It achieved some useful results, but little effective in the co-ordination of priorities for development by the three Services or for production needs. The individual panels of the Services did not play much part in its activities, and the parent body did not concern itself with them till February 1940, when it drew attention to the fact that these panels "have never yet . . . been constituted or allowed to function." Each Service had its domestic lower level panel or committee dealing with its own aspects of radar development and planning, and certainly from the outbreak of war they were very fully occupied and in close contact with their opposite numbers in the other Service departments. In fact these contacts led eventually to the formal establishment of the Inter-Service R.D.F. Board which later became the Radar Board. In addition a special sub-committee was set up known as the C.H.L. Planning Sub-Committee which later became the Low Cover Sub-Committee under the chairmanship of Captain J. H. Hughes-Hallett, R.N. This body submitted its report on the Low Air and Anti-Invasion Cover planned and in process of being implemented, and the Inter-Service Committee agreed that the Army should continue the erection of its anti-invasion stations and that some duplication with R.A.F., C.H.L. stations from Littlehampton to Foreness must be accepted. They also agreed that eventually one Service should take over maintenance responsibility for the whole chain.

Of the main decisions of this body, the allocation of wave-bands in which radar sets for different purposes were to work, was perhaps the most important. The acceptance of the planned allocation by this committee carried sufficient weight to get it approved and implemented immediately.

The committee also made recommendations on the allocation of the various types of radar equipment to A.D.G.B. and to ports at home and abroad. Originally it had been contemplated that the Army would be responsible for long-range warning for overseas fortresses, etc., and for the field forces; but it was agreed that the Air Ministry should assume responsibility for all long-range warning abroad as well as at home.

There were, of course, other useful decisions, but, in review, this committee seems to have suffered from the immaturity of the subject and its expanding possibilities; in its earliest days there was necessarily a considerable tang of technicalities involved. Most surprisingly in retrospect, it was not, apparently, consulted on the policy proposals put forward by the Air Ministry in October, 1939, for the division of responsibilities for radar research, development, supply and control, etc., between the Services.

At the beginning of October, 1939, the Air Ministry made proposals defining the responsibilities of the three Services in connexion with research, development, production, etc., for radar and its general control.

It was proposed that:

(a) Staff recruitment of scientists should be dealt with and allocated by the D.S.R., Air Ministry; that Ministry should define all research policy, putting their programme through A.M., M. of S. and Admiralty, and should bear the whole cost of it.
(b) The valve research and development should continue under D.S.R., Admiralty, for all three Services.
(c) Development policy for their own purposes should be the concern of each individual Service at its own establishments but with frequent informal discussions between them.
(d) Production policy should be confined to the Air Ministry who would enlarge their organization to include representatives of the Admiralty and Ministry of Supply.
(e) The general co-ordination of the whole would be effected by the Inter-Services Committee on R.D.F.

After some discussion and adjustment of details—the War Office, for example, could not agree that D.C.D.,A.M. should be responsible for "releasing Army equipment for production"—the War Office welcomed the proposals and accepted them on 9th January, 1940. In so far as the War Office and the Ministry of Supply were concerned, this arrangement was brought into effect at once and was generally adhered to throughout the war. Research work was distributed by agreement to the Ministry of Supply establishments though the Admiralty continued to carry out their own; the links between the different establishments, however, gradually grew into a flexible but effective means of interchange of information and of mutual assistance.

The next stage in the co-ordination and control of radar policy of the three Services was the setting up by the Chiefs-of-Staff Committee of an "R.D.F. Policy Sub-Committee" in June, 1941, as a War Cabinet Committee to replace the Air Ministry Inter-Services R.D.F. Committee. Air Chief Marshal Sir Philip Joubert was the first chairman but was succeeded by Sir Henry Tizard in September of that year.

This body had but a short life in that form as it was converted into the Radio Policy Sub-Committee in February, 1942, to cover the whole radio field and not only radar. In both its forms this committee did valuable work, perhaps none better than the introduction to its discussions of representatives of the United States from their Embassy. In this it anticipated the close contacts and free discussions of radio and radar matters that came into being soon after the United States entered the war.

In 1940 an inter-Service body had been set up, as already mentioned, to co-ordinate the work of the Services in respect of provision of anti-invasion radar cover; it was known as the "Low-Flying and Surface Cover Committee," later shortened to Low Cover Committee. This body planned the coastal chain of stations for warning of the approach of invasion craft and of low-flying air attack; its functions were absorbed later by the R.D.F. Board.

The planning of this cover is dealt with later in this record and all that need be said here is that the immediate urgency of the threat of invasion admitted of no delay. This caused some duplication of provision of sets for the two distinct purposes and it was not till later that it was possible for responsibility for all the functions and needs of these stations to be placed upon the R.A.F.

It was very shortly after the formation of the revised and re-named Policy Sub-Committee that events caused disquiet in regard to the effectiveness and sufficiency of the Services' radio and radar equipment, and an enquiry was undertaken by Mr.—later Lord—Justice du Parcq at the request of the Prime Minister. As a result of his review the Minister of Production submitted a proposal to the War Cabinet for setting up a Radio Board; this was approved on 28th September, 1942.

The Terms of Reference of the Radio Board were as follows:

"The Radio Board shall be responsible for ensuring that there is a single coherent policy on the development and production of radio equipment, on scientific research for that purpose, and on such questions of inter-Service radio policy as may be determined by the Chiefs-of-Staff Committee. In particular, the Board will exercise the following functions:

(a) To co-ordinate inter-Service radio policy, research, development and production to meet Service and Departmental requirements particularly when conflicting interests and proposals arise.
(b) To determine the order of priorities for research, development and production, referring when necessary to the Defence Committee.
(c) To co-ordinate the activities of the several departments in research and development.
(d) Without disturbing the present responsibilities of the Departments, to ensure that there is adequate forward planning of production.
(e) To ensure the largest practicable degree of standardization in finished equipment and in components.

(f) To determine the distribution of technical personnel between research, development, production, maintenance, operation and other uses.

(g) To determine the policy of disclosure of radio information to the Dominion, Colonial and Allied Governments as far as production is concerned, and to advise the Chiefs-of-Staff on the security aspects of the use of secret radio devices in operations.

(h) Within the framework of the combined Production and Resources Board and other Combined Bodies, to enter into relations with the appropriate United States authorities for the purpose of the exchange of information, the integration of programmes and policy and other related matters.

(i) Similarly to act as the channel of communication with Dominion and Allied Governments on matters falling within these terms of reference.

The Board will make recommendations or submit matters in dispute to the War Cabinet, the Minister of Production, or, where operational issues are involved, to the Chiefs-of-Staff, as may be appropriate in particular cases."

The Radio Board thus became the supreme co-ordinating body in regard to inter-Service radio policy, research, development and production. It took over the whole of the functions previously performed by other committees and bodies, the control of the radio activities of the Post Office and controlled the provision to meet civilian radio needs in this country and, in certain special cases, for the occupied countries of Europe.

It operated mainly through two major committees, the Production Planning and Personnel Radio Committee and the Operational and Technical Radio Committee. Each of these had sub-committees, panels, boards, etc., for special aspects of the radio field, while other committees dealing with specialized matters, such as patents, referred direct to the Board itself.

The War Office was represented on the Radio Board and on O.P.T.E.C. by the Directors of Royal Artillery and of Signals, and the Director of Radar on the Radar Board continued to represent the W.O. when that board was brought under the aegis of the Radio Board. On many of the other committees, boards, etc., the Ministry of Supply provided technical or scientific representation of the interests of the Army.

The Radar Board dealt with the majority of operational problems of radar equipment, the co-ordination of use between the Services and their technical needs. As the Service members of this board also had direct access to advise their chiefs-of-staff, they were frequently able to effect inter-Service agreements or decisions on purely Service matters without the delay of submitting them to O.P.T.E.C. or through that body to the Radio Board for transmission to the Chiefs-of-Staff's Committee.

The chairman of the Radio Board was Sir Stafford Cripps, the then Minister for Aircraft Production, in his personal capacity. Mr. Garro Jones, Parliamentary Secretary to the Minister of Production, and Professor G. P. Thomson were appointed deputies, being also chairmen of the P.P.P. and the O.P.T.E.C. Committees respectively. In June, 1943, Sir Robert Watson-Watt, who had represented M.A.P. until then, replaced Professor Thomson on his resignation.

In May, 1943, in order to improve the organization of radio production, the Minister of Production, with the agreement of the Service and Supply Ministers, set up an executive body known as the Radio Production Executive consisting of the three senior radio production officers of the supply departments with Mr. A. A. Sanders as chairman. This body became an integral part of the Radio Board organization and was given wide powers, taking over some of the sub-committees and reporting to the Production Planning and Personnel Committee.

The Radio Board continued to function effectively throughout the war period and subsequently was engaged upon the change-over to peace-time trade and its needs and the reduction of Service requirements—problems of considerable difficulty and complexity but outside the scope of this record.

One of the earliest actions of the Radio Board was to invite the United States to send to this country a Scientific Mission under Dr. Karl Compton, to discuss problems and interchange ideas with a view to pooling resources and avoiding development policies that would not fit in with the combined working and co-operation of the forces of the two countries.

This mission arrived in May, 1943, and was most successful; it initiated effectively the close co-operation between the two countries in the whole radio field. A return visit at the invitation of the United States was made in November, led by Sir Robert Watson-Watt, which was equally successful in confirming policy, distribution of development and cementing the understandings previously made.

It was to some extent due to these contacts that the Radio Board was able to link up effectively with the United States on all aspects of radio. A somewhat similar organization was set up in America, though minor complications and difficulties naturally arose on account of the differences in lay-out. In the United States the Army and the Navy each controlled its own Air Force and all Army radio, including radar, was controlled by their Army Signals Corps, whereas in this country there were the three separate Services, and in the case of the Army the Corps of Signals had no immediate concern with radar. These difficulties were overcome and effective combined working was achieved which continued throughout the war.

Intermediary bodies were established by our missions and staffs in Washington to smooth out these differences; they also provided British representation on the Allied control bodies such as the Combined Communications Board.

The foregoing paragraphs outline the general growth of the organization for the control of technical and operational matters concerning radar as a whole and should suffice as a background against which the progress and nature of the development of Army radar may be considered.

A few further remarks seem to be desirable to supplement this inter-Service, national and international background, by filling in some of the more parochial and domestic details that form the foreground.

The first item was the creation of the post of Director of Scientific Research for the War Office, which was approved in 1938; this brought the War Office into line in this respect with the Admiralty and Air Ministry. It tended to balance the three Service ministries in their access to advice and assistance from high level scientific bodies and individuals of repute in the scientific world. Further, it gave the Army a fair chance in the competition for earmarking scientists and technicians from the leading research institutions, to undertake advisory duties, investigation of new possibilities and assessment of new ideas and suggestions, when war became inevitable.

This new appointment was filled by Dr. H. Gough as the first, and at any rate up to date, the only incumbent of that post. The War Office, however, soon lost its direct contact with its new source of scientific advice, as he was transferred to the Ministry of Supply on its formation in 1939.

For some time the lengthened chain of access to his advice was tolerated, but the desirability, or perhaps necessity, for direct contact with scientific thought and appreciation un-embarrassed by executive duties became apparent. As a result a new appointment of Scientific Adviser to the Army Council was approved in 1942. Sir George Darwin was appointed to this post but resigned after some six months. He was succeeded by Professor—later Sir—Charles Ellis who held the appointment till after the end of the war. While the S.A./A.C. naturally had little contact with the details of Army radar, he was kept fully informed on the general and policy aspects, and his critical advice and broad views on radar aims and policy were of material value.

With the formation of the Ministry of Supply in July, 1939, the War Office had also lost its technical weapons directorates, and with them the R.E. and S. Board and the experimental establishments, with their staff, and all control of production. Reorganization within the War Office had to be effected and with it new directorates were formed to replace partly some of those that had been transferred to the Ministry. Among these a directorate to deal with antiaircraft and coast defence was formed. This directorate absorbed the operational side from D.M.O., training from D.M.T., and weapons, searchlights, ammunition, fire control appliances, etc., and provided the direct link with A.A. Command and with the Operations Directorate of the Air Ministry. D.A.A. and C.D. linked up closely with the Director of Artillery in the M. of S., but was, of course, separated from him geographically.

On the radar side the need for closer contact with the progress of development, and for closer direction of it, began to be felt as radar possibilities expanded. Towards the end of 1940 the opportunity afforded by the disbandment of the R.E. and S. Board was taken to bring in to this directorate as a deputy for radar, Brigadier A. P. Sayer, who as President of that Board had been intimately associated with this work. This materially helped in determining radar policy and put the War Office more nearly on a footing with the other two Service departments in the more technical aspects of the inter-Service committees and discussions. In 1944 the Deputy for Radar was converted into a Director of Radar, but this directorate remained within the Artillery directorate until after the end of the war.

The A.A. and C.D. directorate reverted to a more normal G.S. form when, in July, 1942, it became the Directorate of Royal Artillery and dealt with all forms of weapons used by the Royal Regiment and its operational and training responsibilities. At the same time its technical "opposite number" in the Ministry became Director-General of Artillery.

On the scientific side of radar, D.S.R., Ministry of Supply had reinforced the establishments considerably and had changed their character to the extent of providing for reseach and similar basic work being undertaken. This was all of value, but the engineering side of the work of development was not provided for to the same extent. In addition the military control of the establishments was soon replaced by civilian, which removed from the design side some of the experience of field conditions of use. On the fire control side, however, the technical military user aspect was still provided by the Artillery Directorate Staff who were associated with radar development.

The links between the War Office and the Ministry of Supply were provided at high level by the Senior Military Adviser appointed to the Ministry and by Sir Robert Sinclair appointed Director-General of Army Requirements to represent the Ministry in the W.O. at Army Council level.

At lower levels direct access to their corresponding members in the other department was permitted at directors' level, but formal statements of requirements for production and supply of equipments had to be transmitted through or by D.G.A.R.

Requirements for investigation or development of new types, new weapons or special devices were usually dealt with between directors in the first instance; but those of importance were formally transmitted at higher level, when the W.O. would indicate their need or the Ministry would submit suggestions or proposals and their assessment of what performance could be expected from them. Much of this could be done in the Inter-Departmental Weapons Policy Committee and the periodical statements of policy submitted by the W.O. after discussions of possibilities at its meetings.

Each department had many domestic committees on some of which the other was represented, but there is no need to detail those concerned with radar. It is, however, worth while mentioning the Scientific Advisory Council, set up by the Ministry, which had such a high level of scientific knowledge and experience available to assist or contribute to the war effort. This body provided a number of committees, among them the "R.D.F. Applications Committee," under the guidance of Sir Edward Appleton; this proved of great value to those concerned with Army radar and provided much useful advice from its discussions.

CHAPTER IV. INTRODUCTION TO ARMY RADAR
1935 AND 1936

The first contact made by the War Office with radio methods of the nature of radar for locating or detecting hostile targets appears to have occurred in January, 1931, when a proposal or "invention" was submitted by two of the scientists at the War Department Signals Experimental Establishment at Woolwich. This was put forward by Messrs. W. S. Butement and P. E. Pollard for record in the Inventions Book maintained by R.E. and S. Board and for consideration by them.

This proposal envisaged the accurate location of ships from a shore station or from another ship, by means of *pulsed* radio transmissions and the reception of the radio echo received back in the intervals between the transmission pulses. It contemplated the use of a high frequency radio beam with a wave-length of about 50 cms. and a rotatable aerial system with reflectors to give a narrow beam. (See Appendix II.)

The R.E. and S. Board referred this proposal to the War Office for consideration, and, as a matter of possible interest, to the Admiralty. At that time the modernization of and provision for Coast Defence, with which the Army was concerned, was at a low ebb, and rearmament hardly considered. The D.S.D. Admiralty expressed some interest if the possibilities were pursued and any useful results obtained, but D.S.R. Admiralty expressed considerable doubts as to the practicability of the system from the scientific aspect.

Some small-scale laboratory experiments were carried out privately by Butement and Pollard in their spare time, but they were not pursued further partly on account of the limited power output then obtainable from the valves available, but also by reason of the transfer of Pollard from S.E.E. to Gun Sound Ranging work. This experiment had not been included in the programme of work of the S.E.E. owing to the growing urgency of the need for development of radio communications for the Army, which occupied the full capacity and facilities of that establishment.

This appears to have been one of the earliest forerunners of the system now known as radar, but there is a reference in the R.E. and S. Board's forwarding minute to a suggestion made by Colonel A. C. Fuller of a somewhat similar nature two years earlier. Another by Mr. L. S. Alder is outlined in Admiralty Signals School Secret Provisional Specification No. 6433/1928, and was mentioned by D.S.R. Admiralty in his reply to the War Office.

Shortly after this the normal contacts of the Signals Member of the R.E. and S. Board with the Post Office Research Establishment at Dollis Hill brought to notice what was referred to as "interference" with Very High Frequency experimental transmissions by the passage through them of aircraft causing "beating" or distortion of the received signals, due to reflections of the radio waves. This was looked upon as of interest as confirming earlier observations by Marconi, but was considered rather an annoying phenomenon and no specific consideration was given to investigating the possibility of making practical use of it.

The Board also had some information on the pulsed radio methods of distance measurement employed by Sir Edward Appleton in his investigation of the

Ionospheric layers in 1931. They were not, however, aware of the decision to investigate the possible employment of radio echoes taken by Tizard Committee, which had been set up by the Air Ministry in 1934 to make recommendations on the lines of research to be pursued to provide urgently for long-range detection of aircraft.

Their external contacts with the Radio Research Board of the National Physical Laboratory, however, did bring to their notice at the end of June, 1935, that interesting investigations were in progress by a small group of scientists under the leadership of Mr. Watson-Watt. Colonel Worlledge, the Signals Member of the R.E. and S. Board, was authorized to report direct to the Director of Mechanization, War Office, who arranged to accompany him on a visit to the Radio Research Board at Slough.

This visit took place on Thursday, 4th July, 1935, and the possibilities of applying the technique under development for long-range air detection, to the short-range and high accuracy requirement of the Army were discussed with Mr. Watson-Watt. Both appreciated the possibilities and were impressed by the importance of this work, and it was arranged to include £3,000 in draft estimates for 1936/37, which were then in preparation, as a token figure to cover initial investigation and experimental work under the R.E. and S. Board on this matter.

The result of this visit of the 4th July, 1935, was therefore the first step in introducing radar to the Army, and the history of Army radar really starts from that day.

Though the records of the activities in this connexion in the remaining half of 1935 are limited it is possible to trace progress with reasonable exactitude. It must be remembered that a strict secrecy grading was applied to this subject and no one except those immediately and necessarily concerned was permitted to have knowledge of this matter or, so far as was possible, of its existence. Service officers and scientists allowed into the picture were strictly limited; copies of reports were rarely permitted and the reports themselves were mostly in manuscript in these early days, and discussion of or reference to them outside those concerned was strictly banned.

Extracts from a manuscript copy of the first report by Colonel Worlledge on the technical aspect and possibilities of this system are given below as a matter of interest, though they refer mainly to the long-range air detection system then under development for the Air Ministry. This report does, however, suggest certain lines for the possible use of this technique for Army purposes, but it must be remembered that the "C" Member of the Board was not intimately concerned with nor aware of the detailed requirements for A.A. gunnery; he was reporting primarily on the general technical radio aspect.

Extracts from the first report on Radar made by Col. J. P. G. Worlledge in July, 1935

"The proposed Radio Method of Aeroplane Detection and its Prospects

General Considerations

1. Mr. R. A. Watson-Watt's proposed method consists briefly of
    (a) 'flood lighting' the horizon over an arc of 180° or 360° with short-wave radiation emitted in rapidly succeeding very short pulses of very high power;
    (b) detecting the part of this radiation reflected from an aeroplane;

(c) determining the time interval between the emission of each pulse and the receipt of its reflection or echo, and translating this into terms of distance.

Facts and Figures

9. *Ranges.* With masts 72 ft. high (service field masts) and an input power of 3 kW. to the Sender, the Maximum Range is about 50–60 Kms. over level ground.

    With masts 250 ft. high, the range would be about doubled and ranges of 100–130 Kms. can be promised.

10. *Sender.* The Sender now used for experiment has an input power of 3 kW. but radiates 200–300 kW. at the peak of the pulse. This sudden intense radiation calls for special valves with large filaments, and further development on these lines is required.

    A Sender can be built into a frame about 4' × 4' × 5', and could be transported, with its power supply in one 3-ton lorry, with a house-body.

11. *Receiver.* This must be specially designed for the purpose. The time interval between receipt of the ground ray (direct) pulse and the reflected pulse is measured on a cathode ray tube. By providing a scale of distances on the tube the distance can be read direct.

    The receiving equipment, complete with aerial gear, could be carried in one 30-cwt. lorry, but to provide sufficient accommodation for the crew and position finding, maps, etc., it would probably be advisable to specify a 3-ton lorry, with a house-body.

12. *Height of Aeroplanes.* Aeroplanes flying lower than 1,500 ft. are hard to detect, but from 2,000 ft. upwards height of flight does not affect the range very much.

Limitations

13. *Jamming.* Effective jamming could be caused by a special enemy aircraft deliberately flown for the purpose, and transmitting on the detection system's wave-length. The only answer to this is to shoot him down. To be effective this enemy aircraft's sender would have to be of very constant frequency, a quality, apparently, hard to achieve in the air. It will be possible, moreover, to change the detection system's frequency over a 2 : 1 range without undue loss of efficiency even with fixed antennae.

Possible developments

15. *Direction Finding.* It may be possible to combine indications giving both direction and range simultaneously on one cathode ray tube. The receiver would be a very complicated one.

16. *Angle of Elevation.* Experimental work on a scheme to measure the angle of incidence of the echo is promising and it is hoped to be able to measure this angle continuously to an accuracy of $0·2°$. A receiver

and antenna array separate from the range receiver and array will be necessary.

Future development

17. It is evident that the system is effective, and by far the most effective of any yet proposed, in that it is or can be made less susceptible to interference and yet allows detection at ranges sufficient to give reasonable warning to the defenders. It has now reached a stage when development towards practical apparatus could be started. A very considerable amount of work yet remains to be done to develop the component parts of the system to the point of construction of practical apparatus fit for use by troops."

Practical experiments and trials were carried out by the Watson-Watt team at Orford and Orfordness in the latter half of 1935, the R.E. and S. Board having some contact with them through its "B" Member, Colonel C. E. Colbeck. There were also discussions with D.S.R. Air Ministry on the subject of Army participation in the developments. These culminated in an informal meeting on 27th January, 1936, between the Board and Mr. A. P. Rowe, who represented D.S.R. Air Ministry and also deputized for Mr. Watson-Watt. At this meeting it was agreed that Dr. E. T. Paris, a Principal Scientific Officer of A.D.E.E., should be attached to the Watson-Watt team sufficiently long to enable him to study the technique thoroughly, and then to make recommendations as to the best method of attacking the Army problems.

A copy of the draft memorandum submitted to the War Office is included here to show the assessment by the R.E. and S. Board of the research and development work probably necessary, pending the detailed review by Dr. Paris, who, it was proposed, should investigate the possibilities. Incidentally it will be noticed that provision in Army estimates 1936–37 for such work, referred to in the foregoing paragraphs, had actually been made to the extent of £1,000 only for the special investigation.

Memorandum by the President R.E. and S. Board to the War Office in February, 1936

"We have now made a further study of 'Cuckoo.' The method has, so far, been devised entirely for long-range detection, i.e. for range up to 130 Km. depending on the height of the aerial. There is no immediate intention to develop it for short-range location unless the Army wishes and is prepared to finance it, but its application to Fortress Defence makes it essential. As a mere sentry it will be adequately developed by the Air Ministry, but it remains for us to supply the missing links to bind it to the defence system.

2. Location is not possible at present at ranges less than 10 Km., this is inherent in the technique now being developed. In order therefore to adapt it to control of searchlights and guns a considerable amount of highly skilled work will be necessary, and we recommend that a preliminary study of the problems should be instituted at an early date.

3. The major items of research and development work necessary are:—

    (*a*) The application of the present method for short-range location.
    (*b*) Method of getting elevation.

(c) Technique for instantaneous translation of oscillograph pattern into Co-ordinates of a point in space and continuous following of that point as it moves at a speed of 250 m.p.h.

(d) Conversion of this translation into instrumental control of searchlights and guns.

(e) Investigation of some method (e.g. direction finding) of monostatic working in order to avoid the well-known disadvantages of the two-station method (the only method possible now).

4. We recommend that we should co-operate with the Air Ministry in developing Cuckoo as a sentry in fortresses and studying the possibility of linking it on to the Defence system. This entails both preliminary investigation of the items specified in para. 3 and also of methods of allying with existing acoustical instruments e.g. 200′ mirror.

5. The form of co-operation we suggest is that A.D.E.E. be charged with the general supervision of the problem of use and application, supplying for that purpose a Scientific Officer for part time. In addition that we should subsidize the Air Ministry to the extent of 3 scientific officers and 2 experimental workers, who would work under the technical direction of Mr. Watson-Watt at the Establishment which we believe is to be set up shortly.

This small staff would work exclusively on our problems and would be altered as and if progress warranted. . . .

6. The token figure of £1,000 for 1936–37 suggested in our previous letter is not sufficient if we are to hasten development on the above basis; £1,500 is a safer figure."

The Army Council addressed the Air Council on 5th February, 1936, and the latter notified their agreement on the 27th February and agreed to all arrangements being made direct between the Royal Engineer and Signals Board and D.S.R. Air Ministry.

As a result, early in March, Dr. Paris commenced his visits to Orford and later to Bawdsey Manor where Mr. Watson-Watt and his R.D.F. team took up their abode in the late summer. The buildings and large grounds of the latter had been acquired for this purpose in August, 1936 and were being adapted to the needs of this special work; it became known as the Bawdsey Research Station, or more officially Air Ministry Research Establishment. The isolated position, or rather the limited means of access to it, was of value from the security point of view and offered good facilities for experiments over and on the sea; essential air co-operation also was available locally. Its very exposed position, however, necessitated the rapid removal of research work and teams on the outbreak of war.

After a month Dr. Paris reported on the 8th April, 1936, that his preliminary investigations indicated that—

"there appears no reason why experimental research aiming at the adaptation of 'Cuckoo' to A.A. work should not proceed at a fairly rapid rate so soon as personnel is available," and—

"that some consideration has been given to the form that the initial experiments might take."

On 8th September, 1936, he submitted his first formal report and recommendations as to the possibilities of applying R.D.F. (Radar) to Army purposes; this was the result of his technical investigation of the problems involved. It outlines the first forms of application that he suggested should be aimed at and indicates the staff required for the initial research and experimental work.

The following are extracts from this report:—

"re 'CUCKOO'

1. It is now possible to make certain recommendations in regard to work that should be put in hand with the object of adapting 'Cuckoo' to Army requirements.

2. Broadly, there are two possible applications of 'Cuckoo' to Army requirements for Air Defence, viz.

    (*a*) for the control of A.A. searchlights and guns;
    and
    (*b*) for procuring early warning of the approach of hostile aircraft to fixed or mobile A.A. defence.

3. The application (*a*), that is, to the control of searchlights and guns, will involve a considerable amount of experiment and research, a good deal of which can proceed in parallel with work of a similar nature that will be done for other purposes. It is estimated that it may be two years before the experiment will have reached a stage at which it will be possible to produce instruments for field trial.

4. The aim of the experiment will be to produce (i) a mobile equipment for searchlights, that is, an equipment capable of determining present line of sight and height from one station which could be located near the gun position.

. . .

6. With regard to the application (*b*), that is, for early warning, it now appears certain that 'Cuckoo' is a definite advance on all sound mirrors, and will ultimately replace them. The development of 'Cuckoo' for early warning in Home Defence is in the hands of the Air Ministry. The present design of Home Defence Stations is definitely 'fixed' and each station is, or will be, equipped with three 250-ft. self-supporting wooden towers.

7. It is, however, possible to develop a mobile 'baby Cuckoo' which would work in the range 3 to 10 miles. This would do the work of pilot locators and small mobile mirrors, and would give warning of the approach of aircraft, their number, and rough bearing (say with a possible error of 5 degrees). The design of the set would not, so far as can be seen, involve any lengthy research or experiment, and it is considered that a first model could be produced at Bawdsey Research Station early in 1937, if certain personnel can be made available. The first model would not necessarily be mobile, but would demonstrate the feasibility of making a set with aerials on 70 ft. masts with a power supply of say $2\frac{1}{2}$ kilowatts, and instruments that could be packed in a lorry. The kind of thing to be aimed at ultimately would be a set that could be transported in two lorries, one for the transmitter and one for the receiver.

9. In addition to the development of 'Cuckoo' for mobile defence, some consideration has been given to the problem of providing early warning at overseas fortress positions (e.g. Gibraltar, Malta, Singapore, Hong Kong). Two courses are open, viz. (*a*) to accept the Home Defence type of 'Cuckoo' as it stands, or (*b*) to attempt to re-design with the object of reducing the size of the masts required for the aerials."

During the period from May to September, 1936, the provision of staff was considered for an Army cell to work under Dr. Paris in co-operation with the Air Ministry scientific staff at Bawdsey, all under the general supervision of Mr. Watson-Watt. Eventually aided by the recommendations from Dr. Paris and with the agreement of D.S.R. Air Ministry, it was decided to transfer two scientific officers and one J.S.O. to join Dr. Paris, and to support them with two assistants, two laboratory assistants, and a motor driver. Treasury approval was formally accorded, retrospectively, to this on 10th February, 1937.

On 16th October, 1936, Dr. Paris was officially detached from A.D.E.E. and joined the B.R.S. as head of the Army cell, the rest of the selected staff joining him on or immediately after that date. Research and experimental work on the application of this new technique to Army needs started effectively from that date. 16th October, 1936, may therefore be accepted as the official date for the start of work to produce Army Radar.

CHAPTER V. THE PERIOD OF INITIAL EXPERIMENT
1936 AND 1937

With the Army cell now in being at the Bawdsey Research Station, work was started in earnest and initial effort was concentrated upon the following:—

(a) the development of a mobile, medium range, Air warning equipment;
(b) research to adapt the new technique to the shorter range and greater accuracy requirements for the control of H.A.A. fire and also for the direction of searchlights.

Of these, the first presented the simpler problem as it had to some extent been proved practicable in the early experiments for the Air Ministry long-range detection type of set. Though experimental work was of course necessary, it was largely a matter of development to produce it in a mobile form suitable for service equipment. Development aimed at a detection range of not less than 30 miles and at being capable of being brought rapidly into action.

It is apparent that the staff at Bawdsey were completely confident of achieving the required results at an early date. Even in October, 1936, at a conference at the R.N. Signal School, the Admiralty representatives accepted the fact that the proposed Army design would meet their needs for a mobile warning equipment for Mobile Naval Base use, and they agreed that work on these lines should not be undertaken by their Signal School, but that reliance would be placed on the Army work at Bawdsey to meet this need.

Early in February, 1937, the design of the transmitter was complete, and Watson-Watt had reported to the Air Ministry that it was ready for contract action to be taken for production of the first models.

Thus early in 1937 the problem of production arose, and for this first experimental equipment the War Office agreed to order or produce through the Air Ministry; this decision was of course very largely influenced by the security aspect. The Air Ministry had already selected two firms of repute—Messrs. Metropolitan-Vickers and Messrs. A. C. Cossor—as the sole providers of their long-range radar equipment under special security arrangements. These firms alone were still to continue the production of any form of radar equipment at this time. The number of these particular Army sets was small and of an experimental nature so that production capacity at these firms was adequate to deal with them. A third firm, The General Electric Co., Ltd., was involved in respect of valve design and production.

In December, 1936, the R.E. and S. Board sought guidance on matters of responsibilities and their division between the Air Ministry and the War Office, in respect of the application of radar to long-, medium- and short-range working. They were in doubt as to whether the medium-range equipment was properly a high priority Army concern.

In order to introduce these problems to the G.S. and the M.G.O. sides of the War Office, it was arranged that representatives should visit Orford and Bawdsey. The visit took place on 14th December, 1936, by the D. of M. (General A. E. Davidson) and M.O. 2 (Colonel K. M. Loch) accompanied by Colonel Colbeck of the R.E. and S. Board. Extracts from Colonel Colbeck's report on 16th December, 1936, are given here:

"Report on the situation at the time of the visit of Director of Mechanisation, Lt. Col. Loch (M.O. 2) and Col. Colbeck (R.E.S.B.) 14th December, 1936.

Mr. Watson-Watt and Dr. Paris showed the party over the Orfordness Station, where work is in progress with 70-foot masts; the 240-foot masts at Bawdsey were seen later on.

A third activity, which is of great importance to the Army, is in the investigation of apparatus that could be used for the control of A.A. guns and lights.

Control of A.A. Guns and Searchlights. Field Equipment.

Would give continuously from one Station:—

Range, present bearing and present elevation of aircraft; sets might be produced by Autumn 1939. No work has been done on the special research and technical development required for this application and the problems differ considerably from the long-range problems.

For the 'Cuckoo' development and application to control of guns, a suitable predictor should be considered now, capable of utilizing data from visual or 'Cuckoo' instruments."

The report finished with the query:—

"Is it worth while putting the utmost possible effort into producing apparatus for the control of A.A. gun fire in view of the importance of being able to bring effective fire to bear on targets not visible from the ground? If so, additional research and technical development staff must be provided by the Army for the purpose as soon as possible. It is possible that complete success might eventually eliminate the necessity for A.A. Searchlight."

As a result of this visit and discussions on the position, D. of M. referred the possibilities of radar for Army use to D.S.D. and D.M.O. and I. on 18th December, 1936. They noted the position and urged particularly the need for means *to engage the unseen target by A.A. fire.* It was also proposed to review the need for the two large sound mirrors, already approved for Singapore defences for early warning of air attack, but which had not yet been built; they were in fact cancelled as a result of the radar progress.

At the Board's request for policy guidance on the Army's responsibility in respect of medium-range radar, the M.G.O. raised this question specifically on 15th January, 1937, but it was decided to postpone action with the Air Ministry until more proof was available from actual trials of the value of radar to the Army. This matter remained in abeyance until April, 1938 and the R.E. and S. Board continued to control development of the M.B. equipment.

The fire control of H.A.A. guns, the primary problem on which the Army cell was working, was more formidable, but work on research and experiment was pressed on. Range accuracy was the first feature on which effort was concentrated, but the angular measurements for bearing, and more particularly for elevation or line of sight, involved considerable difficulties. They evoked many ingenious ideas from those engaged on the work and a number of them were tested experimentally.

The aim, of course, was to devise an equipment for H.A.A. gun site which, as a single source of information, would give all the data required to provide accurately the *present position* of the target. By doing that *continuously and smoothly* it would also provide the rates of change in each of the factors. With this information the calculating machine known as the Predictor could give the *future position* and the *fuze setting information* to determine where and when the shells should arrive and burst. This assumes the continuation of the course and speed of the target aircraft, and in order to reduce errors, the *prediction time* or distance between the present and selected future positions, must be kept to the minimum possible.

As has been indicated earlier, the control of A.A. gunfire in force before the use of radar was based on visual information aided by optical instruments, and the predictors were designed for using information supplied by direct visual following.

Though from the earliest consideration of the possibilities of radar *the need for a special predictor suitable for accepting radar information* had been urged, it was not considered possible to undertake the design of such an instrument until radar had proved itself adequately. Production as well as design facilities were already fully occupied with the greatly increased numbers of these appliances required for the expansion of the A.A. defences, their rearmament and improvement. Early radar development had, therefore, to aim at using the existing types of mechanical predictors and aiding visual methods in the first place, and the replacement of them if possible in unseen conditions to permit of fire by predicted or plotted concentrations.

The ultimate aim, however, of providing full and accurate information continuously and automatically transmitted and fed, in any conditions and of a class at least equal to that of visual methods in the best conditions of visibility, was still borne in mind as the objective of the research and design work.

As a contribution towards the problems involved, Mr. H. S. Young, who had practical experience as a Territorial A.A. gunner as well as being one of the W.D. Scientific Officers in the Army cell at Bawdsey, submitted a useful paper on the application of Cuckoo (radar) to A.A. gunnery on 17th March, 1937. This indicated the advantage to be obtained by the use of radar instead of the visual height and range finders, if its range accuracy could be guaranteed as not worse than 300 yards, as it would be constant at all ranges instead of varying with range. To compete with visual at the shorter ranges he showed that an accuracy of $\pm$ 50 yards was necessary if short-range engagements were to become a practical proposition. He also gave the requirements for measurement by radar as:

Minimum range of operation	3,000 yds.
Probable error in elevation angle	$\frac{1}{2}$ degree.
Probable error in azimuth	$\frac{1}{2}$ degree.

In particular he stressed the essential need for *continuous* laying of the gun if effective results were to be obtained.

This basis was generally accepted at least as a guide or objective to be aimed at in the development work.

Young also put forward a proposal for combining radar with the Mark IX Sound Locator as a quick method of providing a monostatic station for *unseen* A.A. fire control, employing radar range and acoustic angular measurements of bearing and elevation—all read continuously. This proposal was put forward as the only available means in sight for providing for unseen target engagement within a year; it gave prospects of fair accuracy, or at any rate sufficient to permit of fire by plotted concentrations. Serious consideration was given to this suggestion, but it was eventually dropped.

Among a number of ideas and suggestions at this time Pollard had put up a proposal in January, 1937, to combine radar with the 200 ft. acoustic mirror with the object of providing in a simple manner a means of ship location and distant detection of low-flying aircraft. In this combination the reinforced concrete mirror would act as an aerial reflector for the radar and would produce a narrow beam capable of traverse. This suggestion was rejected as no such mirrors were in being and effort would be better concentrated on the development of self-contained radar sets; this was probably the first proposal to use a "Strip" reflector such as, on a smaller scale, came into use a year or two later.

Another proposal of technical radar interest was made by Pollard who put forward a particular form of presentation of echo signals on the C.R. tube with the means of centring the signal break or blip on a hair line on the screen and keeping it there. The electro-mechanical means of controlling this movement of the blip could also effect simultaneously the continuous transmission of the range measurement. This would avoid a part of the time lag caused by telephone transmission of data and would give greater accuracy and consistency of information for prediction. Though not accepted by Watson-Watt as an original invention, it was of value for Army sets and incidentally some two years later when a firm claimed such a device as having originated with them, the Air Ministry called for a copy of this proposal by Pollard to refute their claim.

The first formal Progress Report on the work of the Army cell at Bawdsey was submitted by Dr. Paris on 2nd September, 1937, and it covered the period from October, 1936, to the end of August, 1937. It included reference to Young's Cuckoo-cum-Sound-Locator proposal, the report on which was considered by the Fire Control Instruments Sub-Committee of the R.A. Committee.

This Progress Report indicated the progress made on each of the two lines on which investigation had proceeded:

(*a*) A mobile radio (radar) set for early warning of approach of enemy aircraft to A.A. defences, giving approximate map position and height.

(*b*) A single station radio (radar) method for directing A.A. gunfire.

For the mobile warning type the construction of a completely mobile 13-metre wave-length equipment was nearly finished. The transmitter, with a peak pulse power output of 3 kW., was already installed in its lorry, together with the 5 kW. generator which also supplied power to the receiver. The receiver was also installed in another lorry and included a goniometer and switching arrangements for sense, direction and height finding. Pending delivery of the two Merryweather 70-ft. telescopic wooden towers for the aerials, built on 4-wheeled trailers, the equipment was undergoing field trials at Dunkirk near Canterbury, using temporary aerial supports.

It was anticipated that the complete equipment and the operating team of Royal Signals personnel under training would be ready for full-scale trials by the end of September, 1937. The performance aimed at was 35 miles range for aircraft at a height of 10,000 ft. accurate to the nearest mile, bearing to the nearest 5 degrees and height within 2,000 ft.

For the single station A.A. fire control set, two projects were under investigation:

(i) The design of a 6·8 metre wave-length set.
(ii) The design of a one-metre wave-length search beam set.

Experimental models for (i) had been constructed and trials were in progress to determine the accuracy of range measurements. A range error of not more than 500 ft. was anticipated and the minimum range was expected to be between 5,000 and 10,000 ft. and the maximum range from 10 to 15 miles. Means of measuring azimuth angle were under investigation with good prospects of early solution, but the measurement of elevation angle appeared likely to involve research over a longer period. The use of Cuckoo-cum-Sound Locator was advocated as a short term interim solution for providing a means of unseen shooting.

In regard to (ii) which was a research investigation, it is worth while quoting Dr. Paris's words:—

"It is possible that the best solution of the A.A. gun problem will in the end be found to be some form of pulsed radio search beam, and experiments are now in hand to find what order of accuracy can be attained in line of sight determination by means of an overlapping beam technique."

The selection of a one-metre wave-length for this experiment was then purely a matter of technical convenience. If found promising it was contemplated that a much shorter wave-length would be used and paraboloid aerial reflectors would then be practicable and permit of movement vertically as well as horizontally; the technique for measuring the elevation angles would be the same as for azimuth or bearing angles. Dr. Paris's closing words are also worth noting:—

"The beam method is able to offer the best hope of high accuracy and is the least vulnerable to jamming—whether due to the presence of large numbers of aircraft or to deliberate radio interference."

The first object of the experiments with the search beam set was to determine the degree of accuracy obtainable in angular measurement using an overlapping beam technique. Directional aerials such as the Yagi, produce a fairly narrow beam in the form of a symmetrical and much elongated lobe giving maximum power along its centre line; the effective width in this case was expected to be roughly 12 degrees. With a pair of such aerials close together in the horizontal plane, their beams overlap and the maximum strength of echo signal is to be expected when the target is equidistant from the centre lines of the two beams; any divergence from that position should cause a definite reduction in strength and a sharper change in amplitude than when observing on the maximum signal by bracketing with a single beam only. This overlapping beam technique was a prelude to or a step towards the method known as "split" and later to the development of beam switching.

These experiments were concentrated on the angular measurement of bearing angle which was far simpler to test than the elevation angle, as seaborne targets could be used and movement in the horizontal plane only was necessary. Any results obtained horizontally should also be possible vertically if aerials capable of movement in elevation were provided. This experimental work was being carried on by a team under Dr. Bowen that included both Air Ministry and Army personnel.

In the last quarter of 1937, the Army cell at Bawdsey continued their research and experiment, but in addition a new possibility for employment of radar by the Army was emerging. This was the means of detecting, tracking and accurately locating shipping, which had emerged from the "search beam" experiments.

On 23rd November, 1937, Dr. Paris submitted a memorandum on this new application for consideration: an extract from this memorandum is given below as of considerable interest in view of later developments and effective results achieved.

Extracts from Dr. Paris's Secret Memorandum dated 23rd Nov., 1937.
"R.D.F. and Coast Defence"

"1. The following memorandum has been prepared after consultation with Mr. Watson-Watt, and is forwarded with his approval.

2. In the course of experiments with a radio search beam at Bawdsey, it has been demonstrated that it is possible to obtain echoes from ships in much the same way as echoes are obtained from aircraft.

3. The apparatus used in these experiments was not of a finished description. The transmitter was low-powered and the mechanical design of the aerials for producing the beam, and of the gear for manipulating it, was rough-and-ready. In spite of these disadvantages, echoes from small vessels three or four miles from shore were clearly seen. The apparatus was about 100 feet above sea-level. A wave-length of one metre was used in the experiments.

. . . . .

5. The significance of these observations is that they suggest that it would be possible to develop radio apparatus for the detection and location of ships from shore in conditions of poor visibility either by day or night. As in the case of the R.D.F. apparatus which is being developed for anti-aircraft purposes, range and bearings would be obtained from a single station.

6. The apparatus used in the experiments referred to has now been dismantled but further experimental work with radio search beams will continue under my supervision for Air Defence purposes, although the priority of this work—according to existing arrangements—will be low. In view of the possible applications of the radio search beam in Coast Defence, it is for consideration whether the investigation should not be accelerated.

7. If the work were accelerated I consider that it would be reasonable to aim at the development in two to three years' time, of radio apparatus which would locate ships at ranges up to 10 or possibly 20 miles with an accuracy in range of $\pm$ 500 feet and in line of $\pm \frac{1}{2}$ degree. It is probable that for the best results the apparatus would have to be elevated above sea-level either by artificial means (such as steel masts) or by making use of natural topographical features. A site on a cliff or forward slope overlooking the sea, and fifty to a hundred feet above sea-level, should be satisfactory.

8. With accelerated development it should also be possible to produce within two years a less ambitious equipment which would detect ships up to 5 or 10 miles from shore and locate them with an accuracy of $\pm$ 500 feet in range and $\pm$ 5 degrees in line."

As indicated in that memorandum, the experimental set had been dismantled and the team working on it had been partly diverted to other work of high priority. Dr. Paris, however, was able to keep a small amount of effort applied to remodelling the experimental set with a view to continuing the research work. This effort was inadequate to make rapid headway and the need for additional staff was urged by the Board and was supported by the Air Ministry to whom Mr. Watson-Watt had reported on 10th December, 1937, that in his view, the Army staff at Bawdsey was adequate for the present work on A.A. applications "but that extra staff was necessary for the Coast Defence development and other promising lines of development for Army use."

This matter of shortage of staff for promising work for Army uses again brought to the front the lack, felt by the Board of General Staff, of guidance as to policy and priorities of development. A small *ad hoc* committee with Colonel Lock, G.S.O.1 Fighter Command, in the chair had met on 9th November, 1937, and agreed to the lines of development for A.A. use, but it could not suffice for long, particularly with the new C.D. aspect and essential research items demanding some priority of consideration. This lack of G.S. priority requirements hampered the provision of extra staff and this matter was raised again early in 1938.

The year opened with all the lines of research and development mentioned being pursued with energy in so far as staff permitted. Allocation of available personnel had to be made on the basis of priority of importance of the various items and in this the A.A. needs had to take the first place. Only a very small amount of effort could be spared for the new Coast Defence possibilities and in fact this work had eventually to languish in abeyance pending the arrival of additional personnel.

The medium range warning type in its mobile form and the main part of the A.A. fire control set in its initial form were undergoing practical experimental trials to determine performance, accuracy and suitability. For the latter type also work was being pressed on with the angular measurement problems of which the elevation side was still the major difficulty.

These trials and tests met, of course, with the usual set-backs, delays, unexpected minor faults and difficulties that are inseparable from early experimental work. Though in these particular trials an entirely novel method was involved and unpredictable side issues perhaps introduced more than the usual crop of troubles, the way they were tackled by the Army cell at Bawdsey, and the technical military personnel assisting them, was a very creditable piece of work and was carried through in a time which, on looking back at it, was remarkably short.

It must be remembered that with radar they were dealing with something based practically upon the speed of light for its accuracy, and no standard with which to compare its performance against a moving aircraft was available other than visual following. To eliminate the human element in so far as was possible Kiné-theodolites had to be used from suitable bases at distant sites, most accurately surveyed and linked up by communications, and all observation times had to be completely synchronized. A mass of calculations to convert the "film" positions of the target in space from at least two distant kiné stations, into range from the radar position for comparison, occupied many a midnight session and involved the consumption of much tobacco and other sedatives—perhaps also some stimulants as well. Apart from this, of course, these trials were entirely dependent on good visibility conditions so that the kiné-theodolites could make their records; this naturally accounted for much of the time taken up by the tests.

To close this early period there are two items of interest and importance that mark definite stages in the progress of the work on Army radar that may be included here.

The first is the action by D.M.O. and I. and D. of A. in April, 1938, in urging the development of equipment for coast defence purposes. For the first time in respect of radar the General Staff initiated a specification of requirements to guide development. In this case in fact they provided the complete basis for such work—a specific G.S. requirement was stated, a priority of importance was given and the operational performance to be aimed at was recorded.

The following are extracts from their minutes in the file:—

"The further investigation of ship detection and location should be placed in P* category of importance and should be carried out by the R.E.S.B. It should not interfere with similar work for A.A. which has *first priority*."

. . . . .

"The following gives an indication of our requirements:—

(*a*) *Detection:* With a view to replacing or supplementing observation lights to detect the presence of ships as follows:

(*i*) Motor Torpedo Boats at 6,000 yards.
(*ii*) If failing the above, destroyers at 6,000 yards.

(*b*) *Location:* With a view to replacing or supplementing our existing methods of fire control for close defence and counter bombardment. The following minimum degree of accuracy should be aimed at:—

Range 1 per cent, Line 2 minutes.

The development of the system for 'range' alone would be valuable."

. . . . .

"While the more accurate methods envisaged are being explored, we feel that a cruder set would go far to assist coast fortresses in their problem of watching in the dark.

In view of the importance of this investigation it is considered that the additional staff should be provided as soon as possible."

The second item of interest is the formal acceptance of Army radar as a practical and essential aid to operations. This was the result of the submission to the Treasury, referred to in Chapter III, page 13, which T.I.S.C. approved at their meeting on 18th August, 1938, and covered the large-scale equipment provision for the Air Ministry and for the War Office.

In so far as the War Office was concerned the following summary of the decisions indicates the extent to which Army radar and its development work could be translated into production equipment for supply to the troops.

The immediate expenditure necessary for the extension of production capacity of the "priority" firms (Messrs. Metro-Vickers, A. C. Cossor, and G.E.C.) was approved and also that required for immediate provision of "hand-made" models of equipment for trials and training. The schedule of probable numbers of each of the six different types of set included and their costs was also approved subject to confirmation when actual numbers in detail were known.

For the Army, these approvals covered the War Office in respect of the following equipments:—

G.L. sets—1,000, including 6 hand-made models at £14,000—Total £4,612,500.

C.D. sets—40, including 6 hand-made models at £3,000—Total £33,000.

These costs were inclusive of vehicles, accessories, etc., to be provided from sources other than the "priority" firms. The costs were approved in principle, but the actual numbers, when firm figures were available, were to be referred to T.I.S.C. again.

In addition to these approvals for equipment provision, the Committee approved the proposals for the move of the A.D.E.E. from Biggin Hill, and of the Army cell from Bawdsey, to the selected site near Christchurch. This approval covered the estimated cost of buildings, etc., at £150,000 and the site purchase price of £45,000 for the 125 acres and gave authority for compulsory acquisition if necessary. The works services were approved in principle subject to submission of estimates when completed, under normal procedure.

Further T.I.S.C. meetings during 1938 and 1939 gave approval in detail. At their meeting on 21st December, 1938, an instalment of 500 G.L. sets out of a potential requirement of approximately 1,500, was approved. Later the broad programme put up by the Air Ministry (including War Office needs) was approved at the meeting on 13th July, 1939, which provided for 2079 G.L. and 263 C.D. sets.

The initial research work and development by the Air Ministry had received Treasury approval earlier and had been followed by approval for the original programme of construction of the C.H.—the long-range warning—stations. The addition of the small Army group to the Bawdsey establishment for research and development had also been accepted, but now the War Office was set upon the road for provision for operational employment of this new device by the Army.

This year 1938 marks a stage in the radar story that approximates to the close of the initial experimental period, though research and experiment were of course still forming a large part of the work and continued to do so until the end of the war. However, by this time a good deal of experience had already been gained and practical details of the means of applying radar to Army purposes were accumulating.

It will be simpler and more understandable to carry on the record, from this point, with the individual main types of equipment being dealt with separately.

Those Chapters which deal with the growth and improvement of individual types of equipment will record the Army aspect rather than the details of the scientific and technical advances which brought about the improvements. That is to say, the basis of consideration will be improvements in the form, ease of use and operational performance of the equipment produced by those advances. The Ministry of Supply, which took over the research and development work, has recorded those scientific advances and improved technical methods that are of importance.

From this point then, this history abandons the chronological story of Army Radar as a whole and treats different types of equipment individually. In addition, it records the growth and development of War Office policy on radar, the organization of the Ministry, training, supply and other administrative matters. These too must be separated from technical equipment matters if confusion is to be avoided, and they will form the subjects of separate Chapters.

CHAPTER VI. COMMENTARY

It is intended to include in each main Part of this volume a final chapter in which comments on particular aspects will be made and attention drawn to points of importance either on their own account or by reason of their effect on developments recorded later in the record. At the end of the book itself the more general aspects will be reviewed and, in so far as may be possible, lessons derived from the experience with this special aid to operations will be suggested in the hope that they may serve to aid planning and organization, if and when the occasion should arise in the future, when some equally novel and valuable possibility is to be developed in war-time.

The early parts of Chapter I call for no particular comment—they attempt to indicate something of what radar did and how it did it. Technical details have been avoided as far as possible, but some reference to particular components must necessarily appear if the reader is to have any idea of how radar provides its information and how it differs from normal radio. These should not frighten the reader nor deter him from following the development and appreciating the points that made the great strides forward in this aid to operations. Most of these are included in the Glossary of technical terms, but how and why they perform their functions need not trouble the reader. The interpretation of masses of initials so freely used during the war to distinguish—nominally briefly—various appointments, establishments and individuals, is given in the opening pages of this volume.

No special comment is needed on Chapter II—it is merely the background of the existing defence measures before the advent of radar aids, and serves to emphasize the revolution that this new technique produced. Attention may, however, be drawn to the latter half of this chapter which stresses the fact that the early development of Army Radar was effected entirely by the scientists who were already serving the War Department. Much credit is due to them for their achievements.

Chapter III indicates the growth of inter-Service liaison on radar and higher direction of radar development which eventually embraced also the effective inter-allied co-operation that served throughout the later periods of the war.

It may be noted here that the division of responsibilities proposed at the beginning of the war were not in fact adhered to very strictly for some considerable time. The Admiralty certainly continued largely on their own set course, particularly in respect of production, and to some extent also on research, though this was arranged by agreement between the three Services and the Supply Ministries. On this matter of Research there is always the practical problem of defining the point where basic research ends and applied research begins; the stress of war needs must often require research to be carried straight on through basic work to application and on into the experimental and development stages.

Chapter IV is chiefly a record of events leading up to the introduction of the War Office to the new technique, developed by Watson-Watt and his team, for long-range detection of aircraft, and needs no embroidering here. There are points in it, however, that deserve some attention.

The main point that is worthy of note is that contrary to the general idea of the popular press, the War Office was not slow to take up this new possibility, even in peace-time days of considerable financial restriction. Within a week of the first contact with the earliest experimental work on what was to become radar, the R.E. and S. Board and the W.O. directorates concerned had taken action for provision to be made for an investigation of the possibilities for Army use. Some soldiers at times are apt to carp at the restrictions of financial control in the War Office, but there can be no doubt of the helpful and understanding attitude in this case; it can also be said that similar help was forthcoming for radar throughout the war period, and that it materially eased the burden of those concerned with the provision of radar equipment for the Army.

The provision of the Army "cell" by the Board, from its experimental establishments for work at Bawdsey in intimate co-operation with the A.M. team, proved the value of such staff, experienced in Army needs, being available. In addition to bringing radar to the aid of operations, this had far-reaching effect in initiating the very close relations and liaison between the research and development establishments serving the two Services that persisted throughout the war with mutual benefit.

No apology is offered for the reproduction of somewhat lengthy extracts from the earliest reports, included in Chapter IV. They are of some historical interest and show quite a remarkable appreciation of the possibilities and problems involved, before even a detailed scientific investigation could be made of the possibilities of adapting this new technique to the short range and high accuracy needs of the Army.

Dr. Paris's report and recommendations resulting from his investigations are also quoted in some detail and are worthy of note, as they largely formed the basis on which Army experiment and development work was started.

The first item on which comment is desirable from Chapter V is the agreement of the W.O. to the production of Army experimental sets by or through the Air Ministry in parallel with their own provision. Only very small numbers were involved at that time and the security position made it essential to confine production to the few firms allowed into the secret. The War Office at the time specifically limited their acceptance to the small supplies then required, and the Board drew attention to the apparent lack of adequate capacity to deal with the large-scale provision likely to be required in the future. This method of supply later grew so that all radar assemblies and some complete sets for the Army were produced by the Air Ministry—and the Ministry of Aircraft Production when it took over the responsibility. This first case of very limited production may have been the precedent on which the future system was decided.

This brings up the matter of the security restrictions which were, of course, of vital importance to prevent information on this novel defensive aid from reaching the enemy. That this was achieved to a very satisfactory extent is evidenced by the surprise of the Germans during the Battle of Britain, at always finding our fighters ready and in position to intercept their attacks. Interrogation of captured enemy airmen disclosed that they were convinced that warning of their approach was given from small craft, fishing boats and lightships off our coasts, and this belief was responsible for many of the deliberate attacks on them. That C.H. stations were attacked is true, but the continuity of those attacks was not such as to suggest that the enemy had really appreciated the vital part played by these stations in bringing about his defeat in that first great air campaign. The maintenance of secrecy in respect of radar in those early days was most effective and the secret was well kept even when sets had become fairly widespread throughout the Services. That the restrictions imposed created difficulties is true, but they were amply compensated for by the results achieved. This security restriction did perhaps affect the production side in that it may have delayed the preparations for extended production capacity and the provision of greater numbers of trained personnel for the factories.

A point of considerable interest occurs on pages 28 and 29 in the extract from a report dated 16th December, 1936. This draws attention to the need for a predictor designed to suit the information produced by radar sets for A.A. fire control. Even at that early date it was appreciated that the existing types of predictor were not really suited to radar, and radar information was not suited to a mechanical predictor designed for visual information. The first attribute of radar was its range accuracy, whereas existing predictors were designed to accept accurate angles (bearing and elevation) and "height," the latter having been converted in a "height" finder from relatively inaccurate range and accurate elevation angle. This made necessary the conversion of radar's very accurate range readings by combining them with by no means highly accurate angle of elevation readings, to produce height and ground range—a debasing of the primary accuracy feature. On the other hand the steadiness of information supplied by radar was not likely to be adequate for the effective operation of a mechanical predictor.

A similar point had arisen some few years earlier when the combination of sound locator angular measurements with visual range and height finders was being tested as a means for "unseen" fire control. Young had then devised a special predictor for this purpose which, however, was not acceptable to the predictor authorities who insisted that the standard predictor should be used. This method was not pursued at that time, but if it had been the results would have been equally as unsatisfactory as they were in the case when radar had to be linked to existing predictors.

In Chapter V, page 31, a most interesting forecast of the future by Dr. Paris is recorded. This suggests the narrow beam and ultra-short wave-length working as the eventual solution to the A.A. accurate fire control problem; this forecast was converted into an actual fact some six years later.

Chapter V, pages 34 and 35 are also of interest. The first of them shows the earliest specific statement of operational requirements issued by the General Staff to guide the work of development for Coast radar sets for the Army. This may well be compared with the series of specifications given in Appendix IV, to illustrate the development during the war of the G.S. indications of their operational needs to be met by the designers. The second relates to the approval given by the Treasury for the initial large-scale provision of radar equipment for the Army. The provisional figure approved a year before the start of the war amounted to over £5 million and was increased to over £10 million some two months before the actual outbreak of war. It also provided for the new establishment for Army development work.

PART II
ANTI-AIRCRAFT APPLICATIONS
CHAPTER VII. ARMY ANTI-AIRCRAFT RADAR

The early stages of the investigations of the possibilities of radar being applied to Army uses and the initial experimental work have been described in the preceeding Part. Attention must now be directed towards the consecutive development of each of the main types of equipment.

By 1938 practical sets had been developed that were capable of undergoing trials to prove the performance that could be expected from them, to determine their suitability for field use and the modifications necessary before embarking on production. This proof by practical trials was essential to justify or replace the scientific and technical opinions of the possibilities of these new devices. Facts got from actual use and the results in actual trials would give a solid basis for judgment of the immediate possibilities and a means of assessing the further possibilities of improvement. The General Staff needed such facts to form, with the aid of their technical advisers, a policy to govern the further development of this new scientific aid and its employment as Army equipment.

This Part will deal with the applications of radar to the ground anti-aircraft needs. These needs were, from the start, of the greatest importance and, as has already been indicated, they were given priority over all other forms or uses for the Army.

Medium Range Warning. The responsibilities of the Army for air defence were generally limited to A.A. gunfire against hostile aircraft and the illumination of them at night with searchlights to aid gunfire. In addition the searchlights were required to point out enemy night bombers as targets for attack, or their course for tracking.

Long-distance warning of attack was the responsibility of the R.A.F., as were also the tracking of aircraft with the aid of the widespread network of observer posts, and the distribution of information and warning of approach to particular areas. These responsibilities were well recognized for the defence of this country but were not so clearly defined in 1938 for overseas stations, territories or theatres of operations.

It was the possibility that the Army might require means of providing for early warning of attack on overseas fortresses or other areas that had required the Army cell at Bawdsey to undertake the development of the medium range mobile radar equipment for Army use as well as for the R.A.F. Responsibility for medium-range warning was, however, accepted by the Air Ministry in July, 1938, but it was not until November of that year when trials and modifications had been completed that the prototype sets and the development work were handed over to the Air Ministry staff.

This type of set, referred to as the M.B —meaning Mobile Base—was designed with its receiver and transmitter each housed in a separate lorry which towed a trailer carrying a 70 foot telescopic wooden tower of Merryweather design, for the aerials. The original design was for working on a wavelength of 13 metres with "Figure of 8" illumination (radar transmission) from the transmitter aerial.

The complete set was ready at the beginning of 1938 and trials were begun.

At the end of April, in accordance with the policy of the Air Staff, the set had to be modified to work on $7\frac{1}{2}$ metres and an improved transmitter aerial system provided. At the end of July, 1938, one of the new $7\frac{1}{2}$ metre transmitters was sent to Messrs. Metro-Vickers to guide their production of prototypes for the Air Ministry and in November work on this equipment was handed over to the A.M. Bawdsey staff.

It was agreed that if the need for such sets for Army purposes should arise, the standard type finally developed by the Air Ministry would be acceptable to the Army. Early in 1939 a possible Army requirement of 5 C.H. and 69 M.R. sets for overseas was reported to the Inter-Service R.D.F. Committee, but the R.A.F. took over responsibility for all such stations, whether at home or abroad.

The performance of this M.B. equipment, at the time when Army personnel handed over the experimental sets and the further development became the responsibility of the Air Ministry staff, was approximately as shown below.

Operating crew required	1 N.C.O. and 3 O.Rs. per watch.
Time to get into action from travelling state	30 minutes.
Detection range on aircraft (medium bomber type)	40 to 50 miles.
Bearing accuracy	3 to 4 degrees.
Height reading	within 2,000 feet.

This type of equipment formed the basis for the R.A.F. set known as the M.R.U.—Mobile Radio Unit—which gave excellent and continuous service throughout the war. Modifications and improvements were made to it, including higher and lighter aerial masts, but these developments were not a concern of the Army.

The Problems of H.A.A. Fire Control. The problems of unseen fire control or direction of fire of heavy anti-aircraft guns demand highly accurate equipment to permit of effective engagement of hostile aircraft in darkness or bad visibility; this work had priority for experimental and development effort over all and any other applications of radar to Army uses.

From the earliest days of initial experiment the problems of providing continuously accurate range information did not present excessive difficulty. This aspect of the fire control problem was well dealt with by the Army cell at Bawdsey, and their optimistic assessment of early success was adequately proved by the results of trials against aircraft in comparison with concurrent kiné-theodolite readings during 1938.

The angular measurement of azimuth or bearing angle, and more particularly that of elevation angle, presented much more difficult problems. Not only was continuous transmission of information in both these factors essential but that information had to be of a very high degree of accuracy if effective results were to be obtained against the unseen target. These problems were mechanical as well as radio, though the radio side was primary in the type of set that was aimed at in the first place. It was, however, recognized that the ultimate solution of these problems was likely to be found in the use of narrow "searchlight" type radar beams working on very short wave-lengths, which would permit of the use of a small aerial and reflector system which could be moved in the vertical as well as in the horizontal plane (see page 31). Such methods would bring part of the responsibility for angular accuracy on to the mechanical side of the equipment design.

Though, as has been seen in the previous chapters, initial experimental work was undertaken as a research item on the embryo of such a set, there was not sufficient scientific effort available to make rapid progress on these lines. The fact that no valve of adequate power output had at that time been evolved limited any practical development for equipment purposes being undertaken. That it became a practical proposition some three or four years later will be seen in the following chapters and its effect will be appreciated.

In 1938–39 the urgency of the need demanded development of the best type of appliances that could then be put into practical form and produced in quantity. That the Army cell at Bawdsey achieved as much as it did at this time is remarkable and was appreciated by Watson-Watt who, in a report to the Air Ministry in March, 1938, urging the need for making early provision for large-scale production facilities, referred to "the unexpectedly quick result of the W.O. research, resulting in a practical A.A. set suitable for early production."

The background for the design of A.A. equipment is, of course, the performance of enemy aircraft and the tactics likely to be employed in their attacks. An assessment of the probable enemy methods of attack, speeds, height, etc., was obtained from the Air Ministry in April, 1938, through the War Office A.A. Standing Committee. This is quoted here to show the basis on which, after providing a factor for future improvement in performance, the details of the early Army radar equipments were designed.

"*Data asked for by the R.E. and S. Board to guide design of A.A. Sets*
1st April, 1938

(a) *Practical figures of performance, actual or anticipated, for bombing aircraft by night.*

(i) *Maximum and minimum speeds to be dealt with are:—*

Maximum—350 m.p.h.; Minimum—160 m.p.h.

(ii) and (iii) *Probable maximum and minimum heights of approach, operation and bombing.*

Steep dive 10,000 ft. to 25,000 ft. pulling out at 1,000 ft. at lowest. Angle of dive 15° to 40°. Shallow dive 2,000 ft. to 4,000 ft., pulling out at 500 ft. at lowest.

Height for high-level bombing 5,000 ft. to 25,000 ft. Height for low-level bombing 500 ft. and under.

(iv) *Spacing of attacking aircraft, lateral and vertical, and time interval for successive aircraft.*

It is expected that at night bombers will attack singly but on bright nights they might fly in formation. Singly, time interval for successive aircraft is impossible to predict. If in formation, aircraft may be laterally and vertically spaced to a distance of one span or more.

(v) *Manœuvrability, e.g. limits of quick changes of course and height, including maximum probable dive angle.*

Limits of quick changes of course are being calculated but the maximum dive angle is probably about 40°.

(vi) *Effective "night dope"; nature of night aircraft, e.g. a monoplane with retractable undercarriage.*

Slower obsolescent bombers are painted black underneath. All the new fast types seen have been painted light blue below. It is probable that bombers used at night will be coloured black underneath. It is expected that all night bomber aircraft will be monoplanes with retractable undercarriage in the near future.

(b) *Probable tactics of night bombers to be dealt with.*
  (i) *Approach.* Approach may be high level, low level or by losing height from high level to low level either intermittently or continuously. It is unlikely that aircraft will approach at night below 1,000 ft.
  (ii) *Accurate objective bombing from a height involving recognition of target and steady course or broadcast bombing of area only.*
      By moonlight it is considered probable that precision bombing from a height will be attempted but on dark nights or in bad visibility the enemy would have recourse to broadcast bombing of an area.
  (iii) *Use of dive bombing.*
      It must be assumed that aircraft will be able to carry out dive bombing either low or high. Low dive bombing is considered unlikely at night.
  (iv) *Low-flying attack.*
      As mentioned above, really low-flying attack is improbable at night.

The information given above, obtained from the Air Ministry, covers present day and the immediate future as far as it can be seen, but there is no information which enables the Air Ministry to predict the more distant future with any reliability."

From the information provided by this assessment combined with knowledge of the performance of our H.A.A. weapons—initially the 3 inch and the 3·7 inch, the 4·5 inch in the early production stage which emerged soon after the war started and later some 5·25 inch Naval type guns—it was possible to determine the essential range performance required of the gun-site radar sets. The object to be attained was to enable the guns to engage a target at the greatest range at which their fire could be expected to be effective. This obviously means that the radar set must detect and pick up the selected target at a considerably longer range in order to give the necessary time for the various operations that combine to put the shell in the right place at the right time.

There are roughly four periods of time to be taken into account:—

(*a*) After detection of an approaching target time must be allowed for the selection of the particular target to be engaged and for the fire control instruments to pick it up; meanwhile the gun crews get into action.

(*b*) Time is required to enable the tracking of the target to become accurate and steady and for all the necessary information to be fed into the predictor, and for the predictor to settle down and absorb that information so that it can produce the future point in space at which the target should be met by the bursts of the shells.

(*c*) Time for the fuze setting suitable to the predicted position of the target, and the "drill" operations of loading and firing the gun.

(*d*) Time for the flight of the shell from the gun to the predicted point.

All these time elements are convertible into range according to the speed of the target. They may be divided into two parts for the radar information, as the first part does not require the same high degree of accuracy of tracking as is needed when the prediction information is being produced; this prediction cannot be obtained unless the information supplied to the predictor is highly accurate and consistently steady. The range capacity of the radar may, therefore, be of two classes—accurate over the shorter ranges and of less accuracy at "warning" ranges.

Apart from these more obvious points affecting design of the equipment there are the maximum and minimum rates of angular movement that must be provided for in the gearing of the electrical or mechanical movement of the set or its aerials, and with them the means of keeping these movements smooth to make the transmitted information acceptable to the predictor.

The heights of attack to be expected also materially affect the radar set design but the elevation limit of the guns in action, about 70 degrees, gives the effective upper limit to the radar for accurate tracking of high angle targets, though following with a lower degree of accuracy should be possible, so that a target passing nearly overhead can be re-engaged accurately as a receding target. Low level-attack has a greater effect on the radar—targets are fleeting and much more difficult to pick up as observation may be impeded by ground reflections, distortion of the "beamed" transmission and site clutter. In addition angular rates in azimuth may become excessively high and cause difficulty in steady following, or even in following at all.

Pending experience of actual enemy attacking methods, the information provided by the Air Ministry served its purpose in the development of the early sets. It was, with intelligent interpretations and allowances for improvements in aircraft performance, effective or at least as adequate a basis as could be given on which to base design. There was, of course, ample experience gained during the frequent and persistent attacks that came with the Battle of Britain and the Blitz, to justify the initial design details even though the radar performance was not then all that was aimed at. For the later types that were developed this assessment was modified by the results of practical operational experience. In this the value of the Operational Research Group and their recording of enemy performance and the effects and faults of our radar operation, was very material.

The priority radar problem was that involving the high accuracy requirements of the control or direction of fire of the heavy A.A. guns. The light A.A. weapons also needed aid, but their short range of operation and the low and fleeting targets they had to tackle offered little opportunity for radar control of fire. In addition they operated normally as individual guns and radar aids would be almost useless unless each gun had its own set or, more correctly, its own almost automatic radar sight. Such a scale of provision was prohibitive, and the advantage to be obtained over visual tracer control would hardly have justified it even if production capacity had been available. Some aid was, however, contemplated in the form of radar sets for good range information which at least would assist in checking wasteful fire before or after the target was within effective range.

Other radar aids to A.A. gun defences were required to provide local warning and later to direct the high accuracy gun-laying or G.L. sets on to selected targets for engagement; Tactical control at the gun site and Area control of operations in defended areas also became an essential aid.

Apart from gun aids, there were also the A.A. searchlights to be provided with means of accurate direction to illuminate targets by night. Originally the searchlight was intended to permit of gun engagement by night, but as gun radar control became more effective the primary role of radar-directed searchlights changed over to co-operation with night-fighting aircraft for interception.

The progressive solution of these problems in the development of the different forms of radar sets forms the subject-matter of this Part II, and, so far as is possible, the improved effect obtained by these developments is indicated.

CHAPTER VIII. H.A.A. ARTILLERY RADAR—EARLY TYPES

It will be recalled that by early 1938 the development of an experimental G.L. set had reached a stage at which it was possible to carry out practical trials to prove its accuracy of performance in respect of range information. At the same time the accuracy of the "spot" determination of bearing angle was tested, but there was as yet no suitable means devised for continuous following and reading of these angles; it was, however, anticipated that a suitable solution would emerge from the research and experimental work at an early date. In respect of the third element, angle of sight or elevation, required for complete location of the target in space, an early solution could not be relied upon as this problem presented greater difficulties.

These trials during the first half of that year gave good proof of the range capacity and accuracy of this set; they also brought to light certain points of design in which improvements could be made. They showed the desirability of carrying out more extended tests to ascertain the effects of site, of proximity to guns, of barrage balloons, and of effect of blast on the sets, and to investigate mutual interference caused by adjacent sets.

For this purpose it was necessary to provide mobile sets and a small number of these were constructed by the joint efforts of the Bawdsey Establishment and the A.D.E.E. during the summer and autumn. The first of these was submitted to further trials against kiné-theodolite records of the aircraft tracks, in October, 1938.

The improvement in performance of these mobile and modified sets was very satisfactory. Range accuracy showed only 28 yards' variation from the kiné reading and the "spot" bearing angle measurements appeared to be accurate to within ± 1 degree. These trials also showed that the arrangement of the sets in their cabin trailers was acceptable, though rather crude and austere, for service in the field.

In regard to the proof of high accuracy of range performance of this set it may be of interest to note that over a large series of target runs a consistent difference from the kiné range of only some 13 yards was shown. This led to considerable controversy and argument as to whether or not it was due to the fact that radar reflections emanated from the nearest point of the aeroplane, while the "visual" measurement was from what might be called the centre of gravity, or perhaps better the centre of silhouette. Pursuit of this argument was not encouraged at the time as such a degree of accuracy was adequate for practical purposes.

Others of these sets were employed on the urgent experimental work on continuous following methods for bearing angle and for the elevation measurement system, which by the end of the year were showing greater promise of practical results. In addition, sets were provided as models from which manufacturers could develop the pilot production models of which six had been ordered preparatory to contract action for a full-scale supply. They were also used for the other tests referred to above.

The original experimental work on this type of set was carried out using a wave-length of 6·9 metres, but a re-allocation of wave-length bands was necessary to provide for the growing variety of uses of radar. A scheme had been put forward by Watson-Watt for Army and Royal Air Force types which was finally agreed, with the addition of Naval requirements, by the inter-Service R.D.F. Committee. The G.L. had to be altered to operate in the wave-band from $3\frac{1}{2}$ to $5\frac{1}{2}$ metres. This, of course, involved modifications and more particularly the design and development of new valves; the latter was carried out under Admiralty arrangements in a rapid and very satisfactory manner.

The advantage given by a band-width allocation was that if the sets were designed so that they were all capable of working on any frequency within that band, adjacent sets could avoid interference with one another by operating on a frequency different to that of its neighbour.

Up to this point "wave-lengths" rather than "frequencies" have been referred to; they are of course equally suitable in describing any radio wave (see Fig. 1) as each is a function of the wave form, the shorter the wave-length the higher the frequency and *vice versa*. The $3\frac{1}{2}$ to $5\frac{1}{2}$ metre wave-band expressed in frequencies is a band from 85 to 55 megacycles a second (Mc/s). Practical trials with two of the mobile sets showed that if they were on frequencies separated by 3 Mc/s they could operate without undue mutual interference at short distances apart. This separation was adopted to fix the specific frequencies on which this type of set could operate, thus giving a choice of 11 spot frequencies within the allocated band. Incidentally, it may be noted that a further aid to the prevention of such interference was given by slight changes in the pulse recurrence rate; the normal or mean rate was 1,000 pulses a second.

In February, 1939, a series of trials were carried out to test the value of linking this early type of radar set to the normal visual instruments for fire control. They were held at Landguard Fort where the G.L. I set (experimental model) linked with its external telescope (Modified A.A. Ring Sight Telescope) was associated with a normal gun site detachment with its Telescope Identification A.A. and U.B. 2 Heightfinder, to compare its ability to engage a target with that of a similar normal detachment without radar aid. In reasonably good visibility conditions, the difference in time of pick-up was always in favour of the G.L. aid with an average of between 20 and 30 seconds earlier engagement. In addition, its long-range local warning capacity materially reduced the strain of continuous watch and look-out.

As a result of these trials and in view of the urgent need—which had been emphasized by the stress of the Munich period—for making equipment available for training officers, operators, etc., and for getting it into the hands of troops for practice and experience, it was decided to go to production for a limited number of sets without waiting for the development of the means of providing the full information needed for complete fire control. It was of course fully appreciated that the equipment could *NOT* meet the requirements for engagement of unseen targets, but in view of the time factor this action was considered justified as an aid to and a means of improvement of visual methods of fire.

G.L. Mark I. This equipment was known as G.L. I, or in the official nomenclature adopted later as "Equipment, Radar, A.A. No. 1, Mark I."

It consisted of a transmitter with a "broadcast" transmission from its aerial, housed in a fixed cabin built on a trailer and a receiver housed in a rotatable cabin on a trailer with levelling jack-arms; its aerial frames were demountable, but in operation were fixed to the cabin and carried round with it. An R.A.F. type Meadows generator provided the power supply originally, but a higher power Lister set—an Army development that became standard for a variety of uses by all three Services—replaced it later.

This equipment provided maximum range for detection and pick up of aircraft of about 30,000 yards with an accuracy of not less than $\pm$ 500 yards, and accurate range, read and transmitted continuously to the predictor by standard mag-slip follow-the-pointer dials, from 14,000 yards. It also provided in its Stage I state, spot readings of bearing angle at a maximum rate of one a half-minute, of an accuracy of $\pm$ 1 to $1\frac{1}{2}$ degrees, which were transmitted by telephone; this degree of accuracy was adequate for putting the optical instruments on to the selected target at long range.

The supply contracts for the radio components for these equipments were placed with the priority firms, Metro-Vickers and Cossors, under Air Ministry arrangements, while the cabins, trailers, etc., were provided under War Office contracts (later taken over by the M. of S.) and supplied to the radar contracting firms. These firms produced six pilot models before full-scale production; the pilot models were fully tested and modified as found necessary by the Bawdsey staff who co-operated closely in the development and the trials with the representatives of the firms.

The modified pilot models were passed as suitable in June and July, 1939, and deliveries of the production equipments started in September of that year. By the end of 1939, 59 complete equipments had been delivered and they were followed by 344 in 1940; the total, including pilot and pre-production models and others for M. of S. experimental work, for this Mark I set amounted to 425. It was arranged in the contract terms that additions and modifications should be introduced into the production line if advances in the bearing and elevation measurements and their continuous reading were achieved in time to be incorporated in the later sets.

A change was made in the design in 1940 to incorporate various modifications including higher power transmission and other improvements. This improved model became G.L. 1* which started coming off production in August, 1940; existing sets were also modified to conform.

At the same time a separate contract for provision of a fitting to be added to the G.L. I and I*, started deliveries also in August. This was an important improvement known as the E/F (elevation finding) attachment which provided a means of following continuously, in bearing and in elevation, with a fair degree of accuracy through angles of from 15 to about 45 degrees. This E/F attachment has been largely attributed to Mr. Bedford of Messrs. A. C. Cossor's research staff, who certainly was the designer of the special attachment, though the ground-ray principle of its operation and use had emanated from the Army cell at Bawdsey.

This attachment could be applied to the G.L. I as a modification or addition in the field as it made use of the range C.R.T. for its display without interfering with range reading. Originally it could only provide elevation readings between 8 and 18 degrees, but after discussions with the A.D.R.D.E. staff its scope was extended to operate with fair accuracy but some difficulty up to 45 degrees.

Provision was made for 410 of these attachments for fitting to the equipments already with units and it undoubtedly encouraged attempts to engage the unseen target for which there was no other means available until the Mark II equipment came off production.

In May, 1939, two of the establishment-made pilot model sets were issued to S.A.A.D. Wireless Wing at Landguard Fort for training and instruction of Instructors, and were later fitted in the new service type cabin trailers. By the end of July, another of these sets, including a Metro-Vickers early production transmitter, was issued to the Military College of Science, which enabled training and instruction to be carried out in the more technical aspect for O.M.E.s, artificers and mechanics for maintenance and repair.

The first equipments off production were issued to units, schools, etc., in accordance with a priority list prepared by the War Office (T.O. Directorate). The majority were allocated to A.A. Command units and to Training Establishments in this country as it was useless to despatch them to overseas stations until personnel trained in their use and maintenance could be provided.

In October, 1939, the distribution list was amended to provide for issue to the Field Force. This provision consisted of 30 equipments, to be spread over the months from the end of November, 1939, to mid-March, 1940. Specific limits had to be placed on the frequencies used by these sets as the French could not accept operation in the vicinity of the band 55 to 60 Mc/s owing to certain of their essential communication equipments working on those frequencies and, therefore, likely to experience interference from the G.L. equipment.

Incidentally, it is of interest to note that the French were soon brought into the radar picture and trained on these sets and a number were handed over to them for operational use. Every set sent to our Field Force, and to the French, was provided with a special demolition charge. When our combined forces were overrun in 1940 practically all these sets were lost to the enemy, but in the case of those in the hands of our troops every single set was demolished; unfortunately, one at least in French hands was captured intact.

In regard to the operational effect of this equipment it is, perhaps, of interest to note some points contained in a report on the operation of an early G.L. I set of 6th September, 1939, the first war-time report on Army radar equipment in action. This report was made by Major G. C. Gray, Assistant Commandant of the Wireless Wing, School of A.A. Defence, Landguard; by the end of the war, Gray, by then a Brigadier, had become Director of Radar, War Office.

The trainees at Landguard had rejoined their units on the outbreak of war, but the instructional staff remained for a short time pending removal of the Wing to another more suitable site. Major Gray was authorized to man one of the training sets, established on a gun site at Landguard, with his technical training staff during the hours of daylight.

His report refers to "extensive raids" on September 6th and to "valuable lessons learned" as a result. It is immaterial to the value of the lessons that the raids were non-existent or at least were not enemy raids. The fact was that long-range warning of these raids was due to an error, and a cumulative one at that. Through faulty switching, a means of verifying that aircraft indications came from "forward looking" and not from the rear, some of our own aircraft operating inland were reported as an approaching enemy formation. More of our defence fighters were sent up to increase the force available to intercept, and to the radar, the "enemy" strength appeared to grow; in consequence more defence fighters were ordered up and so the competition continued to build up for a time until the error was recognized and corrected.

However, whether enemy or friendly—and there was no device at that time for radar identification—these aircraft gave Gray and his crew the first taste of G.L. operation against multiple targets, and fast ones at that. During the experimental and development stages of the equipment the lack of fast targets and the need for several targets at a time had been felt by the designers and representations of this need had been made but without effect.

The report brought out a number of lessons, some technical and some operational; of these the need for improved ventilation of the cabins and better lighting for dial reading were indicated, but Gray made no mention of the austere and uncomfortable seating in these early sets—probably the fact of being at war put such considerations of comfort into the background. The following are extracts from the report:—

(a) "Multiplicity of targets completely fogged an experienced detachment in the G.L. receiver. On the range side the high-speed time-base enabled discrimination to be made of individual targets, but the lower speed time-base on the bearing side did not provide the same discrimination, with the result that the targets merged and confusion resulted. It would appear that a high-speed time-base will be required on the D.F. side, unless experiments in connection with directivity show signs of correcting this fault.

(b) "Full speed service targets are desirable in the final stages of training. The operators this morning found that they had much less time than they were normally accustomed to."

and after referring to a technical difficulty in connexion with "locking" between receiver and transmitter,

(c) "With the receiver at a black spot for locking, the application of a man's hand to the locking receiver aerial immediately provided a locking signal. In fact the capacity effect of a man's hand near the aerial did so."

All these and other points and suggestions made were of interest and of value to the technical development staff; some of them resulted in improvements being made in the production sets though most of them had already been foreseen and provided for in the design of those sets. In regard to the two points mentioned at (a) and (b) above, the need for fast and multiple targets for tests had been urged for some time previously; some improvement in this respect was made for later trials but was seldom effected for training purposes.

The last of the three points, mentioned at (c), may sound to the uninitiated as rather a matter of "Ju-Ju" perhaps, but similar strange phenomena occurred in other later sets. In the case of G.L. Mark II, for example, its aerial feeders had to be stroked or otherwise petted to keep them in good temper and operating up to standard. Again the later "centimetric" types of equipment had other idiosyncracies that had to be learned by experience; the "wave-guides" and their joints required a lot of cosseting in the early days. It must be remembered that radar was a novel and rapidly growing technique that was being developed, much of which had to be built up empirically while experience and knowledge were accumulating. The time factor did not permit a complete scientific investigation of all such details before sets were produced, but the theoretical side was soon able to solve and keep pace with the problems involved and translate them into practical solutions for the designers and users.

To give some indication of the effect of the operational use of G.L. I and the improvement produced by the modifications and additions resulting in G.L. I* and E/F attachment, extracts from a Memorandum produced by Brigadier B. N. J. Schonland in charge of the Operational Research Group, are given here in respect of operations in Great Britain, where of course the attacks were most frequent, dense and heavy and the results most easily accessible.

"G.L. 1 (Radar A.A. No. 1, Mark I).

This equipment was designed before the war to provide early warning of approaching aircraft and as an aid to visual methods of fire-control. In this role it performed valuable service in Great Britain, France and the Middle East. It was not intended for complete fire-control purposes but when night bombing attacks began in September, 1940, it had to be used by A.A. Command to direct unseen fire in default of anything else. As it gave no angle of sight, this quantity was obtained from sound locators and with telephoned G.L. bearings and ranges, and a crude height estimate, the predictors were supplied with present data sufficient to enable the rounds to be placed somewhere in the region of the target. 'It was a technique that was complex but crude and clumsy. The data were not accurate enough to be applicable to a precision instrument and they were supplied in a way that made it difficult for a predictor to digest them without severe internal pains. The Sperry voiced its indignation audibly, the Vickers suffered in silence.' The method was widely used through the Autumn. In September and October, 1940, 260,000 rounds were fired and 14 aircraft brought down. (18,500 rounds per bird.)"

"G.L. I with E.F. (Radar A.A. No. 1 Mk. I E/F).

This equipment, which was a modified form of G.L. I and capable of elevation-finding and continuous following in bearing, was extensively fitted and set-up in Britain by the end of 1940 and used for unseen fire-control during the night attacks of 1941. Many technical and tactical problems had to be solved before it could be considered of much use for this purpose. 'It resulted in our entering a world full of troubles hitherto undreamed of; a world of mats, of feeders that had to be "stroked" every day to keep them in a good temper and of calibration difficulties. . . . But it was, for all that, a saving miracle of achievement, that enabled us at least to shoot with some remote hope of success.'

During the year 1941 the efficiency of unseen A.A. fire was improved to a figure of 4,100 rounds per bird."

G.L. II. The design and development of the 5 metre set—a general term for the sets working in the $3\frac{1}{2}$ or $5\frac{1}{2}$ metre wave-band—for providing complete data for the direction and control of fire of H.A.A. guns was, as has already been stressed, the primary problem for our scientists and technicians that formed the Army cell at the Bawdsey Research Establishment. In the earlier part of this chapter it has been shown how the difficulty of providing a suitable means of reading the elevation angle to the target, and of doing so continuously, had made it necessary to put into the hands of troops a set that actually could aid visual methods only, and not provide all the information needed for engaging the unseen target successfully. All the research, development and experimental work up to that time was really aimed at the complete set which was referred to as the G.L. Mark II, and the Mark I was only an early throw-off from that work.

At the time the Mark I was put into production, there was no method available for continuous reading of the bearing angles; observations by bracketing on a zero signal could be made to an accuracy of about $1\frac{1}{2}$ degrees, but they could not be read sufficiently often or regularly to feed into the predictor; this system, moreover, suffered from fading of the signals. In May, 1939, a system had been developed that was showing good promise in an experimental set. In this system the signal obtained from the horizontally spaced direction-finding pair of aerials (see Fig. 8) was fed into a reversing switch, the output from which was combined with the signal obtained from a third aerial. This produced a beam swing, giving the effect of an overlapping beam system. The signals were brought on to a C.R.T. screen superimposed on one another. A colour filter part orange-red and part green rotated synchronously with the reversing switch, so that the signal from the right-hand position appeared red, and from the left-hand position green. Correct bearing was indicated by equality of amplitude of the two signals and due to the superimposition, this meant that true bearing was indicated by the "blip" white to the tip. A red tip indicated that the system was pointing to the left of the target, and right-hand rotation was needed to get correct bearing, while a green tip indicated that a left-handed turn was needed.

This most ingenious device was largely attributable to Pollard. Though with the colour filter it was not easy always to recognize accurately a slight variation in the colouring, it did provide continuous bearing readings to an accuracy of about 1 degree. It was later referred to sometimes as "the red-green monstrosity," but it was the first success with continuous following, and was applied to the improved equipment for both bearing and elevation readings. This was in fact probably the first use of the "split" method though at the time it was not recognized as such. It provided separate signals for comparison, but superimposed them (distinguishable by colour rather than by their separate appearance) on the screen for them to be matched in amplitude, which became the normal method later.

The same method of separated receiving aerials for comparison of direct signals could not be used for measuring the elevation angles, as it was not possible to tilt the cabin and aerial frame in the vertical plane. For this angular measurement, it was necessary to make use of the fact that the signal picked up in an aerial is a combination of the direct ray from the target and an indirect ray reflected from the ground, the result being that the amplitude of the received signal depends only on the height of the aerial above the ground and the angle of elevation of the target. The elevation angle can, therefore, be determined by direct comparison of the signals obtained from two aerials at different heights above the ground. These separate signals had to be brought together through a device known as a goniometer and compared on a C.R.T. screen. It involved many difficulties; the site had to be level and regular for a considerable radius, the whole range of elevation could not be covered by one system of aerials, and the comparison of the signals could not be made on a linear scale as it varied with the elevation angle to the target. The first of these involved surrounding the set with a false "earth" or artificial reflecting surface in the form of a flat wire-mesh mat. The second made it necessary to select a limited arc of elevation angles most appropriate to the effective use of the H.A.A. guns; the selection made at this stage when the full possibilities were still unproved, was the range of from 10 to 55 degrees which would cover the longest effective gun range for first engagement of any target. The third trouble of non-linearity of angular measurement with increasing angles of sight, made difficult the automatic transmission of data for feeding into the predictor or conversion into height. This was eventually corrected with reasonable accuracy by providing and fitting special cams in the control movement. These troubles and other difficulties were, however, cleared sooner or later—in some cases the decision as to whether to go to production or to await complete proof had to be taken: it was a gamble on the accuracy of the scientists' assessments of early effective solutions if long delays were to be avoided—the gamble was, in fact, generally justified by the results.

The systems for the continuous measurement and reading of the two essential angles were demonstrated in experimental form, fitted to one of the pilot model mobile equipments in August, 1939, and tests of accuracy of performance were carried out. This work was interrupted by the move to Christchurch, but was actively pursued there as the item of first importance, in spite of the lack of full facilities in the early days of occupation of the new establishment.

Towards the end of October, 1939, a meeting was held with Mr. Watson-Watt, then D.C.D. Air Ministry, in the chair, with a number of scientists representing A.M.R.E. (then at Dundee), A.D.R.D.E., and the M. of S., as well as W.O. technical artillery representatives and R.E. and S. Board. The whole question of A.A. Radar fire control was considered and the results of trials were accepted as adequate proof of the accuracy possible with this design, with the proviso that proof of performance in elevation above 30 degrees should be obtained and should not be worse than the ± 1 degree achieved at the lower angles. It was also agreed to recommend that this G.L. II type should be put into production forthwith for the full requirements of the W.O.

This meeting also considered the future possibilities of providing for greater accuracy of performance so that unseen radar fire control methods should give results at least as accurate as those of visual methods in good conditions. A narrow "beam" type of set with independence of site conditions and ground reflections was recommended for development, using a 50-cm. wave-length.

On the weight of this body of scientific and technical advice, the General Staff accepted this recommendation as the line for future development for high accuracy fire control.

Before the G.L. II design was finalized for production several improvements were effected.

One of the major points of design represented as essential by the War Office was that all such equipments should be made capable of use in tropical conditions. This was of great importance as equipment would have to operate in any part of the world and uniformity was a key consideration particularly from the maintenance aspect. The R.E. and S. Board had considerable previous experience in making various types of equipment fit for use in tropical conditions, but had to extend its investigations to deal with the novel components and materials used in this new technique. It is interesting to note the result with this particular type during the war. This G.L. II equipment was called upon to operate in conditions varying from the Russian winter with temperatures of 40 degrees below zero to those of the tropical Pacific islands with their high temperatures and great humidity. That the G.L. II did, in fact, compete successfully in all these conditions is a real tribute to the work of the design and development staffs.

An improved system of continuous angular following and reading was introduced; this was the true "split" showing twin signals on a C.R. Tube screen. The "blips" appeared alongside of one another but separate—still tinted by the two-colour filter—to permit of them being easily matched in amplitude. It was found rather better for this purpose to have the "blips" horizontal rather than vertical as it appeared to make matching slightly simpler. The operation of balancing them and keeping them balanced was effected, in the case of bearing, by the mechanical rotation of the cabin and its aerials, while for the elevation reading the balance was effected by turning the handle of the goniometer. Both these actions at the same time operated the electrical magslip transmission gear to follow-the-pointer dials on the predictor. To accept the elevation readings a special addition was provided on the predictor for the conversion of slant range and elevation angle to height, which was the control factor of the mechanical predictors in use, and ground range.

To apply this system to the Mark I equipment already in production was not possible without major redesign and it was decided to concentrate on the new methods for the Mark II type. It was here that the ingenuity of Mr. Bedford of Messrs. A. C. Cossor was of such value, for the Bawdsey cell were enabled to concentrate their efforts on the full-scale application of the more accurate method to the improved type of equipment.

With the addition of direction and elevation finding to the receiver the need for higher power and greater concentration of the transmission had become apparent, so the transmitter for the Mark II had been made more directional and provided with a rotating cabin. The receiver was provided with search aerials for the longer range pick-up, and a separate set of "follow" aerials with a narrower spread or angle of embrace for reception of echo signals for greater accuracy in tracking the selected target. When the receiver switched from "search" to "follow" the transmitter had to conform to the direction of the receiver so that with the maximum power of the transmission directed at the target, the echo signals were naturally stronger.

The G.L. II equipment, officially known as Equipment R.D.F. (later, Radar), A.A. No. 1, Mark II, comprised a transmitter housed in a mobile rotatable cabin which carried its erectable aerial array; a receiver similarly housed with aerials providing the two main arrays; two separate aerials for direction-finding spaced horizontally, and two aerials vertically spaced for elevation finding, all demountable, and a 15 Kva. Lister generator to provide the necessary power. Marked improvement over the Mark I had been made in the comfort of the operators in seating and ventilation, but no material protection against splinters was provided and gas protection was limited to the individual protection given by the Service respirator and to anti-gas paint on the cabins. For accurate fire control working a level site surrounding the set was necessary, and for static sites a wire mesh mat had to be provided to extend for a radius of 80 feet round the receiver; this naturally militated severely against its mobility and suitability for mobile operations.

Its mobility or rather its capacity for movement—without considering the mat—was designed to conform with that of the mobile 3·7 in. H.A.A. gun; its normal wading depth was just under 2 feet in still water, but for special cases and for short periods it could be waterproofed sufficiently to permit of passage through 3 ft. 9 ins. of water with an additional 1 ft. 6 in. lop.

The complete weight of the transmitter unit was 6 tons 15 cwt. and of the receiver 5 tons 8 cwt. Separate presentations of signals were provided for range, bearing and elevation and continuous reading and transmission of each through high- and low-speed magslips to the predictor.

For operation the crew required was 1 N.C.O. in general charge, with three operators in the receiver and one in the transmitter cabins, for each watch.

The accepted performance of this equipment was:—

Maximum detection range —Not less than 50,000 yards.
Accurate fire control range—Not less than 14,000 yards.
Range accuracy —Not worse than $\pm$ 50 yards up to 14,000 and $\pm$ 200 yards up to 30,000.
Bearing accuracy —Not worse than $\pm \frac{1}{2}$ degree up to 50 degrees elevation.
Elevation accuracy —Not worse than $\pm \frac{1}{2}$ degree between 10 and 50 degrees; less accurate outside those limits.

A total of 1,679 sets of this equipment were produced, deliveries started in January, 1941, and were completed in August, 1943. (See Illustration 1.)

That this equipment was capable of being operated to these accuracies is not in question, but it is true that the skill and experience of the crews operating it did not often permit of such accuracy.

It is also true that the nature of the information and the smoothness of its feed to the predictor was not up to the standard of visual, and reduced the overall accuracy of the fire control equipment below that of the best visual operation. It did, however, provide a real means of engagement of the unseen target with good prospects of successful results.

In comparison with the G.L. I* with E/F attachment on the basis of "dead birds," the assessed figures by the Operational Research Group do not show the improvement in effect that might have been anticipated from the much improved and tested new design. The results given in the same O.R.G. Memorandum from which extracts were quoted for the earlier G.L. type, are given below for comparison.

"G.L. II.

This equipment, which was specially designed for fire-control purposes, with a directional beamed transmitter for following aircraft as distinct from searching, was generally deployed in Britain by the middle of 1942 and was in extensive use at home and abroad during 1942 and 1943. During 1942, 26 (actually $25\frac{1}{2}$) aircraft were brought down for an average expenditure of 2,750 rounds per bird. Its introduction was effected with an almost complete absence of trouble owing to the excellence of its design and manufacture and to the large amount of work that had been done by A.D.R.D.E. and in A.A. Command on the technical and tactical development of unseen fire with G.L. Mk. I (E.F.).

For his attacks on London in 1943 the enemy changed his tactics and made use of high speed fighter bombers flying at high altitudes, difficult to predict upon owing to their speed and erratic course. Nevertheless our unseen fire, which had improved considerably with drill and technical modifications, was not significantly less effective than in 1942 (3,200 rounds per bird)."

There are two indeterminate factors in making the comparison, but whether their effect, if assessable, would favour the G.L. II or not is a matter of doubt. The first of them is the fact that a number of radar operators had gained some experience and methods of unseen engagement had been developed; the second, on the other hand, was the experience gained by the enemy which probably resulted in more difficult targets for the guns even before the noticeable change in tactics in 1943, mentioned in the extract above.

The excellence of the design and manufacture of this set is supported by the fact that it remained in very active service throughout the war and in all theatres of operation including the equatorial Pacific Islands and wintry Russia. It was landed on open beaches in the early flights of landing operations and stood up to all conditions and to continuous hard use. It did all this with a remarkable freedom from trouble. It was used successfully for a number of important purposes for which it was never intended, and did so with considerable effect, as for example in tracking the V.2 Stratosphere Rocket in the last days of the war. Even if it was out-dated by the "centimetric" revolution in radar technique, it was never outclassed in the excellence of its design. Even its trailer cabins became famous and were diverted to all kinds of other sets and uses and were in great demand. The Lister generating set introduced for this equipment equalled it in these respects and was adopted by the other two Services also.

Though, perhaps, immature technically on account of the novelty of radar itself, particularly in the light of the revolutionary development of centimetric working, there is no question that the design and production of this equipment were very remarkable achievements.

CHAPTER IX. H.A.A. ARTILLERY RADAR—CENTRIMETRIC TYPES

In the earliest days of the investigations by the Army cell at Bawdsey, the future solution of the problem of accurate angular measurements had been forecast by Dr. Paris, in conjunction with Dr. Bowen of the Air Ministry staff, as most likely to be found in the use of ultra short wave-lengths and very narrow beam transmissions. The very short aerials requiring reflectors of small size to concentrate the beam transmissions would permit of their movement in both vertical and horizontal planes without tilting or turning the set itself. This would not only bring part of the solution into the mechanical field but would also liminate largely the effect of the nature and evenness of the surrounding ground surface.

From the early days Sir Henry Tizard had stressed the need for going to very short wave-length working and urged the importance of development of high power output at such wave-lengths. In this he was supported by other leading scientists concerned with radar, including C. S. Wright, D.S.R., Admiralty, in whose hands the responsibility for research and development of valves was mainly concentrated.

In the autumn of 1939 research work was specially directed to valve design for ultra short wave-lengths with high power output. It is not entirely clear how this work was initiated but it is probable that it was due to Sir Henry Tizard's initiative and C. S. Wright's co-operation and support. At any rate, Professor Mark Oliphant and his party who had been absorbing practical radar at the Ventnor C.H. station during September, returned to Birmingham and with a reinforcement from Cambridge got down to work in the University Physics laboratories. This was the start of the work that gave birth to the most important Radar invention of the war—namely, the Resonator or Cavity Magnetron, which revolutionized radar technique, widely extended the scope of its employment and increased its effectiveness in a remarkable way.

In a very short time sufficient progress had been made to report that the first magnetron valve giving 1 kilowatt output was set up in the laboratory, working on a wave-length less than 10 centimetres.

In May, 1940, it appeared in a hut at Worth Maltravers where A.M.R.E., now renamed Telecommunications Research Establishment (T.R.E.), had been accommodated after their short sojourn at Dundee. Dee and Skinner of that establishment were heavily engaged in getting acquainted with its habits, devising means to apply it, developing the technique for its effective employment and assessing its possibilities. At Birmingham Oliphant's team was embarking on further development while Sutton was developing suitable Klystron oscillators at Bristol and the General Electric Company were tackling the question of crystals suitable for working at these wave-lengths.

By July, 1940, experimental centimetric radar was "on the air" and echoes had been received from cars and aircraft and full efforts were concentrated upon it to bring it into war use effectively. For this purpose all initial development work for experimental types was concentrated at T.R.E., where a Joint Establishment Investigation Group was set up. This was mainly staffed by personnel from T.R.E., but the Admiralty and Ministry of Supply establishments were intimately associated with it and provided personnel to co-operate in the work.

It was this group that demonstrated the possibilities for Naval use which were subsequently developed by the Admiralty Signals Establishment and resulted in the famous N.T. 271 and its successors to which reference is made in later chapters of this record. They also initiated the embryo of a centimetric G.L. set that was sufficient at least to indicate the possibility of developing a potentially accurate equipment.

The progress of the Resonator Magnetron development was closely watched by the R.D.F. Applications Committee under the Chairmanship of Sir Edward Appleton, which held the first of its regular monthly meetings in March, 1940. At that meeting Oliphant had reported that his magnetron was giving an output of 1 kW. on continuous wave and that higher power would be obtained if it were pulsed. In August the magnetron was reported as giving 10 kW. when pulsed and the possibility of obtaining 100 kW. peak pulse output at an early date was reported at the end of October. It will, therefore, be appreciated how remarkably rapid had been the development of this far-reaching advance in radar technique.

A magnetron valve had been produced and known some years before and another valve known as the Klystron, operating on a different principle for very short wave-lengths, was also known, but they were limited to powers of 50 to 100 watts. It was the development of the high power working achieved by entirely new means within the magnetron itself that brought it into the field of practical radar and multiplied the available power output some thousandfold within a year from the start of the investigations. Later this was still further increased and output powers of 500 kW. became available within two years and still greater powers were to follow.

There can be no doubt that this development was a most remarkable achievement and our scientists deserve the greatest credit for it. It is worthy of note that the enemy did not achieve this forward step in the efficiency of radar. They did, however, employ a few of these valves towards the end of the war, mostly recoveries from crashed bombers of the R.A.F. or the American Air Forces, and produced some of their own which were more or less "chinese copies" of those recovered valves.

It must also be stated definitely that this outstanding radar development was a purely British invention. It was disclosed to America freely on the authority of the Prime Minister, in September/October, 1940, by the Mission sent out there under Sir Henry Tizzard. Professor J. D. Cockcroft was one of that party and extracts from his notes on the actual disclosure and presentation of one of the few 9·1 cm. magnetrons then available are worth quoting:—

"Fortified by this (the P.M.'s authority to disclose anything) we got together the famous 'Black Box' collection of samples and reports. At the top of the list was a precious 9·1 cm. magnetron and crystals. . . ."

"Our trump card was undoubtedly the magnetron. We produced it at a meeting in the Wardman Park Hotel attended by Admiral Bowen and United States Naval Research Laboratory officers. I still remember the rather doubtful opening with the United States Officers suspicious as to whether we were putting all our cards on the table. The disclosure was the key point and from then on we had no difficulties. We found the Navy Lab. had been experimenting with klystron 10 watt transmitters, and were intensely interested. We visited the Bell Labs. on October 3rd and left the magnetron over the week-end with Dr. Kelly. Within three days they had it working and developing power, as Bowen saw on October 8th. We were taken on September 24th to Holmdale where we saw Southworth's fundamental work on 10 cm. reception. They also were limited to the 10 watts of the klystron. Our disclosure had therefore increased the power available to U.S. technicians by a factor of 1,000."

In so far as H.A.A. fire control radar equipment was concerned the War Office was asking for the development of a much advanced G.L. set to follow the G.L. II. In August, 1940, the Ministry of Supply still confirmed their recommendation made in 1939 for a set working on 50 cm., for which experimental work was already in hand at A.D.R.D.E., but in September and October, in view of the progress made with the centimetric valve developments, a further request for their advice was made by the W.O. as to the basis on which development of the urgently needed improved type of equipment should be undertaken. There were various competitors to the 10 cm. class of magnetron that were being advocated by a variety of individuals—a 10 cm. klystron was one of them; there was the 50-cm. type already under investigation and proposals were made to develop a set working on 25 cms. while others also were "in the air." The War Office was not then in a position to decide for themselves such technical matters nor to assess the probable improvements in performance of the different possibilities—they had to rely upon the advice of the Ministry in such matters. The War Office asked for this matter to be considered by the R.D.F. Applications Committee and their advice sought. After detailed consideration this committee submitted a recommendation in November, 1940—

"that the maximum effort should now be concentrated on the production of G.L. sets on wave-lengths below 10 cms."

This recommendation was agreed by the Ministry and accepted by the War Office, but even then some of the competitors still had their advocates. The difficulties of decision caused by "many cooks" and "disagreeing doctors" is evidenced by a rather plaintive extract from a letter by D.E.S.E., M. of S., in reply to D.S.R., Admiralty. That letter indicates that the Ministry proposed to adhere to the recommended type employing a resonator magnetron and a Sutton type local oscillator, as being of greater promise for an effective advanced equipment; it ended with the plaint:—

"So many people, however, are interested in and giving advice and instructions on R.D.F. matters that the path is very crooked and ill defined."

In August, 1940, the War Office Panel of the Inter-Service R.D.F. Committee had called for the preparation of a new performance specification of requirements for an advanced G.L. set and this was used as a basis for the development, as then advised, of an experimental 50 cm. set. In November, D.A.A. and CD passed a revised G.S. specification to the Ministry for the future 10-cm. set that was to become the G.L. III equipment. This is given below as issued, though it was amended in detail as development proceeded; it will be noted that the acceptable accuracy of measurement to be attained is *not* given even for range, but at that time the degree of improvement over the performance of earlier types could not be assessed.

"G.S. Specification for G.L. Mark III

To combine a G.L. I or II set for early warning with a V.H.F. set (wavelength 10 cm. or below) for fire control.

        Pick up for early warning—30,000 yards
        Pick up for Fire Control —22,000 yards

Accurate range measurement required from 2,000 to 17,000 yards, though a maximum of 14,000 yards would be accepted.

Beam width 14° desirable; 10° minimum acceptable.

Elevation from 10° to 90° for following;
10° to 70° for fire control.

The same C.R.T.s to be used for the G.L. and V.H.F. parts of the equipment.

(Signed) ———

16–11–40. D.A.A. and C.D."

With the acceptance by the War Office of the 10 cm. wave-length with resonator magnetron for the development of the urgently needed new G.L. equipment, the work on the 50-cm. set at A.D.E.E. was put on low priority and closed down as soon as possible. A little later, development was agreed on 25 cm. for experiment as a possible stand-by in case there should be undue difficulties with the 10 cm. set, which was given the highest priority of all work at the establishment.

The development of production methods for the magnetron valves was organized by the Admiralty and M.A.P. for all Service uses in a surprisingly short time. With the increasing demands from all three Services, however, the supplies of these valves gave cause for anxiety for some considerable time.

The work at Birmingham under Oliphant was helped along towards experimental development of a G.L. set by a team from A.D.R.D.E. under Pollard, but after some two months in January, 1941, they and their initial development work were transferred to the B.T.H. Company's research branch at Rugby. They were joined there by Robinson and Brown from T.R.E. who brought with them the mock-up experimental set devised at that establishment. Pollard's party from A.D.R.D.E. worked in close co-operation with the B.T.H. staff, and it was a strong and capable group that tackled the development problems.

G.L. III. By April, 1941, an experimental set working in a narrow band of wave-lengths around 10 cm., known as the A model, had been completed and demonstrated at Rugby and in May and June trials with it were carried out at A.D.R.D.E. Christchurch. These showed that both bearing and elevation accuracies of about 10 minutes of arc were obtainable and good range following was possible to about 18,000 yards. They also showed that following was good down to low angles and there was no difficulty in following through to the zenith. This set was not, of course, engineered for production nor for service use as it was inadequately water-proofed and unfit for cross-country usage.

While recognized by the War Office and other user representatives as a good "lash-up" that would require considerable redesign and modification to make it suitable for service equipment, its performance was certainly most attractive. It was also appreciated that the great advance in performance demonstrated was attributable rather to the centimetric beam technique than to the form in which it was presented in the A model. The urgency of the need for a fire control equipment giving that class of performance could not be denied, with the experience of heavy night attacks and their continuing recurrence. The time factor weighed heavily and it was questionable whether the proper engineering of a production design of this A model would not give earlier operational advantage than awaiting the development of the form— the B model—contemplated and strongly urged by the scientists and technical

Artillery experts as the proper answer, but which had not by then taken even mock-up form.

This A model was provided only with a 5 kW. magnetron, but provision was made in the design (and in the development contract) for it to accept higher power magnetrons over a range of from 30 to 100 kW. The A model consisted of two parts linked together by the necessary cabling; the receiver, a modified Mark II type with improved presentation and control position, was in a G.L. II cabin trailer while the transmitter and aerial system were fitted to a standard 90 cm. searchlight base, turn-table and U-arms. The aerial system consisted of two separate dipoles with paraboloid reflectors; in the case of the receiving aerial, the dipole was rotated rapidly, slightly offset from the focus of the paraboloid in order to give beam switching reception for readings of bearing and of elevation—right and left positions for the former and top and bottom for the latter. The connecting cables provided the power supply for the transmitter, power for the Selsyns controlling the movement of the aerials, and the transmission of the radio frequency (I.F.) of the receiving aerial signals to the receiver and presentation unit.

The standard of mechanical accuracy of the searchlight turn-table was inadequate for the high accuracy requirements for fire control and the difficulty of ensuring proper weather and water-proofing of components carried on this turn-table, presented awkward problems, but they did not appear to be insoluble.

The contemplated B model was a complete unit contained in a single large cabin fixed on a four-wheeled trailer. The size and, more particularly, the probable over-all weight, were somewhat staggering. There were certainly many easily appreciated advantages in this proposed design. Among these were undercover access to all parts for maintenance and repair, greater comfort of the operators, solidity and rigidity of the whole structure making possible more accurate calibration and collimation of the radar axis with that of visual, providing stable foundations for the mechanical components that had to be of a high degree of accuracy.

In April the War Office asked for the earliest possible provision of four hand-made prototypes of the A type (improved), as a means of meeting a special urgent requirement in connection with the defence measures for the Thames Estuary, and they agreed that a B model should be produced for demonstration and inspection as soon as possible. This would enable a decision to be made as to the form in which the new equipment should be produced, that is to say, whether a partial supply of a properly engineered A type should be made as an interim measure pending the finalization of the design of the B model, or whether the whole supply should be postponed till the B type had been proved. It was rather a case of the best being a possible enemy of the good, and time was apparently on the side of the A pattern.

In addition to this small War Office requirement of the A type, 3 more were required by Admiralty and M.A.P., whose demand, unfortunately, was increased in May, bringing the total up to 17. This produced considerable difficulties and was reported as delaying the development of the B model; the firm meanwhile were strongly supporting the M. of S. in urging the B type as the ultimate and only suitable pattern for production.

In early June a model of the B type was available at Rugby for inspection and was seen by the D. of R., War Office, and by representatives of A.A. Command. As a result it was accepted as the only type to be put into production and the War Office agreed to forgo the 4 A models and strongly urged M.A.P. to accept the B type in lieu of the A models they had demanded; that order, however, was not withdrawn. The R.A.F. wanted them for height determination in conjunction with G.C. I sets and, though warned of their unsuitability, only discovered later their unreliability and the great difficulties in maintaining them. That this diversion of effort affected the provision of urgently needed G.L. equipment for the Army is undoubted and was most unfortunate.

In July an agreed demand was placed for 28 pre-production (hand-made) B type sets, of which the Ministry required 8 for experimental work, and a requirement for bulk production of 900 equipments was stated formally to the Ministry of Supply and ordered on M.A.P. early in July, 1941.

The first 5 of the hand-made models were made available between December, 1941, and April, 1942, as experimental sets for the Ministry and for final proof of the design for full production, but deliveries of the remaining 23 did not start till October and a total of 8 only were supplied by the end of 1942—a most disappointing result from the operational aspect, particularly after the forecasts that had been made by the Ministry. Certainly the constant delays in clearing design and the frequent postponement of delivery dates had increasingly discouraged optimism about them, but that did not help in meeting the night bombing. The War Office had stressed the need for supply starting in time to get sets into action in the winter period of 1941–42, but it was a year later that the first dribble of sets began to make their appearance. These delays and difficulties with production are referred to in a later chapter and all that need be said here is that divided control—between M. of S. and M.A.P.—of production, a lack of appreciation of the magnitude of the production problems and the excessive time taken to finalize the design at the prototype stage appear to have been the chief causes of the delay.

Full supply from production started with 2 only in December, 1942, and slowly worked up to its maximum rate of output towards the end of 1943; the maximum in one year was a total of 548 sets supplied during 1944. The total deliveries amounted to 876 sets by April, 1945, when deliveries ceased. The total of the order had been increased but was subsequently cut owing to lack of production capacity for radar equipment for the other Services; a number of sets were also diverted to aid Russia.

These equipments proved to be robust and gave good service, but they were overtaken by the march of technical progress and were partly outdated before they had got into action. Automatic working was in the air in the latter half of 1942, and though the War Office realized the advantages it offered they could not accept any further delay or diversion of effort in meeting the very pressing operational need for improved H.A.A. radar sets. That delays would have been caused, even by the suggestion of the possibility of introducing such a major change in design, was strongly stressed by the Production authorities. Any form of major modification or addition was ruled out by the General Staff, but had it been possible to foresee the tortuous course of this Mark III production it might have been possible to cut the extent of the order and to replace the latter part of it by a new properly designed type of Auto equipment.

The G.L. Mark III equipment, officially known as A.A. No. 3, Mark II, worked on a frequency around 3,000 Mc/s. at a power of 5 kW., increased later to 100 kW. It consisted of a sheet steel cabin on a 4-wheeled trailer, housing the radar components and the operators. A rotor unit was mounted on an accurate turn-table at the forward end of the cabin and carried the aerial system which projected through the roof and was rotatable with the rotor.

The aerial system consisted of separate dipoles with 4 ft. paraboloid reflectors for transmission and for reception, carried on the rotor cross-arms about which they moved for elevation; for the receiving aerial the dipole was rotated rapidly to give "split" readings for both elevation and bearing, while that for transmitting was fixed.

The rotor housed the transmitter and the gearing for rotation of the rotor and aerials controlled by Selsyn drive; it also carried the Selsyn units for elevation movement of the aerials. Slip rings and cables linked the transmitter and the Selsyn units to the receiver or presentation unit which was situated at the centre of the cabin, leaving a clear space and access for the operators at the rear. The excellent receiver unit for the G.L. III was a joint effort of A.D.R.D.E. and E.M.I. A great deal of work was carried out to determine the best form of presentation and type of control, and the Medical Research Council assisted in devising improved operating conditions. Two range tubes were provided, one for "coarse" reading and target selection by strobe, which enabled accurate range reading to be made on the "fine" tube by centring the "blip" on the cross wire by a hand-wheel which automatically transmitted the range continuously through magslips to the predictor. At the same time the strobing brought side-by-side "blips," due only to the particular selected target, on to the bearing and the elevation tubes. The matching of these signals by hand-wheel turning (see Illustration 16) transmitted the information continuously to the predictor in the same way as for range. The three operators for the presentation unit had comfortable seats, suitable lighting and air conditioning, which also served the cabin as a whole. A fourth member of the crew, for technical adjustment, had access to the rotor unit and to the back of the presentation unit to keep the set up to standard performance or make the necessary adjustments without interfering with the operators (see Illustrations 2, 3, 4, 15).

The narrow transmission beam could be used for searching over limited arcs for pick-up of targets, but usually it was necessary to associate a search and early warning set with the G.L. III for putting it on early to approaching targets. This had been accepted by the G.S. as an essential to avoid complication of the design; the G.L. II was frequently used in this way or a Light Warning set (described in a later chapter). The actual effective beam width was about 8 degrees so that there was no difficulty in operating down to elevation angles of under 10 degrees and up to or slightly beyond the zenith.

It also gave good discrimination between targets if separated by 250 yards in range or 4 degrees in angle.

Its performance may be summarized as follows:—

Range output accuracy	± 25 yards up to 35,000 yards
Range output smoothness	25 yards
Bearing and elevation output accuracy	± 10 minutes
smoothness	10 minutes
Average maximum range for detection (bomber)	35,000 yards

The early models of this new type were submitted to a very full series of trials and tests before it was passed for production; few equipments were put through such a thorough and complete check-up of performance and behaviour, both on site and on the move, and for suitability to withstand tropical conditions. The ease of maintenance and repair, with its ample undercover access for this purpose, were closely studied and adjusted and essential test meters were built in.

It was moved across England and tested by A.O.R.G. on a variety of gun sites to determine any adverse siting effects or other limitations. It suffered no material troubles in its long treks and achieved good performance on gun sites, often tracking hostile aircraft successfully.

It was found capable of withstanding the blast effect of A.A. guns at a distance of 30 yards when firing at 10 degrees elevation and only 10 degrees off line. It was submitted to trials of rough conditions for travel on the "bump" courses in comparison with a mobile 3·7 in. gun and successfully passed them though, in this particular case, through a faulty axle, the gun broke down on the course.

These tests, of course, took time, but it was not this that delayed the preparations for production; the scientific and technical design points affecting accuracy and stability of operation were the primary cause as they took longer than anticipated to determine and to decide what alterations were essential for incorporation in the production design.

The comfortable conditions for the operators encouraged good operation and confidence in the set was established from first entry as there was little of the plethora of switches, knobs, glowing bulb lights and other gadgets as in earlier sets, that tended to give an impression of complication in operation. Generally, operators found it easier than the earlier sets to handle and rapidly picked up a good standard of operation.

The dominant note of the continuous pressure by the W.O. for speeding-up production was always time and the urgency of the operational need. Apart from the needs of A.A. Command in meeting the continuing enemy attacks on this country, the W.O. had to plan for special overseas operations in preparation, for which the earlier types were neither appropriate nor suitable.

With the delay an emergency type had to be improvised and introduced to serve as a temporary substitute; this became known as Baby Maggie, a makeshift to assist the operations in Northern Africa, Sicily and elsewhere. It was to a fair extent independent of site conditions and elevation limits, but it was not a centimetric type nor was it capable of the accuracy of the G.L. III, though it could compete in that respect with the G.L. II, though not in detection range; this gun-laying adaptation will be described in Chapter XI.

It is unfortunate that the assessment of results in terms of "dead birds" for comparison with those already given for the earlier types, cannot be extracted from the same A.O.R.G. memorandum; the G.L. III had not been sufficiently long in action nor in sufficient numbers at the time that compilation was made. A note included therein, however, refers to it as follows:—

"G.L. III Marks I and II.

These centimetric equipments . . . have only recently been introduced into the field and have not had sufficient action to justify report. They are expected to be between two and three times more accurate than G.L. II and to reduce the number of rounds per bird to a figure of from 500 to 1,000, depending upon the type of target and the predictor used."

Another assessment of the comparative value of this 10 cm. type and the improvement to be expected from its operational use was given in a scientific review by Dr. Paris when the Radio Board was discussing the allocation of the then limited supplies of valves and components and considering the available production facilities. On 25th March, 1942, after defining the primary features of the equipment, he gave the following scientific assessment of the improvement to be expected in operational effect:—

"This equipment is thus likely to improve unseen fire by a factor of at least four. Since a further factor of 2 in accuracy will be gained by automatic fuze setting (to which this increased accuracy is appropriate and necessary) and the additional factor of 2 due to the improved rate of fire it produces, there is a potential improvement in A.A. fire against unseen targets by a factor of 16. The effect of avoiding action taken by the target, in the worst case reduces the lethality by two. We may, therefore, expect an overall increase in percentage of aircraft brought down by A.A. fire by a factor between 5 and 8. . . . it is evident that G.L. III is a development of major importance."

A further paper prepared on a scientific basis, by Cockcroft and Schonland in conjunction, in mid April, 1943, to support the G.S. in resisting the suggested elimination or large-scale reduction of production of the G.L. III equipment (a high-level attack due to the limited capacity available in this country and the demands on it by the R.A.F. for their offensive needs), contains the following:—

"*Lethality.* The chance of obtaining a casualty per engagement depends on the accuracy of the fire control, and the number of rounds fired. Both of these factors are determined by the nature of the fire control equipment and the tactics employed by the target aircraft. We will make a comparison between the chances of obtaining a casualty with the existing (G.L. II) R.D.F. equipment and with centimetric R.D.F. equipment, both being used with the same type of predictor, fuze-setter (Molins) and auto-loader. Two (the worst) types of avoiding action by the target will be considered. . . .

Chance of Casualty per engagement by a 4-gun battery for target height of 12,000'

	G.L. II	G.L. III
No avoiding action	1·5 %	7·5 %
Jink on 1st burst	0·5 %	1·8 %
Continuous weaving	1·0 %	1·5 %

The absolute value of these figures may be open to question, but the relative values are reasonably well established. . . . (making allowance for the greater percentage of targets taking avoiding action due to the greater accuracy of fire with G.L. III control) . . .

We thus obtain the figures below:—

	G.L. II	G.L. III
Estimated effect with avoiding action	1·3–1·4 %	2·8–3·2 %

Use of centimetric equipment would thus appear to be likely to result in increase of lethality, ranging from 5 to 2 times that obtainable with present equipment, the lower figure corresponding to the case of the most intelligent avoiding action (seldom encountered). . . ."

It is regrettable that actual figures of rounds per "dead bird" cannot be quoted to give a representative comparable figure to those achieved by the earliest types. Schonland, however, did mention a single action in the memorandum that he quoted as typical; the following is an extract from an Intelligence report that he quoted:—

"An enemy aircraft, believed to have been a Ju. 88, approached . . . from the South at 10.29 hours and flew over the gun defended area in dense low cloud. Six H.A.A. gun sites engaged the raider unseen from 20,000 down to 4,000 feet with 528 rounds of 3·7 in. . . . The plane then broke cloud and was seen by R.O.C. and A.A. sites to jettison four bombs and crash into the sea in pieces off . . . Two rubber dinghies descended . . . and three members of the crew were picked up . . ."

Trials carried out by A.O.R.G. with trained Canadian operators and by C.A.E.E. in conjunction with A.D.R.D.E. in the early months of 1942, showed for the first time that the accuracy of unseen A.A. fire could really approach that of seen fire. Both these series of trials indicated that the overall accuracy of fire to be expected was of the order of that achieved by normal service personnel under good seen conditions. Under trial conditions using specially selected and experienced operators, however, seen fire was still appreciably more accurate.

It may be said that centimetric radar, in the hands of average troops, had brought night, fog and cloud conditions down to the equivalent of clear daylight for Heavy Anti-Aircraft gun fire.

G.L. Mark III—Canadian Pattern. Another pattern of 10-cm. G.L. III set was initiated and produced entirely in Canada; this was the first large-scale development and production of radar equipment in that country and a most creditable effort even though it could have been still more creditable had closer liaison been effected earlier in the design stage. The first supplies of the Canadian pattern—generally referred to as the G.L. III(C)—actually reached this country some two months before the British type began to come off production. As it was adopted as a British Army equipment, it was officially named A.A. No. 3, Mark I, having preceded the British pattern, which became the Mark II.

There is no question of the British type being a development from the Canadian, for it was in fact developed independently. The Canadian designers had worked to a specification of performance given to them by representatives of the Ministry of Supply in 1940 at the time of the Tizard Mission's visit, whereas the British type was based upon an advanced specification prepared some three months later during the absence of that Mission. In addition, the Canadian design and development staffs had not the same extensive experience of practical operations as were available to ours in this country. The Canadian National Research Council's initiative, backed up by the skill and capacity of Research Enterprises Ltd., unquestionably did produce an effective equipment, and it is no disparagement of their efforts to say that the British pattern was superior in performance in the field.

The G.L. III(C) experienced similar delays and difficulties as arose in the case of the G.L. III here. Forecasts of deliveries were similarly over-optimistic and most unreliable, even apart from shipping delays. On the technical requirements aspect there appears to have been a lack of co-operation between the scientific and technical staffs of the two countries during the design stages and particularly in the trial and proof period. In consequence the true capacity and performance of G.L. III(C) was unknown in this country until an early set arrived in January, 1942. Some descriptive pamphlets, with rather vague and incomplete trial-results had been made available and also reports of some independent scientists, but these were really an inadequate basis for judging the suitability of this design.

The War Office, with the advice of the Ministry of Supply, decided to place a provisional order for a limited quantity of this equipment; this decision was influenced by the early delivery dates then promised and the longer time expected to elapse before the British type would make its appearance. That the early deliveries did not in fact materialize—as was also the case with the British set—illustrates the difficulty of G.S. planning for equipping the forces; action has to be taken on the best available information at the time and optimism by the scientist and by the producer in such cases is a menace rather than a help. On the other hand, if scientific possibilities are not accepted and backed up by provisional orders for development and producers are not enabled to get going on preparation for full-scale production, there is the probability that marked advances in operational effect will become available too late. With a probable time lag of some 18 months to 2 years for starting full production of any radar set, as was learnt by experience, chances must be taken in the stress of war and, in such cases, taken only on reliable scientific and technical advice, *but* those advisers must realize their responsibility in giving their advice.

This Canadian G.L. III was provided as a complete unit in two lorries and two large, 4-wheeled-trailers—complete in that it provided a set for local warning and "putting on" the fire control set—and the separate fire control set itself. The local warning set was called the Zone Position Indicator (Z.P.I.) and the fire control set, the Accurate Position Finder (A.P.F.).

The A.P.F. was carried on one trailer in a *rotatable* cabin in which a Plan Position Indicator, operated by the Z.P.I., was installed so that target selection could be made and indicated direct to the range and bearing operators in the A.P.F. The use of a rotatable cabin rather than its aerial was perhaps due to a failure on the part of the designers to appreciate to the full the possibilities inherent in centimetric working. It was an objectionable feature of the design perpetuating the practice forced upon designers with the longer wave-length sets. A rotating cabin is objectionable to the operators and the large mass to be moved tends to make accurate following more difficult and in rapid slewing almost impossible to avoid over-run or lag.

The Z.P.I. was installed in the other trailer but had no display; the aerial system carried on a horizontal frame rotated at 30 r.p.m. at the top of a short tower above the roof of its fixed cabin; for travel these folded down and were fixed to the roof. It operated in the $1\frac{1}{2}$ metre band.

It was most unfortunate that the first prototype model to arrive in this country in January, 1942, was provided for the Canadian Army instead of A.D.R.D.E. as the technical experts and advisers. This resulted in delays in defining necessary modifications and improvements as A.D.R.D.E. were given no opportunity for trials and detailed technical study of the set; they would have been cleared earlier and embodied in the production design had the Establishment been able to carry out its normal functions.

In regard to performance this Canadian design of A.P.F. was similar to the British in accuracy of angular measurement for bearing and elevation, but though range accuracy was similar its smoothness of reading was not quite so good. In respect of maximum detection range and maximum range for accurate engagement it was definitely inferior to the British pattern; the latter was designed to follow up to 36,000 yards and had a detection pick-up range of 27,000 yards (later increased to 35,000) while the Canadian was limited to accurate following up to 18,000 yards and 20,000 yards detection. A comparison in practical operation rather than in trials conditions gave the maximum range for the early models for following of the British as 25,000 as against the Canadian 15,000 yards; this shortage of range capacity materially affected the useful employment of the Canadian equipment against targets at 25,000 feet height or over.

The Z.P.I. warning and "putting on" part of this equipment was not very suitable; it was affected by site clutter and its height coverage was very inadequate and "gappy," which of course placed a considerable limitation upon the performance of the equipment as a whole.

This equipment also had a different form of display to that generally used with earlier British types and with the British G.L. III itself. This, though by no means a fault in design, was a handicap in operation in that it meant retraining our operators to handle this equipment. Instead of the C.R.T. display the signals operated meters indicating which way to turn the hand-wheels to get on to the correct bearing and elevation. This, though quite a good system, was unfamiliar and in general was not liked by the operators who seemed to recognize the C.R.T. "blip" almost as the plane itself, or perhaps more as the image of the plane in a visual instrument or telescope, while the meter seemed much more "impersonal" and its reading unconnected with an aircraft.

A further difficulty arose over the fact that the hand-wheel controls for following the angular measurements were fitted with "aided laying" with the object of smoothing the rates of angular following, and the range measurements were controlled by "velocity laying." Though the A.O.R.G. considered, as a result of trials, that these systems might lead to greater ease and accuracy of operation, no significant difference was found, while the psychological factor and original unfamiliarity tended to militate against this system. The meter reading system had in fact been tested at A.D.R.D.E. in the earlier days in comparison with normal C.R.T. displays and it had been reported upon as showing no improvement upon it.

Eventually 667 sets of this equipment were produced in Canada; of these 600 were against the British order, 65 for the Canadian Army and 2 samples for the U.S.A. Production deliveries commenced, ex-factory, in September, 1942, with delivery in this country in November, and were completed in February, 1945; the maximum yearly output was 313 during 1944. Of the British order over 50 per cent were allocated to Dominions, etc., other than Canada, and to Russia.

In this country these sets contributed materially to the defences of A.A. Command, and in the winter of 1943/44, when most of the available British type G.L. III were needed for operations in Italy and in preparations for operations in Northern France, the defences of London relied mainly on this Canadian pattern for the control of fire of its guns.

This equipment was good, but had better liaison existed in the early days of its development, it is likely that it would have been better. As has been said, this was unfortunate as it tended to depreciate the very fine effort of the Canadian designers; the extent and value of that effort, however, was fully appreciated on this side of the Atlantic.

CHAPTER X. H.A.A. AUTOMATIC RADAR

With the development of centimetric working a new and wider field for progress in equipment design was opened to the scientists and technicians. It was not only the narrow beam transmissions and the greater accuracy of angular measurements that improved performance but the electrical, the mechanical and even the structural aspects of design were simplified even to the extent that the number of operators could be reduced.

Common T and R Aerials, that is to say, the use of the same aerial for reception as well as for transmission, had already been employed in some of the early types of equipment, but in this ultra short-wave band with its high power working, this system was even more effective. It was made possible by the development of a device for protecting the crystal in the receiving side from the heavy transmission pulses. This was due, largely, to a Canadian, A. G. Ward, assisting in research work at T.R.E., who conceived the idea of a device that was to become known as the Gas-Filled, or T-R Switch, an entirely novel conception. The effect of the use of the single aerial system was to reduce the size and weight of the moving parts and thereby to reduce the power required for their movement and control.

The new technique also brought into use the "Wave-Guide," a tube for feeding the transmission pulses to the aerial and conveying the echo waves from them back to the receiver or presentation unit; it replaced the former cable feeders between the aerials and the set itself. In doing this, the connections to the aerial system simplified rotational movement though it involved electro-mechanics in the design of rotating joints. In addition, these wave-guides could deliver pulses direct at the focus of the reflector if desired without an actual dipole. This wave-guide method of feeding the aerial system was certainly "Wireless" in its real meaning and was perhaps somewhat staggering to the uninitiated; they had to accept the fact that "puffing powerful pulses up a pipe" proved most effective. It had, of course, its own special problems and critical dimensions affecting design, but they were mainly solved in a remarkably short time.

With these and other innovations new possibilities were opened up. With the reduction in mass of the moving parts, the opportunity arose of making direct use of the small voltage differences in the split signals produced when the aerials were out of phase or off the true line to the target. These differences could be used to aid or actually to effect corrective movement of the aerial system. In other words, the set could provide the means of continuously directing its aerial system on to the target or could follow the target by itself once it had been put on, whatever its movements, until it was out of radar range.

The possibility of making a radar set follow its target automatically had been recognized before the advent of the centimetric type of equipment, but the large masses to be moved, and more particularly the comparatively wide embrace of the transmissions of the earlier sets, was likely to produce difficulties in that their low degree of discrimination between targets might produce confusion to the brainless robot, and the set might jump from one target to another or dither between them. It was the very narrow beam, used with the centimetric types, giving much improved discrimination that made it a practical proposition for experiment and development.

In so far as this country was concerned, the H.A.A. radar offered a field in which this automatic following might provide dividends of high value in the shape of increased effect in A.A. fire if its accuracy and the smoothness of its data could improve upon that of the average manual operator. Naval high-angle gunnery, similar to the Army H.A.A., was likely to benefit still more in that the stabilization of the gun mountings (compensation for roll and pitch) might be made unnecessary by the use of target auto-following.

In 1942 experiments were initiated at A.D.R.D.E. to convert one of the pre-production models of the G.L. III for automatic following; this was agreed by the W.O., subject to non-diversion of effort from the final clearing for production of the standard set, and to no delay or disturbance being caused to its production which was already disappointingly behindhand.

This was really the first investigation for Army use of automatic following radar and the results of the experimental trials were reported to the R.D.F. Applications Committee and considered at the meeting on 17th June, 1942. That Committee in its report to the S.A. Council summarized the advantages and disadvantages of such systems as follows: "The operational advantages of automatic following are improved accuracy and rates, saving of operators, elimination of the falling off of efficiency found with operators due to battle conditions and fatigue, higher rates and accelerations and quickness in changing targets and settling down of predictors. . . .

Disadvantages may include some increased complexity, accurate machining of certain parts, difficulty of fitting to existing mountings, and difficulty with multiple targets at the same range. Very little evidence as to the effect of jamming and interference is available (at present), it is thought possible that automatic following may be less vulnerable to jamming and interference than manual operation."

In its report for the year 1942, rendered in December of that year, the Committee also made the following remarks:—

"This promises to be of great use in the future, the many advantages more than offsetting the disadvantage of some increase in complexity. Automatic following equipments are being developed at A.D.R.D.E. for Army use, but at present have in a large measure to give way to hand-operated equipments now being manufactured."

By the start of the year 1943 the improvements effected in the design of the two experimental types of auto following modifications for G.L. III set had resulted in a standard of performance that was showing an improvement in smoothness with a consistency and accuracy that was superior to that of normal service manual operation. The substitution of a robot with its unthinking regularity and uniformity of performance for some of the manual operating crew had become a practical proposition; the data transmitted to the predictor was shown to be sufficiently smooth to improve the over-all performance of the radar–predictor link in the fire control system.

At this stage of the war the improved tactics and the higher performance of enemy aircraft was making accurate following by manual methods increasingly difficult owing to the high angular rates that had to be dealt with, particularly in bearing; the auto systems certainly had the advantage in this and could deal effectively with considerably higher rates without loss of accuracy or steadiness.

The provision and training of personnel as operators was becoming something of a strain and, in fact, the personnel question as a whole was very difficult; reduction in numbers would have been very welcome. It was not only in the H.A.A. radar set itself that such relief was needed—the whole train of fire control operations could be reduced with good radar data; the following extract from Brigadier B. N. J. Schonland's memorandum makes this clear:—

"Operational research has shown that the information supplied by Radar equipments (manual operation) has not been smooth enough for the satisfactory operation of the existing predictors and has led to various subsidiary devices and drills for meaning the information, particularly the rates of change. No less than 18 *A.T.S. operators* are involved in the chain from G.L. cabin to gun, all engaged in essential and varied operations necessary to obtain a shell burst at the required future position. It is clear that future equipments, eliminating most of these operators by giving smoothed data from automatic following Radars to *automatic or semi-automatic electrical predictors*, are likely to increase the lethal value of unseen fire very considerably."

This illustrates well the man—or chiefly woman—power solely taken up by the provision and transmission of data for A.A. shooting, and when it is remembered that some 1,500 radar sets were deployed operationally and that the operating crews had to be replaced by reliefs regularly, the personnel requirements mounted up to some 90 to 100 thousand. This personnel question by itself was a sufficient argument in favour of the robot.

It has been mentioned that A.D.R.D.E. were experimenting with two types of auto-following modification for G.L. III; one of these was the true automatic following method of keeping the aerial system continuously and accurately directed on the selected target so that the set practically "locked on" to it, and the output data for the present position of the target were transmitted continuously. The second method relied upon manual following but automatically transmitted such corrections, due to lag or irregularity, as were necessary, and inserted them in the transmission of data system at the magslip dials for elevation and bearing. The latter was therefore an "error corrector" rather than automatic following, and did not effect the same degree of saving in personnel as the former.

The question of auto following for H.A.A. was discussed during the autumn of 1942 by D. Radar with the Technical Fire Control Adviser of the D.G. of A.'s Directorate, and also with C.P.R.S.D. at the Ministry, and Colonel Schonland of A.O.R.G. It was agreed that auto following was an essential for the future, and that more effective results would be obtained from a set specially designed for the purpose, than by efforts to convert an equipment whose design was not really suited to auto following and could not achieve the best results from any modifications applied to it.

Even before these discussions, new prospects had been opened up by the automatic fuze setter and loader (Molins) and the experimental development of an electrical predictor to which radar data would be more acceptable; both would help to eliminate some of the intermediate human links in the chain of data transmission. This wider prospect pointed to the eventual completely automatic chain of operations from the G.L. cabin through the predictor, fuze setter and loader to the continuous pointing of the gun and firing it. Though this had not then been expressed as a specific G.S. requirement, it was recognized as the future aim, and this influenced the decision to call for an automatic following G.L. set designed *ab initio* for the purpose of forming an essential link in that chain.

In September, 1942, the G.S. Policy Statement included auto following as a requirement and the design of a lightweight automatic following equipment was put on the programme of the A.D.R.D.E.; by January, 1943, Cockcroft was able to report that three experimental models (A.F. 1) were being made to an engineered and waterproofed design.

Information had been received during the late summer of 1942 in regard to the development in the U.S.A. of automatically controlled sets for H.A.A., and in October Dr. A. K. Solomon, recently added to the A.D.R.D.E. team with his experience of the American development work, described to the R.D.F. Applications Committee the U.S. sets in being or contemplated. The first type was the S.C.R. 545, an automatic 10-cm. set combined with a $1\frac{1}{2}$ m. set for search and warning. An improved type, the experimental set which was to become the S.C.R. 584 when in production, was an automatic 10 cm. set with the capacity for search and pick-up by automatic scanning over a variable section of the sky. In accurate fire control it was completely automatic in angular measurements which were all effected without provision for manual operation; in selection of targets and range tracking it was operated manually.

Dr. Solomon had been sent to this country under an arrangement made between the United Kingdom and United States for an interchange of scientists, intended to keep the two countries closely linked in the scientific and technical aspects of radar developments. He was the first scientist to be sent; and in fact the only one, as the interchange was never fully effected. There was, however, close liaison maintained by many individual visits in each direction and in addition a number of American technicians and technical Army officers were attached for considerable periods to our establishments and worked in the research and development teams.

As a result of direct enquiries through the British Army Staff in Washington, D Radar was able to report at the December, 1942, meeting of the R.D.F. Applications Committee as follows:—

"Two sets S.C.R. 545 and 584 are being procured for anti-aircraft fire control and should start coming off production in January and June, 1943, respectively. The S.C.R. 584 is the only equipment with complete automatic following and this was included purely with a view to obtaining improved smoothness and accuracy. The resulting economy in personnel, although now recognized as an advantage, was not one of the reasons for its adoption. Future policy as regards automatic following will depend on the operational performance of the S.C.R. 584, but at present the Army Ground Forces are of the opinion that when the present range of sets are in the field they will have all the types they require."

One of these sets was made available to the A.D.R.D.E. in September, 1943, where it was fully tested and submitted to full trials. As Cockcroft says, it created an immediate good impression, particularly since it arrived in charge of a first-class technical officer, Dr. Davenport, with an enthusiastic Army officer, Colonel Warner, to back him up. Subsequently, as will be seen, a number of these sets were made available to our Army for use by A.A. Command and were of great assistance in the battle of the Flying Bombs.

The U.S.A. were ahead of us in the use of automatic following; there was no hope of even development for production of our lightweight set being completed before the end of 1943, and production capacity in this country was so fully occupied that the end of 1944 was indicated as about the earliest possible date by which supply could start. America, of course, had knowledge of our early operational experience and had been introduced by us to the resonator magnetron. They were able to concentrate much of their large available scientific and technical effort and production capacity upon the new technique and the development of the most up-to-date and advanced types of equipment; they were not hampered by commitments in respect of earlier patterns of radar sets and older methods. They also were in the fortunate position of development under the urge of war but not hindered by the close attentions of the enemy with their attacks on production capacity. They had, of course, gained some experience, partly with our aid, of radar and its possibilities before they entered the war and much of their naval radar, with its ship fitting done under peace conditions, was certainly well advanced. It was the impact of war that urged on their radar development and our operational experience and practice that aided them to think ahead and design to make full use of the possibilities of the latest developments. For the H.A.A. duty they certainly tackled the job effectively and produced a very fine equipment in the S.C.R. 584.

British Auto-Following Set. The British automatic-following H.A.A. set was originally referred to as the A.F.1., and as a service type became the Equipment Radar A.A. No. 3, Mark VII, and a small number of "crash" production hand-made sets were given the Mark IV title. Unfortunately, neither of these sets had the opportunity of proving their performance in action against the enemy. No bag of enemy "birds," therefore, can be quoted to confirm its excellence and to compare it with the G.L. III and earlier types. It was not produced before the war ended.

This set was referred to as "lightweight" and that was appropriate to its original demonstration form, but in development it grew in stature and in weight, so that this term was hardly applicable to its final production form, though it was light in comparison with the G.L. III and the S.C.R. 584. (See Illustration 5.)

As a result of the demonstrations of the experimental A.F. 1 set and the photographic film records of its following performance in trials, the War Office requested the Ministry in September, 1943, to arrange for a development contract to be placed for the supply of 50 equipments of this type. The figure of 50 was the minimum number, according to the Ministry, that would interest sufficiently a suitable firm for specially rapid production. No contract had been placed by the end of the year and the War Office raised the matter at D.G.S.R.D.'s conference at the beginning of January, 1944. The Production and the Development departments of the Ministry, in response to enquiries at that meeting, stated that the provision of 24 sets by the end of 1944 was a practical proposition; this was accepted as it would just suffice for the contemplated provision for the Far Eastern Theatre that would have to be shipped at the beginning of 1945. By September, however, M.A.P. estimated twelve only by the end of the year and a fortnight later, on 13th October, the Ministry forecast supply as one set in January, 1945, seven in February, and the remainder by the end of April.

With these postponements of supply the War Office had been obliged to cut out this set from their contemplated provision for the Far East. As it happened, the state of the air warfare out there was by then such that Japanese aircraft were not a material menace to our ground forces and installations; the need for this equipment had waned, but there were plenty of places in this country and in Western Europe where it would have been welcome.

The final manufacturing design of this equipment was not, in fact, completed at the end of the war, though two experimental models for proof and test were supplied in August, 1945, to act as prototypes for the production of the 24 sets of A.A. No. 3, Mark IV, and for modification as a model for the full production of 326 of the Mark VII. Apart from some technical difficulties whose clearance took time, work on these equipments suffered from the relaxation of effort in the change from war to peace conditions. This meant that the Mark IV semi-hand-made pattern did not become available until the early months of 1946 and consequently the full production type, the Mark VII, was not expected to be delivered until late in that year. This lapse of time from the W.O. acceptance of the performance achieved by the experimental model, to the supply of the "crash" pattern—$2\frac{1}{2}$ years, and of probably at least 3 to $3\frac{1}{2}$ years to the supply of the complete service pattern (Mark VII)—illustrates the difficulties with which the General Staff were faced in their forward planning due to the restricted production capacity in this country.

The performance of the A.A. No. 3, Mark IV set is officially quoted as $\pm$ 8 minutes of arc for both elevation and bearing angles between 7 and 85 degrees elevation at rates up to 8 degrees a second; detection range was not less than 30,000 yards, with an accuracy of $\pm$ 35 yards. The Mark VII should provide rather greater accuracy in the angular measurements, and should be fully capable of operation in all climatic conditions, including tropical heat and humidity.

In both the Mark IV and the Mark VII types auto-following in range measurement was provided as well as in the angular measurements. An alternative means of following manually in range was available to the operator for use in cases of interference or difficulty, where the human intelligence could help to maintain following on the selected target through such trouble as might cause confusion to the auto system by itself. In this respect this set was an advance upon the S.C.R. 584, in which auto-following was not provided for the range data; in respect of detection range and long-range following, the advantage lay with the S.C.R. 584, with its larger aerial reflector.

G.L. Mk. III Auto Following Modification. The two types or methods experimented with at A.D.R.D.E. for converting G.L. III to automatic following have been referred to—one true auto-follow and the other error-correction. Of these the former was reported as most likely to give the better performance, but requiring heavy factory or workshop fitting to incorporate the added gear, while the latter, giving an improved performance over manual operation by average operators, could be installed in the field without withdrawing the equipment.

An enquiry as to the production position, as affected by the needs of the other Services as well as those of the Army, was made by D. Radar through the Radio Production Executive towards the end of 1943 and it was found to be impossible to provide capacity for the auto-follow modification without sacrificing the already planned production of the new design A.F.1. set. It was decided to attempt the modification of G.L. III to provide for the simpler form, the "error-correction" system, as it would not materially affect the existing production programmes and could be more easily installed. In January, 1944, however, alterations were reported by the Establishment which were said to remove the auto-follow modification from the class of heavy factory job for fitting and at the same time the error-corrector was reported as being more complicated and difficult than had been anticipated. The Ministry supported Professor Cockcroft in urging the auto-follow system for the G.L. III and abandoning work on the error-corrector. The War Office agreed to the finalization of the auto-follow modification design with a view to its adoption later if the provision of the necessary components could be arranged without prejudice to the production of A.A. No. 3 Mark IV.

The need for auto-following had become increasingly apparent in A.A. Command who were pressing this need with all their power, and rightly so. They urged the provision of modification kits for the G.L. III, as likely to produce a quick result as an interim measure, but they were still up against the problem of production.

At the beginning of March, 1944, the modification was reported as satisfactory and design complete, but production details of a proper engineered design were not yet available and considerable difficulties were encountered in completing the drawings and other details essential for production. The War Office had made it quite clear that they could not accept the modification until a properly engineered and tested design was available so that production could proceed. A late change in design had replaced the "metadyne" system of control by "split-field motors" which were reported as giving improved accuracy and suitable for direct feed to electrical predictors. This further late change in design did not enhance confidence in the earlier recommendations.

The Establishment undertook to make up six sets of modification kits for trial and as prototypes for production; the first of them was expected to be ready in September, 1944, but at the end of December that year the modification was still not ready for production.

This unsatisfactory position with its changes and delays is illustrated by comments made at the end of December, 1944, by the production side of the M. of S., which stated:—

"Development has a long way to go. It has repercussions on the original equipment. The G.L. III is in no condition to take more modification without a number of problems arising."

Incidentally, these remarks also provide an independent assessment of the correctness of the War Office judgment and its desire to have effort concentrated on a set designed particularly for that purpose.

Work on this auto-follow modification was postponed at the end of January, 1945, and in June of that year it was decided to cancel the requirement previously stated for 450 sets of conversion kits. A sad end to a sorry story!

Auto-follow Modification to G.L. III(C). In addition to the G.L. III British type, R.R.D.E. had considered in 1944 a "simple" method of applying auto-follow to the Canadian pattern set. The War Office was anxious that the efforts of the Establishment should be concentrated on urgent new design work for use against ground targets and directed that the modification of the G.L. III(C) to auto-follow should be left to A.A. Command. It had been recognized that this equipment, though temporarily of value in the A.A. defences, was not suitable for retention as service equipment for any length of time, and agreed to this "irregular" means of modifying it subject to proof of sufficient improvement in trials to warrant such work. A.A. Command had already put forward schemes for the improvement of these sets in other aspects and arrangements were made to assist them by the provision of components, etc., if supply were possible. The R.R.D.E. had been in touch with these modifications, but had not the opportunity to tackle them as the official design authority. The War Office, therefore, took the unusual step of relieving that Establishment from all further responsibility for the Canadian type G.L. III in April, 1944.

Unfortunately, the valiant efforts of A.A. Command to add auto-follow did not reproduce the reasonable results that had been achieved with their first experimental set though most of the other modifications proved satisfactory. Their report on the trials of modified sets, included in its conclusion:—

"The reliability of the whole equipment is most unsatisfactory. The reliability of the auto follow is suspect; constant and expert R.E.M.E. attention is necessary to keep it up to a standard necessary for reasonable accurate prediction."

The result was the abandonment of the attempt to convert to auto following the G.L. III(C), even as a temporary expedient. The efforts of the Command deserved better fortune, but it was a case of "repercussions on the original equipment," and if the more robust and reliable British type was suspect of being "in no condition to take more modifications without a number of problems arising," the Canadian pattern, certainly, was itself not only suspect but in fact proved incapable of trouble-free conversion.

A.A. Command, however, was not daunted by this set-back as they again stepped into the breach to attempt the conversion of the British type. As was mentioned in the foregoing paragraph, the production of the official "standard" modification for auto following devised and designed by R.R.D.E. had to be cancelled, but A.A. Command had their own solution to the problem. With the flying bomb menace and the urgent demands from 21st Army Group, the W.O. again agreed that the Command might undertake the provision of kits of modification parts to the extent of 300, and to help in obtaining the parts and components, through M. of S. channels. The number of different items that could not be provided through A.A. Command resources rose to some 230 by the end of November and the project was abandoned.

Automatics versus *the Flying Bombs*. That brings the tale of British auto following G.L. equipment to its end in so far as the war is concerned—a rather sorry story of over three years' frustration largely due to the overburdened production capacity in this country, or at any rate, to the lack of capacity available for Army radar production.

The need for auto G.L. equipment had grown rapidly with the improvement in aircraft performance and tactics, but it became a vital necessity with the advent of the pilotless plane—the flying bomb, with its high speed and low-level approach. That these violent attacks were met by British and American radar aids is a fact, as is also the very material part in the defeat of these attacks played by those radar equipments, but British automatic radar did not contribute to that defeat. The leading place in effective contribution to that defeat is undoubtedly assignable to the American radar equipment S.C.R. 584, which in British hands had become an Army type known as A.A. No 3, Mark V. This in conjunction with the electrical predictor produced by B.T.L. in America and adopted by our Army as Predictor A.A. No. 10, and the radio proximity fuze (dealt with in a later chapter) enabled our guns to take an increasing toll of these flying bombs. That toll rose to the amazing figure of 98 per cent of bombs coming within range of our guns in the later stages of these attacks and on occasions a full 100 per cent in a 24-hour period were claimed.

During these attacks it was seldom possible to allocate "dead birds" to individual gun sites or to specific classes of weapon and their ancillary equipment. A.A. Command and the Operational Research personnel were in a position to observe and assess the comparative value of various weapons and accessories serving them. A.A. Command issued a "Technical Review of A.A. Defences against Flying Bombs" covering the period from June to August 1944 (this did not cover the later attacks which were met perhaps even more successfully) from which it is permissible and of interest to quote some short extracts.

"It is impossible to give accurate figures for the effectiveness of the various weapons and methods of fire control employed during the operation, owing to the extreme difficulty in allocating casualties to specific sites. Reasonable figures can be obtained from analyses of recording van data, and the following r.p.b. figures may be expected.

$3 \cdot 7$ in., V.T. Fuze, Radar S.C.R. 584 and No. 10 Predr. 100 to 150.
$3 \cdot 7$ in., 208 Fuze, Radar S.C.R. 584 and No. 10 Predr. 600 to 800.
40-mm., with normal No. 3 Predictor, 1,500 to 2,500."

and—

"It is impossible to ascribe the success to any one equipment. The most spectacular cause was the V.T. fuze, but these fuzes would not have shown their great effectiveness without the No. 10 Predictor; and the No. 10 Predictor would not have predicted so accurately (certainly not at unseen) without the S.C.R. 584. It was the combination of the SCR. 584, the No. 10 Predictor and V.T. fuze that enabled the H.A.A. gunners to achieve what they did. With these equipments and with $3 \cdot 7$-inch Mk. 2C guns practically the whole chain of operations was automatic, which proved more forcibly than it had hitherto been possible to do, that the ultimate aim must be to complete automaticity."

It is also interesting to note from the assessments of accuracy of the various types of equipment, contained in this Review, that in the early period when the guns were deployed in the inland (Kentish) belt, that the British G.L. Mark III used with the B.T.L. (No. 10) predictor produced results in unseen shooting almost identical with those of the auto follow S.C.R. 584, with the same predictor. In the later deployment along the coast, however, the S.C.R. 584 was distinctly superior with its pick-up range of 30,000 yards as against the 25,000 yards of the G.L. III fitted with the higher power magnetron, and with the self-scanning and "putting-on" of the former it had an advantage in early engagement that was marked. In addition, of course, the automatic following in bearing and elevation enabled the S.C.R. 584 to deal effectively with higher angular rates that at times defeated the manual operation of the G.L. III, or at best caused a deterioration in its angular accuracy.

U.S. Type S.C.R. 584. There is no question as to the overall superiority of the S.C.R. 584 in these operations, and it is much to be regretted that the new British type, the A.A. No. 3, Mark VII, or even its prototype the Mark IV, could not have been made available to take part in them. That they would have shown a performance comparable with the S.C.R. 584, except perhaps in maximum range, is not doubted but actual operational proof would have been most welcome and satisfying to the designers as well as to the General Staff and to the users of Army radar equipment.

The urgent request for a supply of the S.C.R. 584 was made at very high level to the United States in November, 1943, and was most willingly and rapidly met; 135 of these sets were delivered early in 1944 under Lend-Lease, and later a further supply of 165 was loaned by the American forces in this country on the instructions of the Supreme Command A.E.F., to assist in meeting the flying bomb attack as it matured. Of the latter, 75 were subsequently withdrawn for the needs of the American forces in Normandy, but they were to be replaced by some S.C.R. 545 sets; this supply was to be on Lend-Lease, but in fact the sets did not become available.

The performance of the S.C.R. 584 gave a detection range of 49,000 yards on a P.P.I. display and 32,000 yards on a "coarse" range tube with a circular time-base, from which any selected 2,000 yards could be presented on a similar "fine" range tube with a radial cursor manually controlled with "aided laying" mechanism. Following range accuracy (manual) was given as ± 25 yards and accuracy at automatic following bearing and elevation as $\pm 4\frac{1}{2}$ minutes. These figures of accuracy are not strictly comparable with those quoted for the British equipment, as they are in reference to the radar *output* and not the overall input to the predictor quoted for the British type which includes mechanical and transmission variables. The maximum tracking rates of approximately 15 degrees in bearing and 5 degrees of elevation per second were possible. It was a sound, well-engineered equipment proving reliable and trouble free, and was the first type of radar equipment specifically designed as an integral part of an automatic chain of fire control components including an electrical predictor suited to its output.

Automatic radar with a minimum of human aid to operation was established as a practical and proved proposition in the late stages of the war for A.A. work. It had its own particular troubles, of course, but those troubles were largely functions of its virtues; so long as they were appreciated as such and intelligence used in avoiding them, automatic following radar could and did provide for a very material improvement in performance, particularly in the overall performance of the system of fire control applied to Heavy Anti-Aircraft Artillery.

CHAPTER XI. ANTI-AIRCRAFT SEARCHLIGHT RADAR

In Part I where the pre-war provision for anti-aircraft defence equipment has been generally described, the primary role of the A.A. searchlight was indicated as the illumination of hostile aircraft for visual engagement at night by the A.A. guns. A secondary role provided for the tracking of the courses of aircraft for intelligence purposes and also the illumination of hostile targets to assist interception and attack by night fighters; for these purposes many searchlights were dispersed throughout the "Air Fighting Zone" independent of the gun defences. There were, therefore, searchlights deployed for both roles, some for direct assistance to the gun defences and others for the provision of general information and for possible interception and engagement by defence aircraft. The information they supplied was supplemented by, or was supplementary to, that from the widespread system of Royal Observer Corps posts.

Before the war, exercises had been carried out on a small scale that envisaged the employment of night fighters for the interception of bombing raiders, but it took the urge and stress of war to develop it as a practical method of defence. It was only brought to its full efficiency, however, by the development of radar aids both in the aircraft employed and in the means of controlling or directing them from the ground. In this work the A.A. searchlights played their part with the aid of radar; the development of this radar control was initiated primarily for this purpose of interception, though at the same time it was of value for the gun defences.

This form of radar aid was known as S.L.C., short for Searchlight Control, though more familiarly referred to as "Elsie." As an Army equipment it became A.A. No. 2 and was distinguished by a number of different Marks rising to Mark IX at the end of the war. The first seven were all types of $1\frac{1}{2}$ m. wave-length, while the last two operated in the centimetric band and employed automatic following.

In the early days of investigation of the possibilities of applying radar to Army purposes, it will be recalled that the provision for control of searchlights was considered as part of, or parallel with, radar fire control for A.A. guns but that the priority emphasis was on the gun. The searchlights were equipped with an excellent sound locator which in the hands of trained and experienced troops gave very good service; with the increasing dilution of the trained searchlight units from 1939 onwards, it was apparent that this sound locator even with its "visual" reading attachment was becoming ineffective in the hands of war-time personnel.

Professor Cockcroft in his notes—and he may be taken as an independent and intelligent observer—comments on the sound locator control of searchlights as follows:—

"... the great dilution of searchlight personnel reduced them (the searchlights) to almost impotence. During raids searchlight beams waved wildly about the sky but rarely found and held a target."

Similarly Forshaw, then of A.D.R.D.E., expressed the general feeling of the Establishment in some notes from which the following is an extract:—

"S.L.C. grew out of the exasperation we (A.D.R.D.E.) experienced at the futile efforts of our searchlights to pick up the enemy bombers who flew over us night after night during the summer months of 1940."

The original plan for searchlight control by radar means had contemplated the use of G.L. equipment as developed for the guns. By the spring of 1940 this had reached the stage of practical trials which were carried out near Birmingham; these trials envisaged the use of a "master" searchlight controlled by a G.L. set and linked to three or four "satellite" searchlights which were to be directed on to a particular spot in space—of course, a continuously moving spot—to intersect the master beam where the target was held. A form, or rather a number of forms, of mechanical devices to determine the bearing and elevation information for each of the satellites were tried but all introduced too much time lag to be effective, and the only possibility of successful results was when the target was visible in the master beam, when the satellites could be directed upon it.

The radar set for the master beam had, of course, to provide continuous accurate bearing and elevation; the information had to be continuous to ensure pick-up and following when conditions made visual observation impossible.

This scheme was not pursued—not only was it hardly worth while but more particularly such G.L. radar equipments as were available were required for the guns themselves.

$1\frac{1}{2}$ *metre S.L.C.* In April, 1940, the first attempt at radar means of control of individual searchlights, specially designed for that purpose, was mooted by three of the enthusiastic J.S.O.s at the A.D.R.D.E.—Eastwood, Chick and Oxford—and they were given authority to produce an experimental set for trial. Their experimental set made use of R.A.F. standard, but obsolescent, A.S.V. equipment mounted upon a Mark IX Sound Locator, stripped of its sound collectors, but retaining its visual sight and control gear linking it to a projector. It used a single Yagi aerial set at a slight angle to the optical axis and rotated to give "split" readings for elevation and bearing. This did not prove practicable, however, as the rate of rotation was too slow and the cone shape traversed by the Yagi rod during rotation was erratic due to whip. The wave-length used by the A.S.V., $1\frac{1}{2}$ metre, was retained to avoid making alterations in the set. The next experimental model replaced the single Yagi by four receiving Yagis applied to the pairs of elevation and bearing sockets of the locator where the sound collectors had been fixed. These Yagis were all fixed parallel to the visual axis, as was also the single Yagi transmitter aerial; the pairs of receiving aerials provided for split readings by means of a rotating switch feeding each in turn. As Forshaw says, this switch ". . . worked though they couldn't explain it properly to begin with."

The received signals from each pair of aerials were compared—left and right for bearing and top and bottom for elevation—and a signal in the form of a spot of light would appear on the screens of the bearing and elevation C.R.T.s. Separate bearing and elevation operators, by rotating their hand-wheel controls, would bring the spot on to the centre line of their tube screen and by doing so continuously would keep the axis of the locator pointing at the target all the time. The control gear from the locator to the S/L projector ensured that the searchlight axis was also pointing at and following the target. There was in addition a normal horizontal time-base C.R. Tube giving approximate range to any aircraft within the arc of search, and from this the target to be engaged could be selected. When following was satisfactory and the target came within range, the operator on the range or selector tube would open up the searchlight beam by switching on, and from then until ordered to switch off, the aircraft *should* be held in the beam by the radar operators keeping their "spots" accurately centred. This radar method was later adapted for fitting direct on a searchlight projector itself.

In August, 1940, the possibility of this form of searchlight control was brought to notice at the War Cabinet's Night Air Defence Committee and as a result, with the threat of night raids continuing and increasing, an order from the highest level was given that twenty-four of these sets were to be made and ready for use "by the next moon phase." Every effort was made by A.D.R.D.E. to comply with this order by making up and fitting "chinese" copies of the almost unproved experimental model; there was no possibility of enlisting a firm to do the manufacture in time as no drawings nor details were available. That the Establishment with their own resources had several of these sets in the field by the start of "the moon phase," and more before its end, was a very fine effort, but it must be said that only a proportion of them—perhaps some forty per cent—remained in action at the end of the period and that was only achieved by A.D.R.D.E. scientists and technicians nursing them and staying continuously on site to serve, nourish, comfort and maintain them to the best of their ability. That they did not achieve much in the way of searchlight assisted interceptions by our night fighters in that period was not surprising, in view of the lack of training and of organization of the necessary close liaison for this combined operation of searchlights and fighters.

The early operational use of this new device, in what was really only a "mock-up" form, showed that it had possibilities of value, and encouraged urgent development of this type and the working out of improved searchlight tactics as well as an efficient and close link up with the night fighters.

From the scientists' point of view this premature use was regrettable, but with the initiative in the hands of the enemy, any possible means of meeting their night attacks was urgent, and the decision was certainly justified by the need even if it was taking a chance with a half-baked lash-up device.

To quote Cockcroft's notes again:—

"The set was not in any sense designed, but it worked after a fashion ... The result of this (the rush order) was a scramble to try to put the mandate into effect—with disastrous results on the equipment. ... The sets at that time were extremely unserviceable owing largely to their lack of development. They were extremely pervious to water and moisture, exposed as they were to the elements for 24 hours per day. Their phasing switch, an empirical model of Chicks, was a source of trouble and transmitters (R.A.F. type) were continually failing through faulty valves."

This early set, however, formed the basis for the subsequent large-scale production of S.L.C. radar equipments which "buttoned on" to all patterns of Army searchlight equipment; they were also applied to Mark IX locators and to an erectable "Wigwam" structure for static sites.

The scale of provision grew rapidly and with it many improvements in detailed design were effected. A follow-up order for 76 of the experimental or "trials" model was placed with a firm, in parallel with the 24 A.D.R.D.E. models. By the end of the year over 50 of these so-called "trials" models had been issued and a further order for 100 of an improved "pre-production" design were well in hand. Before the end of the year production plans were initiated to meet a bulk War Office requirement of over 2,000 sets which was later increased to over 8,000. These, again, were to a still further improved design resulting from experience in action with the "trials" and the "pre-production" models.

It will be realized that this supply requirement presented a production problem of considerable size; that it was most effectively handled by the Ministry of Supply Production side is indicated by the fact that 8,796 S.L.C. radar sets with a large variety of fittings for the different types of searchlights, locators, etc., were produced between April, 1941, and December, 1943; the maximum supply in one year was 4,160, in 1942.

Another quotation from Cockcroft's notes gives his further comments on S.L.C. equipment and must be given to off-set that quoted above—for here he does appreciate the operational improvement achieved:—

"The S.L.C. programme, meantime, went on its way. . . . The reliability of the sets was steadily improved, but at no time was it a fully satisfactory equipment. Resulting from the circumstances of its birth and hurried upbringing the whole system was full of mismatches, with a result that angular errors were larger than need have been. In spite of this, by 1943 good illuminations of enemy planes were once more being obtained in Kent, Sussex, London and East Anglia."

It can be said that the equipment did, undoubtedly, serve a most useful purpose and provided very valuable aid to our night fighters that resulted in many successful interceptions. The number of "dead birds" killed by these fighters, with the assistance of searchlights, cannot be fully extracted from the total "bags" of the night fighters, but they were an effective proportion. These searchlight (S.L.C.) methods of controlled or visually guided interception were not in competition with the R.A.F. ground controlled interception (G.C.I.) system but were supplementary to it. On occasions particular G.C.I. sets were over-burdened with targets and the S.L.C. system would be allocated specific hostile targets to tackle. Later, on occasions when the G.C.I. sets were seriously affected by special interference known as "Window," the S.L.C. being less generally affected owing to their disposition would become the primary means of control. On the night of 20/21st January, 1944, for instance, over 75 per cent of the hostile aircraft brought down by our fighters were due to S.L.C. aided interceptions.

The official title of this type of radar equipment was A.A. No. 2 with Marks from I to VII; of these Marks I and II were respectively the few "trials" and "pre-production" types which disappeared on replacement by the production types. The latter were distinguished by Mark numbers according to the kind of projector or locator, etc., on which the radar components were mounted, such as the Mark IX sound locator, transportable "Wigwam," 150 cm. projector and 90 cm. projector. (See Illustration No. 6.)

All these S.L.C. sets were identical in their radar parts and all, of course, operated on the same wave-length; consequently, all were liable to be affected by the same jamming or interference, except to the extent that their tactical distribution over wide areas or belts generally made it possible for a proportion to operate effectively, though the remainder might be rendered more or less ineffective for a time. Here it may be said that no true anti-jamming measures could be applied to this set, but a "jammer locator" device was fitted for use in the case of *electrical* jamming from specially equipped hostile aircraft. Had that been attempted, the enemy plane could have been located and followed by picking up its jamming transmission by means of this device and the searchlight beams pointing at it would indicate its direction to assist fighters to eliminate it.

Of the service patterns mentioned above, it will be appreciated that some were directly mounted on the searchlight projectors and others were independently mounted with means of remote control of the projectors that they served. Each method had its individual advantages and protagonists but it took practical experience in actual operations to decide on the more suitable method. The S.L.C. mounted direct on the projector made the alignment of the radar and optical axes comparatively simple, whereas, with the independently mounted type situated at some short distance from the projector but controlling its movement, this co-ordination of the two axes was not so easy. It was essential that the radar beam and the searchlight beam should always point in exactly the same direction otherwise the searchlight when switched on might not illuminate the target even though the radar was following correctly; there would be then no indication of the direction in which the searchlight should move to get on the target. Visual observation of the target in the searchlight beam was necessary whenever conditions permitted and the best position for good observation was some distance from the projector itself. This consideration, therefore, tended to make the independent mounting of the radar preferable, particularly if both radar and visual observation and the control of the projector could be exercised from the same point. The Mark IX Sound Locator converted to S.L.C. (A.A. No. 2, Mark III) offered the chance of this with its over-riding visual control when required but the "Wigwam" type did not. The latter, equally with the direct mounted projectors, required an additional appliance in the form of a Visual Control Pillar, to apply visual aids. This was fitted with binoculars whose movement in elevation and bearing actuated a remote control gear which could over-ride the S.L.C. control of the projector and take charge of the projector movement when necessary.

The necessity for visual control arose partly from the tendency to lag in the radar angular following and consequently in the searchlight beam also, but more particularly on account of the comparatively wide radar beam that did not permit of a high degree of discrimination between two aircraft, flying close to one another as occurs when a fighter approaches its target in preparation for its attack. The beam might illuminate the fighter and disclose it to the enemy bomber at the critical stage of the attack. The illumination of the fighter must be avoided and this could be more certainly ensured by visual control taking over direction at the time of closing in, if conditions permitted.

The question of whether the illumination of the target should continue up to and during the actual attack or not, was a matter for the individual fighter pilot to determine; the majority preferred to have the light doused just prior to the attack. This was effected at the pilot's discretion by special signal, visual or radar; the beam would be doused but the S.L.C. would continue following ready for the beam to be exposed again if necessary.

It will be apparent that the organization, co-operation and tactics of searchlight-aided night interception required considerable practice and development. Some comments by Brigadier Schonland are quoted to illustrate this aspect and the results achieved.

"This equipment was introduced into service in Great Britain in 1941 and extensively deployed at home and abroad during 1942. It was produced at a time when the increased speed of aircraft had rendered the older method of sound location very difficult and has proved extremely successful. It has been used in the main as a method of directing night fighters on to their targets.

The tactics of this operation not only are extremely complex but have had to be altered to deal with the progressive increase of speed of the night bomber. Hunting of the radar beam between fighter and bomber, resulting in illumination of the fighter, has had to be overcome by the introduction of visual control pillars and of special dousing signals. During the year 1943, 63 'visuals' have been obtained by fighters from searchlights, resulting in 17 enemy aircraft destroyed and 3 probably destroyed. The complexity of these operations can be judged from the fact that the ratio of searchlight engagements to attempted fighter interceptions is of the order of 3 to 1, while that of attempts to visuals is about 10 to 1, and visuals to combats 4 to 1.

In the clearer skies abroad, as would be expected, S.L.C. has proved more successful than in Britain. It has received high praises in North Africa and has been of value in the S.W. Pacific."

The standard of performance of this type of S.L.C. is recorded as ± 1 degree accuracy for both elevation and bearing angles and an effective range of 15,000 yards. In actual practice it was frequently found that pick-up on medium bombers was effected at 18,000 yards and occasionally up to 20,000.

The searchlights in use by the Army when S.L.C. was "buttoned" on to them were the 90 cm. and the 150 cm., robust in construction and of excellent design; though both produced a narrow beam, that of the 150 cm. projector was exceptionally fine, approximately $1\frac{1}{4}$ degrees, and clean and it had considerable powers of penetration through cloud. On a particular occasion during trials in the Ringwood area with the early S.L.C. equipment, the target bomber was invisible from the ground owing to a heavy cloud layer with its base at about 9,000 feet. The fighter pilot flying in clear air above this cloud, which he reported as somewhat more than 500 feet in depth, was able to see the bomber well and continuously illuminated at a height of 22,000 feet, from a distance of over 18 miles. This at least was proof not only of the penetrating power of the 150 cm. searchlight beam but also of the good illumination at a high level after passing through that cloud layer; it also illustrates the capacity of "Elsie" for accurate unseen following when operated by well-trained personnel.

Apart from actual performance of the searchlight beam, the robustness of the projector design was an asset when it was necessary to apply S.L.C. to it. Not only were the radar components attached to it but in addition it had to stand up to the weight of three radar operators carried round with it. Though some modifications had to be made later for this loading it is a real tribute to the work of the A.D.R.D.E. designers of these equipments, that these projectors stood up to the job in such a satisfactory manner.

The first introduction of "Elsie" to the troops was of course when the few experimental "trials" models were issued to selected sites in the south, where enemy night bombers usually passed over on their way to Midland targets. Little training of personnel was possible before issue as all efforts were concentrated upon getting the sets into action in the September "moon period" as instructed. The scientist "nurses" accompanying the sets had the added duty of instructing operators from the units and demonstrating the use of this novel equipment, as well as keeping it in action and in working order—by no means an easy task.

These demonstrations normally included actual use in operations against the enemy as the night attacks gave little opportunity for trials with our own aircraft. The usual procedure was to pick up a hostile bomber as it crossed the coast and to follow it until within searchlight range, when the beam would be exposed and the bomber illuminated, if the set was working in good order. The bomber would then usually dodge about but failing to get out of the beam would jettison its bombs and depart homewards. Quite a crop of incidents and stories resulted from these demonstrations—one of which may, perhaps, be mentioned here to end this account of the $1\frac{1}{2}$ metre type of S.L.C. equipment.

On a particular occasion when a number of senior officers were visiting a site to see "Elsie" for the first time, the Junior Scientific Officer who was in charge of the set with two operators from the unit operating the elevation and bearing controls, refers to the visitors as "full of red tabs and scepticism" during his description of the equipment. At that time the projector on which the S.L.C. was mounted was raised some four feet from the ground by a solid pedestal; the J.S.O. as controller was perched another four feet higher with the operators somewhat lower. An enemy bomber was engaged and as usual when illuminated it began to dodge and failed to escape the beam. However, it was not so quick as usual in giving up the contest and when it started to discard, the first "crump" was only three fields away and its second, confirming that it was intending making for home, was very appreciably closer. The J.S.O. at this point found his radar signal was fading and on looking round to see if the operators were functioning correctly, found them both gone but hearing a growing whistle—"I then made a flying leap in the dark for the lee side of the pedestal and at the moment when there was a terrific crump in the next field, I landed on the top of a fairly neat pile consisting of 2 operators, 1 captain and 1 major, 3 Brigadiers and 4 Generals—reading from top to bottom!"

This account may, of course, be somewhat apocryphal or perhaps even slightly exaggerated.

To close this section of Searchlight Radar, extracts from the Despatch on the Operations of Fighter Command, by Air Chief Marshal Sir Hugh Dowding, are appropriate.

(*a*) "A small Radio Location set was designed to fit to the searchlight itself, so as to get over the time lag which was such an insuperable obstacle to the use of Sound Locators. It is probable that if searchlights can substitute the speed of light for that of sound, they may take on a new lease of useful life.

(*b*) . . . What can be done is to fit all searchlights with Radio Location apparatus so that every searchlight beam is a reliable pointer towards an enemy, even if the range is too great for direct illumination. . . .

(*c*) As a result of the experience gained during this period (the night stage of the Battle of Britain), all searchlight equipments have since been fitted with radar control. This, combined with intensified training, has made them, since 1941, extremely accurate."

"*Maggie.*" Here for a short space the searchlight radar story must be interrupted to deal with an off-shoot of this device which has already been mentioned in Chapter X.

"Elsie" seems to have developed some slight irregularity in her marital relations—a few of these "ladies" were encouraged to desert their original "mates," the searchlights, for the more "manly" and "truculent" guns. This change of heart and association resulted in the birth of "Maggie." However irregular this union, the lady can hardly be blamed, and the ingenuity of A.A.

Command in producing this expedient to meet the need of A.A. fire control in positions where the G.L. I. and II could not operate effectively was certainly praiseworthy. Incidentally, this improvised "lady" later produced a "daughter" called "Baby Maggie" who was so far accepted and recognized in official circles that she earned the title of A.A. No. 3, Mark III.

Before the arrival of G.L. III, the conversion of S.L.C. mounted on a Mark IX sound locator was the only means that would enable some degree of radar fire control information to be provided on sites whose nature and irregularity prevented G.L. II sets from operating effectively. It was an improvisation and did not claim to meet the full needs, but it did provide angular data of a higher standard than unmatted G.L. sets and could follow targets through high angles and with little deterioration in accuracy. Its range was limited, but with the aid of a G.L. set for early warning and good range data its operation from some 15,000 yards made fairly effective unseen shooting possible.

The conversion of the locator mounted S.L.C. to operate to a predictor instead of a searchlight involved the replacement of the searchlight remote control gear by magslip transmission for linking it to the predictor. This method was complicated but the conditions for which it was provided could not be met in any other way. Incidentally, of course, the link up of "Magslip" and "Elsie" naturally resulted in the name "Maggie."

An A.O.R.G. report comments on "Maggie" as follows:—

"Trials carried out by A.O.R.G. . . . showed that, on the whole, the accuracy to be expected was approximately the same as that with G.L. Mark II. The chief limitations were the relatively low power, resulting in a short detection range, and the inaccuracy of the elevation measurements (at low angles). The elevations were about correct, however, in the neighbourhood of 14 degrees, so that it was possible to determine a height at this point. . . . At high angles, however, the accuracy of elevation did not diminish as in G.L. Mk.II . . ."

This comparison considers the performance of the G.L. II when provided with its matted surround.

Apart from this country with its few special sites, the only other place where "Maggie" was employed was Gibraltar where level sites were very few; it was, however, very soon replaced by a pre-production model G.L. III.

"*Baby Maggie.*" With this adaptation to fire control and the need, for that purpose, of accurate range information, the A.D.R.D.E. carried out experimental work to improve the set in this respect; for searchlight working there was, of course, no real need for a high degree of range accuracy. In September, 1941, an excellent design was initiated by Oxford and in February, 1942, was undergoing its first practical trials; it showed considerable promise but did not reach its final very effective form until the end of that year.

By that time the need of a light and easily handled fire control set for use in the early stages of landing operations was apparent. The delay in production would certainly not make G.L. III available in time and the Mark II, with its accuracy dependent on exceptional site conditions, would be unlikely to get into effective fire control action in the early stages of such operations when ground air defence measures were most important. No existing equipment could meet this need and as an emergency measure the War Office decided to adopt the improved S.L.C. adapted to fire control use, for this role.

An outline plan for an equipment of this type had already taken form at A.D.R.D.E., which combined some of the mechanical ingenuity of Gibson with the improved S.L.C., including Oxford's automatic range accuracy unit and a higher powered transmitter. As much heat as was possible without interfering with the G.L. III work was turned on to expedite the completion of the design of this set. The technical gunners of the Ministry were naturally not keen on this intermediate step to an improved type of fire control set, but realizing the need for a set that was not site conscious, and appreciating that the W.O. was asking for it only for special and very temporary use, they assisted its development and joined with the G.S. in demanding the lightest possible equipment and the barest essentials in the way of operating amenities. Thus was "Baby Maggie" brought into being.

The set was housed in a thin steel sheet cabin on a two-wheeled trailer which was fitted with three levelling jacks; three operators were provided with seats only some four inches above the floor, a small side door for each and headroom only sufficient for sitting. The main component was a central rotating column which carried the transmitter and receiver inside the cabin and the aerial array above the roof. The range and selector displays were at the forward end and the bearing and the elevation displays at the rear; all were fixed suitably for the operators and were fed through slip rings on the central column and normal magslip transmission to the predictor was provided. A light portable generating set with its power cables was provided, and could be transported inside the cabin so that the whole equipment was complete in the one unit and could be towed by any normal vehicle. It had a ground clearance of only 10 inches and could, with special preparation, wade through a depth of 3 ft. 9 in.—as a matter of fact it almost floated but was very unstable with its top hamper. It was the aerial array above the roof that took up the height, and though the Yagi aerials could be taken down and packed on the roof for travel, the main frame and central column made the overall travelling height over 11 feet.

The performance of this set was originally stated as a $\pm \frac{1}{2}$ degree in accuracy of angular measurement between 20 and 90 degrees elevation, but was subsequently classed as not worse than ± 1 degree. For range, similarly, the accuracy originally was put at ± 50 yards but later raised to ± 75 yards. Detection range was 20,000 yards with accurate following from 18,000. As in the case of S.L.C. no anti-jamming protection was fitted and the effect of ground clutter demanded some care in site selection. The total weight of this set was just over 3 tons and it was capable of being man-handled for short distances.

As so frequently happened the occasion for which Baby Maggie was intended came into view before production arrangements could be made with a firm. The first call for its use, therefore, had to be met by A.D.R.D.E. with its own resources; the essential 12 sets of equipment for this first operation, under the drive of Colonel Raby and the energy of the workshop personnel, were produced in time to take part in the North Africa landing operations—a very fine effort on the part of A.D.R.D.E. workshops. While this emergency construction job was being pushed through, the necessary preparations for contract action were hastened, including some redesign and strengthening of the trailer parts and other details to simplify manufacture. An order for something under 200 of this type of equipment was placed with a small firm who, in fact, did well after a rather shaky and delayed start. This production started in September, 1943 and 172 sets were supplied up to March, 1945, of which 141 were produced during 1944.

No complete "tropicalization" was contemplated for these sets which aimed only at a short operational life.

By the time this supply was about one-half completed, the need for this type had lapsed as the G.L. III type had become available and in spite of its greater size and weight it had been found possible to land it in the early stages of beach landing operations. The supply was however continued up to the figure mentioned mainly for supply to the U.S.S.R. who were anxious for a large number of these light sets.

The A.D.R.D.E. emergency pattern of these sets for the N. Africa campaign were of course not so fully engineered as the later production pattern; their tenderness to rough travel was recognized and users were warned, but service field use cannot or at least does not always adhere to such limitations on speed of movement. That these sets were welcomed and served well in the early days of operations in that theatre was apparent from the special reports received. Several breakages were reported but the troubles were really confined to the structure rather than to their capacity as radar sets; troubles and failures on the radar side were remarkably few and simple to correct. This experience with these "crash" production sets was of value in ensuring that the necessary improvements were incorporated in the production models.

These "Baby Maggies" soon dropped out of the service list of radar equipments and were withdrawn as obsolete. They had served their special but limited purpose and had been used in N. Africa, Sicily and a few in Italy; the special need had then been met by more regular types. They left behind them, however, a legacy in the form of encouragement of the desire, that had been growing for some time, for smaller and lighter radar equipment.

Centimetric S.L.C. After that diversion into the A.A. fire control field and the adaptation of S.L.C. to such uses, the record of the development of searchlight radar aids must be resumed.

With the advent of the magnetron and centimetric wave-lengths permitting concentrated beam transmission, searchlight control was obviously an application that should benefit materially from it. Priorities, however, could not bring S.L.C. into the immediate competition for the limited supply of valves and components nor could experimental effort be diverted from the pressing need of the A.A. guns.

However, this possibility was already in the minds of the War Office who, at the end of 1941, requested the Ministry of Supply to review the possibilities of a radical redesign of S.L.C., including the use of a centimetric wave-length, and to submit their suggestions for consideration. This was mentioned in January, 1942, at a meeting of the R.D.F. Applications Committee, and at its February meeting Cockcroft outlined the following features for consideration in any new design:—

    (1) Circuits for eliminating the effects of jamming.
    (2) Improved methods of following.
    (3) Improved performance at low angles of elevation.
    (4) Better discrimination between adjacent targets.
    (5) Reduction in the number of operating personnel.

All of these features were, of course, mainly attributes of centimetric narrow beam technique, though (2) and (5) might also bring in automatic following. As has been mentioned in a previous chapter the experimental Establishment had already undertaken an investigation of automatic following for H.A.A. fire control and they had also included the simpler problem of searchlight control which was being developed for the Establishment by Messrs. B. T. H.

An experimental 1½ metre set for the latter purpose was reported as likely to be available about June, 1942.

Towards the end of June, 1942, the question of the form a redesigned S.L.C. set should take was discussed in greater detail at a conference when it was agreed that redesign should be based upon 10 cm. working, direct mounting on the 150 cm. projector only and a very narrow symmetrical beam. In addition, in order to reduce the number of operators, trial should be made with a suitable single "joy-stick" control for both angular movements as well as with auto following.

Work proceeded on these lines parallel with the experiments already initiated by the Establishment for automatic following. Included in the requirements of the S.L.C. type, if developed for service use, was the means of automatic scanning in bearing and in elevation to cover a sector of the sky in a limited period of time for detection of aircraft. In the case of the hand-operated type sufficiently rapid movement in both planes was to be possible to permit of scanning by a regular drill for the same purpose.

The War Office was not prepared to consider the application of automatic following to the existing type of 1½ metre S.L.C. as the limitations of that type of equipment with its wide beam would not give sufficient advantage and any available effort should be applied to the 10 cm. type that offered better promise.

In September, 1942, the possibility of applying auto follow to 10 cm. S.L.C. was included in the G.S. Policy statement.

Of the two types, auto and manual, the A.D.R.D.E. obviously took greater interest in auto following; by June, 1943, an experimental set known as S.L.C.8 X, was undergoing tests and trials with aircraft which, by October, had indicated that the auto follow type definitely gave better results than the manual joy-stick control method. It had been found that a very high degree of skill was needed to obtain even fair accuracy with the single operator "joy-stick," whereas the automatics with reasonable skill by the single target selector operator, gave good accuracy. The accuracy of the latter was reported as being well within the spread of the searchlight beam—a matter of 1¼ degrees—so that continuous illumination was almost ensured and with automatic scanning, it was a much superior proposition.

As a result of this and of demonstrations and photographic records of numerous trial runs, the War Office agreed that the auto follow type should be pursued and the experimental S.L.C.8 X became the basis for development of the 10 cm. S.L.C. with automatic following included.

Searchlight radar control, with its simpler requirements but later entry into the centimetric class, had thus taken two major steps forward in radar technique in one bound while the G.L. equipment had been forced to take them in two separate stages.

There were of course a number of points to be cleared before this experimental type could be finalized; they included the capacity of the projector itself to stand up to the continuous and rapid movement for automatic scanning, of its chassis and turn-table to withstand the increased stresses and wear, the suitability of the control gear and similar matters. Some redesign of projector parts and the replacement of the control gear by an improved type were found to be essential. This redesign work for the projector and its mounting was undertaken parallel with the radar side on the basis that projector and S.L.C. should be considered as a single whole in the new design.

This work was of some complexity and no early solution and proof of a new fully engineered design could be expected. It was, therefore, agreed that while this redesign was in progress for the eventual service equipment, which would become S.L.C. Mark IX (officially A.A. No. 2, Mark IX) some models of the experimental pattern should be produced—as S.L.C. Mark VIII—without the major alterations so as to get a few into service as early as possible. (See Illustration 7.)

The experimental model had been tested on an operational site with the co-operation of A.A. Command and two special demonstrations for the Secretary of State for War, the Minister of Supply, senior scientists, members of the staffs of the War Office, Air and Supply Ministries and A.D.G.B. took place in May and early June, 1944, in Hyde Park and were most effective. Fighter Command had provided a very experienced pilot in a fast aircraft, and in spite of his best efforts and most violent evasive action, he was never able to avoid the beam and its continuous illumination. Even with the S. of S. operating the control as his first practical experience of radar and its manipulation, the target was not lost.

Both these types of S.L.C. had good directional control performance as the accuracy of angular measurement in both senses was within $\pm \frac{1}{8}$ degree; this was independent of angle of elevation except at low angles but it was maintainable down to 6 or 7 degrees. In range its performance gave detection at 25,000 yards with accuracy of ± 500 yards, which was fully adequate for searchlight work, and a minimum range of 1,000 yards. In discrimination between adjacent targets it could work to a minimum separation of 300 yards in range or 4 degrees in angle. Automatic or semi-automatic scanning, variable at will, was provided for long-range detection of targets and a single display was used by the operator for searching and for selecting the particular target for engagement. This selection was effected by strobing so that the automatics only paid attention to the signals from the particular target. The single operator could assist the automatics through interference by other planes or intervening permanent echoes, by manual aid. The rotating aerial with its paraboloid reflector was mounted alongside the projector barrel with its radiating axis parallel to the light axis of the projector and moving with it. The radar component assemblies were contained in convenient waterproof boxes, light and easily detachable for replacement as a whole or for access for maintenance and test.

A requirement was stated to the Ministry of Supply in the summer of 1944 for the urgent provision of a small number of the Mark VIII pattern, 50 in all, for training and for operational use in Britain and Europe, pending the introduction of the service pattern, the Mark IX. For this latter type a requirement was stated for 1,000 sets at the same time, but this was reduced a year later to 300.

The "crash" production of the 50 Mark VIII sets was expected to be completed before the end of 1944, but delays occurred and the supply period extended from September, 1944, to February, 1945, which was in fact a very good performance. This supply involved the radar component assemblies, aerial system, control gear, etc., but the whole of the fitting to the projectors was undertaken by R.E.M.E. and was effected rapidly and very satisfactorily.

The production of the Mark IX Service pattern had originally aimed at starting supply in April, 1945, but delays occurred in the testing, modifying and approving the first prototypes. The delivery date gradually receded and the first two sets were only supplied to R.R.D.E. for test and type approval at the end of December of that year. The first delivery from production did not take place until the beginning of June, 1946.

The Mark IX equipment did not therefore obtain any actual war-use proof of its suitability, but the Mark VIII pattern was employed during the operations of 21 Army Group in Northern France, Belgium and Holland. The experience gained with this latter set is a sufficient guide in assessing the advantages of the Mark IX, as it was an improved form of the Mark VIII.

In addition to the operations mentioned above, the Mark VIII was employed operationally by A.A. Command and extracts from the early reports from both these sources are worth quoting here. It should be noted that the 16 sets of equipment mentioned in this report, made in March, 1945, were the first supply off the "crash" production programme and were increased to nearly 40 out of the total provision of 50. There is unfortunately no record of the use of these sets to aid night interception of enemy bombers.

(a) *Extract from a report from* 21 *Army Group*

"Radar A.A. No. 2 Mk. VIII equipments have been used as part of an extended canopy layout for low-level defence of the long, extended, vulnerable area of the SCHELDT Estuary, it has not been possible to try any other employment, and the following report is therefore based on the results of the limited experience outlined above.

Performance. The general performance of the equipment has proved extremely satisfactory. It has produced, in every respect, results which its designers claimed it could produce—in range, accuracy, auto-follow, and stability of radio alignment.

(a) Range.—Ranges to which various aircraft have been followed, averaged 18/20,000 yards for a medium bomber.
(b) Accuracy at low elevations.—Over the sea, targets have been followed, down to about two degrees elevation.
(c) U.H.F.—U.H.F. part of the equipment have presented no difficulties of maintenance. So far not one magnetron has failed in any of the sixteen sets.
(d) Radio Alignment.—The radio alignment of no set has had to be corrected since the sets were first adjusted on their arrival in this theatre.

. . . . .

(b) *Extracts from a report from A.A. Command*

"Four equipments have been deployed at 6–8 mile space intervals at coastal sites in North Norfolk, as part of the 'Gate' anti-Intruder deployment.

Radar performance appears most satisfactory. Initial pick-up and strobing has been effected at ranges up to 22,000 yds. and following out has been continued beyond 25,000 yds. . . . It is thought that (depending on target height) pick-up at 25,000 yds. may be achieved by equipments that are suitably sited."

The full searchlight equipment is completed by the addition of a visual control pillar and the necessary remote control gear; this has to be "double-acting" so that either radar or visual can exercise control at will, though the visual has the power of over-riding control. By double-acting is meant that the visual axis and the radar axis shall always remain co-ordinated whichever form of control is operating and the projector must move in co-ordination with both.

The need for this visual control still remains to permit of the close approach of an attacking fighter without fear of confusing the radar and the chance of causing it to bring the searchlight beam on to the fighter instead of the bomber.

The complete service equipment for an A.A. Searchlight contemplated at the end of the war, therefore, consisted of the redesigned 150 cm. projector and mounting—Mark IX Radar Searchlight Control—Mark VIII Remote Control Gear—Mark V Visual Control Pillar—22 kW. Lister Generator (80 volt D.C.) and its 2,000 C/S alternator.

That brings the record of development of radar applied to the control and direction of A.A. searchlights during the period of the war to a close. It remains to be seen if it is to be "continued in our next," but that is a matter beyond the scope of this volume. It can, however, be said that the future of the searchlight depends upon the nature of future attacking aircraft or other aerial weapons, upon a need remaining for visual indication of hostile targets to the defence aircraft or other weapons in view of the greater possibilities of development of radar applied in other directions and without the need of visual aids and, in so far as the Army is concerned, whether searchlights if retained will remain an Army commitment or not. The utility of searchlights against the future air offensive weapons appears likely to be negligible and if those weapons take practical form the word "utility" may well have to be replaced by "futility" in reference to searchlights as an aid to defence.

CHAPTER XII. ANTI-AIRCRAFT AUXILIARY RADAR

The foregoing chapters of this part have dealt with the major types of radar aids to the H.A.A. ground defences; this chapter will describe those other forms of equipment necessary to enable the fire control sets to function effectively and the different batteries or gun sites comprising the defences of a vital point or area to be controlled and co-ordinated. In addition the radar aids to light and intermediate guns will be mentioned.

Local Warning. The first matter considered must be the question of local warning of approach of hostile aircraft. It will be recalled that the main warning system was always a responsibility of the R.A.F., and all information from that source was made available as rapidly as possible to the ground defences through Group, Area or Sector Headquarters of A.A. Command which operated as part of A.D.G.B. In addition to this general information, local warning for individual A.A. areas and gun sites was essential to enable them to be fully ready for action and pick-up of targets, at a sufficient distance, to allow the "accurate" fire control radar sets serving the guns to track the selected targets before reaching gun range. This distant steady tracking was also necessary to permit the predictor to settle down to absorb incoming information in time to provide its predictions of the future position where the shells were required to burst. This should be done at such a range, in distance or in time, as would enable the guns to make full use of their maximum effective range. This time or range, beyond the effective range of the guns, has also to provide for identification of the aircraft to ensure that it is a hostile target. It will be appreciated that the distance or time for detection of an approaching hostile aircraft is a variable dependent on the speed of the aircraft. In the earlier days of the war, with the lower performance aircraft, a considerably shorter pick-up range than that needed in the later years was adequate. This, however, must be qualified by the fact that the cruder prediction methods then employed required more time than was necessary with the improved methods and newly developed appliances that came into use later.

The earliest types of A.A. radar equipment combined in the one set provision both for local warning of and for fire control, and it was not till the centimetric type, the G.L. III, was introduced that these two functions were separated. These two functions are rather incompatible, at any rate in the mechanical aspect of design; the slow mechanical movements for searching and distant detection, and the high mechanical accuracy for the shorter range tracking and transmission of fire control data, either militate against one another or the effectiveness of one has to give place to that of the other. It was for this reason that the General Staff agreed that the local warning and "putting-on" duties should be separated from the accurate fire control duty of the G.L. III in order to avoid complications and difficulties. They accepted the need for a separate warning and putting-on set to serve the accurate set; this, it was agreed, could be met by the use of an existing early type—G.L. I.* or G.L. II—pending the design of a special set suitable for the purpose.

The Americans also entered the A.A. radar field with a dual purpose set, the S.R.C. 545, which combined an accurate auto follow centimetric type with a longer wave (200 Mc/s) search set and a combined aerial array. They produced, however, in their S.C.R. 584 a set that was capable in itself of long-range search and scanning using a centimetric wave-length for both that and the accurate data provision. This produced a tactical problem that had to be considered, as it denied all information as to the approach of succeeding or alternative targets while the set was engaged on one particular target and controlling the fire of the guns upon it. Their solution to this problem provided for an additional equipment for each group of four-gun sites, to carry on the search for alternative targets and for warning. They were not, however, normally concerned with the more static defences as we were in the defence of vital points in this country, but they did find it necessary to increase the provision for warning when their gun positions in the field had necessarily to be separated by considerable distances, and at times acting independently.

With the increased need for longer local warning, the Army had certainly entered the sphere of responsibility formerly assigned to the R.A.F. in 1939 when the M.B. set design and development was transferred to that Service. Local detection at 20 to 25 miles distance at least was a necessity at the end of the war, and with the increasing speed of jet and gas turbine propelled aircraft, that figure might not have been adequate for long, in spite of reduced "drill times" effected by automatics and rapid settling electric predictors.

One aspect of this local warning auxiliary to the defences is not technical from the radar point of view, but is in fact of considerable importance in the maintenance of the efficiency of the personnel manning the defence. Nothing is more tiring than trying to be alert continuously for long periods of inaction and its attendant boredom. With reliable radar equipment that can ensure ample time for getting into action, considerable relief can be given and the detachments need only be on the alert when a real need for action arises. This aspect has, or should have, an effect also upon the numbers required for manning the defences—it must be remembered that the man- and woman-power absorbed by the A.A. defences in this country became a serious drain upon our resources.

Local Warning Equipment. The first form of this class of auxiliary radar equipment that entered Army service was the A.A. No. 4, Mark I, which was the official nomenclature for the Canadian Z.P. I. set, associated with the Canadian centimetric G.L. III. This has already been referred to in Chapter IX, and it is unnecessary to add much to the remarks made therein. The set was a disappointment and would not have been adopted for the British service had it not formed an integral part of the outfit for H.A.A. fire control. It certainly limited the effect of the fire control part of the equipment and its cover was "gappy" and unreliable, particularly against high targets, and it was very liable to clutter from ground echoes. Still more unfortunately its design brought its optimum operation within the wave-length band allocated to the Identification system and though theoretically it could work just outside that bend it produced difficulties. Though this set remained in service for some time it was relegated to the less important sites and replaced where possible by other types.

The first true development of a local warning set arose from urgent requirements of the R.A.F.—and the anticipated Army requirement—for a lightweight mobile and transportable equipment to provide a minimum performance of 25 miles detection range at 3,000 feet and 45 at 15,000 feet height level of flight. A specification of the inter-Service requirements was prepared by the Inter-Service R.D.F.—later Radar—Board. In this the special requirements of the R.A.F. were the primary consideration; they did not materially conflict with those of the Army and the Navy had only a small interest in such a set and was prepared to accept the resulting development.

As this was the first form of equipment to be specially designed and developed on an inter-service basis, some extracts from the Radar Board's statement of the objects and their specification are worth quoting here:—

"Light Mobile and Portable R.D.F. Air Warning Equipment
(dated 24th November, 1941)

Uses of Equipment.

(a) *R.A.F.* The uses visualized are:—
  (i) For first line cover on sites difficult of access, on which a more bulky type of station could not be erected.
  (ii) For second line cover. . . .
  (iii) To provide cover on a site where air transport is the only immediate means of delivery.
  (iv) For use with Wireless Observer Units in which one light mobile R.D.F. unit might replace 8 normal posts.
  (v) For use inland near to aerodromes and other vital points to provide recognition of intruder aircraft.
  (vi) . . .

(b) *Army.* The uses visualized are:—
  (i) Light mobile equipment mounted in vehicles which can accompany a moving column so as to provide early warning of impending attacks.
  (ii) For second line cover . . .
  (iii) For use in the place of G.L. Mark II as an early warning set for use in conjunction with G.L. Mark III.

(c) *Navy.* The uses visualized are:—
  (i) Light mobile R.D.F. apparatus mounted in a vehicle to provide cover in undeveloped places for early warning.
  (ii) Portable R.D.F. equipment for special landing operations, and various uses at home and overseas.

Specification of Requirements. The requirements of the three Services can be satisfied by a single type of equipment designed in accordance with the specification below.

Range. The minimum range requirements are:—

  25 miles at 3,000 feet; 45 miles at 15,000 feet.

Identification. R.D.F. Identification of friendly aircraft is desirable. If this is done with separate interrogation, the apparatus should be incorporated in such a way that it can either be carried and used or omitted.

Height Finding. The serial system requires to be designed so that a simple aerial structure can be employed and an additional aerial system can be added for use where gap filling and/or height finding are essential.

Transportation. The light mobile equipment should be installed in a 15 cwt. van which should also carry the communication apparatus, the power supply, and plant.

Unit Weights. The equipment should be so arranged that it can be readily removed from the van and be transported by air, hand, or animal transport. All individual units to weigh less than 80 lbs. each.

Communications. Communication apparatus to be incorporated in the vehicle and to be readily removable for use in the portable set. The communication apparatus should be able to operate in close proximity to the R.D.F. transmitter.

. . .

Transmitter. . . .

Height Indication. A Cathode Ray tube is required for height reading.

Operation on the Move. It would be some advantage if the light mobile set could operate whilst on the move, but the mobile station must be designed in such a way that the station is in operation within 3 to 4 minutes of coming to a halt.

Aids to Reporting. . . ."

The urgency of the need for this new type of equipment was primarily an Air Force concern. The R.A.F. had to provide quickly for a wide warning belt deep in desert and trackless wastes where an air threat might mature against vital possessions and territories of great importance. Such a belt could only be established by air transport for a large part of its contemplated length and the greater part of it could only be maintained by air. For the Army the initial need was different; it was a case of protecting moving columns from sudden low-level air attack by providing sufficient warning of the approach of such attack on defiles and similar bottle-necks, where movement might be interrupted. Neither of these uses actually became primary roles of this equipment, but other needs mentioned made use of this light equipment until types of improved performance were introduced.

This requirement was dealt with by the R.D.F. Technical Committee, under the chairmanship of Sir Frank Smith, which included representatives of the Supply Ministries on the development and the production sides. This committee allocated the responsibility for the development of the set to the A.D.R.D.E., who were to have the help of T.R.E. for some of the components and details.

This dual development of the two types of this set became a somewhat complicated business that tended towards competition rather than co-operation between the establishments. T.R.E. took little if any interest in the mobile vehicle type and rejected the designs for the structure for the portable type developed by A.D.R.D.E., though they accepted the latter's design of high-power transmitter, power plant, etc.

The production was perhaps even more complicated in its distribution between M.A.P. and M. of S. and the number and variety of the contractors involved. Supply, test and assembly of components into both portable and vehicle forms was also troublesome, as responsibility for this was allocated in the first place to the R.A.F. Maintenance units. This was cleared to a great extent by the A.M. and W.O. agreeing to a proportionate delivery of components, etc., to Army R.E.M.E. units for assembly, tests and installation in Army vehicles while the R.A.F. Maintenance Units dealt with the portable type in which they were chiefly interested.

Development of the portable type was completed in the autumn of 1942, and to meet the urgent need that then existed—the forthcoming North Africa landings—A.D.R.D.E. and T.R.E. managed to put together a small number of sets, partly from their own workshops and partly filched from manufacturers' prototypes, which were rushed out for use in the operations in North Africa. Thirteen sets of parts for the portable type were provided in this way by October, 1942.

About the same time A.D.R.D.E. had completed their development of the vehicle type, a pilot model of which had undergone tests and flight trials by August, and a prototype vehicle set, using a standard 15 cwt. Morris truck, was made available to R.E.M.E. at Woolwich to guide their installation work as production components were delivered.

The allocation to the Army was initially 800 out of the authorized total provision of 2,000 sets; this figure was increased later to 3,000, though subsequently reduced again. In all the Army received 933 sets of this equipment during 1943–44.

In general terms this equipment in both its forms was a good attempt at a varied-purpose set, but was spoiled by the urgency of the need curtailing proper development. It suffered, by the time it was in service on a fair scale, from the retaliatory action of the enemy in using "window" interference suited to its wave-band. In addition this set, as was to be expected, suffered from ground clutter, particularly in difficult hilly country; A.D.R.D.E. trials, however, had shown that in conditions where there was a considerable amount of clutter, aircraft had been detected at 15 miles at 1,000 feet flying height and had indicated "that some but not abnormal care in siting was required." In Northern Africa and Sicily difficulties with clutter were experienced, but the sets were useful and were liked; few adverse comments were received though some mechanical points were raised.

Though the use of this set as a "putter-on" for G.L. III had been contemplated when the original specification was prepared, and one of the early pilot models underwent reasonably successful trials as a "putter-on" for G.L. III in the late autumn, it was soon appreciated that the range and cover at the higher levels was not really good enough for that purpose. Any attempts to improve it in this respect would reduce its inter-Service performance requirements. Some improvement was effected by an alternative design of aerial framework which enabled the aerial look-out angle to be tilted upwards when desired, by a simple change of the supporting struts, but otherwise the set remained standard; this gave improved high-level at the expense of the lower level detection range. Even with this, however, the results were not ideal for use with the G.L. III, but it had to be employed for this purpose in a number of cases in A.A. Command as the policy of using the G.L. II set with the Mark III could not be implemented owing to diversion of sets to Russia. They served usefully in the field for a number of purposes, however, including service as an aid to mobile G.O.R.s and for warning purposes with L.A.A. formations. (See Illustration No. 8.)

The performance of these light warning equipments gave a range accuracy of 2,000 yards to a range of 65,000 yards and bearing accuracy of 2 degrees; approximate heights were obtainable at 9 and 15 degrees angle of sight. The vehicle type could be in action within 10 minutes from the halt; two operators manned the set, one for technical operation and reading and the other for plotting and radio communication. Of the Marks II, III and IV equipments of this type the Mark II was the rush-preliminary model working on 176 Mc/s. which was withdrawn as soon as replacement was possible by the Mark III, which was worked on 212 Mc/s outside the identification band. The Mark IV was a special modification working on a shorter wave-length of 50 cm. (600 Mc/s) with the object of taking it out of the wave-bands that the enemy were attacking with "Window"; it was not very successful and only a few of this type were provided for Army use.

Gorgonzola. An entirely different type was produced specially for the Normandy operations—a rush-job for 21 Army Group. This was a centimetric equipment known as A.A. No. 4, Mark V, or somewhat familiarly as "Gorgonzola." This used the high power Naval Type 277 set which the Army had adopted for some of the long-range Coastal Warning Chain stations; in that form, used overseas, it was giving detection ranges on aircraft of 100 miles. The R.A.F. had also made use of it for their mobile ground set known as A.M.E.S. Type 14, Mark II, for general Air warning purposes and Coastal warning if necessary.

In view of the threat of "Window" interference by the enemy and other possible jamming of radar sets when deployed on the Continent in proximity to the enemy, the Director of Radar, W.O., requested urgent provision of a centimetric type of warning equipment that might also serve as an aid to Tactical Control of ground Air Defences and possibly for Area Warning as well. Neither the Navy nor the R.A.F. were able to provide mobile sets complete, but the Navy did make available N.T. 277 component assemblies. Time made it impossible to design and produce an equipment specially for the purpose and D. Radar pressed the Ministry of Supply to adopt and adapt this well-known type. This was met with considerable reluctance on the part of the scientific staff on the grounds of lack of range over land and liability to excessive clutter from ground echoes. The former objection was met by the War Office with acceptance of a range performance of about one-half of the over-sea range already proved, and the latter with the suggestion to tilt the aerial structure 6 degrees upwards and thereby reduce the ground reflections.

The N.T. 277 radar parts were housed in a G.L. II cabin—another of the many uses to which this robust and effective rotatable cabin trailer was put—with the tilted "cheese" type aerial reflector on the roof, fed by wave-guide and with motors fitted for power driven rotation of the cabin as well as means of hand control of movement. This was rapidly built up by R.R.D.E. for trials which demonstrated that this set was capable of a performance that was more than adequate. In addition, under Colonel Raby's driving power and persuasiveness, it proved just possible to obtain the various components, parts and mobile cabins, and to rush assembly through the Establishment's workshops in time to provide 21 Army Group with their initial requirements before they had to be ready for D-day. (See Illustration No. 9.)

It was a fine piece of work by R.R.D.E. and particularly by the workshop staff of that establishment, that provided 15 of these warning, tactical control and putting-on sets in time for D-day and followed up by completing the full 22 sets required for the later flights. The result of these efforts were very satisfactory; in fact, it was reported that all the 15 initial sets had been landed and gone into action immediately without trouble. As it happened, the other air warning sets of the R.N. and R.A.F. had been unfortunate in some cases, in getting ashore, and so were lost or damaged. For a time these special "crash" produced Army equipments were the only means available for providing warning of hostile air action. This report and the excellent account of the performance of these sets were specially brought to the notice of the staff and operatives of the R.R.D.E. workshops and the R.E.M.E. personnel assisting them, by the D.C.I.G.S. who visited the establishment and took the opportunity of thanking them for their excellent work.

Supply of this type of equipment was limited to this first small provision, as the development of a tactical control and putting-on set, designed specifically for those purposes, was contemplated and already in the design stage.

As the A.A. No. 4, Mark V, this "Gorgonzola" operated on a wave-length of 10 cm., with a very narrow vertical fan beam, and gave an accuracy of range reading of $\pm$ 1,000 yards and of bearing-angle of $\pm$ 1 degree with a detection range of 55,000 yards for heights up to 25,000 feet. Discrimination between targets was in range 1,000 yards on the P.P.I. display and reducible to 100 yards by reading on the normal time-base C.R.T. which was also fitted; in bearing it was $1\frac{1}{2}$ degrees at 50,000 yards, but increased to 5 degrees at 10,000 yards. Two operators only were required, one for technical operation and reading and the other for "telling" or reporting and plotting. The rate of rotation had to be kept down to 6 r.p.m. on account of the effect of higher rates on the operators.

Time had not permitted the means for the contemplated *variable tilt* of the aerial structure to be devised to enable it to be adjusted to suit the surroundings of any site, but the sets were modified as soon as possible in the field, so as to permit use of the "cheese" being set either horizontally or at 6 degrees tilt, at will, according to the needs of the particular site.

M.Z.P.I. Prior to the introduction of the Mark V type described above, Canada had been developing a 10-cm. warning and "putting-on" set to replace the Mark I (Z.P.I.) associated with their pattern of G.L. III; this was known as the M.Z.P.I. Reports of trials and an examination of the prototype or experimental model showed that it had the promise of being an excellent set and well up to the essential performance now demanded for this role. It was decided to place an order on Canada for 150 of this type of equipment for the British Service, not for use with the Canadian G.L. III, but for warning, long-range detection, putting-on and tactical control. An advance model reached R.R.D.E. for test and for trials in conjunction with C.A.E.E., in the early spring of 1945, and full production was due to start in the autumn of that year. This set did not, therefore, get into the war operationally, but it was an effective design and considerably in advance of any other type in respect of anticipated date of supply. It had facilities in respect of operation in its vehicle or with its display and control transferred to a G.O.R. or a Control Post, and its design had been influenced by practical war experience of the requirements of an equipment for these purposes.

Very Light Set. America at the same time had been developing a number of different experimental types for the warning role, including a handy light-weight set known as the "Little Abner." They had taken considerable interest in our light-weight vehicle and portable set, and had acquired a few of them, but their main design work was able to omit that stage in development and aim, almost at once, at the scanning narrow beam type using centimetric wave-lengths. On both sides of the Atlantic the need existed for a very light warning set, air- and man-portable, requiring not more than two operators, quick into action and simple to operate. It was agreed that uniformity between equipments of this nature for British and for American use should be aimed at, and eventually the development for both was allocated to R.R.D.E., though it had originally been accepted by the United States as their responsibility. The special conditions of the Pacific Theatre of operations not only stressed the need for such a set but also set the standard for tropicalization—unpleasant word—and for unit assembly and maintenance arrangements.

This development did not, however, reach practical form before the end of the war, though R.R.D.E. had initiated a promising design. The pressure of work on that establishment prevented the provision of sufficient effort on design and experiment to produce a speedy solution to the problem.

That must suffice for the local warning and "putting-on" types of equipment. Experience gained in operations strongly reinforced the necessity for equipment for these purposes and though the ideal set did not make its appearance during the war, the development achieved rendered very valuable service in many theatres and gave promise for the future. It would appear that the attempt to combine the two functions at the start of the development was perhaps unfortunate. It seems that a more correct direction for development would have been to concentrate upon the independent warning type for all conditions where the necessity for early local warning existed and to have linked the "putting-on" role with the A.A. gun site tactical control requirements.

Tactical Control Radar Aids. In the early days effective air defence tactical control at H.A.A. gun sites was practically impossible except in the case of visual engagement. With the aid of early radar sets providing range information and some indication of the direction of movement of hostile aircraft, there was some possibility of selecting the target to be engaged, but the plotting of such information, to obtain a picture of what was happening in the air, in the vicinity of or the approaches to the gun site, was neither complete nor a very rapid process. The radar sets for fire control presented their information in a special manner designed to provide the best obtainable accuracy rather than to give a general picture of what was happening. The gun sites were practically independent units and an Area Commander could do little to control their action; the information available to him in his sector or area H.Q. operations room was generally too out of date to affect action and of little more than historical interest. The need for a general radar picture, continuously showing the position of affairs in the air for the gun site control officer, and a still wider picture covering the areas of all his sites for the Superior Commander, soon became apparent.

The first form of Control Radar set that was used was due to the initiative of A.A. Command and was obtained by them from the R.A.F.; this was an early pattern of the G.C.I. set used, as its initials imply, for Ground Control of Interception of hostile aircraft. It was a $1\frac{1}{2}$-metre wave-length equipment with a broadside aerial array continuously rotated, presenting on its P.P.I. display a continuous plan picture of the position of aircraft in the sky over an area surrounding the set. Though the accuracy in detail was not of a high order, the picture painted was relatively accurate and was always up-to-date. These sets suffered considerably from ground clutter and had, therefore, to be carefully sited so that the longer ranges at least should not be obscured or unduly confused.

These sets used for Army (A.A. Command) purposes were officially adopted as Army equipment under the designation of A.A./G.C.I. with the nomenclature A.A. No. 5, Mark I. In all, 16 of these stations were provided between July, 1943, and September, 1944, for large vital areas in this country though only 15 of them were actually installed.

These equipments served a useful purpose in providing the A.A. Defence Commander of a vital area with an overall picture of the development and progress of enemy attacks and enabled him, to some extent, to allocate targets to his individual batteries or to concentrate groups of them to engage targets in particular avenues of approach.

As these sets operated in the wave-band on which the enemy later concentrated his interference efforts, they were adversely affected in the same way as the R.A.F., G.C.I. stations (other than their new centimetric types). They remained, however, in use to the end of the war as no effective replacement had been introduced by that time.

It may be noted that trials in the Newcastle area showed that with adequate direct communications, the A.A./G.C.I set could put a distant G.L. III on to the selected target satisfactorily; this method was, however, seldom used.

The earliest approach to a gun site tactical control set was provided by the Canadian pattern Z.P.I. warning and "putting-on" equipment which provided a display on a large P.P.I. in the G.L. cabin. It was this P.P.I. picture that was the primary requirement for the exercise of proper selection of targets for engagement, the appreciation of likely targets and the time to switch from one to another. It was, however, difficult to accept the necessity for the tactical control officer being cooped up in the dark inside the G.L. cabin. A.A. Command experimented with the removal of the P.P.I. unit to the control post, but the equipment itself, as has been seen, was not very suitable nor reliable.

The use of the light-weight set, as it became available, was applied to aid control and had some degree of success in the field, though A.A. Command did not employ it to any great extent for that purpose as it also had its limitations. A.A. Command were not able to try "Gorgonzola," the centimetric type issued to 21 Army Group, as none could be made available to them. Though its performance showed a marked improvement in range and in bearing accuracy, it could lose high targets at the shorter ranges and its rate of rotation was too low for ideal working in this role.

The experience gained with these and other means or attempts at gun site tactical control, helped in guiding the development of the Canadian M.Z.P.I. for use as a tactical control set. Its make-up in its vehicle was to be such as would permit of the main P.P.I. display being used, either in the mobile cabin with room for the tactical control officer to have access to it without interfering with its operation, or for it to be removed and installed in the command post whence the fire control set could be directed upon the selected target while the T.C.O. could still see the general picture.

Another step forward in the direction of meeting the needs of an area commander was made by A.A. Command in an experimental development carried out in conjunction with Messrs. Pye Radio of Cambridge. It will be recalled that the A.A./G.C.I. sets were liable to clutter trouble which made their siting difficult; this was certainly the case in the London area where such a set could not be sited anywhere near the H.Q. operations room. Transmission through cables from the Hyde Park site to reproduce the P.P.I. picture in the operations room was a difficult and costly business but proved fairly good. To connect a more distant A.A./G.C.I. set beyond the outskirts of London where siting conditions were better was impracticable by cable and Messrs. Pye experimented with a radio link for the transmission. Though this experiment achieved a fair reproduction of the distant P.P.I. picture in the H.Q. operations room, it was not sufficiently good to justify its continuance. The vertical, semi-opaque screen on which the reproduced picture appeared could be viewed from either side and it was possible to mark on its reverse side the changing positions of any aircraft so that its course could be shown and its general changes in direction could be recorded. The screen had, however, to be reviewed in subdued lighting as its marking was rather faint; this prevented it being used fully in the operations room itself, where a number of different plots had to be maintained and watched in normally lighted conditions.

It must be said, however, that this was a creditable effort on the part of Messrs. Pye, and it did emphasize the desirability of large-scale remote displays of up-to-date tactical information for superior commanders.

Development had been pursued in other directions to produce a satisfactory remote display, at a reasonable scale, for reviewing from a short distance, instead of from close up screened from general lighting. The "Skiatron" had reached a useful stage of development some time before the end of the war but was not available in large numbers. A projector capable of reproducing the radar picture on a large screen readable in normal lighting was effectively demonstrated at R.R.D.E. in the summer of 1944. This system was certainly an advance on the Pye scheme in its projection and visibility and showed considerable promise of meeting a real need. No remote display of this class and size became available for use before the war ended.

Light and Intermediate A.A. Gun Radar. Apart from the heavy A.A. guns, the 40 mm. Bofors gun formed part of the defences of vulnerable points in this country and units armed with it were included in field formations. Their role was to deal with the low-flying aircraft by their rapid fire, visually controlled and corrected by observation of tracers; their effect other than deterrent, was achieved by direct hitting only. Sudden and brief engagements—opportunity targets—were their main meat, within their limited effective range of some 3,000 yards. Predictors were provided for groups of these guns but the majority of their engagements were visually controlled.

The possibility of giving radar aids was considered, but it was apparent that the very large provision problem involved was difficult to justify by the possible improvement in fire effect likely to be obtained with the fleeting and dodging targets they had to compete with. Provision for early warning of attack was made by the allocation of light-weight sets on a troop basis but with really low-flying, true "hedge hopping," the warning obtainable was often extremely short and visual watch could not be dispensed with.

The possibility of providing a "radar sight" for individual guns that would automatically give the necessary deflections if the layers maintained the "blip" on the cross wires, was suggested by Shire of R.R.D.E. Such a scheme was only possible with a short-range weapon with short times of flight of its shell. This proposal, however, was not proceeded with even to the extent of producing an experimental model, which was perhaps a pity though there was in fact no chance of going to production for a set of this kind with the many urgent requirements taking precedence over it.

Among these was the more urgent requirement of aiding the Intermediate A.A. gun for which the development of a radar range finder had been in progress for some time. This weapon offered a better return for effort expended on such development and the occupation of production capacity. This 6-pdr. weapon was also a direct hitting gun and therefore demanded highly accurate location, prediction and pointing to achieve its effect. Accuracy in the radar for location and rates of movement alone was insufficient, it had to be complete overall accuracy and without considerable design of a high order the chances of "unseen" direct hitting were small. The capacity of radar at the stage when work started on aiding the intermediate weapon, was not good enough for unseen shooting to approach visual control and the radar aid provided was, therefore, designed to give accurate range only.

This produced the G.R. set, visually directed on to the target by manual control and visual bearing and elevation following fed direct, with the radar range, into the predictor. For this purpose the radar component was "buttoned on" to the predictor and its mobile or transportable mounting. This set was officially named A.A. No. 6, Mark I (G.R.), and operated on a wave-length of 25 cm.; it had a range output accuracy of $\pm$ 25 yards up to a range of 10,000 yards and a rate accuracy of $\pm$ 16 yards a second. One operator for the radar was required, but it needed the other predictor numbers to keep it visually directed on the target. (See Illustration No. 13.)

With the intermediate gun the radar set was applied to the predictor A.A. No. 7, Mark I, and was completely attached to it; it was also applied experimentally to Predictor A.A. No. 3 for possible use with the light (40-mm. Bofors) guns. An emergency experimental form of G.R. set working on a 9 cm. wave-length was introduced and became the A.A. No. 6, Mark III; this set was an improvisation using the radar units of the R.A.F. equipment for "blind bombing" known as H_2S. The radar units were fitted in a metal case that formed the base for the predictor (A.A. No. 3, Mark II) and the predictor itself carried the aerial system and included the radar range unit; the radar, therefore, formed an integral part of the predictor for use with Light A.A. guns.

This equipment was provided to the extent of 24 sets only, built up in the workshops of R.R.D.E. as an emergency means of assisting L.A.A. to meet the flying-bomb attacks. As will be appreciated, this combined predictor/radar was dependent on visual following of the target and it did not, therefore, provide for fire under unseen conditions. It was contemplated that future design, particularly for use with the intermediate guns, would include automatic following in bearing and elevation to permit of unseen fire; this stage of development had, however, not been achieved by the end of the war and its development must be dependent upon the need for and nature of the weapon to be used.

Some rush conversions of available R.A.F. types of equipment other than the H_2S were tried out during the flying-bomb emergency, chief of which were the adaptation of the A.G.L.T. and the A.I. X. These were adapted and used with or attached to the No. 3 Predictor to provide radar range for visual engagements and radar bearing and elevation as well, for use in unseen conditions. These types given the title of Marks in the A.A. No. 7 series, did not in fact get much opportunity for action in the main South Coast period of the battle. As improvised makeshifts, however, they performed fairly well, but it is not possible to give figures of casualties attributable to their use to compare with those of non-radar equipped light weapons. It would appear most unlikely that these equipments will continue in service even if there remains a need for light weapons in the future. These weapons have been out-dated for protection of static vital areas and something more effective will be required to meet the higher speeds now in view and the pilotless air weapons that seem likely to assume major roles in future air attacks. It is extremely doubtful if these weapons have a future sufficient to justify expenditure of effort to provide them with improved radar aids.

That must suffice for the radar auxiliary equipments for A.A. uses; there are other aids in the form of equipments or of additions to equipments, such as those for identification, but being of more general application they will be dealt with in later parts of this book. There is, however, a most important A.A. device which can hardly be called an equipment, namely the Radio Fuze, of which some slight mention has already been made; this too has applications other than A.A. defence, but its importance for this purpose does justify its inclusion in this Part. It will be dealt with in the following chapter, but it is entirely independent of all development work connected with the equipments that have been described so far. To many it may well appear as the greatest triumph of scientific and technical war-time development, and this entitles it to a distinctive position in the record of Army radar development. It is, therefore, included in this Part describing A.A. Radar as it first came into use by the Army against aircraft targets.

CHAPTER XIII. RADIO PROXIMITY FUZE

The use of the Radio Proximity Fuze has already been mentioned and its importance has been indicated in so far as use in A.A. gunnery is concerned. For that purpose this type of fuze may be said to be the last link in the chain of automatic appliances controlling the fire of H.A.A. guns. It completes the operation that starts with the pick-up of the selected target by the accurate radar set and ends by the actuation of this fuze with the bursting of the shell in a position where its fragments can produce lethal effect. This last link in the chain includes the target itself, as it is the target that automatically actuates the fuze when within effective range and indeed cannot help doing so.

Of course, every part of this chain must produce the maximum of accuracy in its own sphere and do so in the minimum of time, so that the contributions of all the links combine to produce the maximum overall accuracy of the system to ensure putting the shell in the right place at the right time.

Here it must be stated definitely that the development of this radio device was initiated in this country. Full details of our early work were given to the scientists of the U.S.A. in 1943, so that they could carry on their investigations and development without having to explore those early stages for themselves. They, having ample scientific and technical effort to apply and the backing of their large production capacity, were able to tackle this work at high pressure and with adequate resources. It was from this source, rather than from our own, that we were supplied with these fuzes towards the end of the war in parallel with supplies to the U.S. forces themselves.

Proximity fuzes, that is, fuzes operated by the target itself, had been "in the air" some years before the war, but owing to the apparent difficulties of the very limited size, application to shell had hardly been contemplated. The A.D.E.E., as the experimental establishment was then named, had been engaged in developing for the Air Ministry a proximity bomb fuze, operated by acoustic means, to explode the bomb as it dropped from above an enemy formation when it came within lethal range of the hostile aircraft. This was at that time contemplated as a possible method of attack to break up an enemy bomber formation or to disorganize it so that our fighters would have greater opportunities of successful attack. It was a case of "bombing the bomber" and some production of these fully proved acoustic fuzes and their "spinner bomb tails" had been put in hand just before the war; they were not, however, used operationally by the R.A.F. The R.A.F. and the R.A.A.F. apparently experienced some forms of attack by the Japanese, of this nature, though there was no evidence of *proximity* fuzes being used. Parallel with this development of the acoustic bomb fuze, the Air Ministry had been developing a fuze operated by a photoelectric "eye"; this, also, was not employed for its original purpose though it was diverted and developed for other purposes, including attempts to apply it to A.A. rocket projectiles but without much success. Proximity fuzes for mines and torpedoes were used against shipping, with magnetic and acoustic operation and it is now apparent that development of several forms of shell fuzes had made considerable progress in Germany during the war, though they had not reached the stage of war use.

Towards the end of 1939, Rothwell of A.D.R.D.E. was experimenting with an acoustic fuze for H.A.A. rockets and shells, and about the same time Butement, also serving then with that establishment, started experimental work on a radio fuze, making use of the "Doppler" effect reflections from transmitted radio waves emitted by the fuze.

This "Doppler" effect—so called because it was first explained by a scientist of that name—needs some explanation as to what it is, but there is no necessity to go into details here; a note is included in the Glossary.

The effect is the variation in the frequency of any wave emission by the movement of the source of that emission in relation to the point where it is received; the emissions may be radio waves, sound or any other waves, and it is this variation that can be used to distinguish an emission from a moving source from that of a fixed source.

The problem at once arose of the small radio valves, components and batteries that would have to be developed as none of sufficiently small size nor of sufficient ruggedness for a shell-head fuze existed. More particularly the question of their design, to enable them to withstand the shock of discharge and the rapid gyration due to the spin of the shell, was likely to raise many problems and involve considerable experiment before a suitable answer could be found. The greater simplicity of the problem of designing a radio fuze for the U.P. rocket for A.A. use—the absence of spin and the much lower discharge acceleration—offered a quicker solution, but such rockets did not appear likely to return an adequate dividend for the effort involved.

Some encouragement to pursue the development of the more difficult problem of the shell fuze was given by the investigation of German diode valves recovered from some of their bombs; these had been found to have withstood the impact of the bomb on arrival. Cockcroft had these tested at Cambridge and found they could stand up to an acceleration of about 10,000 g. as they were of very "rugged" construction. This showed that it was not impossible to build valves suitable for use in shells, and Cockcroft arranged for work to start on development of very small size rugged valves.

Cockcroft also discussed this development of a radio proximity fuze for A.A. guns with Dr. Tuve during the visit of the Tizard Mission to America, and he interested others who were already investigating the possibilities of various forms of proximity fuzes. Tuve agreed to include work on this development for our 3.7 in. A.A. gun shells, in parallel with such fuzes for U.S. guns. This was followed up by continuous close contact and intercommunication at all stages of development and trials in both countries.

In this country two lines were pursued in the early stages of development, the first of which was in reality a step towards the second, namely, a radio fuze operated by a signal from a radar set on the ground when the target radar echo and the shell echo coincided. This was called the Radio Operated Fuze and was simpler than the complete proximity fuze in that it required only a receiver capable of accepting a special pulsed signal to actuate it. Though this type is sometimes referred to as an alternative to the complete proximity fuze, it was not so considered by the General Staff and only partially so by the technical artillery advisers. The prime requirement was always for the full development of the true, self-contained fuze which would be "target operated" without any reliance on assistance from the ground. It was this independent "target operated" type that was the second of the two lines of development mentioned above. The first form was necessary to clear up the difficulties of valve, battery, etc., design to withstand the shock of discharge and other details.

Work started on this development in earnest towards the end of the summer

1941, and the help of two firms was enlisted to assist A.D.R.D.E. in the research and development work and in particular to develop valves of the robust midget type suitable for use in shell from high velocity guns. The design and construction of batteries of minute size but capable of a high output for a short period, aerial design and rigidity of fixing all components inside the fuze and many other problems had to be solved and proved by recovery shoots.

After demonstrations of the R.O.F. type in March, 1942, when a fairly good percentage of rounds were successfully operated in the air by pulsing from the ground, all the available effort was concentrated upon the true proximity type.

Work was slowed up by the move of the establishment to Malvern, and delays in obtaining suitable sites for recovery shoots and for over-sea firing. In addition, the manufacturing firms had produced a 16 mm. valve, which involved an over all increase in the fuze size as compared with the American 10 mm. valve; other difficulties arose over the miniature batteries and the difficulty at that time of getting even drawings of the American pattern "Layer" battery.

These layer batteries presented practical difficulties for service use in that they had a short "shelf" life which would make handling in depots and dockyards very awkward and would severely limit the availability of the fuzes for operations overseas. This position was, however, relieved by the development of a new type of battery in America known as the "Reserve" battery which was suggested by a Canadian; this included an ampoule of electrolyte which was broken by the shock of discharge so that until then with the shell spinning the battery would not be activated. This at once brought the U.S. development into practical politics and the Royal Navy immediately took a hand and led the way in getting a supply of these fuzes from America—as at that time the Naval need was paramount and Army A.A. had to take a back seat. The Naval need was certainly an urgent one with the torpedo bomber, dive bombers and the Japanese suicide enthusiasts all presenting a definite and increasing menace. By October they felt assured of an adequate supply from the United States for their operations, though the American type did not fully meet their specification of requirements.

The A.D.R.D.E. continued to work on the development of these fuzes for all three Services, with priority for Naval use, which was a simpler problem than that of the Army as it did not involve provision for self-destruction, which was an essential for use over troops or populated areas.

With some difficulty it was eventually arranged that our manufacturing firms should abandon the 16 mm. for the 10 mm. valve, and while that changeover was in progress we were able to obtain, through Naval channels, small supplies of U.S. fuzes for test and trials. This helped our development, but by the end of October, 1942, it became evident that we should have to rely upon America for immediate supplies of complete fuzes to suit our different shells, owing to the slowness of development for production in this country. Our development programme had to be amended to longer term work to produce a fuze to fulfil all the operational requirements envisaged by our Services.

The American type fuze was referred to by the letters V.T., which were the normal *development* distinguishing initials like the X.T. for H.A.A. radar sets (the X.T. became in production the S.C.R. 584).

The Army received large supplies from U.S. resources which, as has already been seen, enabled the guns of A.A. Command to take such a very high toll of the flying bombs in their attacks on this country; to this success the V.T. fuze undoubtedly made a very considerable contribution.

It was much to be regretted that no British development of this type of fuze came into operation during the war. Undoubtedly this was due to the lack of sufficient scientific and technical effort and more particularly to the extremely limited industrial development and production facilities available in this country. By the end of the war the British designs were approaching completion and the development of the technique for production of the special valves, batteries, etc., had made some strides forward, but there was still no supply from our own resources. Cockcroft's notes on the position from the end of 1943 include the following comment:—

"The remainder of the story of fuze development at A.D.R.D.E. is of a continual struggle to overcome the disabilities due to poor industrial development facilities. . . .
We may say that we achieved our operational requirements through our keeping in touch with U.S. development and that this alone justified the existence of the A.D.R.D.E. (Fuze) Group.
We have less cause for satisfaction on the technical side and the proximity fuze development was A.D.R.D.E.'s greatest disappointment. We suffered also from being continuously out-paced by American development."

The fuze itself consists of a normally shaped nose-cap suited to the particular type of shell, and contains the radio set complete—transmitter, receiver, battery power supply and aerial; in addition it contains certain safety devices and other arrangements to provide for the special conditions of operational use.

Naval use over sea made self-destruction unnecessary as any unexploded shell would in any case not be recoverable. Army use, however, being generally over land and frequently over populated areas or over our own troops made it highly desirable, if not essential, that the fuze should destroy itself and the shell in the air, if it failed to function near the target; "duds" might be recoverable by the enemy and details of the fuse disclosed.

Another essential device included had to provide for "arming" the fuze or making it alive, at some short time *after* the shell has left the gun. As the fuze is inactive when the gun is fired, prematures in the gun are avoided and the fuze is not affected in the early stages of flight by radio echoes from the ground or other local objects. Different operational uses made it necessary to provide means of varying this arming time to suit different cases. Even for A.A. defence guns, different arming times may be needed, as for example, action against flying bombs at comparatively short range may require a shorter time than against high-level aircraft. There is also the need for being able to adjust the "sensitivity" of the radio echo reception, but there is a limit to this need, because the design of the fuze and its aerial provide for a specific "look-out" angle for its operation. This angle gives an all-round zone for the effective transmission and reception of the radio waves. It is so designed that the shell bursting when operated by the fuze actuated by the target echo, shall include the target in the zone of maximum fragmentation. As different types of shell have different effective fragment ranges the sensitivity of the radio set in the fuze needs setting for each type; these adjustments have to be made at the factory in providing for each different type of shell.

Another consideration affecting the arming time is the time of flight of the shell; the battery when actuated is of course causing the transmitter to emit its radio waves and its life at high power output is short, so that it is desirable that the arming time should not be too short or its power may be reduced too much by the time high or distant targets are approached. The later "Reserve" type battery, however, provided for the full effective ranges of the guns for which this fuze was provided.

The British "midget" (this term was applied to the valves used in the fuzes to distinguish them from the "miniature" types developed for communication sets which were somewhat larger in size) valve manufacturers, unfortunately, would or could not develop the U.S. type of filament and their valve consequently caused a larger drain on the battery so that they did not really match the American batteries. Eventually a British developed reserve battery that should overcome this difficulty was being finalized for production at the time the war ended.

One other point of difference between British and American practice caused some difficulty, or rather added to the extent of the work of American production of fuzes specifically for our types and sizes of shell. The heavier walls of British shell reduced the explosive content in comparison with U.S. shell and further reduction had to be made to provide for the greater intrusion into the explosive space of the proximity fuze than in the case of mechanical fuzes. This was provided for by the use of an explosive "plug" in the cavity when fuzed with mechanical fuzes but removable for fitting the radio fuze; this made a change necessary in the shell-filling operations. It was found in practice that the explosive effect of the reduced filling charge showed little if any actual reduction in lethal effect of the shell and its fragmentation.

In Chapter X some figures have been quoted from the Review by A.A. Command of the Flying Bomb Operations, that give an assessment to compare the effectiveness of the time mechanical 208 fuze with that of the radio proximity fuze; these indicate the advantage given by the latter as an improvement of from 4 to 8.

That Review of these operations also includes the following:—

"*Factor of Improvement.*

Theoretical figures suggest that, round for round, the present Radio Proximity (VT) fuze should show a factor of improvement of about five or six over Fuze No. 208.

It would appear from operational results that this figure is about right, although it is almost impossible to substantiate this by quoting actual figures from the Field.

It was almost impossible to allot casualties to any one gun-site. Furthermore, on many 8-gun sites, four guns fired V.T. and four guns Fuze 208. It must be remembered that the object of the deployment was to destroy Flying Bombs, not to test the effectiveness of V.T. and the best tactical distribution had to be made to achieve the best results."

. . .

"However, there were areas for part of the time where only V.T. fuzes were used, and some indication was obtained that the rounds per bird figure for Fuze 208 was between four and five times greater than that for V.T. fuze.

But whatever was the actual figure for improvement, it is certain that improvement was most spectacular. The results obtained could never have been achieved without V.T. fuzes."

This Review also refers to limitations of this fuze itself and to the operational limitations imposed upon its use.

There were of course limitations and faults, such as a small percentage of "early bursts" and also of "non-starters" or "blinds" that fail to function at all. Such faults or failures are to be expected in all novel devices developed in times of urgent need, when very lengthy trials and test are impossible and the final clearance or reduction of the percentage occurrence of faults cannot be effected in the stress of war. The results obtained with these fuzes as they were, is evidence enough of the excellence of their design and suitability for the war purpose for which they were devised.

So far this fuze has only been considered as an aid, and a very material aid at that, to Anti-Aircraft fire, but it was also applied effectively to other purposes in the Army.

In September, 1943, the D.R.A., War Office, requested the Ministry of Supply directorate concerned to consider the possibility of applying the radio proximity fuze to Field Artillery shell as a means of effecting low air bursts. The A.O.R.G. had assessed, theoretically, the effect of bursts between 20 and 40 feet height, as giving much greater fragment effect than ground bursts against troops in slit trenches; on the moral effect of low bursts, experience had already shown their unpleasantness, particularly when very little above head level.

This was taken up with the Americans who had also appreciated this possibility, and arrangements were made at once for the fuze to be adapted to suit our Field Artillery 25 pdr. shell. This was effected with remarkable speed and supplies were made available in both countries for trials. Here at the School of Artillery, Larkhill, their limitations and the tactical doctrine for their operational use were determined and defined. The primary problem was to decide the most effective height of burst which would decide the sensitivity of the fuze most suited to field use; crest clearance seemed at one time to present a problem, but the variable charges of the 25-pdr. supplied the means of avoiding this difficulty in many cases.

These fuzes were made available in time for them to be used with effect in the operations in Northern Europe and in the Pacific areas. The initial supplies were not large but grew fairly rapidly and considerable experience was gained of their use; from general reports it was apparent that they were very effective and a valuable asset to the gunners in the field.

The application of this type of fuze to mortar bombs was also mooted and considered; the problem did not produce much difficulty from the radio aspect, but the means of applying it to the bombs raised matters of some complication from the design point of view. It was not possible to divert effort from the field gun needs at the time and no fuzes for British mortars were made available for use in the war.

Throughout the experimental and development work on these radio proximity fuzes, the strictest security measures were applied and the number of people permitted to have any knowledge of the subject was closely restricted. In addition no operational use of the fuzes was permitted, either by America or by this country, without the agreed permission of the Combined Chiefs of Staff.

This high degree of security was fully justified by the great operational importance of this device and the need to obtain the full effect of this novel weapon by adequate supplies being available rather than wasting the surprise effect by frittering away small supplies in minor actions. It was also justified by eliminating the possibilty of premature disclosure of it to the enemy by recovery of unexploded shell and perhaps giving them time to copy and reproduce it. There was, too, the possibility of the enemy being able to develop an antidote to it in the form of some radio counter measures, though this did not appear very likely at the time and was not experienced in the war.

There is no question that this security restriction was effective and necessary, but it added to the difficulties of interchange of information and ideas on development and design progress between us and the United States. It did in fact contribute to some "differences" between the two American Services which involved us in having to tread somewhat delicately at times on the subject. Those difficulties, however, were a small price to pay for this remarkable device and we owe the United States a debt of gratitude for the way in which they aided us in providing for our needs when we could not provide for ourselves.

In regard to the C.C.S. release for operational employment of these fuzes, authority was given in stages. The Navies, firing over the sea, were freed first as the possibility of recoveries was practically nil. For Army A.A. use we were permitted to use them firing out to sea or, with the threat of the flying bomb attacks, for use limited to this country. Use against the enemy ground forces was generally withheld until the Northern Europe campaigns were started, though some use of them may have been made before then for some operations against Pacific islands.

With that general description of the development and provision of this remarkable device, this chapter must be closed. It will, however, perhaps be permissible to mention two of the American scientists—Tuve and Salant—who so willingly gave us their help in this work and were largely instrumental in solving the special problems of our shell fitting, advising on and supporting our requirements. We owe them much and fully acknowledge how much they did to help us—we are very grateful to them.

From what has been mentioned in this chapter it will be appreciated that the failure to develop and produce these fuzes in this country was not only a disappointment to the A.D.R.D.E., but must be a matter of great regret to all concerned.

CHAPTER XIV. COMMENTARY

The first point in this Part II on which some small comment or observation is desirable is the division of responsibilities between the three Services in respect of Air Defence. The conditions of this country with its proximity to enemy or potential enemy territory were the primary basis on which all defence measures were designed; the allocation of functions for the defence of the United Kingdom was applied also to overseas territories, either from the start or shortly after the actual outbreak of war, but in operations in the field they were not so directly relevant.

To the R.A.F. fell the responsibility for the whole of the Air Warning measures, their co-ordination and the distribution of information. In the United Kingdom these functions were exercised by the organization known as Air Defence of Great Britain (A.D.G.B.).

The Navy did not come into the defence picture for the United Kingdom except for a few special cases of primary import to its own interests; the Navy was concerned with its own protection and that of its convoys at sea.

The contribution of the Army was the provision and manning of the ground defences sited to protect vital points or areas. The operation of these defence weapons was the function of Anti-Aircraft Command, the military formation that formed an integral part of A.D.G.B.

Radar was the saving grace—the means of providing that first essential, the distant detection of enemy attack; on that warning depended the effect of all the other active and passive measures of defence. In addition it was radar that grew to serve and to improve increasingly the various active measures and methods to defeat the attacking enemy. This Part II has endeavoured to sketch the growth and development of Army Radar applied to A.A. ground defences.

The development of the medium range warning equipment—the M.B. set mentioned in Chapter VII, taken over by the R.A.F. after initial work by the Army cell, raises a point of minor interest. The warning range of some 40 to 50 miles was considered in 1938 as beyond the local needs of H.A.A. gun sites, but by the end of the war such a range would not have been thought excessive, at any rate for control of ground defences in important vital areas. This illustrates the improvement in aircraft performance and speed during the war period, and the consequent need for extended range of H.A.A. Radar.

The difference between the accuracy requirements of radar equipment for the R.A.F. and for the Army and its direction or control of H.A.A. gunfire, should be fully appreciated. The H.A.A. targets are moving in three dimensions—in fact, Time may also be included as a fourth—and the accuracy of the measurement in each of them must be of a very high order if the shell is to arrive and burst at the proper place and time within effective lethal distance of the target. Radar is not the sole concern in achieving this effect, but as has been seen it grew to be the key factor eventually in the automatic chain of appliances—all suited in speed of operation and in standard of accuracy to the radar data transmitted to and through them—that pointed and fired the gun.

In radar equipment itself, the radar alone was not the key to accuracy—the mechanical side had a large part to play. Radar and Mechanics must combine, each with the maximum of refinement and must balance one another if the best results are to be obtained. This point is stressed here because it is frequently assumed that accuracy is almost entirely achieved by the radar technique; in point of fact the mechanical aspect was often of greater concern in production and manufacture than the radar assemblies but did not appear always to have been appreciated in the selection of firms nor at times by the firms themselves.

The assessment by the Air Ministry of the performance and tactics of enemy air attack, quoted in Chapter VII, is of interest. The only comment necessary is that it proved to be a sound and effective basis for design that continued to be adequate well beyond the time when our scientific watch on enemy performance during the war could point to changes and improvements needed, and our designs of equipment in general kept well ahead of, or at least in step with, enemy improved performance, if not always in up-to-date supply to the troops.

In Chapter VIII the decision to introduce the incomplete G.L. set as service equipment calls for some comment. As is indicated, this partially developed set was only intended as an aid to visual methods and as an immediate means of introducing radar to troops in the field. Some post-war opinions have expressed doubts of the correctness of this decision, but those opinions appear to ignore the conditions of stress and urgency of need at the time. Time did not permit of waiting for the ideal, or even for elementary means of providing full data, to emerge from the scientists' researches, and no one could estimate a date by which it would emerge; the need to provide the troops with the best equipment available at that time was the urgent need.

The problems of providing accurate angular measurements and of continuous following and reading them were the biggest "headaches" for the scientists. Those in close touch with the work at that time do not blame them for the time taken to solve those problems, and they appreciate fully the difficulties and their efforts to overcome them.

An acceptable solution was achieved late in 1939, though it was not possible to incorporate it in the G.L. I., as had been provided for; it was a real *tour de force* to get the Mark II type incorporating the solution into production and supply early in 1941. This complete equipment certainly benefited from the experience gained with the early type and the fire control methods developed with it. Wisdom after the event does not necessarily prove the correctness of the decision taken, but it would certainly have found it difficult to justify a delay of 18 months before any radar equipment got into the hands of the A.A. gunners.

The first operational report on radar in action—nominally against the enemy —which is referred to in Chapter VIII, is of some interest as it was the first of a series that became a routine matter in A.A. Command; it also linked up with the reports by the Operational Research Group on the effects and errors of our ground defences and the performance and tactics of enemy aircraft. These reports and the observations of scientists during action played a very considerable part in guiding new development as well as in devising methods to improve handling of the different parts of the fire control appliances.

The points raised by Gray about the operating conditions led to an investigation by medical and scientific advisers which materially influenced future design. They showed that a higher standard of operation was achievable and maintainable for longer periods by careful planning of the seating, position of hand-wheel controls, and displays and by proper lighting, heating and ventilating of the cabins. The G.L. II showed a very marked advance on the austere conditions of the Mark I and subsequent equipments improved matters still further.

Chapter VIII, includes an independent opinion of the merits of the design of the G.L. II set, and that opinion was fully confirmed by users of the equipment over a considerable period. Further confirmation could be cited from a very independent source, namely Professor Mark Oliphant, who, on his return from visiting Australia and the Australasian Islands, reported that of all types of radar equipment—Naval, Air Force, Army and Australian—in that theatre, the British G.L. II was functioning the best and giving the least trouble.

Apart from the excellence of its design, its performance was inherently capable of providing all the needs for fire control, but it was to some extent disappointing in its performance in the hands of the troops. The standard of the average operators was not such as to produce the results of which the set itself was capable when in expert hands. As will be seen in Part V, in trials with highly trained radar and predictor crews, the accuracy and the smoothness of the data supplied was satisfactory.

It is of course a commonplace that the skill and experience of the user of any weapon or device is the determining factor in its efficiency in action. With novel appliances such as this it is only to be expected that the overall efficiency will be comparatively low; for this equipment a rough estimate would put it at not better than 60 per cent of the instrumental capacity of the radar set.

Chapter IX introduces the revolution in radar technique effected by the research and development of the means of ultra short-wave working at high powers. This is attributed mainly to the resonator or cavity magnetron work done by Oliphant and his team, but the other developments of Klystron oscillators and crystals for the centimetric working contributed materially to this great step forward. It was a remarkable effort that resulted in a magnetron valve being "on the air" only nine months from the start of the research work, a War Office decision to base design of the improved G.L. set upon it within 13 months of the start and an experimental set demonstrated within another six months. The first pre-production model was in fact available for test and trials in 26 months from the start of the research work. There certainly was no delay in these early stages, but the later stages unfortunately did not maintain that rate of progress.

It is not easy to attribute this delay to any one specific source. Some delay was, undoubtedly, caused by the diversion of effort to the A type model for the R.A.F.; the finalization of the design in the testing and modification of the prototypes for production certainly took longer than it should have done and probably the large number of sets ordered by the War Office, involving the two Supply Ministries in complicated organization of large groups of manufacturing firms, contributed to the delay in supplying the troops with this British type G.L. III.

There was a very regrettable absence of proper co-operation in the early days between the Canadian authorities and scientists and the War Office and Ministry of Supply in the initial stages of the development of the Canadian pattern of Centimetric G.L. set; on both sides insufficient information was supplied, or at any rate did not reach those concerned in time. This certainly depreciated the value of the initiative and effort put into this work in Canada. The equipment was good, but with a little aid from the practical experience gained in this country it could have been much better.

The Canadian equipment filled the gap in our defences when the British type had to be largely diverted to the use of the Field Forces in Northern Europe.

The development of Automatic Following Radar for Army use—dealt with in Chapter X—commenced before the G.L. III set had got into full production; this development was included in the G.S. Policy statement of September, 1942, as an aim for further advanced equipment. Its possible or probable utility for H.A.A. fire control was one of the reasons for the suggestion for keeping down the number of G.L. III sets ordered.

The initial experimental work to prove the adequacy and suitability of this system was effected by improvisation in adapting a G.L. III pre-production model; this offered earlier indication of the performance attainable than by designing a set for the purpose. The War Office had accepted this method only as a guide to the possibilities and not as a means of modifying these sets for service equipment. Experience with many classes of equipment—not only Radar and Radio—had shown the frequency of failures and troubles caused by major modifications to make an equipment perform functions for which it had not been designed. The W.O. aimed at an equipment designed from the start for auto following provided that the experiment with the G.L. III showed sufficient promise to justify such work.

Dr. A. K. Solomon—mentioned in Chapter X, had joined A.D.R.D.E. under the special scheme for interchange of scientists between United Kingdom and United States; he was, however, the only one who came in on Army Radar. His experience of development of auto following in America was valuable and he started the work at A.D.R.D.E. with a team including Dunworth and others of the Establishment. When he was transferred later to the A.S.E. to help with Naval needs, Dunworth continued the work at A.D.R.D.E. Apart from the experimental conversion of the G.L. III, three experimental patterns of sets were developed under contract with a firm. One of these known as A.F.1 was accepted as the basis for design and put into production; an emergency form was to become the Mark IV, and after proof, to be the model, when modified and cleaned up, for the eventual service pattern that would be the Mark VII. That not even the Mark IV got into operational use against the enemy was regrettable.

With the impending delays in the production of these sets, efforts were made to adopt the modifications to the G.L. III for auto follow; the War Office agreed to this provided that the A.F.1. type was not delayed thereby. The actual course of the modifications recommended was very crooked and variable —changes in advice from the Ministry of Supply as to which type and unreliable information as to the position of the availability of components, parts, etc., prejudiced this work. Neither of the types ever came into service and the wasted effort was the result of "snatching at straws" in the hope of obtaining some operational benefit to offset the delay in supply of the new model.

The early forms of S.L.C. call for little comment—Chapter XII gives the general picture of the rush development. Here was a case of deliberate clipping of the wings of the scientists and technicians in order to meet an emergency in operations; however desirable a fully developed and properly designed set may be, it is useless unless it can be provided *in time*. To do them justice the scientists accepted the need and adapted themselves to that point of view and rushed the job through; the set worked, even if it did not work as well as it might have done if time had permitted fuller experiment and development.

The control of searchlights presented a simpler problem than that of H.A.A. gunfire—the highest degree of accuracy is not so essential as there is the width of the searchlight beam to play with in ensuring illumination of the target—and this naturally simplified the development of the means of automatic following.

The auto fittings and assemblies were neat and compact and were easily attached to the standard projector and its turn-table; it certainly was a very good job particularly in its final service form; its emergency Mark VIII form proved itself in action against the enemy, but was not, unfortunately, given the opportunity of demonstrating its suitability as an aid to night interception.

Radar Tactical Control of H.A.A. defences was never fully developed during the war—improvisations and diversions of equipment from other uses were tried but the real needs were neither met nor fully defined. Available facilities and effort, particularly production capacity in this country, did not permit of tackling this problem by special design. The Canadian M.Z.P.I. centimetric type certainly offered the nearest approach to such a set at the end of the war. Whether future needs can be defined sufficiently, and development effort applied to the design of equipment, is a matter beyond the scope of this record; if tackled it would appear essential that the needs of static defences should be divorced from those of mobile conditions.

The final chapter of this Part deals with one of the most outstanding developments of the war—the Radio Proximity Fuze. This device formed the final link in the automatic chain between detection of a H.A.A. target and its destruction. In addition it opened up a wide and profitable field of use against ground troops which was only explored to a very limited extent just before the end of operations.

In so far as this country was concerned—and it was this country that initiated development of this fuze—it was also perhaps the most outstanding failure "to produce the goods."

To close this Part the following figures have been given by the G.O.C.-in-C., A.A. Command as the total bag of enemy aircraft due to the A.A. fire of his command during the war. Destroyed 822; probably destroyed 237; damaged 422—in addition over 1,970 flying bombs were brought down.

PART III
COASTAL DEFENCE RADAR

CHAPTER XV. 1½ METRE COAST DEFENCE RADAR

In Part I it has already been recorded how the possibilities of detection and location of surface vessels from the shore by means of radar was brought to notice towards the end of 1937. This was the result of experimental work at Bawdsey with a rather primitive "beam" set; the appreciation by the General Staff in April, 1938, of the value of radar for defence of ports and harbours, and their directive to guide development has been quoted in Chapter V.

These early experiments, and the scientific assessment of the possibilities arising from them, pointed to the early achievement of long-range detection and warning of approach of surface craft with sufficient accuracy of location to track and plot their courses. It was estimated that practical equipment for this purpose could be developed within a year or so from the time additional staff was made available for the development work. It was also estimated that equipment of greater accuracy for directing and controlling the fire of Coastal Artillery weapons could be developed from the simpler detection type within a further year.

With the backing of the General Staff the necessary authority for provision of extra staff for the Army cell at Bawdsey was obtained and experimental work was restarted in the autumn of 1938.

This application of radar to all coastal defence uses by the Army was originally referred to as C.D.—Coast Defence—which then covered all forms whether simple detection or accurate location for fire control. This may lead to some confusion in referring back to old reports and files of that early period as the types were distinguished later and C.D. then came to be applied only to those detection and warning sets that were not actually associated with the gun defences of ports, harbours, etc. The types that formed part of the defences of such places, whether for warning, for fire control, or for other purposes in connexion with the artillery weapons, came to be known as C.A.—Coastal Artillery—equipment.

It is true, of course, that some early C.D. sets were also employed for C.A. purposes and later that there were similar if not identical equipments for both purposes; still later, however, the C.D. set practically disappeared from Army use and responsibility, first in this country and then generally overseas as well. In the following descriptions of the development of these radar sets the two different appellations will be used from the start for simplicity.

This chapter will be confined to the C.D. class which is the simpler of the two, as the complications involved by the high accuracy required for fire control operation are absent; further, early development for this type formed the basis on which the first C.A. equipment design was built up.

The development of the C.D. set started from the experimental work on a very short wave-length (1·2 metre) beam set, undertaken primarily as a matter of research for the improved means of determining with accuracy the angular measurements for A.A. equipment and the means of continuously reading those measurements.

With approval for the extra staff for the Army cell in May, 1938, the selection of personnel mainly from Army establishments began and a sufficient number were assembled by October, 1938, for this C.D. development to be tackled properly. The small team allocated for this work was led by W. S. Butement from S.E.E. and took over the work that had previously been in the hands of a small Air Ministry team, including one or two members of the Army cell, under the leadership of Dr. Bowen.

The position of this investigation early in 1939 was as follows:—

(a) Improvements had been effected in the experimental 1·2 metre narrow beam set, including increased power output, but it was still not producing the results of which it was capable theoretically; this was partly due to the Yagi aerials and their critical dimensional features which were not fully understood at that time. Further work on this set was abandoned early in 1939.

(b) A beam set working on 18 cms. with 10-ft. paraboloid reflectors, was still not ready for trials by February and by then the promise of a third type was such that it was decided to put this very short wave-length set into cold storage for a time and concentrate all available effort on the third type.

(c) This set was a new design working on $1\frac{1}{2}$ metre wave-length with a large broadside aerial array carrying a series of dipoles so arranged as to give "beamed" transmission. Included in the design was a mechanical switching device that moved the beam horizontally through a small angle on either side of the centre line. This device produced a double-echo signal on the time-base and by turning the aerial, the two echoes could be balanced in height or amplitude; when so balanced, the true azimuth position of the target was on the centre-line of the aerial system. This gave a much greater degree of accuracy in determining the angle of azimuth or bearing to the target and in addition provided the means of following continuously with good accuracy.

This was in fact the true "split" method that made possible an effective advance in accuracy of angular measurement and continuous following.

Confidence in this new design was such that several transmitters had already been ordered on the priority firms and one or two receivers had been built at the Establishment for initial full trials.

By May, 1939, preliminary trials had been carried out and the results obtained justified the optimistic forecasts of the scientific staff. Actually, these trials made use of the Yagi aerial for transmission, as the new transmitter array was not ready, but the receiver and its aerial system were complete. These trials showed that the "split" systems made continuous following a fairly easy matter and a good standard of accuracy was obtainable. Against shipping targets an angular accuracy of 15 minutes of arc seemed to be possible and a detection range of 17,000 yards on a ship of some 2,000 tons was obtainable from a site less than 60 feet above sea-level; accurate angular measurement was shown to be possible up to 12,000 yards.

These were, of course, only preliminary results and would require full proof, but they were sufficient for an immediate assessment of performance that could be guaranteed from the complete set, as more than meeting the first requirements stated by the General Staff (see Chapter V) and as likely to meet the range needs for existing Counter Bombardment as well as those for the Close Defence weapons.

They also gave good justification for pushing on development of this type —including increased power output, the combination of transmission and receiver aerials in one array, and adequate screening to reduce "side-lobes" and unwanted "fixed echoes" from local objects or ground features. Wire mesh screening used for this latter purpose acted also as an aerial reflector and was so employed for the first time.

Three valuable results of these trials were obtained that were independent of the primary object of producing a suitable C.D. equipment.

(a) The first of these was the experience of reading to abnormally long ranges occasionally; these experiences were the forerunners of the later world-wide investigation of what was called "anomalous propagation," which in certain conditions appeared to cause the radar waves to bend so that readings were obtained of echo signals from ships, far beyond the horizon. The following are extracts from reports made in June, 1939:—

"Echoes have been observed from sailing yachts at distances ranging from 10 to 12 miles. These were large enough for bearings to be taken, but it was noted that the height of the echoes diminished later in the day although the echo from the Naze tower, at a range of approximately 11 miles, increased in height during the same period. These results are of interest in that the more distant yachts were below the horizon unless their masts were at least 200 feet high. The cause of the variation in echo height during the day is also of interest as the cause is not obvious, though it was noted that the days on which the yachts were 'seen' at these distances were clear and warm."

and:

"Another interesting point which has been observed during these trials is that it is possible to obtain range and bearing apparently accurately of a ship proceeding into the river mouth towards Harwich after it has passed out of sight behind the Felixstowe headland (Cobbold's Point)."

This last, however, can hardly be attributed to anomalous propagation.

(b) The second result incidental to these trials was of far-reaching importance, particularly so for the Air Ministry and its Air Defence responsibility. This was the effective detection and tracking of aircraft flying at low levels equally as well as, if not better than, shipping. It will have been noted that the C.H. stations—the Chain Home long range detection and warning stations—could not pick up aircraft flying at low levels, or only do so at much reduced ranges; there was, therefore, a channel of unobserved approach available to the enemy if he appreciated this fact or found means of ascertaining it.

This result from the preliminary trials of the C.D. set was reported at the beginning of June as follows—though of course the A.M. personnel at Bawdsey were aware of it and witnessed the trials in progress.

". . . On Aircraft, an even greater mean accuracy appears to be attainable, since the echoes are generally clearer and more easily equated for height. The method automatically provides 'continuous following'. . ."

and:

". . . A seaplane flying at a height of 500 feet has been successfully followed, with accurate azimuth, up to 20 miles, and detected with approximate azimuth, up to about 25 miles. These results are such as to suggest that this set may be used to supplement the main chain for the detection of low-flying aircraft up to ranges of 50 miles, if placed on cliff sites 200 feet or more above sea level, or alternatively, on towers."

The Air Ministry naturally wanted to duplicate this experimental equipment as rapidly as possible, to concentrate on trials to prove its performance capacity against aircraft from different heights of site above sea-level. For both Army and R.A.F. it seemed highly probable that ranges from the low Bawdsey site were only limited by the optical horizon and that higher sited sets would be capable of longer range detection. It was proposed, therefore, that the second "Army" set should be built in a movable form so that trials at different coastal height levels could be carried out rapidly.

(c) In July a further new possibility of aid to Army C.A. uses came to notice when it was reported from Bawdsey, that:—

"A chance opportunity of a practice shoot from Brackenbury battery of the Harwich defences was taken of observing the echoes from the columns of water and spray raised by 9·2 inch shells striking the water. Although the splashes were some four to five miles distant from the set, large echoes were seen and persisted for an appreciable time—long enough to obtain bearings and range."

This, of course, was not a concern of the C.D. set as such but was of great interest from the point of view that this set was to be the basis on which the more accurate type for fire control—the C.A. set—was to be developed. It gave promise of radar observation of the fall of shot and, thereby, correction of fire in addition to control or direction of fire.

Another technical development about this time is worthy of note, though it also was applied only to the C.A. type of set; this was the "spiral time base" (Fig. 4) devised by Butement, which could give a much longer time base on the C.R. Tube screen and, therefore, a much larger scale for reading the range. As compared with the normal straight-line base of about 9 inches in length, the spiral gave up to 7 feet if required, and though this did not increase the electrical accuracy of measurement it did materially increase the accuracy of reading.

In July, 1939, a decision was taken to go to Development Contract for Production for a small supply of the 1½-metre sets with some modifications and improvements resulting from the trials mentioned above. This involved the construction and proving of a complete set from which the priority firms would be able to produce drawings for their production. In order to reduce the time by which they could start, the services of both A.D.E.E and of S.E.E. were enlisted to construct such parts, component assemblies and units as were beyond the capacity of the Bawdsey establishment itself without delaying matters. These early sets were required for full-scale trials to determine the full Artillery needs, for further experimental work, for training and to provide tested prototype models for full-scale production of equipment for the Army. This decision aimed at clearing up all details of design and having proved models ready for the contractors by the end of October, 1939.

This initial production proceeded but not as a separate Army contract as the Air Ministry combined this requirement with their own for the similar type that they were developing for detection of low-flying aircraft. This latter type became known as the Chain Home Low—C.H.L.—and varied but slightly in its presentation, using a P.P.I. presentation to deal with the fast-moving aircraft, while the standard range presentation was more suited to shipping targets of the C.D. set. Even at this early stage the Army set became the C.D./C.H.L., thus marking its ability to detect aircraft but retaining its primary function of warning of approach of surface craft—probably the first step towards the co-ordination and combination of the two functions which eventually led to the complete control and operation of the "Low" chain by the R.A.F.

The experimental development of the C.D. set to represent the elementary form of the future C.A. type was demonstrated to certain G.S. and Technical Artillery representatives at the beginning of August, 1939. Representatives of the training branches concerned and the Commandant of the Coast Artillery School had originally been included in the party, but were excluded at the last moment for unknown reasons—probably the security aspect of the Bawdsey Station combined with the difficulty of accommodation, imposed a restriction on the numbers.

This demonstration was arranged in conjunction with a practice shoot from Brackenbury battery (9·2 in.) of the Harwich defences and it gave a good indication of the capacity of the set in respect of ranging and azimuth tracking and a striking demonstration of its capacity for observation of "fall-of-shot." For the first time, also, the flight of shells through the air was seen on the tube occasionally, which provided some food for thought. As will be seen later, though this was not employed for C.A. purposes, it became of particular interest for other Army uses though for A.A. purposes it was occasionally an annoyance.

In that month also a special demonstration of the C.D. (experimental) set in detection of surface vessels and aircraft was given for Mr. Winston Churchill. Some palpitations were caused to Butement and his assistants when Mr. Churchill could not spot the target in the observation telescope which was directed by the radar set. Fortunately, it was soon found that the accuracy of direction on that occasion was so great that the cross hairs in the telescope were actually obscuring the aircraft target and a slight movement disclosed it. This was almost too much of a good thing for such an occasion as the set certainly could not live up to that standard of performance in practice.

There is one further trial that must be mentioned which took place in the middle of September, 1939, and was, in effect, a true war-time trial, though no enemy craft actually participated, as the conditions very closely simulated enemy activity in an unexpected manner.

This was a specially arranged trial of the C.D. set, at the request and for the personal benefit of Admiral Sir James Somerville, to ascertain the capabilities of these sets against submarines. At two days' notice Butement was sent back to Bawdsey from Christchurch and got the set working in time for the Admiral's visit. The Admiralty had arranged for a submarine to be off Bawdsey and in radio communication with that station, but apparently information as to its presence in that region did not reach all concerned. The trials were interrupted for a while by a bombing attack by one of our aircraft on this submarine which was ordered to take cover by submerging, while the keen but aggressive aircraft, after some communication difficulty, was warned off the course by the Admiral's effective naval phraseology. The trials then proceeded and were sufficient to prove there was real value for anti-submarine operation even in this rather primitive form of set. The result was that a strenuous job of work under difficult conditions was provided for some of the "newcomers" from research laboratories who had just joined the A.D.R.D.E. radar family. That they put the job through with skill, ingenuity and enthusiasm proved them to be a valuable reinforcement to the Establishment and perhaps gave them some appreciation of the difficulties of service construction and operating conditions.

The outbreak of war had now intervened and brought with it a hasty evacuation of Bawdsey and the consequent disturbance of work. But it had also brought a valuable addition to the scientific resources to help on Army radar work under the control of the Ministry of Supply.

The research and development work at Bawdsey ceased on the outbreak of war, the A.M.R.E. departed northwards to Dundee and the Army cell in a variety of transport took itself and much of its gear south-west to Christchurch, where it arrived at the still uncompleted new establishment at Somerford. However, they had it to themselves for the time being as the move of the rest of the A.D.E.E. from Biggin Hill was postponed until the accommodation could be made ready to accept them.

The group working on the C.D. development were, if possible, worse off than those in the main Establishment. Their detached site on the low cliffs at Steamer Point was even more behindhand and facilities, apart from a few bare laboratory buildings, were practically non-existent.

It was surprising that the disturbance to the radar work caused by this move was not much greater, and it was due to the excellent spirit, keenness and drive of all grades of these ex-W.D., but now M. of S. personnel, that they got their work started again so rapidly in such difficult conditions. It was no uncommon sight to find scientists felling trees, technicians erecting protective fencing and draughtsmen digging drains or shelters; each lent a helping hand to speed up the full resumption of work, and all accepted the rough living conditions in the unfurnished headquarters building named "Bure Homage," and were even glad of the feeding provided by Joy's Transport Café. It was *not* an easy time.

It was not for long, however, that they were left to themselves, for at the beginning of October a party of new scientific recruits arrived in the form of Professor J. D. Cockcroft's party from the Cavendish Laboratories, Cambridge, and others to contribute their aid. These newcomers in their more-or-less natty suitings found it hard at times to distinguish the gum-booted old hands from the navvies and building works' staff.

Cockcroft, his Cavendish team and the others from various sources, had been booked by Dr. Gough, now D.S.R., Ministry of Supply, for reinforcing the Radar Establishment, and a very valuable addition they proved to be. Cockcroft and some of his party had visited Bawdsey on two occasions before the war and had been given a slight introduction to Radar.

A large-scale practical introduction for 80 or more physicists involving a month's working in C.H. stations had been planned by Watson-Watt to start on 1st September which, in fact, proved a very suitable date! Cockcroft and others studied radar at the Rye C.H. Station and then inspected the experimental C.D. set at Bawdsey, where they were present at the demonstration to Admiral Somerville.

As a result Cockcroft had a job on hand for his group. It was an urgent and most important task—to meet the Naval need for the protection in the Orkneys and Shetlands at the earliest possible date in view of the submarine activities of the enemy.

This job, in fact, was the building and installation of radar sets, copies of the experimental Bawdsey set, which for this purpose was called the C.D.U., to detect submarines from Fair Isle and the Shetlands. Watson-Watt had asked Cockcroft to take it on with his Cavendish team, who had already unshipped Butement's experimental set at Bawdsey, transported it under their own power to Cambridge and started making up copies of it with the aid of Messrs. Pye Radio with modifications of their own, before the A.D.R.D.E. really knew anything about this emergency work.

This party was soon brought down to Christchurch where they could be helped by the experience in radar development and by the administrative arrangements available at the Establishment.

The incomplete Establishment at Christchurch had the R.E. and S. Board behind them, able to bring in the aid of its Experimental Bridging Establishment for workshop help in the heavier engineering and mechanical work. Between them they provided heavy gear, radio parts, accessories and tools by various devices, *e.g.* by raiding G.L. Mark I production in hand, by filching or scrounging turn tables and aerial frames from other supply sources, and generators wherever they could be obtained. Tool stores of both establishments provided a portion of the tools and materials needed to equip the party, and a sweep of all the ironmongers in Christchurch and Bournemouth supplied the rest.

Discussions with Butement and his team saved them a good deal of technical trouble and the financial, travelling and stores arrangements were cleared for them by the Commandant A.D.E.E. The selected party departed for the North on 27th October, 1939, to get on to the job, which promised to be no easy one with the approach of the season of gales and the lack of communications in those parts. There were perhaps some sighs—either of relief or of regret—when they had gone, and settling down in the new establishment and the pressing experimental work could go ahead. However, in four or five days' time a telegram from the North arrived asking for the immediate despatch of some small tool or gadget that had been forgotten; unfortunately, the only address indicated was "Cockcroft, Edinburgh." Four hours on the long-distance telephone failed to contact anyone who knew of his existence, but with the aid of the Admiralty a signal was got through to him to tell him to whom his gadget had been consigned. History does not record what happened to it, but it is rumoured that this introduction to Army code addresses and strings of initials speeded Cockcroft's departure from Edinburgh.

Extracts from some of Cockcroft's notes on this emergency work, which was undoubtedly a stiff one on the radar side, let alone the local topographical and weather difficulties, are quoted here:—

". . . Ratcliffe had surveyed Fair Isle with Admiral Somerville and had made a great impression on that Officer—being voted worth a guinea a minute. I recruited at Cambridge G. C. Evans, a Johnian Plant physiologist, Donald Carmichael an anthropologist, and J. A. Lewis, a civil engineer lately returned from the East. They were put into the R.N.V.R. to take charge of the stations, and became the first contingent of 'Col. Miles' private army'—Colonel Miles being the Marine Officer (and a wireless expert) given charge of the stations.

Skinner and Dunworth went to Sumburgh Head on Shetland and selected a site close by the lighthouse. Kempton went to Fair Isle where conditions were made more difficult by having to tranship stores from Lerwick by drifter, with further transhipment to flip boat on arrival at Fair Isle. The winter was the worst of the war, with high gales and snow. Materials for the stations had to be hauled by oxen up a gradient of one in four. Labour was scarce and difficult and we dropped a long way behind target dates. Sumburgh was on the air by the first week in December, 1939. The first Fair Isle station worked by 16th February, the second by 23rd February.

The performance of the stations on submarines was good; Fair Isle detected broadside on submarines at ranges up to 25 miles. Aircraft were detected at ranges up to 70 miles, and it was very soon found that the greatest use of the stations would be in giving warning of low-flying attack on Scapa Flow . . ."

The success of these three stations, however, led to the provision of a fourth C.D.U. station at Saravoord, in Unst, a still more difficult site on top of a peak 1,000 feet up, to reach which a road had to be built. Three more sites were reconnoitred and selected in March, but the installation of the sets could by then be left to Naval installation parties as they had gained sufficient experience. They certainly did good work in keeping these improvised stations in action.

While this emergency Naval work was being done by Cockcroft's northern party—Dunworth, Kempton, Skinner and others—a further demand on his services was made, this time by the Air Ministry, in mid November, 1939, to meet the growing threat of the magnetic mines dropped by low-flying aircraft that was taking high toll of our convoys along the east coast. He with Shire and Ashmead were first required to rush up improvised C.H.L. stations at Foreness Point and Walton-on-Naze to cover the Thames estuary, and later to supervise the installation of three other stations at Happisburgh, Spurn Head and Shotton.

Again more rush work and more scrounging, but the job was done with the aid of an Air Ministry erection gang from Kidbrooke, learning the work under Shire, Ashmead and Cockcroft himself. Foreness was on the air by 1st December, Walton followed in a fortnight, and Shotton was functioning by 27th December; the other two followed in the first ten days of January, 1940.

Cockcroft was asked to take on another seven stations, but it was now felt that the R.A.F. could get down to the work for themselves, and this further diversion of scientific effort from Army needs was avoided. In January, 1940, all these emergency diversions were concluded and most of the team, after a short spell of leave, returned to A.D.R.D.E., Christchurch, to take up the pre-arranged war-time duties.

These stations became the first part of the low-flying chain that eventually covered the coasts of this country to form the essential supplement to the C.H. system. These early and somewhat improvised stations were, like the C.D.U., based upon the experimental Army C.D. set and eventually developed into the Air Ministry C.H.L. type.

One other point—though not really concerned with Army radar—emerging from this work of the Cockcroft party and its co-operation with the R.A.F. must be mentioned as it was of far-reaching effect. Largely at Cockcroft's suggestion the new Foreness station was used to control fighter interception of mine-laying aircraft *from a single station*—a new conception. Cockcroft had the reward of "seeing" the first successful interception controlled by this station, made by Squadron-Leader Pretty. This was the embryo of the R.A.F. Ground-Controlled Interception—G.C.I.—system that later covered this country and contributed so much to the defeat of the night bombers.

These excursions into the Naval and Air Force fields of activity may appear to have little claim to be recorded here, but they were in fact all based upon the Army development of the C.D. type of equipment and effected by special scientific personnel allocated to Army Radar work. It was a case of Inter-

Service co-operation, with the War Office and the Ministry of Supply, meeting these urgent operational needs of the other two fighting Services as they could not tackle them for themselves at that time. The diversion of material, mechanical equipment, components, etc., as well as the occupation of these scientists, naturally had some delaying effect on the development of the Army C.D./C.H.L. set and its provision. This anti-surface-vessel equipment, however, was of secondary importance in comparison with these emergency requirements of the Naval and Air Force at that time. This delay, however, was felt in the latter half of 1940 when the threat of invasion emphasized the urgent need of warning of approach of invasion craft to our shores.

The development of the $1\frac{1}{2}$ metre C.D./C.H.L. was completed and pilot models began to become available late in 1940. The earliest were required for development work for the C.A. fire control type as well as for training operators and mechanics and for practical operational trials and experience. Most interest for C.D. was, perhaps, centred upon the model in mobile form, as it was essential for the selection of sites on which the permanent structures to house the equipment were to be built. This siting problem could not be solved without test and trial as this equipment was susceptible to clutter due to unwanted echoes and reflections from local objects, owing to its "side-lobes"; "wave clutter" also was particularly troublesome on low sites.

The initial aim in providing the C.D./C.H.L. sets was to establish *continuous* warning cover from north of the Thames estuary southward and westwards to the Isle of Wight. To extend further north along the east coast was found to be impractical owing to the low levels of the coast, but two sites just north of the estuary were selected that would require the construction of towers on which to raise the aerials of the sets sufficiently to be effective.

An extension of this scheme along the whole of the east, south, and west coasts followed the enemy occupation of Norway and Northern France. It did not attempt, however, to provide a complete chain of continuous surface cover but to give warning cover at all beaches where landings might be effected and their sea approaches.

A plan of the original cover provided along the south-east coast is included as Appendix IX. From this it will be seen that the cover is *not* complete—there are three specific "gaps" and no means of filling them was then possible, without very considerable structural work.

It is, perhaps, of interest to note that two of the three gaps in the cover occur at the positions where two successful invasions of this country had started many years before.

The first was in the Richborough area where nearly 2,000 years ago Julius Caesar's Roman Legions made their landing.

The second was in the Pevensey or Norman's Bay neighbourhood where William the Conqueror is said to have landed the majority of his Norman followers some 875 years before this radar cover was even contemplated.

As to the third gap, the largest of them all, it was wide open on both sides of Dungeness. This, it will be remembered, was an area in which great defensive effort was applied nearly a century and a half ago at the time of the Napoleonic threat. Though that threat did not materialize into an actual landing, many raids and incursions by the French have been experienced in the vicinity throughout our early history. Was this wide-open gap in the most modern means of warning of approaching attack an omen? It certainly was very ominous and the cause of much concern. Was it to be the scene of Adolf Hitler's attempt? The *post factum* answer is not entirely definite, but as that attempt was never put to trial it does not matter now.

That yawning gap, however, was closed in 1941 and the other two, also, when a remarkable stride forward in radar performance was made possible by the production of the "resonator" magnetron valve and the rapid development of more effective equipment was made possible. A new radar era was opened and its C.D. aspect is described in the next chapter.

CHAPTER XVI. CENTIMETRIC COAST DEFENCE RADAR

The revolution in radar technique brought about by the development into practical form of the resonator magnetron has been mentioned in earlier chapters —here we are concerned only with its effect on coast defence equipment.

The first point to note is that this class of equipment was the first of all the Army types to benefit from the new possibilities opened up. That this should have been so does not mean that effort was diverted from those other types that had been assigned higher priority, such as the H.A.A. fire control equipment which still ranked first of all. The fact is that this C.D. role requires none of the complication of design that is involved in providing the high degree of accuracy necessary for C.A. fire direction or control and the still greater complications of providing "three dimensional" accuracy for H.A.A. operation. It was, therefore, far easier to meet the C.D. operational requirements, and it happened that it was possible to do so by making use of equipment designed for naval ship-borne use and made available to the Army by the good will and co-operation of the Admiralty.

This naval radar set was known as the Naval Type 271 or more generally as N.T. 271, and it immediately gained a great reputation. The Army in applying these sets to its own purposes retained the standard form of its radar components but housed them more suitably for shore use. Operationally and technically it became famous in the Army; the R.A.F. also had great help from it and its successors.

It is as well to remind readers that the detection and tracking of shipping off our coasts, which initially was effected by the Army C.D. stations in the Coastal Chain, was of great importance to the Navy. All reports of shipping went direct to the naval plotting rooms at the Naval Area H.Q., from which control of convoys and other sea movements were exercised. The Admiralty was, therefore, deeply interested in the efficiency of the coastal chain, and their agreement to the diversion of their new type of equipment for this purpose served their requirements as well as helping the Army.

The first introduction of the War Office to this naval 10-cm. equipment was effected at the invitation of D.S.D. Admiralty in March, 1941, when Brigadier Sayer, the Radar Deputy to D.A.A. & C.D. visited the Admiralty Signal Establishment (A.S.E.) at Eastney. He was accompanied by Major Moth, G.S.O. II for C.D. and C.A. operations, and as it happened, Sir Henry Tizard was also inspecting this new equipment. All three visitors were much impressed by the prototype set that was demonstrated to them. The informal discussion that took place after a good lunch was most helpful and fruitful. The immediate result was a provisional agreement to supply six sets for early delivery for trials and experiment for the Army; this was confirmed within three days and arrangements were made for their delivery to the A.D.R.D.E. as sets became available. The A.D.R.D.E. was asked to provide them in suitable form by fitting them rapidly in mobile cabins for trials and to provide for a narrow symmetrical beam by the use of paraboloid reflectors, instead of the fan beam used for ship-borne sets.

The development of this N.T. 271 equipment had been a rapid and very practical piece of work by the A.S.E.; it was largely due to Dr. S. E. A. Landale and the team working under him, with the energetic support of Captain Willett,

R.N., the Captain Superintendent. The A.S.E. had started from the point reached in the early experiments at T.R.E., at Worth Maltravers (Swanage), were the Joint Establishment Investigation Group was tackling the problems of how best to apply the new resonator magnetron to practical equipment (see Chapter IX).

Not only was its development rapid, but its finalization for production and production itself followed suit, and the supply of service equipment had certainly started by March, 1941—a most remarkable performance when it is recalled that Oliphant's new magnetron first appeared at T.R.E. in May, 1940. The first set made available for experimental trials for the Army reached A.D.R.D.E. in June, 1941, just over a year from the first appearance of a practical magnetron.

In its naval form the main radar assemblies, suitably boxed, were carried below deck in very compact yet accessible form; while the aerial was carried on a small pedestal mounting fixed above deck, on which the aerial could be rotated or traversed for search or following. The aerial assembly consisted of separate T. and R. fixed aerials each with a "cheese" reflector or rather a single "cheese" divided into two by a horizontal plate. These reflectors, being parabolic in the horizontal plane only, gave a very narrow beam horizontally, but a wider vertical spread in the form of a fan. This vertical spread provided for the pitch and roll of a ship, so that a target once picked up should not be lost by roll taking it off the target; it thereby avoided the additional complication of providing for stabilization.

The "fan" beam was not required for Army C.D. shore stations where pitch and roll was seldom experienced. It may be noted, however, that the fan beam was employed later in a limited provision of a special Army equipment referred to in Chapter XII under the name "Gorgonzola"—an unofficial title—which was applied to it and indicated its parentage or relation to the "cheese" of the original N.T. 271 set.

The available power output of this set was about 7 kW., and its range capacity was dependent on the height of its site above sea-level as its limit was approximately the visual horizon. It was not provided with any means of accurate angular measurement such as "split," but its narrow beam gave a fairly sharp "peak" signal and accuracy of approximately 1 degree was obtainable and fully adequate for detecting and tracking targets but not, of course, for engagement by gunfire.

Further development of this naval type later produced an increase of power output up to between 70 and 100 kW. and still later a higher power type—known as N.T. 277—gave from 350 to 500 kW. Both were eventually used by the Army to replace the lower power 271; the former was called the medium power type and the latter the high power.

For the modification and fitting of the 271 components to provide a set for practical trials, D. Radar, War Office, discussed proposals with the S.R. directorate of the Ministry of Supply and representatives of A.D.R.D.E. It was agreed that it should be tackled as a "rush" job and, therefore, it required the use of existing equipment or equipment parts. Further, to permit of trials at a variety of sites, it should take mobile or at least movable form and the need for a symmetrical beam, as narrow as could be provided easily, was agreed.

The Establishment tackled this job rapidly and effectively, provided for mobility and overcame all difficulties of rotation of the aerials by installing the whole set in the rotatable G.L. II receiver cabin. This permitted the aerials and their 7 foot paraboloid reflectors, which were demountable for travel, but fixed outside the cabin wall for operations, to be fed direct as the set, aerials and cabin rotated as a whole. This cabin gave ample space for operators and their plotting and its accurate turn-table and hand-control provided for accurate movement and the necessary connections for telephone and power supply. It was a rapid and good improvisation—in fact the job done by the Establishment was of such a standard that the word "improvisation" appears somewhat derogatory, for these sets justified themselves as service equipment and remained in action for a considerable time.

After initial tests this set was sent first to Dover for operational trials in July, 1941, with the intention of trials later at other sites, including Great Ormes Head for C.A.E.E. and C.A.S. This form of the equipment became the Army C.D. No. 1, Mark IV, though the first experimental set was usually referred to as the 271X.

This experimental model sited on the cliffs at Lydden Spout (Dover), at a height of some 330 feet above sea-level, immediately proved of great value to the Dover defences. G. C. Varley, of the Operational Research Group, A.D.R.D.E., as it was then called, was in charge of the set and its trials, in close co-operation with the Commander Coast Artillery, Brigadier Raw; he reported at the end of August, 1941, as follows:

"Operationally N.T. 271X was a great advance on previous sets in maximum range, discrimination, counting and accuracy. For the first time reliable cover was obtained across the Channel, so that not even E-boats could go between Calais and Boulogne undetected. Large ships could be watched at anchor in the outer harbour of Boulogne."

and:

"Already, by 10th August the set had had great successes, plotting an enemy convoy in daylight and giving an hour's warning of an E-boat attack on one of our convoys. The Navy (Admiral Ramsey was then Vice-Admiral, Dover) considered the set was vital to operations in the Channel."

Brigadier Sayer of the War Office discussed this set with Admiral Ramsey and Brigadier Raw and in view of its local value agreed that the set should remain in operation at Dover. He called a conference in September, 1941, at which the Admiral took the chair and the R.A.F. was represented by Air Marshal Sir Philip Joubert, C.-in-C., Coastal Command. The views of the War Office that additional sets should be provided for the coastal chain for convoy protection up the Channel and along the east coast, as well as further sets for the Dover defences, was supported; the provision of a special set for R.A.F. experimental trials against aircraft and for control of interception was also agreed. Professor Cockcroft undertook that the necessary modifications and installation work should be carried out by A.D.R.D.E.

The proposed programme for the immediate reinforcement of the chain put forward by the War Office as a result of this conference was agreed by the Inter-Service Low Cover Sub-Committee. This provided for the installation of nine additional sets by 1st January, 1942. As a result the Dover defences were improved and the three "gaps" in the cover, referred to at the end of Chapter XV, closed.

The W.O. request for more sets from Admiralty sources could not be met completely by the date aimed at and the A.D.R.D.E. could not compete with the full number of installations and modifications in that time. Later the requirements were increased considerably and recourse was had to contract provision for fitting and installation in the mobile cabins.

Though the proposed programme could not be fully carried out it is worth while noting that by January, Dover itself was equipped with two sets in addition to the original experimental set, and a third had been established at Fairlight to operate in collaboration with the Dover defences, though it was actually in the Newhaven Naval Area. As will be seen later some of these sets were of operational value very shortly afterwards. Foreness, Newhaven, Ventnor and Beachy Head followed during that month.

This account of the development of C.D. in this country must be interrupted at this point for mention of an urgent overseas demand. On 1st October, 1941, signals from Gibraltar were received by the Admiralty and the War Office in regard to attack by Italian 2-man torpedoes, and the need for immediate provision of means to detect their approach; the use of sets of the N.T. 271 was suggested as a possible solution.

A meeting at A.S.E. was held at once and it was agreed that this set was the only type available that *might*, perhaps, meet this need, but that it should be fitted with larger paraboloid reflectors. The maximum size that the design could accommodate was 4 ft. 6 in. diameter, but even this required special machining of the cross-arms. Brigadier Sayer for the War Office arranged to provide Ordnance mechanics for the work at A.S.E., and for the training of two officers—one an I.F.C., R.A., and the other an O.M.E.—who would accompany the set for siting, erection, trials and local training of operators. The Admiralty were arranging for a destroyer to be ready to sail on 27th October, 1941, to take the equipment, stores and officers. A.S.E. undertook to provide the set ready packed, complete with spares, stores, etc., required to maintain it in action, and the materials for housing the set to give it protection from the sea and weather.

At the same time the Admiralty required a second set to be provided for immediate despatch by air to Alexandria where an Air Force officer would take charge of its installation and the training of operators, etc.

That this emergency job was completed, and the equipment for Gibraltar was on board ready to sail within a month of the demand, was evidence of the excellent co-operation between the Services and the helpful attitude of the A.S.E. Similarly the Alexandria set was specially packed for carriage by an aircraft detailed for the purpose in time for despatch.

It is doubtful whether these sets achieved any success in this special role, but it is certain that no other equipment in being at that time could have done so. In Gibraltar the set was a considerable asset to the defence of the Fortress in other more normal ways, but in Alexandria little was heard of what happened with this set. In any case, it is now well known that very serious loss, from attack by these submersible machines, was sustained in that harbour.

Continuing the record of the new C.D. equipment, operational successes were obtained with air strikes against shipping detected and tracked by these radar sets. In fact, though before August, 1941, enemy shipping used the Straits only by day, by October practically all day movement had ceased; this was in no small measure due to the improved radar cover and its aid to attacks by cannon fighters. From this time on night convoys began to be the enemy's normal method of use of the Straits and this gave our M.T.B.s the chance they had been waiting for. The enemy was soon forced to counter this form of controlled interception actions by increasing the size of escorts until the M.T.B.s seldom had the chance of successful attack. Controlled cannon fighter strikes by night were tried for a time, but eventually the initiative was left to the Dover coast guns or the coast guns in combination with M.T.B.s. The effect of these actions, and the disturbance to the enemy's important traffic by sea, must have amounted to something considerable in expenditure of effort to get his convoys through the Straits, without taking into consideration the actual sinkings and damage inflicted.

The effect on Coastal Artillery actions as distinct from C.D. uses will be mentioned in the chapters dealing with the C.A. types of equipment, but there is one special action to which reference must be made now, as it was the C.D. type that played the primary part.

This was the action on the 12th February, 1942, when the *Scharnhorst*, *Gneisenau* and *Prince Eugen* made their dash up Channel from Brest. Land-based enemy jamming of an intense nature was operated from across the Channel to make all 1½ metre C.H.L. and C.D./C.H.L. sets unworkable, thereby preventing detection or warning by these sets of the Southern Coastal Chain, but the 10 cm. sets *were not affected*. The 10 cm. set just installed at Ventnor was unfortunately out of action that morning due to an outbreak of fire the night before, but it is not likely that it could have picked up these vessels hugging the French coast, even from its high site.

Two of these sets had been installed in the Dover area and there was one at Fairlight, east of Hastings. It was this last set (K.7) that obtained the first definite detection of the ships, picked them up and plotted their track at 10·50 hours, at a range of 67,000 yards on a bearing of 136 degrees.

The K.7 (Fairlight) station report was not received at Dover Naval Plotting Room nor at the C.A. Operations Room, owing to the direct telephone line not having been installed by this date; it was, however, retransmitted from Newhaven, but not received by C.A. Ops until just before 11.30 hours. No early warning had therefore been received in C.A. Ops. Room until one of the Dover sets, K.148 (Lydden Spout) picked up the plot at 11.30 hours at a range of 14,000 yards bearing 166 degrees, and this plot was identified by the Naval plotting room to C.A. ops. room as "hostile" at 11.31 hours. This set continued to follow and track the enemy force till about 12.45 hours when it was well out of range of the guns at 65,000 yards. The other station K.147 at Fan Hole, also picked up a little after K.148, and both these stations reported occasional fall-of-shot observations. The plots passed continuously by these C.D. No. 1, Mark IV sets to C.A. ops. room were passed on to the Eastern Fire Command, one of whose batteries (9·2 in.) was able to engage these targets; these were given as a location, course and speed to assist the engagement as the only radar battery range finder, an early naval pattern—Type 284—was not performing well.

The account of this action is recorded in more detail in the following chapters on C.A. equipment for the control of fire of the coastal guns. This action, however, illustrates the value of this new type of set, even if the full benefits obtainable were not made available at the time due to the lack of communications and to other causes, none of which were failures of the radar.

It should be noted that these 10 cm. sets and the N.T. 284 (50 cm.) were entirely unaffected by the enemy's jamming attack on the normal 1½ metre stations of the coastal chain.

Reverting to the low-cover chain and the improvement to be effected by the replacement of C.D./C.H.L. sets by the new centimetric sets, the C.D. No. 1, Mark IV, it will be appreciated that the longer range given by the latter type made it unnecessary to replace every one of the earlier type sets. In respect of the stretch of coast covered by the original chain, only 6 of the new centimetric stations were needed in place of the 15 old type, and they gave more complete and effective cover than was previously possible. With these improved stations not only were the gaps mentioned closed but practically double cover was given at each of them. In addition there was double cover along almost the whole of the convoy route as well as long-range detection well beyond the route, sufficient to give ample warning of hostile attack.

All the coastal stations were given numbers and a letter prefix—M in the case of the old type, the K for the new; these are used through this part of this history.

With the increased requirements for this type of equipment to extend the coastal protection of this country and its coastal shipping, and to provide for overseas needs as well, it was essential to develop a design specially for the purpose rather than adhere to the improvisation adopted for the early rush provision.

The use of essential components of the new 10 cm. G.L. Mark III antiaircraft equipment had been contemplated for this purpose with the object of uniformity or a measure of standardization of components, but it was now apparent that this would not be possible on account of the delay in supply.

The Ministry of Supply (A.D.R.D.E.) proposed to undertake a complete new design, but the War Office objected on the grounds of delay and duplication of work and of stores and spares. The Naval type had already proved itself suitable and adaptable to Army needs and was in full production on a scale that could be extended to meet the Army needs as well as those of the Navy. The Ministry were, therefore, requested to develop a simple form of set, employing the N.T. 271 essential radar components, suitable for easy and rapid installation and for transport to overseas theatres.

A.D.R.D.E., taking their cue from the word "simple" and realizing the need for speed, produced a design known as the "Gibson Box," which was made up and demonstrated in experimental form. This was based upon the furniture removal container, capable of being transported on a trailer, lifted by crane for shipping and erection or rather placing upon its operational site. It had installed in it the 271 radar gear and was fitted with a simple hand-turning arrangement for the aerial and its reflector projecting above the roof. All components including the aerial structure and a supply of spares could be packed inside for travel and in operation plotting space or "office" was available. This set employed a short length of "wave guide" giving a single aerial and single 7 foot paraboloid reflector for both transmission and reception.

This pattern was at once approved and adopted, and was most satisfactory. The set complete in its box could be established on site in a very short time, and material protection could be provided by locally constructed traverse walls, if required, up to roof level. Alternatively, the whole set could be unshipped from the box and installed direct in a permanent structure, when the only part that would appear from the outside would be the aerial reflector.

This pattern of equipment became the C.D. No. 1, Mark V, but when installed in a permanent structure it became C.D. No. 1, Mark VI.

Further Admiralty development brought in higher power working. The first increase put up the transmitted power from 7 to 70 kW. or rather more;

this became known as "medium power" and the addition of a star to the Army title—thus C.D. No. 1, Mark V*—distinguished sets working on this medium power. A further increase to give a power output of 350 to 500 kW. was identified by a double star to the Mark number of the equipment. These increases of power gave greater ranges, or where the range was already limited by the horizon, gave stronger signals for the maximum range readings and thereby greater certainty of detection of distant targets. Conversion to these higher powers produced no difficult problems in these equipments.

With the provision of these Mark V and VI sets the mobile emergency type, the Mark IV, was discontinued, but they were retained in service for special use.

For low-lying sites of importance, such as those along the East Coast, sets intended to guard and guide our coast-wise convoys through "E-boat alley" —the north and south bound routes off the Norfolk and Suffolk coasts—it was necessary to provide artificial height by means of towers 200 feet high, to get a greater horizon distance. This produced a problem by the desirability, if not the necessity, for keeping the top weight down to the minimum and doing the operation of the set in its office at ground level. The aim was to install the aerial gear only at the top, fed with remote control of rotation from the ground. This involved the use of wave-guide feed for over 200 feet. After experience with a long wave-guide at Foreness, where the tower height was only 60 feet, Cockcroft advised that this was a practical proposition and installation was started with an experimental set-up on one of the 240 ft. stages of the high towers of the C.H. station at Bawdsey to prove it. For some reason this hung fire badly and the erection of the towers at other sites had to proceed as a matter of urgency; losses in convoys off this stretch of coast line, known as "E-boat alley" from the frequency of attempts by the German light craft and their mining activities, were increasing and distant radar warning was impossible without extra height.

Unfortunately, the experience at Foreness was not repeated with these higher towers and a variety of difficulties had to be overcome. Power losses in the wave-guides were excessive, moisture in the guides caused some troubles and the rotating joints others, turning gear packed up or rapidly wore badly— in fact, there was a real packet of trouble. This was tackled hard, but involved time and that the Navy could not spare, so an improvisation had to be adopted which meant putting the set up top and the operators too—an unpleasant business with that long ladder climb in the dark of a cold and squally winter's night; the lifts installed were temperamental and usually down at the bottom when wanted at the top, and *vice versa*. By degrees, however, these difficulties were overcome and these special K stations, equipped with the high power equipment were eventually brought into fully effective action and provided cover to the convoy routes.

By this time a scheme agreed by the three Services had been implemented, which transferred the responsibility for manning, maintenance and operation of all coastal warning and detection sets, whether for air, for surface, or for both purposes, and the control of shipping and other Naval needs, to one Service only, instead of the Army being responsible for some and the R.A.F. for others. This change and simplification of responsibilities has been mentioned on page 120. The Army transferred its other coastal stations to the R.A.F. in 1942, but undertook to complete the "tower" stations before passing out of the picture. This transfer, which was completed in 1943, did not affect the coastal sets included in any of the Port defences, and they remained in Army hands.

The extent of the Army's provision for this low cover chain, in this country and for the overseas needs which were small in comparison, may be summarized as follows:—

C.D./C.H.L. stations fixed complete with accommodation, etc.	120 between the end of 1940 and September, 1941.
C.D. No. 1, Mark IV sets, mobile trailer types.	50 between May and August, 1942, in addition to the 12 made up by A.D.R.D.E.
C.D. No. 1, Marks V and VI, self-contained transportable type.	205 between September, 1942, and February, 1944.
C.D. No. 1, Mark VI Tower stations.	13 between September, 1942, and July, 1943.

In addition there were the conversions of these stations to medium power and in the case of the Tower stations to high power working.

A further contribution by the Army to the final United Kingdom coastal cover was the investigation into the *optimum* performance of these sets and the means of checking them, devised by the Army Operational Research Group. This led to a greater understanding of their capacity and had a marked effect in keeping them up to standard performance; some remarks on this work will be found in a later chapter dealing with some of the work of this Group. A further contribution from the same source established the means of assessing the size of vessels from the radar signals which was a valuable addition to the operational information obtainable from these sets, particularly for naval use.

To those who planned, provided and originally operated the Army "K" stations, and particularly to those who devised the means of keeping them up to their peak of performance, it will be of interest to know that technically these stations, after their transfer to the R.A.F. in May, 1943, were maintained in an excellent state, and that operationally they served the large variety of needs of their own and Allied Air Services very successfully and also met the needs of the Navy most effectively. The stations were then in charge of No 73 Wing of No. 60 Group R.A.F., and the following are extracts from reports and from appreciations of their work, during the last 8 months of the war.

(*a*) *Review of maintenance performance by* 60 *Group R.A.F.*

"Analysis of unserviceability (of Type 54 stations—old 'K' stations) for the period 1st January to 30th April, 1944.

Station	Total hours U/S
Benacre	5·59
Skendlebury	12·48
Dimlington	17·05
Bard Hill	18·02
Trimmingham	31·22
Bampton	45·55
Winterton	45·59
Hopton	55·29

Above figures show a minimum serviceability of 98% and a maximum of 99·8 %"

(*b*) On the operational side from the Naval aspect, the following are extracts from a message from C.-in-C. Nore, Admiral of the Fleet Sir Jack C. Tovey, G.C.B., K.B.E., D.S.C.

"Naval Operations Rooms and Plotting Rooms in the Nore Command have a warm appreciation of the value of the East Coast K Stations . . . the stations have won a deserved reputation for prompt detection and tracking of E boats. . . . the Radar tracks of their movements have been of great assistance in determining where mines may have been laid, and, in the time-honoured phrase, 'The convoy has always gone through.'

The routine day and night plotting of friendly vessels has been just as important though perhaps less exciting. On many occasions friendly ships have been warned of impending danger. In general, the continuous Radar picture of all shipping movements provided by your operators has greatly facilitated naval movements and operations.

This would not have been achieved without a high degree of efficiency on the part of the technical, operational and maintenance staff both at your headquarters and at the stations. I am very glad to have this opportunity of saying 'Thank you' for their fine performance in keeping the stations so continuously on the air."

CHAPTER XVII. COAST ARTILLERY RADAR

Fire Direction. The direction or control of fire of coastal guns is a considerably simpler requirement than that for H.A.A. artillery—it has only to deal with accurate measurements in two dimensions and the rate of movement of the targets is small in comparison with that of aircraft. To obtain effect, however, the coastal guns must produce direct hits, and that demands high accuracy of measurement of both range and bearing and steady continuous transmission of data so that the future position where the shells strike shall coincide with the movement of the target. In place of the Anti-Aircraft predictor for working out the future or predicted position, coastal artillery is served by a Table, Fire Direction that plots continuously the full data supplied, automatically determines course and speed and provides the future positions of the target at which the shells must arrive. This appliance is generally a fortress or fire command equipment that can serve all or any batteries allocated to the defences. Individual batteries are also provided with special plotters so that they can operate with their own battery radar set if required; this plotter, as its name implies, records graphically the data supplied and geometrically determines the future position.

In previous chapters references have been made to the proposed means of developing an accurate set for this purpose by refinement of the design of the C.D. type; the first of these was in Dr. Paris's report dated 23rd November, 1937, and the resultant G.S. requirement of performances, dated April, 1938 (see Chapter V).

Trials of a "mocked up" C.D. set, in July and August, 1939, indicated the effect of some of the refinements and brought to notice special possibilities of probable value to coastal artillery operation (see Chapter XV). Radar refinements cannot determine the overall accuracy obtainable and in this case the mechanical side had a very material part to play. In fact, the radar performance of the C.D. set needed comparatively little modification or refinement for meeting the C.A. requirements of accuracy, but the stability of the aerial system and its steady and accurate movement required considerable improvement and a higher degree of refinement; improved means of reading range measurements and the automatic transmission of range and bearing data, continuously, were necessary if full value of the radar performance was to be obtained. The development to produce the C.A. set was, therefore, mainly a mechanical and structural matter.

On the radar side of the C.A. No. 1 set—the title given to radar fire direction equipment—several of the necessary refinements had been devised or were in process of formulation when the Bawdsey team had to migrate to Christchurch in September, 1939. The large scale range display given by the spiral time base initiated by Butement was taking practical form in the hands of Newsam, Denman and Beale of his Bawdsey team, and the final tidying up and removal of the last "bugs" was effected at Somerford, by Tempero and Forsyth. Butement's mechanical switch for beam-switching for bearing angle measurement was replaced by diode switching, devised by Ashmead and Eastwood, as it was found to have greater reliability. Discrimination in range was improved by shortening the pulse length, and other refinements in details of the radar make-up were also effected.

On the mechanical side a good deal of stiffening of the heavy broadside aerial structure was necessary and reduction in windage by an improved framework with flattened tubular members was effected. The tower for the aerial system, its turn-table and the turning and control gear had to be stiffened and strengthened to ensure steady movement and prevent over-run and back-lash when changing direction or switching from one target to another.

The structure or emplacement for the equipment, to suit the radar and the siting in conjunction with the battery it served, was designed by the War Office Works Staff in very close co-operation with the radar designers and the Artillery directorate of the Ministry of Supply. The standard type proved suitable for most sites but provision had to be made for special low-lying sites by the raising of the set on a tower of some 60 feet in height.

Early in 1941 the design work had been finalized for production and two pilot models were supplied in the summer, for final proof and trials, to clear the set for full production. One of these models was tested practically by the Coast and Anti-Aircraft Experimental Establishment, which had by that time been moved to Llandudno; another was tested by the A.D.R.D.E. at their Steamer Point, Christchurch site, and as no major faults were found and but few minor modifications had to be made, it was agreed that production could go ahead.

The set from C.A.E.E. was transferred in August to the Coast Artillery School, also established at Llandudno, and it had been installed in its new structure and was in operation in November. Here it was used to devise and define the drills for operation, to determine its performance in the hands of normal service operators and to develop the tactical methods for employing it as an important new aid to coastal artillery. At the same time it was used for training purposes and continued to be so used until it practically wore itself out; this is dealt with further in Part V, in Chapter XXVIII.

This particular pilot model and the one at the A.D.R.D.E. were in fact the only sets of this type to be used by troops; the latter—as will be seen later in this chapter—was the only one to take part in operations against the enemy, but it did so only after it had been modified to 10 cm. working. What had happened was that the employment of 10 cm. wave-length technique had arrived and had been proved so superior that this $1\frac{1}{2}$ metre set was outdated before it had come into being. Though this equipment was never introduced into the Service it was officially entitled to be called the C.A. No. 1, Mark I. As it was never issued for operational installation and use, there is no object in defining its performance in detail; naturally, it suffered from some of the troubles of the C.D./C.H.L. and its "beamed" transmission, and though its range performance was good it had not the discrimination of a "narrow-beam" set.

It had, of course, been contemplated for some time that a very short—an ultra-short wave-length would, eventually, be employed for this class of set. The priority requirement for applying 10 cm. working was for the urgent needs of anti-aircraft fire control and development for that use appeared to offer the best chance of applying its major items or assemblies—if not the equipment as a whole—to the C.A. fire control role. Here again the policy of uniformity in Army equipment, or parts of equipment, was aimed at. However, during the autumn of 1941 it became increasingly apparent that the prospects of early production of the 10 cm. G.L. III were deteriorating and that delay was inevitable. In any case, the priority claims of A.A. gave little hope of this type becoming available for C.A. purposes for at least two years. The War Office radar directorate had already had its appetite whetted by the results obtained with the N.T. 271 equipment, as modified for C.D. purposes, and the advice of the Ministry of Supply was sought as to how this need could best be met with the G.L. III type ruled out of consideration.

A recommendation to adopt the 50 cm. wave-length set that had been developed experimentally at A.D.R.D.E. for A.A. fire control (see Chapter IX) was rejected on the grounds that the production position was most difficult and no Army equipment of a new type would become available much, if at all, before the G.L. III for C.A. purposes, and the latter appeared to be largely outdated by the 10 cm. sets already in production and supply to the Navy. The other alternative recommendation, that the Establishment should, themselves, develop a high-power 10 cm. transmitter for incorporation in a new design, was also rejected on the grounds of time and duplication of development as the Admiralty were already well ahead with their contemplated higher power designs.

The War Office then asked for a review of the possibility of applying 10-cm. working to the C.A. No. 1, $1\frac{1}{2}$ cm. set by incorporating essential radar components of the N.T. 271 set. It had been ascertained from the Admiralty that it was likely that a number of these sets could be made available to the Army at a regular rate and increased provision could be arranged to follow in three months' time, if an order were placed on which the existing production contracts could be extended.

The A.D.R.D.E. reported through the Ministry that this conversion was practicable and presented no great difficulty though some problems such as "wave-guide split" would have to be solved, but they were hopeful of producing solutions at an early date. This, in fact, they achieved, and the experimental set at A.D.R.D.E. was "mocked up" for 10 cm. working and tested at Steamer Point satisfactorily.

On the production aspect the position of the Mark I was examined by the M. of S. production directorate in detail and it was found that little of the production work already completed, or in hand, would be wasted; much of it could be used for the 10 cm. Mark II, some would be modified and some diverted to other purposes. In addition the changes to be made would not interrupt production to any material extent.

This conversion to 10 cm. working was, therefore, agreed and accepted. In view of the lighter aerial loads involved it was decided to use the existing "Adamson" turn-table and its control gear only for the initial supply, and a more economical design would be introduced as soon as possible for the majority of these sets.

C.A. No. 1, Mark II, became the title of the early supply of the 10 cm. wavelength equipments and Mark III was applied to the later models with the improved turn-table and control gear. (See Illustrations 10 and 12.)

The Mark II supply started with 10 sets for proof, pilot models, experimental work and training, in June, 1942, and some few were made available for priority operational stations, Dover and Gibraltar being supplied in this way with one early model each. A further 8 equipments were issued to operational sites during July and August and the flow of provision was well maintained to complete the programme. A total of 99 sets were produced between August, 1942, and June, 1945; the United Kingdom requirements were completed during late 1943 and the provision for Ports Abroad and for supply to Russia continued up to June, 1945.

With the buildings constructed by "Works," towers, turn-tables, etc., erected by Ministry of Supply contract, installation of the radar sets carried out by R.E.M.E.—often assisted by the coast gunners who would operate them—

and checked by C.I.E.M.E. before they were passed for becoming operational, this complete provision proceeded steadily. Eight of the installations (only one in the United Kingdom) had to include a 60-ft. tower on account of low sites. (See Illustration 11.)

Later medium power—70 kW.—was applied to all these sets as was done in the case of the C.D. types, but high power was not applied to C.A. No. 1, with the exception of one set at Dover as an experiment. Medium power provided quite adequately for the full-range capacity of the longest range C.A. guns, as was proved at Dover, and the need for stronger signals at long range was not apparent.

The performance of these C.A. No. 1, Marks II and III was officially recognized as—

Detection range and accurate following on a site 200 feet above sea-level—
on M.T.B.. . . . . 25,000 yards.
on Destroyers . . . . 40,000 yards.
Range accuracy between 2,000 and 36,000 yards . $\pm$ 50 yards.
Bearing accuracy . . . . . . $\pm$ 10 minutes.
Discrimination
in range . . . . 400 yards.
in bearing . . . 5 degrees.

With experienced operators these standards were generally improved upon, particularly in bearing, and frequently in the discrimination between targets; while the bearing accuracy did not approach the 2 minutes of arc specified in the original G.S. statement of requirements in April, 1938, the equipment achieved good results.

The burden of provision of these C.A. equipments fell mainly upon the Ministry of Supply Production directorate (D.E.S.E.) rather than upon the Ministry of Aircraft Production. This production and its contracts covered the heavy and bulky structural work as well as the large mechanical components which, in fact, comprised the major part of the equipment. It involved the co-ordination of supply from a variety of sources—the receivers from M.A.P. contracts, transmitters, etc., from Admiralty sources on a planned allocation a month, and the structural and mechanical parts and appliances from M. of S. contracts. In addition, a number of Service stores from Army sources were required and the structures or emplacements to house the equipments had to be built under arrangements made by the Director of Fortifications and Works, War Office.

The responsibility for the phasing and co-ordinating of supply lay with, or perhaps was assumed by general agreement by, D.D.S.E. of the Ministry of Supply directorate, Brigadier C. M. Simpson. Certainly from the War Office point of view this single authority for the whole production was most satisfactory; it provided the forecasts of provision for the equipments as a whole, and thereby enabled a priority order of installation, based upon operational needs, to be formulated and construction work to be organized to meet the dates by which equipment would be ready for installation at each site. The planned programme was adhered to with but minor changes and a few small delays. This was due primarily to the work of D.D.S.E. as the co-ordinating authority.

This provision of the C.A. No. 1, Marks II and III equipments, once the pilot models had been cleared for production after practical trials, can be said to have proved one of the most satisfactory of any Army radar equipment throughout the war period. The rate of supply averaging only some 3 sets a month was, perhaps, not spectacular, but the regularity and reliability of the forecasts of supply were, at any rate from the aspect of the General Staff, most helpful.

Before the full-scale production got into its stride, the early converted experimental model from A.D.R.D.E., Christchurch, was transferred to Dover for operational trials and practical experience.

This reached Dover in March, 1942, and was used in actions against enemy vessels from July onwards, from its emplacement at South Foreland. This set was referred to as B(p)X—the "B" numbers indicated the type of radar station at which 10 cm. battery fire control sets were installed; the "X" was added officially to denote that it was an experimental set, not a standard service type.

Major P. C. Varley of the O.R.G. also took this set under his wing as he had already done with the early 271 X type, and after installation got it working with crews he trained in its operation.

It certainly had plenty of operational experience at this active station, as will be seen from the selected summaries of Dover defence actions in Chapter XVIII. It produced results that were promising for the Service pattern sets that were being installed a little later. This early rousing of confidence in the performance and possibilities of new devices or equipment is, of itself, of value as it enables the new sets to be used to their full operational capacity as soon as they have been installed and tested.

The performance of B(p)X was a considerable improvement on that of the N.T. 284—the Naval type working on a 50 cm. wave-length—that had been installed by local arrangements with the idea of providing accurate range-finding for the coast guns. The latter did not prove much of a success for this purpose even after it was "hotted up" and provided with "split" in an endeavour to improve its angular accuracy. B(p)X was converted later to medium power working and was kept in action until, after surviving the effects of splinter damage from enemy shelling on two occasions, it succumbed as a casualty to the fire of the enemy battery near Cap Gris Nez. Both experimentally and operationally, nursed and sustained by Major Varley's untiring attention, it had served Dover well.

As a special case, partly for concealment, one of the early C.A. No. 1, Mark II sets provided for the Dover defences was installed in the old lighthouse at South Foreland, with the aerial inside the lantern and the set in the ground-floor compartment. This involved some adaptation which was carried out, with local assistance, by A.D.R.D.E. It was found impossible to replace the steel-work supporting the lantern roof and this caused some variation in azimuth reading, but it was constant for particular bearings and could be allowed for in transmitting information. This set also suffered from enemy fire, but that was due to misalignment caused by a shell burst on the cliff face below that disturbed the foundations of the lighthouse itself; it was corrected by lining up and adjusting the set within the tower.

Another special installation occurred at Gibraltar where, instead of construction above ground, excavation in the rock provided the standard operating chambers and gave good material protection. This was the only C.A. fire control set required for the defences and it was the first to be provided overseas; one of the earliest sets was made specially available for despatch and erected under local arrangements. No particular points arose in the installation of sets in the standard design of emplacement, nor were any material difficulties encountered even with the 60 foot tower sets though they were not a simple job.

Few of these equipments were in action against the enemy other than those at Dover, and though the defences of that station were considered to some extent abnormal, the experience gained there in the use of radar aids for coastal artillery action was of the greatest value. The Coast Artillery School appreciated this experience and kept in the closest touch by frequent visits and attachments of members of its staff so that the new—or more correctly the revolutionary —methods and their effect could be reflected in the revised doctrine for the defence of ports and harbours, in the training of R.A. personnel and in defining operational requirements of radar equipment and its accessories.

Fire Command Equipment. The equipment provided for the Fire Commander's Post was classed as C.A. No. 2 to distinguish it from the C.A. No. 1 battery set.

The object of this set was the detection and tracking of surface vessels at long range to give warning of their approach so that the batteries could be ready to engage them when they came within range. It provided the means by which the whole water area with which a Fire Commander is concerned, and the approaches to it, is kept under continuous observation so that he can select and allocate to individual batteries the targets they are to engage. By its means he can indicate to any battery the location, course and speed of a target so that its fire control set can pick up the specific target ordered. It enables the Fire Commander to watch the course of the action and if necessary to control it by using the fire power available to him to the best advantage. When the conditions within the area for which he is responsible permit, the F.C.'s set could, if desired, assist in the correction of fire by observation of the fall of shot, but that is not a primary concern of the Fire Command. The long-range detection and tracking capacity of this equipment is of value, also, to the Naval and R.A.F. components of the defences for interception and attack by surface craft or aircraft, if so decided. All information received is passed immediately to the C.A. operations room and thence to the adjoining Naval plotting room.

The first type of set provided for this purpose was identical with the C.D./C.H.L. and was similarly emplaced as close as practicable to the F.C. Post; no further reference to this $1\frac{1}{2}$ metre equipment is necessary as it has been dealt with adequately in Chapter XV.

The replacement of these early sets by the 10 cm. type C.A. No. 2, similar to the C.D. No. 1, Mark IV, was effected and again, as early as was possible, sets of the C.D. No. 1, Marks V and VI type were introduced and, similarly, modified later for medium power working; high power was not applied to them.

These 10 cm. wave-length equipments had the official title of C.A. No. 2, Mark 1, and were installed in the Fire Command post itself wherever possible. In cases where old pattern or improvised F.C. posts were in use and these sets could not be accommodated, they were installed in a special annexe or were operated from their containers sited as close as possible to the post.

These C.A. No. 2 sets were provided with an additional device known as the L.17 unit, of Admiralty design to match their Type 271 equipment. The additional presentation provided in this unit gave a larger scale time base for 1,000 yards range on either side of the target signal break. This made for greater accuracy of reading, improved discrimination between targets and improved observation of shell splashes.

The standard performance of these sets without the L.17 unit was:—

Range accuracy	$\pm$ 200 yards on the 15,000 yards time base;
	$\pm$ 500 yards on the 75,000 yards time base;
Bearing accuracy	$\pm$ 1 degree;
Detection range from 200 ft. site	25,000 yards on M.T.B.;
	40,000 yards on Destroyers;
Discrimination . . .	400 yards in range, 3 degrees in bearing.

With medium power (70 kW.) working the above ranges were increased by 5,000 yards; with the L.17 unit discrimination was brought down to about 200 yards in range.

The narrow beam transmission had an effective width of 6 degrees approximately, used common T and R wave-guide and aerial reflector (paraboloid) with hand turning.

Fall-of-Shot Observation. A further very marked advance in fall-of-shot observation was made by the development of an experimental set at A.D.R.D.E. This worked on a wave-length of 3 cm. and had a remarkable new form of presentation.

Some development work on this ultra-short wave-length had been carried out at T.R.E. in 1941, and they provided some basic components for experiment early in 1942. The aim of development was chiefly to provide a more satisfactory means of observation of fall-of-shot in direct relation to the target. Instead of the angular measurement between line to target and line to splash and the difference in range to target and to splash all measured *from the set*, a gridded presentation was to be the basis on which observation would be effected. This would show all echoes from target, splashes and any other object at the same time, so that their relative positions on the sea surface could be observed directly.

Such a form of presentation was produced by the rapid and continuous scanning of a small area by a very narrow beam. The area scanned was 2,000 yards long in range and six degrees wide, and with the target held at the central point any shell splash within 1,000 yards plus or minus and three degrees right or left for line would appear on the "grid" on the C.R.T. screen. Its error could, therefore, be read in direct relation to the target itself, in the same way as points on a gridded map can be related.

The target echo appeared as a short horizontal line on the grid and so did the splash echoes, though they were usually somewhat less well defined. It was certainly a most effective display and a beautiful technical achievement. A diagram illustrating this grid presentation is included as Fig. 6.

The scanning was effected by wobbling the end of the wave-guide feed horizontally at the focus of the reflector; at first a paraboloid was used but this was improved upon by an elegant strip reflector of some 12 feet aperture, narrow vertically but long horizontally. This was mounted on one of the now famous G.L. II trailer cabins with the complete set inside. The accurate rotation of the cabin could maintain the target signal on the centre cross lines of the grid and the scanning aerial covered the area around it.

This experimental development was carried out by Kempton and his team which included Lieutenant Vollum of the United States Army attached to A.D.R.D.E. as one of the U.S. Electronics Training Group; he helped this development materially as also did Ashmead's aerial party and Farley working with Vollum. Much credit is due to Kempton and his team for this valuable development.

The experimental set was made available for trials by C.A.E.E. and C.A.S. at Llandudno in March, 1943, where it proved most satisfactory, giving a range accuracy of 25 yards and bearing accuracy of about 3 minutes of arc relative to the target. It gave a 25,000 yards range on 6 in. shell splashes.

A demonstration given to the War Office representatives was most effective and the set was "sold" at once. Incidentally, this demonstration was also witnessed by the members of the American Scientific and Technical Radar Mission under Dr. Karl Compton, who were most impressed by it. They obtained a promise from the War Office to have a model of this set sent over to the States as soon as one could be made available.

As a result of this demonstration and in order to get experience with the set in operations, arrangements were made for its early despatch for operational trials at Dover and for six additional copies of it, or rather improved models of more robust form, to be built. These were to have direct electrical transmission of information instead of the telephone "telling" of bearing and range of the first model; the provision of a remote display for use in the F.C. post or other position as required, was also to be provided.

The set was provisionally and very temporarily named C.A. No. 3, but was usually referred to as "Charlie"; it was sent to Dover in July and as was becoming customary, was taken charge of by Varley. Sited near the Eastern Fire Command post controlling Wanstone 15 in. and South Foreland 9·2 in. batteries, it was found that from its height of 340 feet above sea-level, it could "see" 15 in. shell splashes at 34,000 yards with a big signal and 9·2 in. shells gave an ample size of signal for good reading at 31,000 yards. The coast gunners liked the display and found the set a considerable factor in still more effective shooting.

The first of the additional sets built by R.R.D.E. was delivered in November, 1943, and all six had been provided by April, 1944. The first two were ordered to Dover and two others to Ventnor for operational use in connection with the invasion of Normandy and operations in the Channel generally. One, as promised, went to the United States and the other to Australia in view of the Pacific operations, but no news of its employment nor of development from it was received.

At Dover these sets (B.X. and B.Z.) were used for battery fire control as well as for fire command duties and it became apparent that its accuracy in range and in tracking was in advance of that of the standard C.A. No. 1, Marks II and III equipment. Though no replacement of the latter type could be contemplated at that stage of the war, this new 3 cm. type would certainly have been adopted as the normal equipment for C.A. fire direction had the need for active harbour defences persisted. It was, therefore, brought into the class of C.A. No. 1 and became C.A. No. 1, Mark IV. At Dover it continued to operate until all enemy activity in the Channel had ceased.

The Dover sets and the two provided at Ventnor were of material aid in covering, counting and checking all convoys and invasion shipping. The Ventnor sets proved of the greatest service in recording with precision and reporting the numbers of craft in convoy—a typical case dealt with 83 craft of different sizes, all but one being counted at over 28 miles distance—and the disposition of all returning convoys from Normandy. As a result, a saving of some 40 per cent in turn-round time was effected, the docking authorities being able to allocate berths considerably ahead of the arrival of the convoys, and the supply services being ready with their cargoes for shipment or personnel detailed and ready to embark.

These sets were also required, incidentally, as a matter of scientific interest, to check cases of abnormal propagation and the meteor conditions in which they occurred; no practical information with the 3 cm. transmissions had been obtained previously, but it did not appear to conform to the performance of transmissions on 10 cm. This is referred to in a later chapter dealing with the A.O.R.G.

A further small programme of production of this type of set, in a special form, was attempted towards the end of 1943, when the needs of operations in the Pacific and South-East Asia areas were accorded high priority. The War Office had submitted a requirement for 6 in. coastal guns and transportable mountings for defence of temporary anchorages or bases for these operations and radar equipment to serve them was also required.

The conditions of handling and installation were severe, particularly for the radar sets, which would require a reasonable height above sea-level to meet the warning and range needs of the guns. This might necessitate transportation by man-loads through jungle and up rough and trackless hills, and air-transportability was also an essential requirement.

After discussions with D.G. of A.'s staff and the R.R.D.E., it was agreed that the only practicable solution was to use the new 3 cm. type, and to modify it so that it could be broken down into 200 lb. load units, completely tropicalized, and to provide for it a temporary and completely austere tented shelter to give some small degree of protection from weather. This was authorized in October, 1943, and design and development work were undertaken at R.R.D.E. as a priority job; a production requirement of 24 of these equipments—to be known as C.A. No. 1, Mark V—was stated and delivery by the end of December, 1944, was given as the target date that must be met.

This provision and date were agreed by the Ministry who proposed to have the majority of the display units made up by R.R.D.E. in order to save time. There was, however, a long delay in allocating a contractor for this production work. In the spring of 1944, the production forecast was 12 sets only by the end of December, 1944, and this was acceptable—though regretfully—as the number of batteries contemplated had been reduced to six from the original 12. The number of radar sets required was based on replacement of whole units rather than repair or replacement of individual components, etc., on site; all repair and detailed check of boxed assemblies was to be effected at base.

Soon, however, even this reduced provision slipped further back and by the autumn the delivery date had gone back to the end of March, 1945. With these delays the War Office need for this form of set waned to some extent and with the change in the position and outlook in the Japanese theatre of operations, S.E. Asia Command intimated that they were not contemplating the use of these guns and their accessories, nor making provision for them in their operational plans. Though this need had fallen away, the War Office had another operational need of urgency and value to our field armies that it was hoped to meet by the use of these radar assemblies, and continued to press for their production to be expedited. This new requirement is dealt with in Part IV.

A demand for some of these equipments for adaptation for use in Naval vessels in the Pacific and Eastern fleets was raised by the Admiralty in the late summer of 1944, but it had been made clear to them that they were not suitable for ship-board use and would need extensive re-design of many of the units and the whole of the aerial gear. The demand was renewed later when the absence of a real Army need for S.E. Asia Command was apparent and it was agreed that 8 of the 12 sets should be diverted to the Navy who would effect the modifications needed for ship-borne use.

The diversion of the very limited production capacity by now available for Army supply to this special form of 3 cm. set for the specialized S.E. Asia conditions was unfortunate, but could not have been avoided. Had it been possible to foresee the lapse of that requirement, the production effort could have been made use of for a more normal form of equipment. This would in fact have provided the Army with a standard production model of the best C.A. set in existence and such a production design would in fact have been more easily adaptable to the Naval purpose.

That completes the tale of the development of the C.A. radar equipment for the British Army up to the end of the war. There is, however, another type of equipment designed in Australia before the war for their own coast defences, of which mention must be made; no actual experience of it was gained in this country. This set was called the Sh.D.—presumably Ship Detection—and though intended as a fire control set it did not conform to the single-station type considered essential here. It was really a "range-only" set and needed two stations to operate in conjunction to obtain a location by range co-ordinates instead of bearings. It was developed to employ American valves and components, and as an early type was quite a meritorious achievement. With the limited production capacity available for such work, Australia gallantly offered to make a few of these sets available for the defences of Singapore, and this offer was accepted if we were not able to equip that station with a British pattern by the time Australia could supply. They were, however, not provided in time to be of use in Singapore and little information of their performance and operational effect was received from Australia.

In Canada the coastal defences also relied upon their own production—in this case the Canadian pattern G.L. III set was applied; no reports of its suitability were received, but the performance of its A.P.F. component should have proved adequate.

CHAPTER XVIII. RADAR EFFECT ON C.A. OPERATIONS

To give some idea of the effect of radar on C.A. operations, and the improvements produced by the various stages of development of radar equipment that have been described in the previous chapter, some extracts from "Action Reports" of the Dover defences are recorded here.

Dover was of course in a unique position, and no other station had the opportunities for action against the enemy that naturally fell to the Dover defences nor, incidentally, did any other station experience the severe retaliatory fire from enemy coastal guns that fell to their lot with those opportunities.

Covering the narrow waters of the Straits which became a vital sea route for the enemy after he had occupied Northern France, Dover was able eventually to employ its coastal weapons offensively in interrupting movement along that route and making it costly to the enemy. In addition, Dover covered the nodal point of our vital convoy route from and to the West. At this point enemy coast guns could bring our convoys under their fire and could employ their light craft to attack them or to mine their path; it was Dover's primary defensive objective to protect these convoys.

These reports of C.A. operations and their variety serve best to illustrate the increasing effectiveness of our coast artillery due to the introduction of radar aids and they show how the development of improved radar equipment was directly reflected in the performance of those weapons in action against the enemy.

Being in this position of activity, Dover was used very largely as a practical trial station for new and even for rough experimental sets, to prove them not only in the hands of the troops but in their hands in action, and under enemy fire. In this work the co-operation of the Coast Artillery Commander—Brigadier C. W. Raw—and his units was close, willing and most helpful. The acceptance of representatives of the A.O.R.G. and of their assistance and advice materially helped the scientific assessments of the value of the new types, and of embryo or experimental equipments. In particular, the brothers G. C. and P. C. Varley of that group were enabled to do very valuable work by this co-operation and they, in turn, repaid that assistance by their work in keeping these sets operating to the best of their capacity and "mothering" them in action as well as out of action.

The Naval authorities—the Vice-Admiral Dover, in Command—fully supported Brigadier Raw in this helpful attitude and contributed materially to the successful collaboration between the two Services and the scientists.

The extracts from "Action Reports" that follow have been selected chiefly from those in which the Eastern Counter Bombardment Fire Command and 540 Regiment R.A., under Lieut.-Colonel J. H. W. G. Richards, R.A., were concerned. So far as it is possible, they are representative of a number of actions that took place in the different stages of radar development. They aim at showing the effect of the radar equipment employed rather than the full effect of the firing, though this latter is in fact the "eating" of the "pudding" that is supposed to provide the proof.

(*a*) PRE-RADAR PERIOD. Between August and the end of December, 1940, there were twelve actions at Dover against enemy E-boats; all were daytime visual shoots and no radar equipment of any sort was available. The targets were all at extreme range and after a few rounds they retired out of range.

Results. No known casualties; no damage claimed.

Note. Actions unaided by radar occurred elsewhere but none appear to have produced casualties to the enemy.

(*b*) EARLY RADAR PERIOD. The installation of $1\frac{1}{2}$ metre C.D./C.H.L. sets produced little material effect on operations, though they could assist visual methods by providing good range information. Their valuable capacity for providing early warning of impending chances of action were appreciated at the time, but confidence in their reliability had not been established sufficiently for any relief of look-outs or duty watches to be permitted, so no material advantage from these sets for coast artillery had been achieved before the improved type —the 10 cm. set—arrived and put this first form into the background.

At Dover two of these $1\frac{1}{2}$ metre sets had been provided at Lydden Spout and at Fan Hole and, in addition, a Naval pattern set working on a 50 cm. wave-length had been installed under local arrangements to act as a battery range-finder. This set did not prove satisfactory nor did it effect any improvement even in conjunction with the C.D./C.H.L. sets; the accuracy of performance was not sufficient to warrant attempts at unseen fire control—a role for which they were not intended.

No radar-aided actions are reported from Dover. Later, in Malta, where the only radar equipment then available was of the same $1\frac{1}{2}$ metre type, a violent close action did take place, most successfully, when the Italians made a determined attack on the Grand Harbour with small and fast motor craft and man-directed torpedoes. Radar detection of these small craft does not appear to have been effected, though their base, or mother ship, lying well out of range, seems to have been detected. Radar can, therefore, claim no part in the effective destruction and defeat of this attack.

(*c*) EARLY CENTRIMETRIC PERIOD. Centrimetric radar appeared first as the C.D. No. 1, Mark IV or N.T. 271X, provided at Lydden Spout (K.148), and St. Margarets (K.147) in the Dover defences in the late summer and autumn of 1941. Though *not* truly suitable for fire control they were employed for that purpose for want of the more accurate battery sets. Their performance in long-range detection and tracking alone made an immediate improvement in the defences as a whole, as no vessel could then traverse the Straits undetected and opportunities were afforded for successful attacks by light Naval and air craft.

(i) The first radar shoot by the Dover guns took place on 27th November, 1941, when Lydden Spout battery (6 in.) engaged a group of E-boats. Plots by K.148 (Lydden Spout) were transmitted to C.A. Operations Room, whence predicted location and time were passed to the battery. Only five rounds were fired before the enemy passed out of range of the guns.

The second took place on 6th February, 1942, when Fan Hole battery (6 in.) engaged E-boats moving at 22 knots. In this case ranges and bearings were passed direct to the battery plotting room. The fire—15 rounds only—appears to have been effective, or at least menacing as the enemy turned sharply to starboard and retired rapidly out of range.

Note. In neither of these actions were casualties claimed. The second action shows an improvement on the first in the saving of time by direct transmission of information to the battery for plotting and determining a suitable predicted point and time. In neither of these actions was radar employed as a specific range-finder for the guns.

(ii) 12th February, 1942, brought the first big radar controlled action when South Foreland battery (9·2 in.) engaged the *Scharnhorst*, *Gneisenau*, etc.; Wanstone (15 in.) battery had not been completed by that time. From the radar aspect this action was the first in which fall-of-shot observations were obtained.

Local warning was obtained by K.148 at a range of 46,000 yards at 11.30 hours and at 11.31 hours Naval plotting room identified it as "hostile," and gave its composition; they had received the plot picked up by K.7 (Fairlight) at 10.50 hours through Newhaven, but it had not reached the C.A. operations room. Due to this delay South Foreland was not ready for action till 12 noon and the elementary battery set (N.T. 284) could not get warmed up to operate till 12.15 hours. Plots were passed direct to F.C. post, South Foreland, continuously as to location, course and speed from K.148, N.T. 284 occasionally and from K.147 when it could pick up and follow. The battery opened fire at 12.19 hours and continued until 12.36 hours when the targets passed out of range; N.T. 284 could follow no longer, but K.148 continued to follow up to 65,000 yards. Two salvos only were picked up by the radar, one enabled gun range to be corrected by an increase with which the next salvo was reported by the radar as "hit or near miss." The number of vessels, including escorts, made radar fall-of-shot observation difficult particularly with operators who lacked experience in such observation.

The battery fired 33 rounds and obtained three direct hits on *Gneisenau* during this action—as confirmed later. The radar sets were "patchy" in their performance, due to lack of early warning—K.147 was off the air for maintenance and the N.T. 284 also, and took some time to warm up—K.148, however, operated very well throughout the action and, in fact, was really the basis on which the fire was controlled.

Note. An unfortunate series of events marred this first and only action against enemy heavy capital ships by coastal artillery. One of the radar stations at any rate had amply proved its value and as a result pressure for full provision of radar aids for Dover and other important defences hastened the supply of new sets.

(iii) A later Dover action on the night of 2nd/3rd July, 1942, by which time the experimental C.A. No. 1 set, B(p)X was installed and was used for the first time, shows an improvement in the fall-of-shot observation. Of 20 four-gun salvos fired, six were reported "on target," four as "probably on target," three as minus, one as plus and one as right—seven only were reported "unobserved."

Note. B(p)X—a battery fire control set—was only taking part in this action for a short time while K.147 lost the target for a few minutes; this is quoted simply for the fall-of-shot improvement obtained.

(*d*) BATTERY FIRE CONTROL RADAR PERIOD. The experimental centimetric set erected as B(p)X was employed as an operational battery set between July, 1942, and January, 1943, when the first production equipment was installed at Wanstone to operate with that battery; this station was referred to as B.5 and took over battery range-finding duties on 2nd March, 1943. Further C.A. No 1 and C.A. No. 2 sets were added to the Dover defences to complete the requirements of the batteries and fire commands; the number available for fall-of-shot observation was increasing and some of the F.C. post sets were being completed with the extra L. 17 panel. While the C.A. No. 1 usually worked through the fortress plotter, individual sets could work direct to their batteries if so desired.

(i) With the improved accuracy of early rounds produced by the use of C.A. No. 1 sets now available, the percentage of shell splashes observed rose considerably as the following figures show:—

Action on 10th/11th November, 1942. All 9·2 in. salvos observed—4 minus, 2 plus, 2 on target. Two only of 15 in. salvos unobserved out of 15.

Action on 10th/11th December, 1942. 26 salvos of 9·2 in.—5 unobserved, 7 on target, 4 plus, 10 minus. 18 salvos of 15 in.—2 unobserved, 4 on target, 4 plus, 8 minus.

Both these actions were at long range, targets took sharp evasive action but hits were scored as one ship was observed on fire. Escorts to the main targets adopted close formation abreast of target which often made fall-of-shot observation difficult.

(ii) An action on 2nd/3rd March, 1943, is notable as it was the first in which a standard battery fire control set—C.A. No. 1 Mark II—which had been installed at Wanstone as B. 5, was employed in its proper role. In addition a success was achieved and for the first time, also, the sinking was actually confirmed from another source. Up to this time some seven sinkings had been caused by the guns, but no independent confirmation was obtainable and they had been classed as "probable sinkings" only; radar had in most cases reported the target echoes fading and eventually disappearing, and in some cases immediate photographic reconnaissance had failed to find the vessel engaged in any port—this, however, was negative information and not acceptable as positive confirmation.

In this entirely radar controlled engagement, Wanstone (15 in. battery) was not available as its pieces were being changed, so the whole brunt fell upon South Foreland 9·2 in. battery. The target was a merchant vessel of some 200 feet in length escorted by 6 other vessels and a number of E-boats. Range-finding was by B. 5 through the fortress plotter and 6 other radar sets were available for observation of fall-of-shot.

In all, 177 rounds were fired and 22 salvos were reported by radar observation as "on target," and 5 as direct hits. After 48 minutes' action the speed of the target was reduced to 3 knots and shortly after she was stopped and the escort was very disorganized. Later another vessel proceeded from the spot where the stopped target had been observed and it was engaged till out of range. It was not possible to say that this was not the original target, as radar conditions had become somewhat anomalous, and though the target echoes had faded and disappeared it could not be verified that it had sunk. In the meantime enemy signals had been intercepted which showed that a vessel had been damaged and survivors were in the water.

A few days later, however, the sinking of this target was confirmed from a reliable source; a most satisfactory postscript to a well-conducted shoot.

(iii) Combined operation. Another radar controlled action which took place on 5th July, 1943, is quoted as an example of a different kind of operation. This was a combined action in which the C.A. guns co-operated with our M.T.B.s and covered their approach.

Radar warning enabled our light Naval craft, in two groups, to get well out towards their selected points of interception by the time the guns opened fire. The targets were two destroyers proceeding at 25 knots on a "snaking" course to make ranging difficult. After eleven minutes' engagement, gun range was increased by 1,000 yards and two minutes later by another 1,000 to occupy the attention of the enemy while the first group of M.T.B.s made their attack. This was repeated later for the second group.

Though neither of the attacks achieved success, they were able to make them unobserved and to return unscathed. To this extent it was a successful operation on the radar side and, incidentally, this action provided some actual proof of the accuracy of the radar fall-of-shot observations; the M.T.B.s observed a number of salvos and their visual estimates were found to agree effectively with those of the radar.

(e) 3 CM. FALL-OF-SHOT PERIOD.

(i) On 3rd/4th August, 1943, "Charlie," the experimental fall-of-shot set, was in action with the other radar sets and proved very successful. The target was a 4,000 ton vessel—D. 55—from Boulogne, attempting the passage of the Straits with 3 others and escorts. After 15 minutes' engagement by South Foreland battery—all salvos observed—the large vessel stopped and was seen to be on fire and burnt for 90 minutes before its echo faded and disappeared as it sank. No direct confirmation was obtained, but no trace of this vessel was found in any port afterwards and "presumed sunk" was recorded.

(ii) Another notable engagement occurred on 21st January, 1944, when the 6,500 ton vessel *Munsterland* was sunk in attempting the passage of the Straits. On this occasion, owing to very thick weather, the vessel could not see the gun flashes and could not, therefore, take effective evasive action.

Wanstone opened fire at 36,000 yards and its *first two salvos were straddles*. This battery fired 75 rounds all told and 9 straddles and 4 direct hits were reported. Fire had been opened at 05.05 hours and at 05.30 hours the target slowed and circled, eventually it was reported stopped and drifting at 06.00 hours. By 06.40 hours the echoes had been reduced considerably and radar stations reported the target aground. Air reconnaissance at first light confirmed that she had sunk and was lying with decks awash and upperworks above water; they were able to photograph her and read her name, *Munsterland*. Another smaller vessel was also reported with a heavy list, ashore and on fire, west of Calais. This was one of the escorts which had been reported as hit and ashore at this position by radar.

Apart from the actual sinkings achieved in this action, and the verified value of the radar information, the coast artillery had provided themselves with an excellent "datum" mark at operational range which was available to them right up to the end of the war and proved of great value.

Note. In these actions the "straddles" obtained with the initial rounds proved the ability of the battery sets, and the excellent and consistent fall-of-shot reports from the different types of set observing gave the opportunity for full confirmation of the value of the new 3 cm. type and its effective method of display.

(f) COMBINED BATTERY FIRE CONTROL AND OBSERVATION OF FIRE.

Further proof of the C.A. No 1, Mark IV, set was obtained in an engagement on 22nd/23rd July, 1944, when this set, operating through the Displacement Corrector, acted as battery fire control set for South Foreland and also supplied direct the fall-of-shot information to that battery. In this role it proved itself as the complete battery fire control equipment and the means of observing and correcting fire.

(g) FINAL ACTIONS.

The final actions of the Dover guns cannot be called typical or representative—they are unique in the history of coastal artillery—but as radar made them possible and gave such essential aids to their remarkable success they cannot be omitted from this record.

The official report on the actions from the 1st–5th September, 1944, is reproduced here as no transcript could be as effective as this plain, straightforward—almost bald—report.

"COAST ARTILLERY ACTIONS 1ST TO 5TH SEPTEMBER 1944

Part I—Night 1st/2nd September 1944

1. Information had been received from R.N. that the enemy was likely to attempt a mass evacuation with all his vessels remaining in Boulogne. PRUs had shown that there were no large vessels in this port, but that there were a large number of trawler type auxiliaries, E/R boats and smaller craft.

2. On the night 1/2 Sep 44 at about 2155 hrs Radar detected small craft collecting outside Boulogne. When collected, the convoy moved northwards in several groups. Some of these groups were 10–15 strong and consisted of trawlers and E/R boats, etc., in about equal proportions. Altogether between 30 and 40 craft appeared to leave Boulogne.

3. The first group, which was considerably smaller than the other groups and contained no trawler size vessel, was not engaged by coast artillery but was attacked by light naval forces just west of Calais.

4. About 2245 hrs a second group of about 15 vessels left the Boulogne area and by 2330 hrs was off Cap Gris Nez and in range of 540 Coast Regt. R.A.; Radar identified this group as 5 or 6 trawler size, 5 or 7 E/R boats and a few smaller craft.

5. Fire was opened by South Foreland bty (9·2") at 2335 hrs followed at 2340 hrs by Wanstone bty (15"). The action against this group was continued until 0004 hrs when light Naval craft attacked successfully. The convoy was then about 5 miles west of Calais.

6. During this action several echoes were seen to be fading on the Radar and at the end only 1 trawler type vessel could be located. There also seemed to be fewer of the smaller vessels. Five vessels are claimed as sunk in this group.

7. Hostile Batteries replied in a counter battery role at 2352 hrs and were identified as A.2, A.3 and A.6. Wanstone bty was switched from an antishipping role and engaged A.6, and the Royal Marine Siege Regiment (2-14") engaged A.2 and A.3.

8. By this time two further groups had left Boulogne and rounded Cap Gris Nez. The leading group turned round at 2359 hrs and returned about 1½ miles towards Cap Gris Nez. It was then joined by the following group and the combined party set off east once more.

9. This group was engaged by South Foreland bty between 0010 hrs and 0130 hrs when it passed out of range. From results observed on Radar a further five vessels of various sizes are claimed as sunk. In one instance a hit was observed on a trawler when another vessel came alongside presumably to help. With the next salvo Radar recorded a hit on both vessels which immediately sank fading from the tube.

10. Rangefinding in this action was BZ to S. Foreland bty and B5 to Wanstone bty, both through D.C.C. Fall-of-shot was given by F.1, BX (until put out of action) and BZ, all giving excellent results. It is considered that as a result of this action, altogether 10 enemy ships were sunk and others damaged.

11. S. Foreland fired 123 rounds and Wanstone 17 rounds in an anti-shipping role and 42 in a counter battery role. The Royal Marine Siege Regiment fired 29 rounds in a counter battery role. Both R.M. Siege Regiment and Wanstone were ranged on to the hostile btys by using a Radar datum (wreck of s.s. *Munsterland*) as a witness point.

12. The hostile shelling was very heavy in 540 regimental area and 44 shell holes were found, in addition to which there were a large number of air bursts. The hostile fire was also exceedingly accurate and S. Foreland bty was consistently straddled. There was heavy damage to buildings and a large number of communications were cut. The majority of the latter were, however, maintained by alternative routes but communications could not be re-established with R.M. Siege Regt. till after the action. F.1 and BZ suffered minor damage from splinters and BX was damaged sufficiently to put the set out of action. The C.A. plotter at Wanstone was put out of action by a cut cable. No. 1 gun S. Foreland bty was out of action for approx. ¼ of an hour as a result of a near miss and No. 2 gun was put out of action for the remainder of the action owing to damage by shell splinters to the pump house and cage hoist. Considering the severity of the hostile shelling the casualties suffered in 540 Coast Regt. R.A. were remarkably light. They consisted of one man seriously injured (leg since amputated) and 5 men suffering from minor injuries and shock. All ranks carried out their duties under these hazardous conditions in an exemplary manner.

13. The last round from the hostile batteries fell at 0213 hrs.

Part II Afternoon 3 September 1944

1. At 1245 hrs on 3 Sep. 44 a hostile bty identified as A.6 opened fire on an eastbound convoy off S. Foreland. Except for one round which fell in Langdon Bty, causing considerable damage to buildings but no casualties, the remainder of the shells fell in the sea, doing no damage. It was, therefore, decided not to retaliate with counter battery fire. However, at 1417 hrs, before the all-clear had been sounded, shelling recommenced from A.2, A.3 and A.6 and was concentrated on the Dover area.

2. At 1431 hrs the Royal Marine Siege Regt. opened fire on A.3 and at 1440 hrs Wanstone engaged A.6. At 1452 hrs, as A.3 had ceased fire, the R.M. Siege Regt. were switched to A.2. Wanstone ceased fire at 1513 hrs and the R.M. Siege Regt. at 1530 hrs but the enemy continued till 1556 hrs. Immediately our guns commenced firing the enemy ceased firing on Dover and concentrated on 540 regimental area. Considerable damage was caused in Wanstone bty but there were no casualties. There was also a lot of damage in Dover with casualties to service personnel, one being killed and 2 injured. There were also some minor casualties from air bursts in Deal. The R.M. Siege Regt. fired 23 rds and Wanstone 22 rds whilst the hostile btys fired approx 33 rds.

Part III Night 4/5 September 1944

1. At 2315 hrs on 4 Sept 44 hostile btys identified as A.2, A.3, and A.6 opened fire on a convoy off Dover. Wanstone bty immediately engaged A.6 and the R.M. Siege A.2. The last hostile round fell at 0019 hrs but our guns continued until 0135 hrs. From this it is presumed that our fire had been sufficiently effective to deter the enemy from continuing the action. Further

damage was caused in 540 regimental area and BZ was hit by splinters and seriously damaged, but there were no casualties. One shell landed on the cliff face immediately above the offices of HQ., C.A. Kent, causing considerable minor damage but no casualties. There was considerable damage in Dover but no casualties. A M.M.S. was hit in the harbour suffering one killed and two injured. During this action Wanstone fired 35 rounds and R.M. Siege Regt. 15 rounds whilst the hostile btys fired approx 60 rounds.

2. At 2359 hrs on 4 September 1944, whilst the action described above was taking place, a hostile track was detected by Radar about two miles N.W. of Cap Gris Nez. Size estimates identified this track as 2 E boats and after consultation with the R.N. it was decided to engage with S. Foreland bty.

3. Fire was opened at 0005 hrs and continued on this target till 0035 hrs. In the meantime another track identified as 4 E-boats had been detected near Cap Gris Nez at 0015 hrs and S. Foreland bty was switched to this target and continued to engage it till it passed out of range at 0101 hrs.

4. Rangefinding for this action was carried out by B5 through the Fortress plotter and fall-of-shot by F1 and B(p)9, all of which gave good results. One of the two E boats in the first track sank at 0040 hrs and this was later confirmed by the R.N. Several near misses were recorded on the other track and three E boats were probabaly damaged. During this action speeds were experienced of up to 40 knots. S. Foreland bty expended 85 rds.

5. The results of the series of actions outlined above are considered most encouraging and the behaviour of all ranks under heavy hostile shelling was in accordance with the best traditions of the Royal Regiment of Artillery.

(Signed) C. W. RAW, Brigadier,
Commanding C.C.A. Dover."

From the foregoing samples of engagements in which the Coast Artillery Regiments and their weapons took part, it will be apparent that they contributed to the successful outcome of the war. It is difficult to assess the true value of that contribution or to allocate the share in it to the radar aids provided. Certain it is that little could have been achieved without radar, but it is equally certain that no small measure of the success was due to the spirit of the coast gunner—all ranks from the senior commander to the most junior in the ranks —in accepting these new devices, absorbing and proving them and adapting their own methods to obtain the best value from radar.

As has been said, Dover was more or less a unique station and had unique opportunities, but the Gunners were not unique—they were the ordinary personnel of the Royal Regiment and as such they took a grip on their opportunities and made the most of them in a typical manner.

They were subjected to heavy enemy fire which, though at first mainly retaliatory on Dover, Folkestone and Deal, became more and more concentrated upon the areas of the active batteries—Wanstone and South Foreland in particular. They were not equipped to retaliate to such action in kind as their job was to close the Straits to shipping, but at the end they did get one opportunity against the enemy guns that had pestered them for so long. Wanstone was able to reach the enemy battery that had been specially annoying and was allowed to engage it in the last actions. It had the satisfaction of causing it to cease fire and it obtained a direct hit on one of its guns as was ascertained when those coast batteries were captured.

Associated with the defences of Dover were some special units of the Royal Marines which manned long-range guns on railway mountings. They did not form part of the normal defences but were primarily concerned with counter bombardment action against the enemy batteries, and took no part in the anti-shipping operations. They were, however, aided in the final actions by the Dover gunners in observing and "datuming" by radar on the remains of the *Munsterland*.

That brings the story of the development of Army radar for coastal purposes to an end—an end in so far as the war was concerned. What the future holds for radar applied to this operational form of Army activity remains to be seen—it is not a subject on which prophecy would be appropriate to this record—but it can be said that radar had revolutionized coast defence measures and increased the effect of coastal artillery weapons to an extent undreamed of before radar was made available.

The following views and comments are of interest and may fittingly close this chapter.

(a) Brigadier B. N. J. Schonland, in charge of the Army Operational Research Group, expressed the following opinion as a result of the careful scientific assessment of the effect of radar up to the end of 1943; by that time the C.A. No. 1, Mark IV (3 cm. set) was only in its experimental form.

"Coast Artillery (Radar) Fire Control

These equipments installed at important gun-defended ports have proved extremely successful both in performance and reliability.

Radar fire control of coastal batteries in the neighbourhood of Dover has virtually closed the Straits to all enemy vessels over 2,000 tons. Unseen fire at long range, controlled by Radar, has superseded fire-control by visual methods, even by day.

The sets have also been of great value in ensuring co-ordination in attack between coastal guns and light naval craft.

The Radar apparatus is giving ranges accurate to 25 yards and bearing accuracy between 5 and 10 minutes of arc. This is somewhat more accurate information than is warranted by the ballistic errors of the guns at the range of engagement (35,000 yds.).

The installation of a new set (C.A. No. 1, Mk. IV) which gives accurate position of the fall-of-shot has enabled unseen gunfire to reach a standard of accuracy actually higher than that of visually controlled shoots."

"General Remarks on Radar with Coast Artillery

The Radar fire-control equipment at present available to the coast gunner has given him a counter-bombardment equipment which is completely satisfactory in all respects but one. The exception is the observation of fall-of-shot in relation to the target, which cannot be satisfactorily observed on the C.A. No. 1 Mk. II or III equipment at the same time as the target is being followed. With the development of a set capable of acting both as a rangefinder and as a fall-of-shot observer (now provided as C.A. No. 1, Mk. IV) the long range coast-gunnery problem by night and day will revert to one of gunnery and not of range-finding."

(b) Brigadier C. W. Raw, Commander of the Dover Coastal Artillery throughout the war, commented upon radar and its effect, as follows:—

"The adaptation of Radar to early warning, range-finding and fall-of-shot detection has been by far the greatest advance ever made in Coast Artillery. It has revolutionised all our ideas and has enabled us to assume the offensive rather than remain always on the defensive.

In all its three roles of early warning, range-finding and fall-of-shot detection, radar is a tremendous advance on any previous instruments available with the one exception of bearings, in which visual instruments are at present still in advance of radar. The fact that visual instruments require good visibility, however, really nullifies this advantage.

The future development of radar sets for Coast Artillery should be towards providing:—

(*a*) Greater reliability.
(*b*) Increased discrimination and range.
(*c*) A presentation which is virtually optical allowing identification of targets.
(*d*) Accurate and quick means of assessing target size.
(*e*) Suppression of wave clutter and unwanted echoes.
(*f*) Ready means of altering frequency in order to counteract jamming.
(*g*) Reducing the effects of anomalous propagation so far as they are confusing, but utilizing the advantage of greater detection."

(*c*) Brigadier C. O. Olliver, Commandant Coast Artillery School, has given the following views on Coast Artillery radar:—

"The effects of Radar on Coast Artillery can be divided in actual and potential effects, because during a large part of the war C.A. has suffered under necessarily low supply priorities. During the war, Radar has proved to be an essential C.A. weapon, and leads one to wonder how anyone ever managed without it when it did not exist.

Considering first the Early Warning equipments. These have given as their first great advantage the reduction of strain. No longer does that great essential, early warning, depend on a cold and tired look-out peering into the night or the fog. The Radar set can see through either.

Coupled with the first is the possibility of surprise of the enemy: the strain is transferred to him. A prowling E-boat close inshore knows that, as like as not, the first searchlight to expose will expose *on* him without sweeping about looking for him, and with proper drill a salvo will probably be on the way too.

In addition there are the Fire Direction Sets, with which he may be engaged with fire in the thickest fog or smoke, and these sets enable the fall-of-shot to be determined with at least the accuracy of visual observation, and with the latest type of set, very much more accurately.

The P.P.I. display provides the Fire Commander with a tactical chart which keeps itself up to date, and with the latest type of Skiatron tube it is a large-sized chart.

To attempt even to summarize the effects on C.A. procedures seems almost impossible, for Radar has revolutionized Coast Artillery. The salient points are as follows:—

1. Night and day cease to be differentiated.
2. Targets can be engaged earlier, because course and speed and probable point of engagement may in some cases be worked out when the target is still twenty miles out of range.
3. Fully adequate warning is always assured in any conditions of visibility. Duty watches can sleep.
4. Radar can be used to get searchlight and guns on a close target before exposing, with a resultant moral effect which must be devastating.
5. The accuracy of position-finding information is, in the case of the latest equipment, far better than that of any other type of position-finder."

CHAPTER XIX. COMMENTARY

The responsibilities of the three Services in connection with coast defence were generally well understood, but the advent of radar had brought the R.A.F. more specifically into the picture. The Navy had the responsibility for off-shore active measures against enemy shipping and for protection of our coastal convoys while the Army provided the gun and searchlight defences of ports which in emergency extended also to possible invasion landing-points along our coasts. The R.A.F. provided warning of air attack and active measures to deal with it over and beyond our coastline; the latter had to be co-ordinated with the Naval measures and particularly so in the case of enemy air mine-laying and attacks on our convoys.

Apart from protection from enemy interference with these convoys, the Navy were concerned with their movement and control; in both protection and control the aids brought by radar were of great importance. In this respect radar practically replaced the former Coastguard and Coast Observer organization, or at least greatly extended its effective range and efficiency. With the Army coastal radar stations spread along parts of our coasts, their functions of watch and warning of approach of enemy surface craft could be equally well applied to the location and tracking of our convoys. These stations, therefore, served the Naval needs as well as those of the Army; Naval "tellers" at each station reported shipping movements to Naval area headquarters at the same time as the Army personnel reported to local Army defence headquarters and when necessary to the C.A. operations room of adjacent defended ports.

The addition of low air cover to the surface cover by the R.A.F. at first produced some duplication of effort in establishing radar stations as the sets for both purposes were basically similar though differing in detail—mainly in the form of presentation suited to the greater speed of the aircraft. However, as soon as the early emergency stations were well advanced and the imminence of the invasion threat was reduced, the simplification of the coastal radar system—the Low Cover Chain—was tackled and eventually the integration of the needs of the three Services was complete and the R.A.F. became responsible for all operation, maintenance and manning of these stations for the operational needs of all three Services. Materially this was made possible by the improved availability of P.P.I., C.R. tubes that were originally in very short supply, and by the reduction in the number of stations by the introduction of the N.T. 271 equipment; operationally it was made possible when proof became available that the high power version of this set could deal adequately with long range aircraft detection and tracking.

Whether this simplification of the system effected any saving in man power is a matter of some doubt; certainly a saving was effected in the provision for maintenance—especially by the reduction in the number of stations—but the R.A.F. scale of manning was generally considerably higher than had been found adequate by the Army for surface watch only.

No further comment on the C.D. aspect appears necessary, but it is worth while stressing the improvement effected by the use of the N.T. 271 centimetric type of set, and the difference in the cover provided by a few of the new type stations in place of that given by a number of the $1\frac{1}{2}$ metre pattern has been described in Chapter XVI. This improvement was effected by lower-power sets and, with increase in power available later, it was still further improved.

The high-power stations were proved to be suitable for low air cover over the sea with their capacity for detection at 100 miles and more; the medium power sets had capacity also but there was no need to use them in this way.

The high-power stations on 200 foot towers along the East Anglian coast presented many difficulties and problems, but when these were eventually cleared the stations provided surface cover over and beyond the convoy routes along the very exposed E-boat Alley.

It is not practicable to reproduce the map showing the sites of all the stations in the low cover chain in this country but some idea of its extent can be gathered from the totals of stations that were established. As finally planned, 105 stations were installed in addition to 53 early type that had been eliminated by the centimetric sets; of these 105, 65 were released after a time from surface-watching duties and remained in action for air purposes only. Of the total, 45 were planned as high-power stations, of which 13 were sited in the Humber, Yarmouth and Harwich areas, 5 in the Dover area, and 12 along the rest of the South Coast.

The record of the development of the C.A. type sets calls for little comment as the picture is reasonably complete. It was fortunate that the Naval type 271 made its appearance in time to prevent further work on the $1\frac{1}{2}$ metre pattern.

The exploitation of the possibilities of 3 cm. working was initiated by the scientific staff of the A.D.R.D.E. as a matter of research and not as a result of a G.S. requirement; this is a specific case of an advance brought to notice by the Ministry and its taking the initiative rightly to carry out the investigation. The Ministry and the A.D.R.D.E. can justly take full credit for this achievement —it resulted eventually in the "ideal" C.A. set.

Chapters XVII and XVIII link up the improvements made in development with their actual effect in operations against the enemy. The C.A. problem was, of course, much simpler than that of anti-aircraft fire control but it is not possible to record the bag of ships sunk against the number of rounds fired. The extracts from the action reports do, however, show how the improvements made in the radar aids to C.A. operations had their effect upon the overall efficiency of the heavy coastal weapons. The total of ships sunk by the Dover defences cannot be determined as fact, but there were a number of cases where sinkings occurred but no independent or positive information in confirmation could be obtained. The appellation "presumed sunk" is unsatisfying but cannot be helped—even without taking them into account the Dover gunners can rightly claim to have achieved very material success that contributed to the enemy's defeat.

The matter of observation of fall-of-shot calls, perhaps, for some remarks. Such observation is an essential to good shooting as there are variables that affect the gun and the travel of the shell through the air; the wear of the gun, the nature of the shell, the meteor conditions and other factors all contribute to slight variation in the range, and in some cases in the line, of the point of arrival of the shell. If the splash caused by the shell striking the water can be observed and measured accurately the necessary corrections can be applied to bring the rounds on to the target.

Such observation had been shown to be possible in the trials of the early

C.D. set in July, 1939, and had been proved increasingly effective in operations at Dover. It should be noted, however, that a narrow-beam set like the N.T. 271 type can only observe on shell splashes if the shell strikes the water within the effective width of the beam or if the splash persists long enough for the beam to sweep over that point. In the Dover actions several sets would be told off specifically for such observation and would search ahead of or astern of the target vessel itself.

In the case of a battery fire control set such as C.A. No. 1, Mark III, such searching is not possible as it would interrupt the steady and accurate following of the target essential for good fire direction; fall-of-shot observation by the battery set can only be effective if the splash occurs in the beam as a short or an over. The 3 cm. "Charlie," when it became a battery fire control *and* fire observation set was able to do both jobs and do them better by reason of its special "make-up." It had the capacity to follow the target steadily and accurately by the movement of the whole aerial system, and at the same time to watch over an area all round the target by means of the rapid aerial scanning; the two functions did not militate against one another. In addition the shell splash could be related directly to the target and did not need measuring from the shore station.

The offsprings of "Charlie," therefore, became the complete answer to the coast gunners' needs, including checking the day-to-day accuracy of the gun performance.

There is one thing that distinguishes the development of Coastal Artillery radar during the war from that of the Anti-Aircraft equipment and other types, and that is that the full requirements had been completely provided for in design and had been proved in operations against the enemy. The equipment had reached a pitch of perfection that was ahead of the immediate needs of the guns they served and had surpassed the accuracy of visual methods.

There were, of course, improvements that were still desirable in accessories, as, for example, large-scale displays for remote use by the Fire Commander and perhaps desirable also for the Coast Artillery Commander. The latter might also be served by a complete picture, always up to date, of the whole water area over which his weapons can operate—possibly the Fortress Commander might, also, be so provided. If desirable, there is no difficulty in its design, but with the slow rate of ship movement in comparison with aircraft it is perhaps doubtful if such an accessory can be classed as necessary.

It will have been noted that no radar provision was made for A.M.T.B. defences. In general it appears very doubtful if radar fire direction for these weapons should be attempted—detection and warning of approach can be met adequately by the local Harbour Fire Command equipment from which it should be possible to direct the searchlights and to provide range information as well to the guns. That, however, is a matter for the future and depends upon the nature of the weapons employed and the nature of the enemy's small craft likely to attempt close attacks. There was experience during the war of new types of very small craft partly or completely submersible, but radar cannot compete with under-water detection and some other means must be found to deal with such targets.

One final comment is desirable and that is on the subject of radar in fixed defences. It is suggested that "fixture" should be avoided in so far as radar equipment is concerned—continuous exposure to the weather and to salty atmosphere is not good for radar equipment and there appears no necessity for it in peace time and no necessity for much of it, in many cases, in war. The experience gained during the war with the use of mobile or transportable sets does not bear out the necessity for such equipment to be "fixed." Many sets during the war were installed, but very few ever came into action and their fixation limited their availability for replacing or supplementing sets at active stations. Prepared protection for the selected sites, with the necessary communications, should suffice and there is little reason in most cases why the transportable sets should not be withdrawn to protective storage except in real emergency threatening the particular defences.

Such an arrangement would make peace-time numbers of sets for training quite small while war reserves could also be limited and issued as the threat developed to the particular defences likely to be affected.

The last remark on C.A. radar to be made is one of regret. No record of the radar pictures of an action in progress is available. A film was taken of all the information appearing on the presentation of a radar set, at Dover, which was used to direct, observe and correct fire on an enemy vessel which was eventually sunk. Unfortunately, this film suffered an accident and was spoilt; no other action occurred to give a second chance of making a film. Such a record would have been of intense interest for demonstrating radar performance and the effect of corrections applied during the action. This loss was a great pity and is much to be regretted.

PART IV
MISCELLANEOUS APPLICATIONS
CHAPTER XX. IDENTIFICATION

From the earliest days of radar as a practical aid to defence, the need for some means of distinguishing between friendly craft and those of the enemy had always been appreciated. This need for some method of determining with certainty and at the maximum radar range, whether a target indication on the radar presentation was from a friend or from a foe was a real operational requirement.

The problem of enabling a radar station to effect such discrimination was always a difficult one to solve and involved much scientific and technical effort, and the devices that were developed occupied an enormous amount of production capacity throughout the war. No real approach to what would be an ideal system had emerged by the end of the war, nor was there any indication that such a solution might eventually be found.

To approach the ideal a "positive" method is necessary, that is to say, the echo signal from a hostile craft must be inherently different from that from a friend. There is, however, no specific distinction between such signals nor is there any special characteristic in the reflection from a hostile craft that can be used to identity it. In the absence of a "positive" system the only alternative is to use a "negative" one which means that our own craft must be specially provided with means of producing a characteristic signal on or associated with the radar presentation, which will distinguish it from the signal produced by a hostile craft.

Such systems were referred to as "Identification of Friend from Foe," or more generally, I.F.F.

It should be noted that the I.F.F. facilities and the need for them were much more vital to the other two Services, and the Army was naturally the junior partner in this respect. Failure to recognize a hostile craft may involve the Navy in a loss equivalent to a whole division, but for an A.A. gun site the loss caused is negligible in comparison, though the vital point it is helping to protect may of course suffer. The Army, therefore, could not lead the development of I.F.F.—the needs of the other two Services more than covered those of the Army—but they assisted in the fullest measure in the development of the projects and their application.

It will be appreciated that the operation of an identification system which involves the transmission of a radio signal from our aircraft or ships must provide as much protection as may be possible against its use by the enemy to track and locate them; special precautions have to be taken to reduce to a minimum this liability. A further danger is the possibility of the enemy reproducing the means of transmitting the identification signal from his own craft and, thereby, make his attack under the protective cover afforded by Identification.

From our own point of view the working of such a system demanded that it should not be dependent on the pilot or crew of an aircraft—and similarly that is desirable for ·surface craft also—as they may well be fully occupied fighting, or coaxing a damaged craft home when the need for identification is greatest. This requires automatic functioning and was provided as an essential part of the special equipment. This automatic functioning also made it possible to cause the identification signal only to be emitted when called for by our defence radar sets; the pilot or other member of the crew, therefore, was relieved from all responsibility for identifying himself other than for ensuring that his I.F.F. appliance was switched on when coming within range of our defences and switched off when outside that range or when over enemy territory.

These considerations outline briefly the major requirements that have to be met and the remainder may be covered by the phrase, simplicity of operation, reliability, speed of reading the special signal and its attribution to the appropriate radar target echo. They produced a problem of some considerable complexity for the technicians and the solution was made no easier by the security aspect, which was of course vital to successful operation. It was not to be expected that a simple system could survive for any great length of time, but its safe life might permit of an improved and more secure system being developed for its replacement.

One other consideration must be mentioned here, and that is the primary essential principle of an effective identification system, namely, *uniformity and universal use*. We in this country, of course, with our Dominion forces and Allied personnel joining our forces, gained much practical experience of the operational essentials of such a system and had appreciated the operational limitations of our earlier systems. When America joined us in the war, we already had a much improved system under development and well advanced for introduction. They had developed a system based partly upon our experiences but mainly on theory, without large-scale operational proof of its suitability.

Agreement between the United Kingdom and the United States on the operational essentials, and the adoption of our new system for universal use by the Allies, presented problems perhaps even more difficult to solve. Agreement was, however, achieved and our system known as the Mark III was accepted for universal use, though in the South-West Pacific area America retained the right to employ its own system, known as the Mark IV. Such use of their system would rule out co-operation by our sea and air forces unless the Americans could develop and provide the necessary component assemblies to fit our radar sets to enable them to operate with their Mark IV. We could not contemplate the adoption of this system either from the operational or from the technical and production aspects since our Mark III was on the stocks and supply just starting and the Mark IV certainly had not the same degree of security.

Even when the Mark III supply was starting, we had a still more advanced system, the Mark V, under consideration and in the initial stage of tentative design. This was agreed by both countries as the future universal system to be developed and adopted. With their large capacity for scientific and technical development and their great production facilities, the U.S.A. undertook to carry out development and production for our use as well as for their own needs. This was a great boon to us as our production capacity was by then inadequate for our needs.

The extent of the American undertaking will be realized when it is appreciated that the production of the Mark V appliances would occupy over one-third of the enormous capacity in the United States for radio and radar production; the figures reached astronomical proportions.

Actually, this Mark V system never came into use even in its partial or incomplete form: it was the Mark III system that saw us through the war and served its purpose well.

The development of these identification systems can be described briefly; as has been seen there were five types that were distinguished by official Mark numbers, but of these the first never matured into practical operational form for all our radar equipment and the fifth had not emerged from the development stage by the end of the war. The fourth or early American type is of little moment, so far as this record is concerned, as it was never adopted for our use even in the South-West Pacific area.

In the earliest days of radar development the possibility of equipping our aircraft with a di-pole aerial—of a length that would be most appropriate to the radar wave-length—incorporated in the wing or fuselage structure was considered. Such a member would give the optimum reflection signal for the particular wave-length and thereby produce a signal that would be stronger or of greater amplitude than one from a normal aircraft not so equipped. To "mark" this increased signal, it was proposed to include in this special member a gap that could be opened or closed mechanically. The opening and closing could be effected automatically and the duration of the "closed" and the "open" positions could be varied to permit of some elementary coding; as the coding would be affecting the radar signal blip, the number of different codes would have to be small to make reading simple. Theoretically this appeared to be fairly simple but practically it failed on account of the number of different wave-lengths used by the various types of radar sets requiring identification.

This conception, however, was of interest in that it made use of the normal radar transmission and its reflection back to the set; it was a true radar method.

I.F.F. Mark I. It was decided that the only means of identification was to provide our own aircraft with special equipment that would give a characteristic signal on the radar presentation; in those early days this was solely a matter for the Air Ministry and its long-range determination of whether targets were friendly or hostile.

This operational need was first raised, officially, after the Home Defence exercises held in August, 1938, when none of the shorter range sets were in existence. The Bawdsey research station at once made up some models of the special equipment for fitting in aircraft and demonstrated their performance in October of that year. Some six months later 30 aircraft fitted with these sets were included in similar exercises in May, 1939, and as a result the decision was taken to go to production to provide for about 950 aircraft to be fitted. Operational use of this, the Mark I identification system, started in January, 1940.

This I.F.F. equipment fitted in aircraft consisted of a combined receiver and transmitter that would receive the pulsed transmissions from the C.H.—long-range detection chain—stations and automatically cause similar pulsed signals to be sent out in response. The C.H. radar stations would receive these return signals in addition to the ordinary aircraft reflection signals and as they were directly transmitted they were somewhat stronger and, therefore, distinguishable from the reflected signals. This type of set became known as a "Transponder" and in improved form was the basis of all I.F.F. systems subsequently used.

The Mark I responded only to transmission in the C.H. wave-band—22 to 28 Mc/s—and only those stations could receive its identification signals.

The aircraft set could transmit any one of three codes, which were not provided for security purposes but gave the means of indicating the class of aircraft—whether fighter, bomber or coastal craft.

Though limited in its use by the restriction of its very narrow wave-band, it provided for the first and most important need of identification at long range; in addition, long-range information as to the class of our aircraft identified was of some control value.

I.F.F. Mark II. In February, 1940, on completion of the provision of the Mark I equipment, the manufacturing firm was immediately instructed to prepare for the production of the improved type. This Mark II pattern had wider application as its transponder could be actuated by radar transmissions in any of three frequency-bands 22 to 30, 39 to 51 and 56 to 83 Mc/s—which covered the shorter range sets as well as the C.H. stations; the third of these bands was that allocated to the Army G.L. sets. In addition the re-transmitted signals could be sent out in any pre-selected one of six codes which in this case were primarily a security measure.

With the shorter range equipments now partially provided for, and the need for identification of surface craft as well as aircraft, the number of equipments required had risen to 13,000; this quantity as well as the more complicated equipment involved presented a considerable production problem. The design had been accepted in March, 1940, and production was so well advanced that operational use of this type, in replacement of the Mark I, commenced in October of that year, a fine production effort.

This was an advance upon the Mark I but it still could not compete with the whole series of wave-bands of sets requiring to identify targets for themselves. In 1942 a temporary addition was made to permit of identification by certain particular radar sets in aircraft and ships, which incidentally brought in certain ground stations also. Two types known as Mark II, G and N, provided for identification being extended to cover the 200 Mc/s band; it brought in the G.C.I. sets and permitted also direct identification by S.L.C. and C.D. sets and gave the Navy special identification powers that were essential to their operations. In some cases it was necessary to provide the identifying stations with special transmitters known as "interrogators" and special receivers known as "Responsors" to operate in the Mark II wave-bands; in these cases it was necessary to co-ordinate the identification signal with the radar echo signal on the presentation unit.

This method of extending the application of the identification signals to sets whose radar transmissions were not within the effective wave-band was the forerunner of future I.F.F. systems, for with the increasing number of types of radar sets requiring identification facilities, the method of direct response to the radar transmissions began to cause serious troubles in operating the system. While the Mark II was satisfactory as an interim measure it suffered from both over interrogation and from continuous interrogation. The former was due to the number of sets in an area all of whose transmissions might be actuating the transponder and the latter to the fact that any radar set required to follow the target would be actuating the transponder continuously and could not stop doing so. There was also the difficulty at the radar set end, in that the strength of the "stray" identification signals might make accurate following of a target echo signal very difficult, if not impossible, and for detection sets might obscure the echo signal and prevent early detection.

Much valuable experience in operational use of I.F.F. was gained with this

Mark II type and that experience was effectively made use of in the development of the Mark III.

I.F.F. Mark III. The Mark III system was based upon the use of a wavelength band within which no radar set was permitted to operate—with one notable exception, namely, the A.S.V. (Air detection of Surface Vessel) then in use, which was of vital importance in the anti-submarine operations and convoy protection.

This restriction on a wave-band in a zone already somewhat crowded by different types of radar equipment, emphasizes the great and growing importance of effective identification. That such restriction, initially, caused some troubles in removing equipments from that band was only to be expected, and it was fortunate that centimetric radar was already taking the place of the $1\frac{1}{2}$ to 2 metre sets thus helping to clear the I.F.F. band which was, in fact, effected with considerable rapidity.

The restricted wave-band was from 155 to 185 Mc/s and with a 3 Mc/s frequency spacing to avoid mutual interference, ten-spot frequencies were available to allocate to the different operational functions of radar in the three Services. In many cases spot frequencies could be shared by two Services where geographical separation reduced mutual interference and confusion; Army C.A. sets were able to use Naval type I.F.F. units, for example.

With the actual radar sets excluded from working within the I.F.F. band, the transponder fitted in the friendly craft had to be actuated by a special transmitter fitted to the radar sets; this was called the "interrogator." With it a "responsor" had to be provided to accept the I.F.F. signals and to present them on the display in the radar set. This display was in some cases made on the radar selector C.R.T. or in others on a separate C.R.T.; the interrogator and the responsor were served by a separate aerial, usually a beamed or directional type, though in many cases in the early days of I.F.F. Mark III, "all-round" looking or wide-angle aerials had to be used by sets already in service. The latter was the case with the British G.L. Mark III in which the radar aerial system rotated but not the cabin itself, and to provide synchronous rotation of the I.F.F. aerial would have involved a major modification. Time did not permit of this being done before the new I.F.F. system had to be brought into action in this country; later during 1943, provision was made for a simple independently mounted I.F.F. aerial giving directional interrogation, to be erected at a short distance from the set.

The "all-round" aerial method permitting discrimination only in range, caused considerable trouble by over interrogation. A further trouble was caused by sets keeping their interrogators switched on continuously, but that was soon eliminated by operating instructions requiring switching on only when a specific identification was necessary—a matter of drill.

The transponders were designed to provide any one of six different coded signals; these signals appeared on the display as various combinations of long and short markings. Any one of these six could be selected and pre-set as the signal for the day or specific codes could be allocated to particular classes of operation. Normally one code was retained, available to the pilot of an aircraft by pressing a button switch, for S O S purposes. When actuated the transponder would sweep through the whole of its band width so that its signals would be received by all the responsors operating on their allocated I.F.F. wavelengths.

This system had not a high degree of security with its limited number of codes. An equipment in one of our aircraft lost to the enemy would, of course, enable him to employ it to simulate a friendly craft though his lack of knowledge of the effective code of the day was some restriction on its use.

Certain German radar equipment operated within the I.F.F. wave-band and would, therefore, interrogate our aircraft if their transponders were switched on, but working instructions required them to be switched off while over enemy territory and only to be switched on when within effective I.F.F. range of our defences.

As has already been indicated, the Mark III system continued in use as the universal system for the Allies throughout the war and in spite of its deficiencies compared with the later system that was being developed, served us well.

I.F.F. Mark IV. As the American system, the Mark IV, was never introduced for use by British radar equipment, no particular comments are necessary. It was, in fact, less secure than the Mark III, but operated on the same principle of an actuated transponder emitting the response signals.

I.F.F. Mark V. As has been indicated the conception of the much-improved system to replace the Mark III was taking shape in 1942 and individual items of design were being considered theoretically with a background of war experience. Little practical development had been achieved, though some experimental work to prove possibilities had shown promise of leading up to the required results. With the U.S.A. undertaking full responsibility for finalizing designs and providing for production, the United Kingdom contribution to the project resolved itself into provision of practical war experience of operational needs and conditions; it supplied a team of Service, scientific and technical personnel to co-operate in America with the development of this system.

The discussions between the United States and United Kingdom groups were by no means short, nor were they always easy, but when the intricacy of the problems and the technical difficulties are considered, the time that elapsed before the main details were agreed and settled could not have been expected to be less. The eventual aim was to have "bread-board" models of the main units available early in 1945 so that we in the United Kingdom could carry out the necessary development of the displays for the different types of Service equipment and of the necessary inter-connections from these units to our radar sets. It was hoped to have all equipments in the Far Eastern Theatre of Operations—Pacific Ocean, South-West Pacific and South-East Asia Areas—early in 1946 when it would become the sole I.F.F. system in use against the Japanese. In actual fact, however, the Japanese surrendered before this system could be introduced.

This Mark V system provided a much greater degree of security; it provided for a larger number of codes and used different frequencies for the interrogation and the response signals. Its operating frequency was high which enabled finer beams to be used with greater directional accuracy and, thereby, greater discrimination between targets and less liability of obscuring or missing a hostile craft that would not be showing the I.F.F. coded signal.

The responsibility for defining the War Office policy for providing Army equipment with the means of target identification, within the agreed system (I.F.F. Mark III) for universal use, was delegated to the Director of Radar.

The policy laid down by the Director defined the provision to be made according to the functions of the equipment; all early warning, putting-on and tactical control sets whether for A.A. or C.A. uses, all A.A. searchlight control sets and those H.A.A. fire control sets capable of picking up their own targets, were to be provided with the means of identification but no other types of set. Provision was to be made in the design of the I.F.F. components for the simplest form, generally consisting of an independently mounted aerial system with a narrow beam to give discrimination in bearing as well as in range. This was to be rotated or directed independently of the main radar set and interrogation was to be made only when a specific target was to be challenged; this was to be effected by means of a special switch. The coded response display in the set was to be convenient to the radar presentation unit but not necessarily incorporated in it. Discrimination in elevation was not required nor was co-ordinated movement (electrical or mechanical) of the I.F.F. aerial with that of the radar set, except in special cases where it could be incorporated in the main aerial system without involving complication or delay in fitting. The main object, apart from the essential need for effective identification, was simplicity in design, speed of production and the possibility of using one design of independent unit for "buttoning-on" to several different types of equipment; adequacy rather than the ideal had to be accepted.

Similar arrangements for the contemplated Mark V system were defined towards the end of 1944, but electrical or mechanical control of the directional aerial independent of the radar aerial was required. The only work required for our Army equipment to be carried out in this country was the design and provision of the inter-connections between interrogator and display units suited to our types of equipment. An order of priority for the different types of Army sets for this design work was laid down, but the desirability of the greatest possible measure of uniformity was stressed. In addition, full instructions were to be prepared for R.E.M.E. to fit this facility to sets in the field. This was essential as supply would first be made to the Pacific areas direct from America for operational use against Japan.

It may be noted, though it was of no material concern to Army radar, that this advanced I.F.F. system was designed to provide an additional facility valuable to the Air and Naval Forces. This was its use for "homing" on a beacon signal. Before its introduction homing facilities required a special beacon to operate in the wave-length band of radar sets in aircraft or ship and involved a larger number of types of beacon. The use of the I.F.F. made it possible for any type of craft to operate on one type of beacon. Apart from being the Universal I.F.F. system, it also provided Universal Beaconry and the title became I.F.F. Mark V/U.N.B.—the U.N.B. representing United Nations Beaconry.

CHAPTER XXI. INTERFERENCE

Natural Causes. In earlier parts it has been mentioned that most obstructions to the passage of radio waves cause them to be reflected; ground and wave "clutter" have been referred to as confusing or obscuring echo signals from aircraft or ships. All ground surfaces may produce clutter, but it varies in intensity according to the nature, texture and aspect of its surface in the same way as light is reflected in varying intensities by different surfaces and materials. Again, birds may provide echo signals that are annoying and occasionally even sufficient to obscure signals from hostile craft. Seagulls have been followed on the radar presentation to ranges of five or more miles and clouds of small birds at times have obscured approaching air targets. This happened on several occasions on the East Coast during the later stages of the flying-bomb attacks when millions of starlings, that apparently favour Orfordness as a dormitory, were roused by the noise of approaching "doodle-bugs" and rising in mass formation seriously affected the pick-up and following of these targets. Wave clutter produced by reflections from the sea surface, particularly when rough, would often make following of targets to short range difficult, and this, incidentally, was largely responsible for one of the "gaps" in the original coast chain that is illustrated in Appendix IX. Abnormal propagation also produced echoes from objects far beyond the horizon that were at times confusing.

These and others are natural effects, not caused by the enemy but inherent in the use of radio waves and their reflections. Many of them are countered or reduced to proportions that can be worked through by means of narrow beam transmissions and careful design to reduce side lobes. Others can be eliminated by local screening, effected by a wire mesh screen close to the radar set, that prevents most of the low angle part of the transmission from reaching the short-range sources of clutter and their reflections from reaching the set. This confines the clutter to very short range and, therefore, it does not materially affect the longer range pick-up and following.

The centimetric type sets are affected in ways that are less noticeable in longer wave-length working, as for example, by reflections from storm clouds, heavy rain and other atmospheric disturbances. The longer wave-length sets, like the G.L. Mark II, on occasion pick up emanations from the sun in periods of sun-spot activity, and there were "ghost echoes" on both G.L. and C.D. sets that caused some confusion or were mistaken for target echoes, followed and reported as hostile till recognized by their rate of movement as due to some other cause or atmospheric effect.

With the very short centimetric wave sets, such as the C.A. 3 cm. set, it was possible to discriminate between different degrees of clutter from ground surfaces and to eliminate much of the weaker by means of an attenuator and to present the picture in such a way that much of the clutter did not appear on the tube screen. On the other hand these extremely short wave-length types were affected by storm-cloud reflections and, as reported from India, were occasionally "blotted out" by heavy sand storms.

Another means of eliminating ground clutter in certain cases made use of the "Doppler" effect to distinguish echoes from moving targets from static echoes. The static signals were not allowed to appear at all and the only responses shown were those due to moving objects; it was the *movement in range* of the object in relation to the radar set that produced a special signal and allowed the clutter to be removed.

Scientists were continuously engaged upon investigations for the reduction, removal or elimination of unwanted echoes and the clutter they produced; this need was always in their minds. They realized fully the difficulties of the users and the progressive development of radar equipment showed much improvement in this respect, but the need for further improvement remained when the war period closed; it is not a simple problem that still faces them.

Deliberate Jamming. Turning from natural causes to those of a more deliberate and intentional nature, a complex field of activity is opened up that is of even greater importance to the operational use of radar. Here is radar war—a war of wits and of scientific effort to attack the effectiveness of the enemy's equipment and to protect that of our own from his efforts to nullify it. In this battle of radar, this country certainly led the way and, except for occasional tactical or local successes, the enemy was always kept a few jumps behind and suffered accordingly.

Jamming and anti-jamming—the offensive and the defensive—are the main subjects to be considered and they lead on into a separate field in which radar deception plays its part, but that is seldom a concern of Army radar.

In these activities the Army's part was primarily defensive, so that its chief concern was anti-jamming measures to protect its radar from enemy attacking efforts. The Navy, also, was concerned with anti-jamming measures but had opportunities for attacking enemy radar and also to employ deception. The R.A.F., on the other hand, were able to employ counter measures against the enemy's radar to a greater extent and to attack it offensively; their offensive jamming activities were probably at least as great as their defensive anti-jamming measures and they added "spoofing" and deception to offence.

Deliberate jamming, for clarity of description, must be divided here into two classes, the first electrical or radio jamming and the second "Window," which was a code name given to an artificial means of causing confusion or of obscuring the radar screen by special reflecting material so that the radar set should clutter itself up by a large number of spurious echo signals.

Radio Jamming. In connection with radio jamming, it will be recalled that a tactical success was gained by the Germans in the escape up Channel of the *Scharnhorst, Gneisenau, Prince Eugen* and their escorting light craft. That particular success was achieved by the use of jamming transmitters established on the French coast, mainly in the vicinity of Boulogne and Cap Gris Nez; these special transmitters were operated on a band of wave-lengths suited to our Coastal Warning Chain Stations which operated on and about $1\frac{1}{2}$ metres, and the jamming spread well to either side of that wave-length. As has been seen, the few Army radar sets then operating on a centimetre wave-length were not affected. It is very doubtful whether the enemy had by then discovered this new installation and its revolutionary very high frequency working. A new radar era had opened and it is known that he had not the technical knowledge resulting from research that would enable him to produce sufficient power at the very high frequency to jam these new stations effectively.

In this area, also, the Navy undertook jamming operations against the enemy's radar controlling the fire of their long-range guns against our convoys passing through the Straits. This was successful in reducing shipping casualties, but it was a continuous battle of wave-length variations by the enemy and the automatic following of these changes by the jammers on our side.

These two examples of offensive jamming were special cases made possible by the proximity of the two coasts; in no other theatre of operations was there any jamming approaching that experienced across the Straits. Long range ground-based jamming becomes most uneconomical and uncertain at long ranges as the power output necessary to be effective increases very rapidly with range. There were indications that attempts at jamming were made and were experienced with our $1\frac{1}{2}$ metre sets in Malta; at first they were apparently from a high-power jammer established in Sicily, but later reports were received that suggested attempts were being made to employ air-borne jammers, but they were not very effective nor very intelligent.

This possibility of air-borne jamming had been recognized from the early days and a large amount of effort was naturally expended on preparations to meet it, should it occur, and to reduce its effect on our defensive equipment. The staffs of all three Services put such protective measures on the highest priority for radar research and development; no employment of air-borne jamming was indulged in by our forces during the period before our change-over to full offensive operations, as we had no wish to encourage the enemy to adopt such measures at least until the balance of offensive power was definitely in our favour.

Anti-jamming. Defensive anti-jamming measures or palliatives to reduce the effect of jamming on equipment already in service, and the design of new types of equipment to provide against enemy jamming, was a very complicated matter. It will be remembered that radar operates on the reflection of its own transmitted signals and, therefore, if someone at a distance were to *transmit* a similar signal of sufficient power, directed on to the radar receiver aerials, that signal must appear on the radar screen. It cannot be prevented from appearing unless the false signals are inadequate in power, are on a different wave-length (or the set can change its wave-length to avoid it) or the radar receiver "look-out" angle is very small and the jammer does not operate in it.

An air-borne jammer cannot be directed at individual ground sets and must, therefore, transmit broadcast or over a wide angle to embrace all sets within its range. This multiplies the power output needed to obtain effect, for the scattered and widely spaced sets will each receive only a small part of the transmitted power. That air-borne jamming can be effected is true, but a very large effort is involved if it is to be effective.

In order to devise the best measures for A/J protection it was essential to determine how best to effect jamming. The scientific staff allocated to A/J work at A.D.R.D.E. was divided into two parts, one to devise the worst possible forms of jamming and the other to devise the means of defeating it, or the most effective palliatives to permit radar sets to continue to operate in spite of the interference. It was not a case of just reproducing the forms of jamming that the enemy had employed but of providing against more effective possibilities that he might conceive, if he had the intelligence and capacity to go into the matter to the limit.

R. G. Friend of A.D.R.D.E. led these investigations and produced a variety of very effective jammers that could make the radar operators' task most difficult, if not impossible. Not only were the operators disturbed but the scientific staff devising the means of combating jamming were caused many headaches. This work was certainly done most fully and effectively and the investigations, in fact, went considerably further than the enemy was ever able to apply in practice. Apart from the Army aspect, the work of this group at A.D.R.D.E. was of considerable value to the Navy and the R.A.F. both in A/J measures and in offensive jamming.

This record is not the place for detailed consideration of the different A/J devices that were applied to our sets nor of the various means of jamming possible—the reader would be involved in highly technical matters and fogged with "chokes," "filters," "back-biasing," "short time constant couplings," etc., that are of little interest to other than technicians. Here it should suffice if a short general description of the forms of jamming and the results of the protective measures are noted.

The first form of jamming is by C.W., continuous wave transmissions on the carrier wave frequency of the radar; this is what might be called the brute force method, which achieves its effect unintelligently by the high power transmitted. With comparative low power reaching the radar set, the effect is to cause target echoes to appear below, as well as above the time base and as the received power increases the true echo signals are reduced until they appear only below the time base or disappear altogether.

This rather crude form can be improved and become somewhat more refined by modulation; as the modulation frequency is increased so the pattern on the C.R.T. screen varies from a series of rather dithery lines across the tube, through deep criss-cross lines to a phalanx of vertical lines, and it becomes increasingly difficult, if not impossible, to recognize true target echoes.

Other forms of jamming are produced by "noise" modulation and by frequency modulation; the former is one of the worst forms to compete with, but it is also considerably more difficult to produce effectively.

All the forms of jamming produce their characteristic patterns on the screen and these were given pet names by the operators or were named by the scientists, so that reporting of the type of jamming experienced could indicate simply the particular form and enable experts to assist, if necessary, or the group of scientists, maintaining a continual watch for enemy jamming, to pick up and analyse its nature. Some line diagrams of the appearance of the radar presentation when some forms of jamming are being experienced, with their pet names, are shown in Fig. 9.

The protective measures, applied to the earlier types of G.L. and warning sets, generally comprised two alternative components that could be brought into action when needed and, dependent upon the actual type of jamming being experienced, the operator could select whichever gave the better results. All the early pattern of sets had been provided with the means of meeting C.W. jamming in their original design and some additional protection, made available by the investigations referred to above, was provided for those types still required to be kept in action.

The application of these devices was not possible for S.L.C.; the make-up of this searchlight control equipment did not permit of these devices being added. A different type of appliance with a different object was provided; it did not attempt to eliminate the jamming but instead aimed at using it to indicate the position of the enemy aircraft that was emitting the jamming signals, so that it could be eliminated by our night fighters. In effect this appliance was a "jamming locator" and not an anti-jamming device. When switched on it employed the emissions from the jamming aircraft to produce a blip on the selector tube instead of the blip normally formed by the reflection from the aircraft; this enabled the searchlight to be continuously directed at the jammer. This device was known as "Jill"—the phonetic J/L—and so named was suitable for association with "Elsie."

To illustrate the action of the J/L device a line diagram of the picture on the signal selector tube of S.L.C. is given in Fig. 10, to show one form of jamming and its effect with the J/L switch off and with it on.

It must be appreciated that no S.L.C., with "Jill" switched on, can operate to follow any target other than the aircraft emitting the jamming, if that jamming is sufficiently powerful. As it can give no range, it is of no value to apply Jill to warning sets or to fire control equipment; its only object is to direct the searchlight *towards* the source of jamming to help a fighter to find the jammer aircraft. The jammer could stand off or cruise round out of range while other aircraft approached undetected.

Apart from these special additions as palliatives—for they cannot be said to have eliminated the effects of jamming without loss of efficiency by the equipment itself—there are other aids to A/J protection. Some are available in the set as designed and others inherent in the nature of the equipment and its characteristics; of the former the power to make small changes in the working frequency of individual sets is of considerable value and enhances the value of the added measures in many cases. Narrow beam working was of assistance in that jamming out of the actual beam needed a very great additional power to be effective, which would of course be a considerable handicap to airborne jamming, at least. An actual comparison of effective performance for the same jamming effect in, and 90 degrees off, the beam of a particular set illustrates this point. A 100 watt jammer giving effective results when *in* the narrow beam at a range of 90 miles can only produce equal effect when 90 degrees off the beam, at a range of $\frac{1}{2}$ mile. It is obvious that effective jamming of a number of sets scattered over a wide area would involve such a vast effort as to make it almost impracticable.

This narrow-beam working was a characteristic of the centimetric type of Army equipment and, in addition, the extremely high frequency at which they operated involved the use of components including valves, that were highly frequency-conscious, and largely unaffected by external emissions that were even slightly off their specific frequency. In this respect this centimetric revolution in radar technique automatically provided a measure of security from jamming. It may be added that a halt was not called on this degree of security, but further advances were made by provision for varying the frequency by a tunable magnetron should the need for further protection arise; they only became available, however, in the last stages of the war and then only in very limited quantities.

Mutual Interference. Before leaving this aspect of interference, it must be mentioned that a large proportion of the cases of interference reported by stations in the earlier days were attributable to effects other than those of the enemy. In Fig. 9 diagram (*f*) illustrates the type known as "running rabbits," which was due to the effect produced by one of our own radar sets on its neighbour; a case of mutual interference. Careful planning was necessary to arrange that adjacent sets of the same type operated on slightly different frequencies— in the case of the G.L. Mark II sets a separation of 3 megacycles was found sufficient to prevent undue mutual interference; every set was equipped with the necessary critical length feeders to enable it to operate on either of two well-separated frequencies, and seven different frequencies were available to this type. Similar arrangements were made for other types according to their natures and needs. With the entry of American equipment into the field and in this country, there was a good deal of adjustment necessary; in particular their searchlight control radar, S.C.R. 602, was particularly awkward in the vicinity of our S.L.C.

It was not only other radar sets that produced interference, other sources caused trouble, perhaps worst of all being badly adjusted I.F.F. interrogators and transponders. Apart from the planning mentioned, careful maintenance and frequent check of all forms of radio sets was essential; a continuous watch and monitoring of transmissions had to be maintained to analyse the nature of interference and determine its source. In this the Services and the G.P.O. worked in the closest collaboration.

This jamming and interference and particularly its threat, naturally produced many problems and involved much effort in experiment and design and very considerable production capacity. There is, however, no question that all this was well worth while even though the full jamming battle was never joined. The menace was present right up to the time when the enemy was forced upon the defensive and could not apply effort to attack our radar seriously by radio methods. He did, however, attempt to attack our defence radar by the interference method known as "Window," and achieved some local success, but not sufficient to neutralize our defences entirely.

Interference—Window. "Window" does not depend upon the transmission of radio waves to create disturbance but achieves its object by providing a mass of reflecting material in the air so that the radar set itself creates such a quantity of reflection echoes that it clutters up its own screen and confuses or obscures the true target echoes.

The name "Window," as has been mentioned, was but a code name that conveyed no indication of its subject or nature; this was one of the security measures taken to guard against premature disclosure to the enemy. The maintenance of secrecy in regard to this method and its possibilities was of great importance and all experiments, trials and development were conducted with that background. The intention was only to employ it against German radar on a large scale at the start to support important offensive bombing operations and to obtain the maximum effect by ensuring that its use should come as a surprise. It was realized that much of our own radar equipment was wide open to this form of interference and that retaliatory measures were to be expected. It was, however, to be anticipated that the surprise employment of Window would give us at least a short period in which to exploit our advantage without serious counter effects by the enemy. The decision as to when first to make use of this device was taken by the Defence Committee of the War Cabinet on the recommendations of the Chiefs of Staff. The primary object was to reduce the casualty rate of our bombers in the heavy, continuous and concentrated attacks on the German war potential and communications. That it was effective was proved both by the reduced casualty rate and by the consternation of the enemy at the disturbance caused to their radar defences, which was apparent from intercepted radio reports and conversations.

The offensive use of this device was of course not a matter for the Army, but defensive measures for the protection of our radar against the enemy use of Window were very much their concern. Here again the Army aspect of protection made it necessary for the A.D.R.D.E. to investigate the optimum type and size of Window material and the most effective tactics for employing it. This was done in conjunction with their opposite numbers in T.R.E. and to the A.D.R.D.E. was due a large measure of the credit for the development of the best methods of tactical employment of Window.

The form of Window that was devised to give the most effective results was made of metallized paper and it was cut to form strips of particular dimensions. For maximum efficiency, that is for the maximum echo clutter for a given weight of material, the metallized paper strips had to be of a length which would be a half-wave dipole for the particular wave-length of the radar equipment to be attacked. The width of the strips would be decided by practical—manufacturing and handling—considerations, and to some extent by the band of frequencies to be dealt with, but it would only be a fraction of the length.

Strips cut to suit the wave-length of a particular radar set would also be partially effective against equipments using shorter wave-lengths, but it loses its effectiveness against sets on wave-lengths that are appreciably longer than that for which the strips are designed. The method of use to give effective results is to provide the material in packets which open up when dropped from the aircraft; each of these packets must contain a sufficient number of strips to produce a combined signal equal to that from an aircraft itself. The number needed in each packet varies according to the radar frequency aimed at—for the 5 metre G.L. Mark II only a few are needed as compared to the 10 cm. G.L. Mark III, which would require packets containing many thousands of small strips.

When dropped in rapid succession the packets open up and the dipole strips spread out gradually and sink slowly. How long they remain sufficiently dense for each packet to give the full signal response depends on the wind strength, but it may be 10 minutes or more and the rate of fall is only about 250 feet per minute; their horizontal travel is, of course, that of the wind at the height concerned.

Apart from the necessary density of strips to give a response equivalent to that of an aircraft, there is also an optimum density of package dropping, to produce echoes at all ranges and in every direction, so that all sets concerned would be completely cluttered up and made temporarily useless. This is a matter that is dependent upon the particular type of set and its design—matters of beam width, pulse width, receiver design and of the form of presentation used. It is unnecessary to go into details here but the narrower the beam the less is it affected; the shorter the pulse width the greater the chance the radar has to observe through gaps in their spreading pattern. As to presentation, all that need be said is that the P.P.I. type is more seriously affected than the range tube form; the latter has the power of discrimination between signals of different sizes, whereas the former necessarily marks—and retains for some time—the markings of all signals of and above the minimum strength so that there is no discrimination possible. In Fig. 5, showing diagrammatically the P.P.I. presentation, the target marked C is shown as just emerging from a small patch of clutter formed by Window. (See also Illustration No. 17.)

The above gives some indication of various methods of reducing the effects of Window attack by instrumental means; some were not applicable to the older types of equipment. In new designs the aim of the designer may be reduced to the simple conception of making it necessary for the enemy to use the highest possible density of dropping to achieve complete cluttering up, or even to make it impracticable. The user must try to work through it and though much of this clutter is most annoying and confusing, it is a matter of intelligence and determination on the part of the operator to keep the equipment in action as effectively as possible, and to obtain results in spite of the enemy's efforts.

One final point should be appreciated and that is that a variety of types of equipment on well-separated wave-lengths is in itself a measure of protection. Window jamming may be practical against any one of them but it can hardly be considered against all of them, at one time, at maximum efficiency. There is also the fact that advantage may be obtained in some cases when a large number of similar sets are in use in an area, even if all are on the same wave-length. Unless the whole sky over the area is completely covered at effective density of Window—a practically impossible proposition—some sets are likely to be less affected than others. There were specific cases in the war where, in the presence of hostile Window or "Duppel" as the Germans called it—aimed at our equipment in the $1\frac{1}{2}$ metre wave-length class, particularly the G.C.I. and S.L.C., some of the latter were able to continue working with fair efficiency owing to their dispersion, though the few G.C.I. sets were made practically ineffective. On the night of 21st/22nd January, 1944, when the enemy supported his attacks by Window dropping, individual searchlights were able to illuminate enemy aircraft and as it was a clear night, other searchlights could pick up visually the targets so illuminated. With the G.C.I. badly affected the S/Ls provided the necessary indications for our night fighters, with very good results.

It is not the intention of this general description of Window, and the mention of palliatives and means of working through its effect, to imply that this form of interference was anything but a very serious menace. It is certain that had the enemy applied such methods in the days of our defensive struggle, we should have suffered much more severely. Much of our development and progress in design of radar was influenced, to some extent at least, by this potential menace, though the primary influence at the time was the improvement of efficiency for normal use of the radar equipment. As has been seen, that improvement did in itself contribute towards the countering of this form of attack; future designs have to take it into serious consideration. The need for human intelligence to aid automatic radar through trouble of this sort is certainly one of the essentials for fire control purposes. Faced with the problems of Window, the scientists have no easy task to tackle.

CHAPTER XXII. MINOR APPLICATIONS

The preceding chapter has indicated how radar equipment can be attacked by two different methods; one by deliberate radio emissions to produce a pattern on the radar display that will obscure or confuse the normal echo signals, and the other by providing masses of reflecting material so that the radar itself clutters up its own presentation. In that chapter and in earlier ones, the adverse effects of unwanted echoes from natural objects, from ground surfaces, waves, buildings, etc., have been stressed.

These effects may be applied in some cases for useful purposes though generally at a much lower degree of intensity or of density of the signals. Some of these uses emerged from the investigations carried out with the object of reducing the effects of enemy action and some of them from the general need for reducing clutter. Some of the inherent powers of radar to induce and accept echoes from objects other than ships or aircraft were developed for specific purposes, and the power to accept injected signals as in radio jamming was also made use of for training purposes.

Special Reflectors. Artificial reflecting surfaces, which may be said to have their adverse counterpart in Window, were used from the earliest days for experimental and test purposes. In the first instance they took the form of small free balloons carrying crossed dipoles appropriate to the wave-length of the set under test. Moving slower than aircraft, they provided the means of comparing radar range readings with those of visual instruments; later they formed the initial targets for the development of the methods of angular measurement and of comparing them with visual methods. More accurate proof of performance was of course provided with aircraft as targets and Kine-theodolites to check photographically the accuracy and the continuity of accurate reading.

With equipment in the hands of the troops, the need for field check of the collimation, or agreement between the axis of the radar set and that of the visual instruments for fire control, was met by the use of small captive balloons with a metalized surface forming part of the R.E.M.E. "Calibration" parties' equipment. Calibration was the term generally used, but to the gunner "Collimation" was more correct for describing this functional check and adjustment. Some difficulties were experienced with these balloons due to the confusing reflections from their cables unless special non-reflecting nylon cables were provided. These were overcome later by the use of an oscillator or signal generator suspended from a balloon, producing a stronger signal than the reflections.

At a later stage when centimetric radar was in being—though some of the older types of equipment also made use of them—free balloons carrying all-round-looking "corner" or tetrahedral reflectors became the normal collimation targets for field use. As the relationship between these aerial reflectors and "Window" was so obvious, great care had to be taken to prevent them falling into enemy held territory; special restrictions had to be placed upon their use if the conditions of the wind made it possible that some of them might be carried far enough to fall into enemy hands. The "corner" reflectors did not give any direct indication of the actual critical wave-length of the sets for which they were used, and as soon as the R.A.F. had employed "Window" operationally against the enemy, the restrictions were relaxed.

Similar aerial targets were employed for determining meteorological data and were most effective; in fact, radar with their aid materially helped the determination and provision of meteor information in the field. With the G.L. Mark III type of equipment, single station working was possible, as the set could track these free balloons accurately beyond the range of visual instruments and to great heights irrespective of light, fog, or cloud. Wind direction forces at different heights were, therefore, obtainable at any time desired from a single point or station, so that local up-to-date information could always be made available.

These corner reflectors erected as survey beacons showed promise of providing the means of speeding up artillery survey by making observations possible in darkness or bad visibility, and even of assisting larger-scale triangulation. Their capacity for giving maximum reflection generally marked them from surrounding ground clutter and made them distinctive. That their useful employment for these purposes could not be achieved before the end of the war was due to the radar sets rather than to the reflectors. The degree of accuracy of the azimuth or bearing readings was not high enough for accurate survey, but the attainment of an appropriate degree of accuracy in a set specially designed for the purpose is not impracticable as a future development—a combined visual and radar beacon might simplify rapid survey in the future.

Injected Signals. Similar methods to those employed for radio jamming were used with very low power from small sets that could be used for "on site" training and practising operators on their own service equipment. Such sets were, of course, quite distinct from the more elaborate trainers provided for schools as "class room" trainers. These small field trainers could be carried by one man walking about within 20 or 30 yards of the radar set, and its signal transmitted through a light cable provided the bearing operator with signals on his tube for practice in following accurately and smoothly; others of somewhat larger size could be wheeled about in a special "pram."

Range-following practice needed slightly more elaborate devices in the trainers, as the range signals had to be made to simulate the time taken by the outgoing pulse and the return echo from an aircraft. This was provided for by means of a "delayed pulse oscillator," a device which was actuated by the pulsed transmission from the radar set but imposed a slight delay in giving its answering signal. The degree of delay—a very minute fraction of time—could be varied to provide appropriate signals on the range tube to represent echo signals from aircraft at different ranges. In some cases the signals injected into the radar sets were conveyed by cable from the field trainer and in others by low power radio transmissions accepted by the aerials and receiver of the set. By the use of a tethered balloon and a means of raising and lowering a signal generator, or delayed pulse oscillator suspended from it, the elevation operator could also be given training and practice, but this was mainly intended for S.L.C. training.

Another useful employment deriving from radar jamming or interference from another radar set, was of value operationally in watching the activities of enemy coastal radar across the Straits of Dover. In the same way as "Jill" was used with S.L.C. equipment to locate or point to a jamming aircraft, so the powerful centimetric sets of the Dover defences were able to pick up signals from active enemy radar equipment (or harmonics of their transmissions) and thereby obtain accurate bearings on active sets. We could, therefore, observe the periods of activity of each enemy set and this became of considerable importance during the R.A.F. offensive operations in preparation for the D-day landings; it gave a good check on the effectiveness of our air attacks on these radar stations which it was necessary to obliterate, or put out of action, in order to reduce the enemy's appreciation of the real points where the major landings would be made, and to deny him effective warning of the approach of our invasion craft.

Normal Reflections. Coming to reflections from objects other than the normal aircraft and ship targets, the location of shell splashes for coastal artillery fire correction has already been described. It will be recalled that the earliest observation of these reflections was made during trials at Bawdsey in 1939, and at the same time reflections from the shell itself during its flight had been detected and air bursts also which caused some confusion occasionally in H.A.A. fire control radar operation.

The ability to observe and locate accurately the burst of a shell in the air by radar was of considerable value in the test of time fuzes. With the aid of radar, the fuze scale shoots could be carried out independent of cloud conditions or of visibility and at maximum heights; in the case of the radio proximity fuze, tests of premature action and of self-destruction could also be made. This was of considerable value as a time saver with accuracy comparable with visual observation; this method appeared likely to supersede the acoustic method.

The reflections from projectiles in flight as distinct from those from their bursts, was made use of in the first instance to develop means of testing the muzzle velocity of shells in the field by tracking them for a short distance after discharge. The ballistics of the weapon and its projectile are, of course, affected by wear in the barrel of the piece, and recalibration at intervals is essential if accuracy of shooting is to be maintained. Generally this involved periodical check of the weapon by an Ordnance Workshop Detachment with special apparatus, but means for making radar ballistic tests in the field at the gun site tended to save much time and disturbance. A radar set of adequate accuracy and mobility, so that it can be moved up to the guns in position, could provide for this need. Trials were carried out with an existing type of radar set, but one designed for the purpose would seem desirable. It is possible that the capabilities of radar to aid ballistic tests may be exploited still further with advantage in the future.

One of the most interesting applications of this trajectory tracking by radar was that employed towards the end of the war for detection and determination of the trajectory of individual V.2 rockets, the large Stratosphere rockets used by the Germans intensively against this country. A number of types of set were tried, but the most successful proved to be the early Army 5 metre type, G.L. II. This excellently designed and engineered equipment was specially modified and deployed on selected sites on our Eastern and South-Eastern coasts and also in Belgium and Holland for this purpose. A large part of the work and the operation of tracking was carried out by A.A. Command in conjunction with A.O.R.G. and special communications for rapid reporting were installed, including a cable link across the Straits. An officer of A.A. Command, reporting upon the effect of radar and its development on the operations of the Command throughout the war, remarks, "Perhaps the finest story of all is the use of radar against the V.2 rockets . . ."

Early warning of discharge of a rocket was immediately notified to other watching stations, two or more of which would track part of the trajectory, or select points on it, and these co-ordinated plots would be extrapolated to give the later part of the downward course and the arrival area—not a pin point—could be determined. From the tremendous speed of travel of these projectiles the length of warning time that could have been given was too small for any effective local protective action to be taken even if instantaneous transmission could have been arranged. Plans were made for testing the possibility of offensive action to destroy these devastating projectiles in the air by close concentrations of shell splinters from bursts of H.A.A. shell in zones through which the trajectory would pass; this, of course, involved trajectory tracking and extrapolation to determine these zones. This method was not tested practically before the rocket attacks were stopped by the firing sites being overrun by our forces in Northern Europe. Whether action of this nature could provide any really effective answer to such weapons has yet to be proved —there is also the question of whether the lethality of the falling shell fragments would not produce as high casualty figures among the population as the V.2s themselves.

In this connexion, though from the opposite points of view, the employment of radar for guiding a projectile on to a specific target has received considerable attention; this also requires trajectory tracking to bring the projectile on to its target. The primary problems of all these projects are not radar nor radio matters but lie in the aero-dynamic field; they are inter-Service matters and not purely Army concerns.

A number of minor applications of radar to Army purposes have been mentioned and there were others, if not in being at least in the possibility stage. Enough has been said to indicate how radar was increasingly entering Army service apart from the major applications that have been described in the earlier Parts of this record. There is, however, one matter of future potential value that should be mentioned here. This is the detection of particular targets from the air or from the ground by discrimination between their echoes and those from ground surfaces or other unwanted reflecting objects.

Discrimination of Ground Targets. At the first meeting of the W.O. Radar Committee before the war, a question was raised as to the possibility of detecting from the air large metal structures, such as an important bridge; at that time it seemed to be most unlikely. Later during the first half of the war this possibility was raised again in the hope of being able to detect concentrations of tanks, and with the considerable advances by then made in radar technique, trials were carried out by Cockcroft in conjunction with T.R.E., who provided an aircraft fitted with a 10 cm. H_2S equipment—a down-looking set that could distinguish built-up areas from open country and aid recognition of bombing targets. No success was achieved with tanks, even in open country, and it is doubtful if the 3 cm. type, used later for bomber target recognition, which gave improved definition of towns, water courses, etc., was ever used for this purpose in the Northern European campaign.

About the same time that 3 cm. working was being considered for R.A.F. purposes, A.D.R.D.E. had demonstrated their experimental set on this wavelength at Llandudno (see Chapter XVII) which later became the C.A. No 1, Mark IV. This showed that the set could discriminate between different degrees of ground clutter and could, in fact, provide a picture on its display screen that could be related to the ground features shown on a map or chart. The use of this by the Navy was suggested as a means of assisting approach to and recognition of selected landing sites on the enemy's coastline, but the use of the R.A.F. H$_2$S type had already been arranged for this purpose.

This set, however, did give promise of being able to discriminate between degrees of clutter, and opened up the possibility of extending the utility of radar for the Army into the field of ground operations; these are described in the next chapter. Incidentally, it may be noted that the A.S.V. set used by aircraft could detect surface craft and submarines from the air, but in this case the sea surface produced more or less uniform clutter or background which could be eliminated from the "picture" so that detection of ship echoes was not obscured.

CHAPTER XXIII. FIELD ARMY APPLICATIONS

Towards the end of 1943, experiments and investigations were carried out at A.D.R.D.E. with narrow beam centimetric types of set that were primarily intended for anti-aircraft or coast artillery purposes, and new possibilities began to emerge. These investigations were aimed at the reduction of clutter effects and the means of discriminating between different intensities of clutter. They also aimed at distinguishing moving objects from static bodies, and a third had as its object the improvement of the means of tracking the trajectories of projectiles in flight, particularly those of the smaller shells and mortar bombs, and to locate ground bursts.

The scientists at A.D.R.D.E. soon appreciated that these possibilities might be translated into practical propositions of value to the armies in the field, and brought them, through the Ministry of Supply, to the notice of the Director of Radar, War Office. The value of such radar aids to field artillery was immediately appreciated and the work was urged forward on high priority.

Thus was the gate opened into a new and most important field for radar to assist the field armies in their operations. Unfortunately, however, the development and production of equipments for this purpose was so delayed by the inadequacy of the production capacity by then available for Army purposes, that none of these types of equipment were supplied to 21 Army Group before the end of hostilities. Apart from the failure to help operations against the enemy, this delay denied to our designers the truest guide to the value of such sets to the troops.

For Army radar this failure was almost the biggest disappointment of all. Here, at last, was the opportunity for it to take on a truly offensive role, putting it on a par with Naval and Air Force radar, but adequate production facilities could not be provided in spite of the urge and pressure put upon this operational requirement.

At the beginning of 1944 there were three separate types of experimental set that were selected for development at high priority for use in the field. The first of these was intended for the detection and location of ground burst shells in relation to some specific point recognizable on the radar screen; this point might be merely a "witness" point in some relation to a specific target or preferably the target itself. This type was given the title of F.A. No. 1 in the radar equipment family, the F.A. of course representing Field Artillery to distinguish it from the A.A. and the C.A. types.

The second was commonly known as "Watch-dog," as its function was to detect and give audible, visual or other form of warning of detection of moving objects; it became officially F.A. No. 2. The third form of equipment, F.A. No. 3, was intended for the location of enemy guns and mortars by tracking the trajectories of their shells or bombs and determining rapidly the origin of the trajectory, which would be the site of the weapon firing them.

Each of these types required different radar composition and technique; they were designed individually and as time was of the greatest importance, no attempt to combine the functions of any two of them was permitted, though it was appreciated that such combination might well be the ultimate answer. The development of each type must be dealt with separately in their numerical sequence.

Field Artillery Fire Correction. This set was a direct replica of C.A. No. 1 Mark IV, but for the fully mobile form in which it was required for use with the field armies it was modified or rearranged so that it could be installed complete in a half-tracked vehicle for the necessary cross-country performance and a measure of armoured protection.

This set operated on a 3 cm. wave-length and produced a very narrow beam transmission; this radar beam was moved rapidly 3 degrees on either side of the centre line of the aerial system and thereby scanned continuously an area of ground limited by the vertical spread of the beam and the lateral scan angle. In addition the traversing of the aerial or set as a whole provided the means of sweeping over any part of the area around the site on which the set was in action, and the whole of the swept area was subject to the detailed scanning as the set traversed.

The presentation of the echo signals obtained was of the gridded form as Figure 7. The duration of each individual echo signal is kept to the minimum possible to avoid afterglow, but the rapid scan of the beam repeats the signals continuously. This confines the echo signals to the minimum area of the tube screen and reduces their furry outlines to some extent. In addition the contrast between different degrees of strength of the echo signals can be accentuated and the unwanted weaker echoes can be eliminated or reduced by attenuation of the signals.

The stronger echo signals remain on the presentation and may be co-ordinated with ground features, particular objects or targets, though direct recognition of a target without other aid, such as visual observations, is rare. Once a particular signal group or "blob" has been identified as a particular point or object it can be noted and used for reference as a witness point or a means of fixing the radar picture with the map or temporary operational grid. If set up in daylight and "fixed," the radar set can operate and observe by day or by night, in fog or in smoke without difficulty.

In the same way as the C.A. No. 1 set, "Charlie," could locate shell splashes in the sea, this F.A. No. 1 could observe shell bursts on the ground and locate them equally accurately in relation to the target or witness-point. In the case of the shell splash in the sea the majority of the echo signal appears to emanate from the splash itself, while in the case of ground burst shell it was at first doubtful if the major part of the echo came from the fragments of the shell or from the earth thrown up, but later trials showed that the thrown-up earth was the primary cause of the echo signals.

This capacity for observation and location of shell bursts in relation to a target or other known point, provides the means of correction of fire in unseen conditions, and of doing so with great accuracy.

The identification of static target "blobs" on the screen is, as has been said, rare unless some special strength of signal or other feature distinguishes it. Movement can be classed as a special feature in this connection and that is recognizable in the radar picture by comparison with static echoes, though the nature of the moving object may not be so definitely identified. This may be of value by night or in bad visibility as the movement can be plotted and fire directed upon the future position of the moving objects for an accurate predicted concentration and results can be observed.

Early trials were carried out at the School of Artillery, Larkhill, in February, 1944, and the assistance and co-operation of Colonel H. W. Taylor of that School materially expedited both the trials and the practical appreciation of the possibilities of radar aids to artillery in the field. Kempton and his party from

A.D.R.D.E. were able to demonstrate with the experimental set that moving vehicles could be detected and tracked at ranges up to about 20,000 yards, and that ground bursts of 5·5 in. shell could be seen and located at over 14,000 yards. It was also found possible to discriminate between different intensities of clutter and that some clutter "blobs" could be identified with tanks, vehicles and guns and others could be attributed to particular ground features or structures.

In the open plain country these early results were rapidly improved upon with experience, and the direction of fire of 25 pdr. as well as 5·5 in. guns on to a recognized target direct, or by witness-point shooting, and the correction of fire by observation of the shell bursts, became a practicable proposition. It was also found possible to locate air-bursts, and development in that direction might, it was considered, be of value in connection with the use of radio proximity fuzes by field artillery.

While recognizing that the tactical employment of this new aid to field Army weapons was as yet in its infancy, its potential value was so considerable that the War Office at once pressed for urgent development into production form on the highest priority. In doing this it was urged that all elaboration or modification not absolutely essential for reliability should be omitted from the first models and the design, generally, should be identical in its radar composition with the C.A. No. 1 model used in the trials. The set had, however, to be housed in a vehicle more suited to work in the field and with a cross-country performance on a line with that of field artillery weapons. This required some modification in lay-out and special construction for the vehicle body to accommodate it and to carry the armoured protection which was considered essential. The decision on the type of vehicle to be used took some time as the supply of suitable vehicles, in view of the urgent demands of 21 Army Group for completing their invasion needs, was not a simple matter. This naturally caused some delay in development and further delays occurred later in attempting to meet the degree of armoured protection that was required. A definite requirement for provision, however, was stated by the War Office at the beginning of July, 1944, for 12 hand-made or "crash" production sets for the earliest possible delivery, to be followed by 40 sets in full production form.

Early forecasts of delivery given by the Ministry of Supply—though not by the Production Liaison branch with M.A.P.—suggested that the 12 hand-made sets might be expected to start deliveries before the end of the year.

Delays and postponements were continually being notified, and at the end of 1944 the first delivery for test was given officially for the first time as June, 1945; by the end of January it had gone back to September with completion of the order by the end of that year, but in August it was hoped that perhaps the first set for the War Office might be ready in February, 1946. None of these sets got into the war. A pitiful record and a disappointment to all concerned.

It should be mentioned that attempts were made to provide some few sets, in the C.A. No. I cabin trailer form, for extended operational trials at the School of Artillery and for training purposes. The War Office diverted some of these sets from the C.A. role but the number available was very small; being entirely without protective armouring they were not suitable for full use in the field against the enemy, but some trials were attempted by 21 Army Group in rather difficult country.

Detection of Movement. The second type of Field Army radar set—"Watch Dog"—provided for the detection of movement in any zone in which its beam could search. It has been mentioned that the F.A. No. 1 set could detect movement, but it was not suitable for searching an area for movement, as its results were dependent on recognizing the relative movement of clutter "blobs" and, therefore, needed time for that recognition involving a series of angular steps to cover an arc.

Watch Dog employed the Doppler effect and applied it to the pulsed transmissions of a standard centimetric type of radar equipment, a medium power version of the famous N.T. 271. With all static echoes cleared from its presentation, or rather their signals neutralized, the signals of echoes from *moving* objects only could appear and actuate the warning apparatus that was connected to the set. These signals could be used to light a warning light, to operate a buzzer or whistle or other audible warning signal.

The movement to be detected by this method must involve change in range from the set—a vehicle moving along the circumference of a circle of which the set is the centre is *not* detectable—and naturally the maximum rate of change of range is given by a vehicle or other object moving directly towards or away from the set.

The Doppler signals give no accurate indication of range, but the narrow beam spread of the transmission from the set gives the direction in which movement is detected. The set being capable of sweeping can be used for searching for movement and it can, therefore, act not only as a warning appliance but also as an indicator to a set of the F.A. No. 1 type, of the direction in which to observe for the accurate location and tracking of the moving target; in other words, it can act as a sentry and as a "putter-on." Of itself, it has value simply as a warning of movement in a certain area, as, for example, on a known stretch of road used by supply columns, and can, therefore, provide for profitable harassing fire by night, as, if previously registered by the guns and observed by this radar set, fire would only be opened when it was known that targets were using that particular piece of road. Its use, however, in conjunction with the F.A. No. 1 is a much more effective method, as not only can the fire be directed upon any point where movement is observed but the point of engagement and time can be predicted and the effect of fire can be observed.

This radar set was contained in a small rotatable cabin, on one side of which was mounted its paraboloid aerial reflector; one operator only was required. The small cabin could be mounted upon a light truck chassis and, to reduce the height of the cabin, it was accepted that an arc of search of some 220 degrees would be adequate; this allowed for the blanked arc due to the driver's cab and protection. For the future, if this type were to be used, any standard form of light vehicle could be adopted. Movement could be detected up to ranges of 30,000 yards, provided no crests or other ground features intervened.

In the same way as in the case of F.A. No. 1 pressure was exerted by the War Office to get 12 sets produced rapidly and hopes, encouraged by the Ministry of Supply, put the end of 1944 as the time that they would be available. A definite order on the Ministry was placed in July, 1944, for 40 of these sets to follow the 12 "crash" or pre-production sets. Similar difficulties and delays occurred but eventually one set was supplied in March, 1945, for test and two more by April, but none of them had overcome the technical troubles that arose in the production form which caused further delay. By August, with the European side of the war finished, the order for 40 was reduced to 17 and two months later to 9, of which 3 were for further experiment and development by the A.D.R.D.E.

This set in a properly designed form did not get into the war and the opportunity for practical proof of its value was lost. One experimental set was for a short time used with 21 Army Group, but proved unreliable even in the hands of special personnel, and no true test of its capabilities could be made; actually the unreliability of this particular model tended to give a wrong impression of its potential value.

Before leaving this sorry story, it may be mentioned that Kempton had demonstrated the capacity of Doppler working on 3 cm. pulsed transmissions in some experimental tests at Malvern in 1943; these gave definite short-range detection of vehicles, cyclists and individual men in an area ordinarily completely swamped by clutter. Some two years earlier, also, the Marconi Company had demonstrated a mock-up of a Doppler set on 50 cm. wave-length that could give warning of moving cars to a range of about one mile.

Neither of these trials could justify an operational requirement for development for such short-range use at that time, when all efforts had to be concentrated on the urgent high priority needs. Kempton's work, however, formed part of a general investigation of a basic character, that aimed at reducing clutter effects or permitting working through such effects, and as such was rightly continued by the Ministry.

Mortar Location. The third type of radar set intended for field Army use aimed at tackling the mortar menace; these mortars had become a major factor in field operations and were responsible for a large proportion of the total casualties inflicted on our troops. Any method by which this menace could be reduced would have been most welcome and a variety of means were investigated. A few that gave some promise of useful results were given high priority for development, among them being the application of radar to this purpose.

The detection of shells in flight by radar had been possible from the early days and it was known that the trajectory of a projectile could be traced and plotted. If the plot of a part of the trajectory could be extended backwards to its origin with sufficient accuracy the location of the weapon could be determined and the weapon dealt with appropriately. This was the general aim at A.D.R.D.E. in the experimental development of a radar set to meet this need.

The mortar and its bomb presented special problems. First the mortars could pack up and move position rapidly and, therefore, location and transmission of information had to be effected in the shortest possible time if effective counter-action were to be taken. Then the mortar bomb itself, in size and shape, was not such a good reflecting object as the larger shells, or at any rate was not so good on some wave-lengths; there were other factors also that made special investigations necessary before development could be commenced.

Trials in the later part of 1943 with a 10 cm. G.L. III showed that the bomb could be followed in flight, certainly, up to a range from the set of 5,000 yards, or that a number of spots on its trajectory could be located. Trials with the U.S. type of automatic following G.L. set (S.C.R. 584) gave a more defined trace of the trajectories of individual mortar bombs, but with salvos it tended at times to dodge from one bomb to another and at low elevation angles ground echoes tended to divert it from following the bomb. Both these types were actually employed in the field for this purpose, for want of a specially designed radar set, and did in fact give some useful aids.

Short trials with a 3 cm. set did not produce such good results though it had been anticipated that the shorter wave-length might be more suitable for this projectile.

The A.D.R.D.E. turned their attention to the development of a 10 cm.

set, employing the N.T. 277 radar assemblies, the high-powered version of the N.T. 271. They aimed at a special form of presentation to make the reading of the trajectory rapid and accurate so that the location of the mortar could be read off the C.R.T. presentation itself, without calculations or comparison of traces.

The general idea of this was to employ two aerial reflectors, one with its axis slightly elevated, back to back and rotated rapidly on a vertical pivot. This would enable each to give a series of spots on the trajectory at ½ second intervals; the signals from each would produce its own trace or series of spots on the C.R.T. screen and the two would, of course, be practically synchronous. They would appear separately on the screen though associated with one another, as one trace would refer to range and bearing, while the other would bring in the height element. With the fairly rapidly rising curve of the start of the trajectory of the mortar bomb, the "height" curve or trace would be markedly steeper than that of the "bearing" trace and the maximum separation of the two would be about the peak of the trajectory. It would not, of course, be the full length of the trajectory that would be picked up, as the siting of the mortar was usually behind cover and the ground clutter at low elevations would obscure the beginning and the end of the trajectory. Sufficient of the trajectory, however, should be picked up to ensure that the curves of the traces could be extended backwards with accuracy. This extension backwards of the two curves would produce an intersection and with the difference in slope of the early part of the two traces, that intersection should be fairly well defined. That backward intersection would, of course, be the origin of the trajectory, or in other words the mortar site, which could be located in range and bearing on the C.R.T. screen. The accuracy of location was, therefore, primarily a matter of accurate reading and to improve this an "expanded" presentation was to be provided on which the two traces would appear on a larger scale; this would permit finer determination of the point of intersection and finer reading of the location of that point.

It should be remembered that with the continuous rotation of the aerials, any projectiles in the air within the arc over which the set was observing would appear on the screen and all active enemy mortar sites within the swept area covered by the set could be located approximately, or, by concentrating on any one, more accurate location of the selected active site could be effected. Similarly salvos from a mortar site would not cause difficulty to this set and the added or thickened traces might even help to get the location more accurately.

That general description of the radar aspect of the F.A. No. 3 set, as aimed at in the development work, shows the possibility of a radar aid to counter the mortar menace. Its range performance was confidently expected to be at least 8,000 yards with such projectiles and the location accuracy of the mortar was similarly expected to be better than a box of 50 yards sides.

The set complete with operators' cabin and essential armouring was to be installed on a half-track vehicle chassis, with the rotating aerial system at the rear, covered with a canvas housing that would conceal and disguise the nature of the vehicle and its contents.

It must, unfortunately, be recorded that this equipment never appeared in production form, and no practical field experience of its suitability and value was obtained. Of the three Field Army types of radar aids described in this chapter, this was, perhaps, of most urgent need, and in the summer of 1944 it had appeared to be the most advanced of the three in practical design form so that it was expected to be the first to be supplied. There arose, however, a number of mechanical problems as well as radar troubles that proved unexpectedly difficult to clear. The first model was actually completed before the end of 1944, but failed to produce the results obtained experimentally due to a considerable number of items that required rectification. Many of them were minor matters but some were more serious and this model never came up to specification.

The initial order placed had been for six "crash" production prototypes followed by 34 (later increased to 37 to provide for M. of S. needs), but at the end of March, 1945, the War Office order was cancelled leaving six available to the M. of S. for experiments and revising design. Any development or improvement that was effected later, however, is not the concern of this record. What is of concern is the fact that the introduction of this radar aid, for the field Armies in their operations, was not supplied before the war ended. This concern does not refer only to the failure to produce the goods, even in elementary form, to help on those final stages of the war; from the technical aspect also—the proof of the real value of radar in offensive operations—the loss of the opportunity to gain practical experience to guide future development was a severe blow.

CHAPTER XXIV. COMMENTARY

The ability to identify an unseen aircraft as hostile, at the longest distance that a radar set can detect it, is an essential counterpart to the advantage given by radar. Without it the value of radar would be reduced to a small proportion of its capacity, as action against a detected target cannot be taken unless it is known not to be friendly and that knowledge must be definite. The air was frequently pretty full of aircraft of all types, our outward-bound and returning bombers, fighter sweeps or protective escorts, surface-craft detection patrols, etc., which could not be continuously tracked; they often gave an opportunity for hostile craft to follow or accompany them in as "intruders" and an undetected intruder might achieve much before it could be dealt with.

Chapter XX has described the need and the problems of identification and the extent to which they were solved during the war; it will be appreciated that no positive method of doing this was produced nor did the possibility of such a method appear likely to emerge.

Chapter XXI has dealt sufficiently with the matter of jamming and with interference by Window, but it has not, perhaps, stressed sufficiently the full threat that existed to our defences in this country; we had a taste of it in the "little blitz" in the winter of 1943-44, and would have suffered considerably more had the enemy been able to apply such methods in the earlier days. Window in particular was a very serious threat and easier to operate effectively than jamming, and it is difficult to provide adequately against it. It is at least surprising, if it is true that the Germans were aware of the effect of Window in 1941, as is reputed to be the case, that they neither made use of it nor made preparations for its use until after we had given them some good doses. The reason for this is said to have been the ostrich-like attitude of Goering and his immediate advisers and their depreciation of the ideas and suggestions of scientists.

Successful radio jamming from the air involves a very considerable effort, but Window can be achieved with effect for a considerably smaller expenditure —both are real threats and must always be taken seriously and provided for in new design.

In Chapter XXII some applications of a minor nature are mentioned which make use of some of the adverse effects of jamming, odd reflections and interferences—in smaller doses—for useful purposes. No particular comment is needed except to say that many of them did lead on to new uses for radar to aid the operations of the Army.

The "corner" or "tetrahedral" reflector is worthy of some note as it provides the best means of concentrating the reflections of radar transmissions. Two reflecting surfaces at right-angles to one another give a stronger echo signal than a flat surface, and three such surfaces, forming a hollow tetrahedral, increase it still more. It was this right-angularity between the walls of buildings and the ground or road surfaces that acted in this way to distinguish built-up areas by the H_2S equipments of the R.A.F. for recognition of bombing targets. It was applied in made-up form for various Army purposes such as "datum" points for lining up radar sets, meteor balloon reflectors, etc.; hung from balloons they presented their hollow "corner" reflectors in all directions.

Another use was made of them which almost provided a means of identification of our M.T.B.s in their attacks on enemy shipping and E-boats in the Straits of Dover. In this form, rotets, as the two-faced reflectors were called, rotated on a small mast to give an intermittent strong echo by which they could be tracked by the radar set through the echoes of enemy craft.

This type of reflector also offered opportunities for deceiving the enemy and was so employed in the early stages of the Normandy landing operations. It provided the means of making a few small craft appear on the enemy's radar as a larger and heavier force approaching the coast, thereby suggesting, for a time at any rate, that parts of the coast other than Normandy were threatened; this helped to delay his realization of the real decisive point of invasion. Such deceptive measures did not fall to the lot of the Army, but it was fully exploited by the Navy and to some extent by the R.A.F. as well.

The attempts to open up a new field of activity for radar to aid the operations of ground troops are described in Chapter XXIII, but it is rather a sorry story as equipment could not be produced and supplied to the troops in time for it to help them. Development was rushed under the urge of the G.S. appreciation of the valuable operational possibilities and the desire to get at least embryo equipment into action to prove it by the stern test of operational performance. Delays were due chiefly to the very limited production capacity available to the Army in those late days of the war.

Further development of the designs was contemplated after the war ended, but that is no concern of this record. What is of concern is that these radar aids did not assist our Armies in the field at the time when the Army was taking primary place of all the Services in actually finishing the job by hard fighting in direct and close contact with the enemy.

That radar can provide valuable aids in the field is a fact, but the form that it will take as equipment is a matter for the future. The embryo sets of the war are not the final form such equipment is likely to take. They were put to production as they were to save time in order to test their operational value in war. Had time permitted it is probable that some of their functions, at least, would have been combined in a single set as, for example, direction, observation and correction of fire might well have been supplemented by a Doppler display unit to enable it to search for movement and put itself on for fire action. These matters, however, are, as has been said, for the future to determine.

PART V

WAR OFFICE RADAR RESPONSIBILITIES

CHAPTER XXV. RADAR RELATIONS

Some slight outline has already been given of the general arrangements and organization for the control of radar development and its application; there are, however, certain points in connection with Army radar and its direction into useful channels, which call for reference in greater detail here.

In this chapter will be included some brief notes on the co-operation of the War Office on radar matters with the Dominions and Allies. In subsequent chapters of this Part will be discussed General Staff radar policy and the War Office concern with training, operational research and maintenance and supply. The link-up between the War Office and the Ministry of Supply will also be mentioned, but the organization of the latter will be dealt with in Part VI.

Dominions, Colonies, etc., Radar aid. The first efforts within the Empire —other than those in the United Kingdom—to lend a helping hand with radar development for Army purposes were those started in Australia; mention has been made of the Sh.D. set in Chapter XVII. This set was intended for the defence of Australian and Australasian ports and harbours, but Australia offered to provide a few equipments for aiding the defences of our Far East outposts. Though this aid was gratefully accepted for the Singapore defences, it was not used as sets did not become available before the Japanese had over-run and captured Malaya.

South Africa followed closely in providing locally developed sets of coastal warning type which were in operation before British types could be supplied. In addition, South Africa made a most valuable contribution in North Africa by providing a number of radio personnel with some knowledge of radar, to undertake the maintenance and repair of Army radar equipment and to assist, if required, with R.A.F. sets. This was of great value as the supply overseas of trained United Kingdom maintenance personnel was extremely limited in the early days when the majority of our resources had to be applied to the defences of this country. Perhaps the most important contribution made by South Africa was in the field of Operational Research, where B. N. J. Schonland —rising to the rank of Brigadier—was loaned by the South African Government to take charge of this work; some details of its achievements in the radar and fire control field will be found in Chapter XXX.

Canada came strongly into the radar picture in 1940–41 with the development on its own initiative of a centimetric H.A.A. equipment (see Chapter IX) an ambitious undertaking but an excellent effort on the information available to them—and its large scale production and supply to our troops as well as to their own. Subsequently they undertook further development in closer liaison and our designers and technical A.A. experts, which produced the M.Z.P.I.—a centimetric warning set that most nearly met our needs for a warning and tactical control equipment. Canada also undertook to provide for her own needs in respect of surface craft warning and the protection of her harbours, as might be necessary, without calling upon this country to allocate British equipment for those purposes.

In the opposite direction, this country supplied the Dominions (other than Canada) India and threatened Colonial and other overseas territories, with British types of radar equipment for their protection and for the protection of convoy routes. Canada was self-sufficient and South Africa required but little help from this country.

Allocations of British equipment were made by the General Staff on priorities in which the Inter-Service Defended Ports Committee had a considerable influence on the decisions. The allocation of sets made in late 1939 covered only the primary fortresses and defended ports; the provision was as follows:—

Gibraltar	G.L. I sets, 4; C.D./C.H.L. sets, 8
Malta	G.L. I sets, 6; C.D./C.H.L. sets, 11
Aden	G.L. I sets, 2
Singapore	G.L. I sets, 12; C.D./C.H.L. sets, 31
Hong Kong	G.L. I sets, 6

These allocations were subsequently revised as the course of operations changed—Gibraltar and Malta received a large proportion of the figures shown above, but the provision for the Far East was not made before the Japanese attack, as many sets had to be diverted for this country's anti-invasion needs and to provide for the convoy routes round the Cape. In those cases where supply had not been made until later, the C.D./C.H.L. type was replaced by the new standard centimetric types and the G.L. II was issued in lieu of the earlier pattern.

The R.A.F. had, of course, also contributed to these defences with their air warning sets—the C.O.L. which was the overseas form of the C.H. type, some M.B. sets and their C.H.L.

With the R.A.F. carrying the general responsibility for air detection and warning overseas as well as at home, the Army's provision was limited to the A.A. gun and searchlight radar sets and to coastal sets forming part of, or detached from, specific port defences.

Parallel with these operational allocations overseas, it was arranged that early production—or pre-production—models of each new type of radar adopted by the Army should be supplied as samples to Australia and, if particularly so desired, to Canada also. Later India came into this picture also, in order to keep them up to date in developments and enable them to prepare their personnel for the new types to be supplied. Training sets were of course also provided to India and a few other overseas centres.

Periodical distribution of handbooks and technical documents was also made to overseas authorities and formations for the same purpose; in the case of the Dominions with Military H.Q. in this country, distribution was made through them. In addition their representatives were enabled to attend W.O. radar committee meetings, while the Ministry of Supply brought them into their radar progress meetings and technical discussions so that they should have full information of policy and of development progress.

Allies

(i) *U.S.A.* Considerable mention has already been made of the .close liaison that grew up between this country and the United States and of their considerable aid to us with anti-aircraft radar in the flying bomb period and in the supply of radio proximity fuzes. Their great production capacity and also their large scientific effort were of assistance to us in the radar field, but there were limitations imposed upon our acceptance of their designs as standard

Army equipment. These were chiefly on account of the difference in detail in components that made interchangeability with our types impossible. We had to rely upon supplies of spares and parts from the United States to keep equipments provided by them in action. Though possible, with their build-up of supplies in this country for their own forces, it was liable even so to cause an added drain on shipping facilities; it could not be contemplated as anything but a temporary expedient to meet a special urgent need and to tide us over a difficult supply period. Further, the equipment developed in this country was by no means inferior to that of the United States—it was the delay due to the limitations of production that made the expedient necessary and we were most grateful to America.

No specific mention has been made in earlier chapters of our aid to the United States in the early days of their entry into the war. With the Pearl Harbour disaster, American radar was suspect and the basis of use of the information it supplied was seriously in question. An immediate examination of the Pacific Coast radar system and that of the vital Panama Canal area by Watson-Watt, resulted in drastic alterations and replacements, and this country at very short notice collected from its then rather meagre resources a number of surface warning sets, C.H.L. from the R.A.F. and C.D./C.H.L. from the Army, and rushed them off to the States. Though a comparatively small contribution it was the quickest means of providing adequate cover to the Canal's Pacific approaches.

British Army radar was originally represented on the British Army Staff at Washington by a staff captain trained as an Instructor Fire Control. He was naturally representing other aspects of A.A. operations as well as A.A. radar; but had little experience of its other forms and uses, and was not fully in the picture of G.S. radar policy. Full representation of that policy as well as of the various types in being and in development was provided by the appointment of Major A. A. Eden in 1942, to the Staff in Washington as a G.S.O. II. His experience in the radar branch of the War Office gave him a proper background for the liaison work and formed a valuable means of transmission of information on radar matters between the two countries. One of his early duties was, at the request of the U.S. Army authorities, to inspect the system of coastal warning sets in the Canal area, and he was instrumental in making a marked improvement in their operation and particularly in the effective transmission of information from the sets to reorganized plotting and control stations. This appointment was later raised to G.S.O.I, and an additional appointment for a G.S.O. II approved; Lieutenant-Colonel J. A. Fisher relieved Lieutenant-Colonel Eden and Major Waldock from the W.O. radar branch filled the junior post in the autumn 1943 and succeeded Fisher as G.S.O. I some 18 months later.

In addition to the Army Staff at Washington, the Ministry of Supply were kept in close touch through their Supply Mission, which included representatives of the research and development aspects. The radar representatives on the Army Staff and the Supply Mission kept in close touch and assisted each other in collecting and in passing radar information in both directions, which materially aided the collaboration between the United States and the United Kingdom.

(ii) *U.S.S.R.* The links on radar matters with Russia were practically confined on our side to providing and on theirs to receiving and asking for more. This applied to equipments as well as to information and they had none to give us nor was there any apparent reciprocation in respect of other information to counterbalance our radar "gifts." Radar was one of the key war devices or weapons that we placed at their disposal freely in order to aid the combined Allied efforts against Germany.

Army radar was naturally involved in this as well as Naval and R.A.F. types. Originally the U.S.S.R. Military Mission in this country formed the contact for us to demonstrate and explain the equipments, but later a Scientific and Trade Mission were more concerned with the details and working of the equipments, though the Military Mission dealt with the quantities.

These demonstrations and explanations led at times to some strange proceedings in which technical details got beyond the interpreters of both sides —though it must be said that they did remarkably well considering their own difficulties. A case in point occurred at Earls Croome where "Baby Maggie" was being demonstrated and examined in detail. After a short while the interpreters dropped right out of the picture and two Russian scientific technicians, knowing no English, carried on with two of the younger scientists from A.D.R.D.E. who had no Russian. It was remarkable how the information was got through, for the fact remains that it did and the Russians had a real understanding of the set and its working by the time they left.

Perhaps the first introduction of a G.L. set into the U.S.S.R. was even more surprising. In this case a standard set was specially modified with Russian range and other scales, with "Arctic" grease for its bearings and the replacement of a few components unsuited to low temperatures. This was despatched in a northern convoy, accompanied by Captain Salt, a technical officer trained in operating, maintenance and repair with an experienced artificer to assist him; they were to set up, operate and demonstrate the equipment and train a number of Russian personnel on it. They had to report to our Military Mission which at that time had been moved east from Moscow. They were separated from the equipment on this long journey and in spite of repeated enquiries, even at the highest level, they were unable to make contact with it for over three months. When at last they were permitted to reach the set they found it set up and working after a fashion, manned by two Russian majors and a captain with a scientist helping by keeping up the temperature to only some 20 degrees of frost by various stoves, fires and fur rugs. The Russians had, of course, been supplied with instructional handbooks and technical pamphlets, but it must be conceded that it was a remarkable effort on their part.

In regard to the types and numbers of sets that were provided for shipment to the U.S.S.R., they had to be found from the production provision already made for our own needs—we were not able to undertake any extension of contracts for supply to meet extra demands. It should be noted also that we could only undertake to supply for shipment from this country and not for the numbers delivered at Russian ports—the difference being the losses in transit due to sinkings in convoy on the northern route. Little if any news of the behaviour of these sets in Russian hands was received, and no indication was given of their effect in action. The types and quantities supplied were:—

G.L. Mark II   204; Baby Maggie   50;
G.L. Mark III British   50; Light Warning Set   30;
Samples of C.A. No. 1, Marks II and III; C.D. No. 1, Mk 5;
S.L.C. (1½ m.).

(iii) *Other Belligerent Allies.* Allied contingents and formations that formed part of our field Armies and were required for A.A. defence operations were, in the later stages of the war, equipped with up-to-date radar sets in the same way as our own troops. A Polish contingent in the Middle East and North Africa formed a Heavy A.A. Brigade and were equipped with the British type G.L. III radar as well as light warning sets. They eventually formed part of the Central Mediterranean Forces and operated in the Italian campaign. Few if any of the other Allied contingents were required to use Army radar; it will be recalled that the French had been brought into the early radar picture before the collapse in 1940, but apart from that they had no army radar. Nor were the Greeks, Dutch, Belgians, Norwegians, Czechs, nor any other co-belligerents. China, towards the end of the war, sent over some technicians or scientific students to learn about radar and its operational use and it was agreed to demonstrate and explain some early sets to them, but no actual supply of equipment was made.

(iv) *Non-Combatant Allies.* Apart from operational Allies some provision was made at later stages of the war to other Allies. The largest provision of this nature was made to Egypt by the transfer of equipment for anti-aircraft defence of the Delta area and of the Cairo and Canal zones. Still later the coastal artillery defences at Alexandria with their radar equipment were also taken over by the Egyptian Army under the guidance of the British Military Mission in Egypt.

Our oldest ally, Portugal, was also provided towards the end of the war with some radar equipment and Turkey was supplied with a small number of sets and given instruction in their use and maintenance. These were all special and individual cases and, with the exception of some of the equipment given to Turkey, did not affect our urgent needs nor our production arrangements.

From the foregoing remarks it will be realized that the liaison with our Allies was fairly widespread on radar matters but was limited, in so far as the "junior" members of the co-belligerents were concerned, by the security aspect— only the need for effective operation of H.A.A. defence justified, at that time, the spread of information on the subject. In respect of the "senior partners," it will have been appreciated that with the U.S.A. we received reciprocal treatment of great value.

It may be mentioned here that after the war some up-to-date automatic A.A. radar equipment was demonstrated successfully through Europe by a mobile "circus" which showed it in action and discussed it in detail in Switzerland, Belgium, Holland, Denmark, Norway and Sweden.

CHAPTER XXVI. ARMY RADAR POLICY

Before the formation of the Ministry of Supply, proposals and new ideas for novel aids, new techniques or inventions likely to assist military operations, were considered and their possible value assessed, by the technical weapons directorates and specialist branches in the M.G.O.'s department of the War Office whose duty it was to advise the General Staff on such matters. With the support of the G.S., investigations and experiment would be undertaken on such proposals as were likely to be of value to the Army. It was not until practical proof of their value, as a result of experimental trials, became available that the G.S. could be advised as to the direction in which development was likely to be most profitable and as to what useful possibilities might be expected to emerge from further research and experiment. The General Staff could not, therefore, at any rate in cases involving a completely novel or complex technique, initiate and define a policy to guide development in any but the widest and most general terms.

The G.S. had the ultimate responsibility for laying down such policy but in the early days of an investigation it would be the technical personnel controlling the investigation who, being fully aware of the general needs of the Army, were well able to direct the initial stages of experiment and trials. As soon as the practical proof began to emerge, they were in a position to bring forward facts and advise the G.S. effectively and thus help the formulation of policy.

With the formation of the Ministry of Supply and the transfer to it of the technical directorates from the W.O. there was at least physical separation of the G.S. from its advisers on technical matters. Close contact was, however, generally well maintained, though with the stress of war the need for day-to-day contacts increased and the organization had to be reinforced by creating special directorates and appointments in the War Office. These were both operational (G.S.) and semi-technical and linked up with their opposite numbers in the Ministry to form the direct channels for contact and discussion. Neither the Ministry nor its individual departments could usurp the responsibilities of the General Staff, though they could provide advice on scientific and technical matters and their possibilities. The Ministry could, of course, initiate research and experimental work or other investigations provided that essential effort was not diverted from the urgent needs stated by the General Staff. Research was the responsibility of the Ministry—the War Office could not indicate the direction in which research should proceed though it could point to the apparent needs for improved performance of its equipment.

The separation of the technical directorates from the General Staff led to a gradual deterioration in the focus of the guiding policy, or perhaps more in its translation; for a considerable time, however, the momentum of the old association within the War Office was sufficient to carry it along in the new Ministry.

The result was that the single authoritative voice expressing policy and all operational and technical requirements was replaced by two tongues, not always quite in unison, and their composite utterances at times were interpreted differently or with some alteration in stress on the different aspects. With research the concern of the Ministry there is no doubt that their direction of this work was sound and valuable, even if the duality of direction was at times rather conflicting. On the whole it may be said that this dual control of policy for Army radar functioned in a reasonably satisfactory manner, and that the co-operation between the two departments was generally close and effective.

From the start of the investigations for applying radar to Army purposes up to the end of 1940, it may be said that the General Staff was only in a position to accept the results of development presented to them and not to guide development, though it could indicate generally its priority needs. With the appointment of a Deputy to the Director of Anti-Aircraft and Coastal Defence in the War Office, for radar duties at the end of 1940, the G.S. began to have closer contact with the research and development work and to obtain a view, ahead of future possibilities, so that they were able to formulate their policy to meet operational needs. In this contact the Ministry was most helpful, permitting direct access to their directorates controlling the work of the A.D.R.D.E. and even to the establishment itself and its trials. More effectively still the Ministry accepted this representative of the War Office as one of the group to discuss the periodical programme of work for the establishment. This put the War Office in a position of having their policy translated direct to the Research and Development Establishment and their urgent requirements accorded appropriate priorities in its programme. By this close liaison, thanks to the Ministry, the General Staff were kept in the closest touch with developments and future possibilities and the Ministry directly informed of G.S. requirements and aims.

The responsibility of the General Staff extends beyond the defining of the operational requirements for a new equipment: the acceptance of an experimental model or prototype for production as Army equipment is their concern. The ultimate decision to accept or to put back for modification to improve performance lies with the G.S., though some part of the proof of adequacy of the design will usually be delegated to the technical military advisers. If the full standard of performance previously specified has not been attained, the G.S. will have to weigh up the limitations of the model against the operational urgency of getting improved equipment into the hands of the troops—the time factor *versus* performance; this requires the best available factual information and *responsible* advice.

With the decision taken to proceed to production and supply the G.S. has to supplement the qualitative with the quantitative requirements and justify them—in peace-time mainly a financial matter, but in war the operational need may well be predominant. With that requirement defined and passed to the Ministry, the whole responsibility for production passes to that Ministry and the War Office only comes into the picture again for the receipt of supplies as they come off production and for their distribution to formations, training, etc., as required by the operational needs and situation.

From 1941 the War Office began to define their operational requirements for radar in greater detail and to initiate policy that grew with experience, to cover all aspects of radar for Army use and to guide development, provision, operational use and allocation. This policy was built upon advances in the technical field, the limitations of available production capacity, inter-Service needs and priorities and particularly on the general strategic directives for the conduct of the war—this last formed the background against which the policy of the General Staff was stated and kept up to date.

Policy Background. It has been shown that Radar was applied primarily to air defence purposes both by the R.A.F. and by the Army. In 1939 Army radar had expanded its useful capacity to shipping detection and anti-invasion warning purposes and was developing it for improving coastal artillery fire; in these forms it became a material aid to the Navy in the control and protection of convoys and local anti-U-boat operations. The development of Army radar had, therefore, played its part in the primary strategic considerations in the early defensive period of the war.

Even in those early years the future offensive use of radar was envisaged and development, with that object in view, was started, but its application for aiding our ground forces was not then a practical proposition. By 1942, however, Army radar was emerging from its youthful stage of growth and with the advent of the centimetric era, the promise of extension of its useful applications was increasing and research and experiment were probing new fields of possible utility.

By July, 1942, the trend of the general directives issued at the highest level, for the application of our war effort as a whole, had reached the stage of calling for the maximum possible provision for the offensive both direct and in support of land operations, while retaining the essential minimum for the air defence of this country, for securing our vital communications and interrupting those of the enemy. Both the Navy and the Air Force could contribute radar aids to offensive action and their opportunities naturally gave their requirements priority in the competition for capacity for production which was already becoming saturated with the expanding programmes of radio and radar requirements.

In the early months of 1942 the Chiefs of Staff had furnished the Radio Policy Sub-Committee with an outline of the strategic requirements, and on the 27th of April that Sub-Committee had submitted a statement of priority requirements for development and production for the three Services in respect of radar, or R.D.F. as it was then called. This is recorded here as the first co-ordinated statement of radar priority items for the three Services, and in fact the only statement of this nature that was formally produced.

"R.D.F. PRIORITY

Offensive uses of R.D.F.

(a) Accurate location and range finding ship to ship, *and shore to ship*, for attack of surface vessels, seen or unseen.

(b) Improvements in A.S.V. (apparatus for detection of surface vessels from aircraft), including developments to aid blind or bad visibility attack on ships by aircraft.

(c) Priority to be given to those developments of radio navigation which employ the simplest and most mobile ground stations. Hence priority of work on beacons and H_2S. Beacon methods also needed for accurate homing.

(d) *Accurate location of ground targets.*

Counter Measures.

(e) An adequate staff to be devoted entirely to developing methods and equipment for interfering with enemy use of D.R.F. and *for, preventing enemy interference with our R.D.F.*

Defence.

(f) Highest priority *for night defence to be given to improvement of S.L.C.* and centimetre A.I.

(g) *Mobile* G.C.I. and *general warning systems* to have priority over static equipment.

(h) Highest priority to be given to R.D.F. *Developments to improve accuracy of short-range gunfire.*"

The Army application of radar, other than aids to A.A. guns and coast warning sets, both of which had, of course, to continue in development and production, was included in five of the items (shown by italics in the sub-paragraphs of the statement) and possibly in a sixth if research could produce practical results. Item (a) brought coastal artillery fire into the foreground, (e) in its latter part was an essential protective measure and (f) included the combined use of searchlights and night fighters to combat the night bombing raids. Item (g) had general application to Army equipment while (h) embraced improvements to Heavy, Intermediate and Light A.A. gun fire to increase their effect. Item (d) pointed to research for the reduction of ground clutter to permit of observation and location of ground targets from the ground, as well as their observation from aircraft; this would bring Army radar into offensive use by our ground forces.

These inter-Service priority requirements were considered by the Minister of Production to be "broadly in accordance with the strategic requirements" but as "insufficiently precise in respect of an order of priority for the individual items, and its adequacy as a guide for the distribution of effort on development and for production." As a result, on the recommendation of the Minister, the Radio Production Executive was established in the autumn of 1942, under the Radio Board which had by then replaced the Radio Policy Sub-Committee, to be responsible for the co-ordination of production and the allocation of capacity and resources. The three senior radio production officers of the Ministries of Supply, of Aircraft Production and of the Admiralty were the members, with an independent Chairman. Representatives of the operational aspects from the three Services were *not* officially included.

Though this body was effective in co-ordinating the production facilities and capacity and the manpower available for production, it did, in fact, tend to divorce production priorities from those stated for the supply of operational equipment; those priorities were not always, apparently, carried through to the production and supply stages.

Early in March, 1943, the Chiefs of Staff issued a revised outline of strategic priorities to guide the Radio Board in its planning for the future. This directive stated the four primary principles in their order of priority, as follows:—

1. Defeat of U-boat;
2. Assistance to Russia;
3. European offensive;
4. Pacific and Far East offensive.

For these the Army radar equipment in production and under development —A.A. local warning and fire control, A.A. searchlight control, coast warning and coastal artillery fire control, mobile light warning—with the improvements that were in process of incorporation, were available for their normal defensive roles. Assistance to Russia involved no special research or development, but the Army's contribution provided for the supply of equipment designed for our own use. The needs for the Pacific offensive did not involve major new design but rather an intensification of the means of resisting tropical conditions and the reduction or breakdown in weight and size, wherever possible, for transport and air conveyance. There was still no practical proposition for radar aids to the ground forces in their operations, as distinct from normal air protection and protection of base ports, etc., against enemy attacks. The next six months, however, were to see the emergence from research and experiment of embryo types for aiding the operations of our ground forces.

In late 1943, the strategical directives required the maximum of concentration of effort against the Germans in 1944, while fulfilling the planned contributions to operations against the Japanese. They also pointed to the need for reducing development effort and production capacity occupied by those items that could not come into effective operational use by the end of 1944—later extended to mid-1945—against Germany. In special cases of potential war-winning weapons (including radar), this time limit was not to be strictly applied, and special equipment for the Japanese war was also exempt, though the end of 1945 was the general limit for high priority development, and supply.

The interpretation of these general directives for the Army radar field is exemplified by the G.S. Policy Statements detailed in the following paragraphs. They were further translated in detail in the priorities assigned to the different items in the programme of work of the A.D.R.D.E.

G.S. Policy Statements. In the summer of 1941 the War Office prepared a general review of the radar position and its immediate future possibilities, and with it was an outline of the policy for the development and improvement of equipment. This was really the first of a series of policy statements initiated by the General Staff to indicate to the Ministry the needs and priorities of development for Army radar equipment. These statements were issued at intervals, as required by the march of events, fresh operational possibilities or special operations in contemplation. They were originally issued independently but later were included in the general series of policy statements issued through the War Office Organization and Weapons Policy Committee.

A selection from the series of radar policy statements, or in some cases extracts from them, is recorded here to illustrate the development of G.S. policy during the later stages of the war.

(i) *November*, 1941

"This policy provides for equipment for the following purposes:—

(a) Local Warning of approach of enemy aircraft . . .

A set to an inter-Service specification is now in the production stage; . . . For the Army this set is intended for inclusion in the equipments of Light A.A. Regiments and for use with mobile Heavy A.A. units.

(b) Provision of accurate data to enable H.A.A. guns to engage enemy air targets by unseen fire . . ., and to provide accurate range-finding against visual targets.

. . . The G.L. Mark III (10 cm.) set now clear for production should become available at the beginning of 1943. It is more accurate and will supersede G.L. Mark II.

(c) Provision of continuous and accurate range for Light and Intermediate A.A. guns to improve visually controlled fire.

The development of an accurate equipment (25 cm.) for incorporation in the Intermediate role Predictor is in hand.

(d) Development of searchlight control . . . to assist engagement by night fighters.

The programme of provision of S.L.C. (150 cm.) is about one-third complete.

(e) Warning of approach or of passage of surface craft and their tracking...

The adaptation of Naval type 271 (10 cm.) approaches completion and a considerable number of coast watching stations are already installed.

(f) Accurate location of surface targets and the control of fire of coast artillery guns; this includes correction of fire by observation of fall of shot in relation to the target.

C.A. No. 1 sets, which make use of the Naval type 271 (10 cm.) are now coming into supply.

(g) Radio proximity fuze to improve the accuracy of shell bursts.

Development approaches the stage of practical adoption.

Note.—This was *not* realized—this item was subsequently dealt with in another section and not included in later radar statements.

(h) Means of identification friend from foe.

The Inter-Service (and Inter-Allied) policy provides for the use of I.F.F. Mark III; the necessary interrogators and responsors for . . . Army sets are in production in some cases and in others development approaches completion.

(i) Protection of our equipment from effects of enemy jamming.

. . . the development of protective measures has been intensified. Certain palliative measures have already been applied . . . Inter-Service investigations and research are in hand to provide more complete remedies or protection against possible future forms of jamming.

For the Army the main policy . . . has been to adopt centimetric wavelength working, which is being expedited.

Anti-jamming measures of all natures have been given the highest priority in the Research and Development programme.

(j) Area control of static A.A. defences.

This at present is limited to the use of an R.A.F. type (G.C.I.) adapted for Army use in large G.D.A.s."

Note.—This statement did *not* place the items in an order of Priority.

(ii) *September, 1942*

1. "The highest priority of effort will be given to the provision of protection against the effects of enemy jamming.

2. The A.A. and C.A. fire control sets now in production will be accepted as adequate for the present and development will be confined to minor modifications rather than to new equipments.

3. The centimetric wave-length for searchlight control and for air warning will be developed; . . .

4. Projects which lead to simplicity in apparatus, increased reliability and reduction in personnel for operation will be pursued. Automatic following for G.L. and S.L.C. might be able to qualify under this head.

5. Existing equipment of the other Services will be adapted or adopted if possible, in preference to new development.

6. The investigation of the possibility of applying R.D.F. aids to A.F.V. recognition and combat will be expedited. . . ."

(iii) *November, 1943*

1. "The highest priority will continue to be given to protection measures against enemy jamming.

2. The development of centimetric wave-length equipment for Army purposes is to be pursued as a matter of urgency.

3. Existing equipment on 10 cm. wave-length for A.A. and for C.A. fire control will be accepted as adequate. Design on 3 cm. wave-length will be pursued in the first instance for the C.A. mobile application.

4. Automatic following to improve operation of Service Radar equipment will be developed to obtain better value from the capacity of the equipment.

5. The application of Radar to Field Army purposes will be investigated as a matter of importance.

6. All development work is to be directed towards simplicity in apparatus and maintenance, reliability in Service conditions including tropical, ease of operation and reduction in operators. In particular, attention is directed to the need for reduction in weight and size, improved mobility and portability.

7. Research and development work that is unlikely to mature in practical form in 1945 should *not* be classed as high priority."

(iv) *April*, 1944

1. "The highest priority will continue to be given to protective measures against enemy jamming.

2. The development of centimetric wave-length equipment for Army purposes is to be pursued as a matter of urgency. Includes:—

    (*a*) Searchlight Control
    (*b*) Putting on for G.L. equipment.
    (*c*) Area warning and tactical control.

3. Existing equipment on 10 cm. wave-lengths for A.A. and for C.A. fire control will be accepted as adequate. Development of equipment on 3 cm. wave-length will be pursued particularly for Field Army purposes; the design for fire control of mobile C.A. weapons required for Far Eastern theatres already well advanced will be completed.

4. Automatic following to improve operation of service Radar equipment will be developed to obtain better value from the capacity of the equipment.

5. The application of Radar to Field Army purposes will be investigated as a matter of importance. The possible applications urgently requiring investigation include:—

    (*a*) Trajectory tracking of mortar bombs, shells and rockets for location of weapons.
    (*b*) Location of airburst for ranging Field and Medium Artillery.
    (*c*) Check of muzzle velocity of guns in the field.
    (*d*) Detection of moving vehicles.

6. In all development work, while maintaining the full performance required, the need for simplicity in apparatus and maintenance, reliability in service (including tropical) conditions, ease of operation and reduction in operators is stressed. In particular, attention is directed to the need for reduction in weight and size, improved mobility and portability.

7. Research and development work that is unlikely to mature in practical form in 1945 should not be classed as high priority."

This sequence of policy statements makes it quite clear that the threat of jamming was never lightly considered; it was always recognized as of primary importance. From the time that the first serious tactical use of jamming was experienced in February, 1942, the highest priority was assigned to the research and development of protective measures. Even before that, some palliatives had been introduced for Army sets that were most exposed to the effects of cross-Channel attack and the earliest available centimetric sets had been provided and deployed in that area as a more effective measure against jamming.

This series of statements illustrates the development of General Staff policy in respect of Army radar. The series started from the time when the value of 10 centimetric working had been established and the decision taken to adopt it for Army equipment.

The 1941 statement, rather tentative in form and matter, really marks the change from the "Acceptance" to the "Direction" period of policy formulation by the G.S. It was not a case of going against the recommendations of the Ministry but of the acceptance by the General Staff of its responsibility for deciding the operational requirements of this particular form of Army equipment, while having regard also to the needs of the other two Services and the combined radar policy.

The development of the policy shows the increasing desire for centimetric wave-length working for the major forms of Army equipment for priority operational purposes. It shows the increasing appreciation of the value of automatic working H.A.A. fire and searchlight control, and in 1944, the importance placed by the G.S. upon the development of radar for Field Army use. Towards the closing stages of the war, the limitations imposed by the time factor and by the increasing restriction of production capacity, made it necessary to urge concentration upon types that could be provided in practical form by the end of 1945, rather than longer term research and development projects.

Though these statements do not refer directly to production, the policy was naturally intended to cover production and supply to the troops; the formulation of policy was itself materially affected by that aspect. The production problems are dealt with later but their influence on policy, even as early as 1941, is worth noting. In the statement issued in 1941, a W.O. note on the factors governing future policy states:—

> ". . . the tendency towards saturation of radio production capacity in this country . . . (points) to the need in all the Services for concentration on as few types of equipment as possible."

In addition the difficulties then being experienced in the supply of trained operators and of skilled maintenance and repair personnel are also mentioned as affecting policy. These difficulties in their qualitative aspect were, however, largely overcome by the excellence of the training arrangements, but the G.S. policy stressed the need for "simplicity in apparatus," "increased reliability" and "ease of maintenance," to reduce maintenance and repair.

The man- and woman-power situation also made it necessary to aim at a reduction in numbers required to operate the sets; this, in the 1942 statement, is used as a partial argument for developing automatic working which appears for the first time in that issue. In subsequent issues this automatic following requirement is more justly attributed to the need for improvement over the standard of performance given by the average manual operators, for the equipment itself had greater capacity for accuracy and for smoothness of output than was being achieved in practical use by average operators.

It will be noticed that policy in respect of identification (I.F.F.) only appears in the earliest of these statements; this was because the Army had to follow the other two Services in their essential needs in this respect and could not initiate policy. The General Staff agreed that no further definition of policy for Army identification was necessary as the decisions of the Radio Board covered the requirements of all Services and the detailed implementing of that policy could be left to the Director of Radar to define. This continued for the preparations for the inter-allied introduction of the Mark V system that was to replace the Mark III as the universal form.

A series of specifications is given in Appendix IV to illustrate the growth in radar performance required to meet the improved capabilities of our H.A.A. guns and their accessories as the war progressed. They also show the development of direction by the General Staff to the scientists and technical staff of the Ministry and its establishment, in respect of operational needs.

It may be noted that the first specification, marked A, is headed G.S. Specification (*Amplified*). This was an "accepted" specification, following proof of performance in trials in which the minimum acceptable ranges and accuracies had been achieved. It contains, in addition to the technical artillery requirements for complete "unseen" fire control, the mechanical, vehicle, transmission, etc., details, but the cabin and trailer design details have not been included—a surprising omission but in fact already well known at the time the specification was prepared. The transmission and some of the other details were standard equipment accessories and had to be acceptable by the radar equipment in their standard form; many of these were, of course, included in the specifications for later designs but will be found to have been omitted in this Appendix in order to save space and unnecessary repetition.

The later specifications will be seen to have gradually taken a more effective form. The system was for the General Staff to state its requirements in an "*Outline*" specification, dealing with range performance and service condition as affecting design. This *outline* specification would then be passed to D. of A., Ministry of Supply, for amplification with the necessary technical details of accuracies, consistency, transmission rates and other details. The result would be what was known as an *Amplified G.S. Specification*; examples are given by items C and D; in the case of item E, the final form of the specification for passing to the A.D.R.D.E. only is given.

It should be noted that this dual form of specification only applied in cases where fire control was concerned or where radar equipment affected the fire control of guns. It will be seen that item F, dealing with the later form of searchlight radar control, is a complete specification issued by the General Staff without apparent aid from the D.G. of A.'s directorate. That directorate was concerned primarily with the weapons and their control and D.G. of A was *not*—perhaps unfortunately—the technical military authority for all forms of radar for Army purposes.

It may be said that this variation in procedure was perhaps more apparent than real since the assistance of D.G. of A's representatives was always available and welcomed; even if the specifications appeared simply as of G.S. origin, they had generally been agreed or helped by that technical directorate.

Some of the equipments were inter-Service in their use and consequently, as in the case of the light warning equipment, their development was governed by an inter-Service specification.

This series of specifications are samples only, and most of them deal with the growth of the G.L. type of set.

There is, however, one further addition to the H.A.A. fire control series that might be mentioned here without going into details. This is an outline specification prepared in 1944, for a radar unit to form part of or to be associated with the new electrical predictor, then contemplated, to provide for the latest conditions of higher speed and rates. This required the design of the predictor and of the radar to be completely co-ordinated. Radar information was to be the primary factor for the operation of the predictor but with visual methods as the secondary source—both being synchronous, so that transfer of control from one to the other would be instantaneous. Automatic search and scan, detection at long range, following in all senses at high rates and high acceleration, regenerative tracking from the predictor or "tracker" and the provision of a local and a remote P.P.I. presentation, as well as other refinements, were aimed at.

Here at last was the opportunity for radar and predictor to be designed to suit each other. It was not entirely the requirement suggested in 1936 but it was an improvement upon it. Practically, it combined the two key components effecting accurate prediction, the radar and the predictor—without human intervention, and also provided for true tactical control of local operations.

This new design had not emerged by the end of the war; whether it matures later does not concern this record but the indication of this requirement shows that the General Staff had appreciated the future possibilities of the fully automatic chain of H.A.A. fire control operations and had visualized and perhaps anticipated, the needs of the future

CHAPTER XXVII. SIDELIGHTS

United Kingdom–United States Liaison. When the United States joined us in the war, the broad strategic outline plans were of course decided by Combined Planning Staffs and co-operation at all lower levels was developed. In the radio and radar fields this co-operation became very close and increasingly effective; it owed much to the visit to this country of the Scientific Mission under Dr. Karl Compton in May, 1943, on the invitation of the Radio Board, and to the return visit by representatives of that Board to the States some six months later. The opportunity was taken to discuss freely the policy and programmes for research and development of radar and the operational needs to be provided for. In the discussions on radar matters the War Office was represented by the Director of Radar who was fully informed of policy, the operational needs for Army radar, and the research and development programme then being pursued.

The equipment requirements and the research and development items for the Armies of both countries were considered in detail. It is of interest to note that both countries were working on very similar lines, if allowance is made for the fact that the United States Army had to provide for its own Air Force, which was not the case with us.

Of the eleven items in the United Kingdom (Army) research and development list, six were agreed, one (auto-following) was already in progress, and one (reduction in size) was in its early stages in the U.S. list and the three others were special modifications to existing United Kingdom equipment.

Of the thirteen items in the United States list, five were not included in the United Kingdom list as being R.A.F. or Naval responsibilities, one was excluded as already provided, one was excluded (unseen A/T fire) as impracticable of effective development in the near future, and six agreed with the United Kingdom list.

The results of these visits included some measure of avoidance of duplication of research work, appreciation of the practical experience in operations gained by this country, and recognition by this country of the value to the combined effort of the extensive research and development facilities and production capacity of the United States and great appreciation of their willingness to make it available to us. In addition it undoubtedly helped towards the co-operation in these technical matters so essential to the forces of the two countries operating together, by reducing, if not eliminating, the chances of chaos by mutual interference affecting radio and radar operation in the field.

Inter-Service Priorities. In the summer of 1943, with the increasing trend towards offensive uses of radar, the question of comparative importance of the priority items under development at the M.A.P. and M. of S. establishments was raised, at an O.P.T.E.C. meeting, with the suggestion that it might be necessary to divert scientific staff from one establishment to the other. The Ministry of Supply representative resisted the suggestion of any transfer from A.D.R.D.E. as they were already insufficiently staffed to meet all the War Office priority needs. In this the War Office representative supported the Ministry and it was agreed that Sir R. Watson-Watt, in his capacity as chairman, should investigate the two programmes of work concerned.

In August, he reported "that the relative departmental priorities were all well considered, systematically revised and authoritative" and indicated that in his opinion "they were equally justified as items of first importance." At that meeting the War Office protested against a proposal to "milk" the A.D.R.D.E. of staff by transfer to T.R.E., at least until it had been made clear what the effect would be on urgently needed Army equipment, and the comparative importance and urgency of the work for which the additional staff was required at T.R.E. Eventually this matter was adjusted by an agreed re-arrangement of the programmes of the two establishments and the transfer of one senior scientific officer to T.R.E. In November, however, another attempt to "milk" A.D.R.D.E. was made by the Admiralty, but by this time the possibilities of using radar in offensive operations by the Army had been demonstrated. The D.C.I.G.S. was able to advise the Ministry of Supply that he was impressed by the many possibilities for the use of radar in offensive operations by armies in the field, "and in his opinion, future development in this field is of vital importance." He also indicated that he was prepared to support the Ministry in resisting further reductions in the staff of A.D.R.D.E.

The foregoing instance appears to be the only case in which the Radio Board or its O.P.T.E.C. committee attempted a direct comparison of the importance of work in progress at the R. and D. establishments to meet the urgent needs of the Services. The terms of reference of the Radio Board (Chapter IV) put the onus on that body for the co-ordination and determination of priorities of research, development and production of the needs of the three Services, but formal comparison was never made.

Individual items of research and of development were discussed by the O.P.T.E.C. committee, but on the production side—the P.P. and P. committee and the R.P.E.—the War Office was not represented and no directive from the Radio Board appears to have been communicated in respect of priorities of importance and the allocation of production capacity, for the three Services.

Quantitative Requirements. The basis on which the G.S. calculation of requirements was made was, generally, the number of units, weapons, gun sites, batteries, or of other appliances to which radar was linked, such as the predictors, searchlights, etc. The number of G.L. I sets required, for example, agreed with the number of predictors that would be available by the probable date that the improved G.L. II would be coming into supply; S.L.C. sets matched the number of searchlights needed, coastal artillery batteries for counter bombardment and for close defence of harbours required each its own C.A. sets, but this figure was reduced in cases where conditions permitted the serving of several batteries by one radar station.

The totals of individual types in some cases reached large figures; often the initial requirements were reduced later for various reasons or had to be extended to provide for additional weapons or changed tactical needs. In some cases diversion to meet Allied needs reduced the numbers available for our own and occasionally production had to be stopped before full provision had been made, in order to free production capacity for other urgent work.

A detail of the production figures for the different types of Army radar equipment is given in Appendix V: only the major types are included and the actual numbers of equipment supplied and notes against certain items indicate changes from originally stated requirement or diversions to other than our Army needs.

There was often much unnecessary labour involved in detailing the requirements down to the last individual set. The word "unnecessary" has been used advisedly because in nearly every case of radar provision the eventual number of sets supplied to the Army did not agree with the original figure of requirements. In the usually long period between the passing of the order to the Ministry and the delivery of the last set, conditions had altered the required numbers sometimes upward, sometimes downward, for reasons entirely unpredictable. In several cases, also, advances in technique and development had rendered a type already ordered out of date before some at least of the equipment had been manufactured; that is one of the difficulties with such a novel and rapidly developing appliance as radar equipment.

In retrospect it seems strange that round figures, downward to the nearest ten or hundred for example, were not agreed as the reasonable basis for ordering. The "odd" figures involved a considerable amount of extra labour in the calculation of the spares, components, valves, and other bits and pieces for which there were a number of different scales or rates of wastage. These different items ran into several thousands in some sets and they had to have a factual basis as the component supply position was a very big factor in the rate of manufacture of the sets themselves. Round figures for the number of equipments demanded would certainly have reduced this effort and would have made easier the ordering of components by the manufacturers. In this respect the General Staff must bear the responsibility—they should have tackled this matter with the Finance Branches who would, undoubtedly, have accepted a "rounded" figure for ordering provision on the Ministry if the proposition had been put to them.

Probably the chief difficulty from the G.S. point of view was the "time" factor—the time by which supply would start and the rate at which supplies would be delivered. The complexity and novelty of radar equipment was such that the production firms and the Ministry officials were generally unable to give any really effective dates before the production flow was well into its stride. There were frequent cases of optimistic forecasts that were quite unjustified and most misleading. That such forecasts were furnished by representatives of the development directorates in many cases is true, but they should have been in a position to ascertain the facts within their own Ministry. The General Staff were not adequately informed of the true production position, and had no direct official access to the production authorities dealing with radar; they had permissive contacts with the Ministry's production directorate which itself had but second-hand information on the radar side, though it dealt with other parts of the equipment.

The result was that operational planning was affected by erroneous provision information and, in consequence, demands were made for larger numbers of equipment in cases when a new design was ripening and might have replaced the later part of the supply of the older type with advantage, had the production time been more realistically estimated.

This lack of liaison on production matters also resulted in the position that War Office operational radar requirements did not appear to carry their priorities beyond the development stage into the competition for production capacity. When the Radio Production Executive was formed the representation of the Army's urgent operational needs was certainly no better than third hand, whereas those of the other two Services happened to be directly represented by members of the body itself. Undoubtedly certain Naval and R.A.F. offensive requirements were of the highest priority from the operational point of view, but some of the Army needs in the last eighteen months of the war were certainly approaching that standard.

Whether or not there was a lack of recognition of the priority of certain Army radar needs, the fact remains that production time for Army radar was the limiting factor in equipping our troops with up-to-date appliances. Towards the end of the war, radar aids to Army offensive operations that would have been of material assistance to our field Armies in the last stages of the European campaigns did not become available to our troops.

Emergency Provision. That special or abnormal action was taken by the General Staff, on occasion, with the aid and good will of the Ministry of Supply and its establishments to make provision for special occasions is true. That it did achieve its object is illustrated by the cases of "Baby Maggie," an emergency requirement for the North Africa and Sicily landing operations, the 10 cm. detection sets at Dover provided with special valves as a safeguard against enemy jamming, the provision of special 3 cm. C.A. No. 1, Mark IV sets to operate in the Dover and Isle of Wight areas for the invasion period, and the "crash" production of "Gorgonzola" for 21 Army Group. The three latter items were made available in record time to aid the Normandy landing operations. The diversion of the Establishment's workshop facilities from its experimental work was amply justified by the results achieved.

In connection with the preparations for the great Normandy invasion operation, it may be mentioned that early in 1944 a small body of scientists and Service officers concerned with radar, led by Sir Robert Watson-Watt, were allowed full knowledge of the plans of the invasion operations. They were put in the picture completely, so that they should be in a position to advise how radar could best serve and assist those operations, particularly during the difficult periods of the crossing and approach, and the extent to which radar deception could be applied effectively to mislead the enemy. The Army radar representatives were, the Director of Radar, War Office, with Brigadier Schonland of the A.O.R.G. and Professor Cockcroft of A.D.R.D.E., who were able to assist in the formulation of recommendations that were in several instances acceptable and proved effective. The majority of the recommendations were concerned with the Naval and Air Force provision for jamming, deception, accurate navigation, target location and the recognition of specific landing-places; the Army radar aspect was not really at issue. Schonland and Cockcroft particularly, as scientists, were able to contribute materially to the development of the appliances and methods recommended. The two aids mentioned in the previous paragraph—10 cm. tunable magnetrons for the Dover cross-Channel watch and protection from possible jamming and the special pairs of 3 cm. sets of high discrimination which had already been installed—were welcomed as a valuable aid to the operations.

Modification Control. Another aspect of G.S. policy that should be mentioned is the need for maintaining the uniformity of each type of equipment and to limit modifications and alterations to those proved by the official design authorities and accepted as essential for the equipment or its performance. Changes made locally without authority defeat the essential uniformity and interchangeability of equipment and upset the test, maintenance and repair organization. Frequently such changes lead to trouble, particularly in the case of equipment of the complexity of radar sets whose design is dependent upon a careful balance of interacting components, both electrical and mechanical. Changes made without full knowledge and experience may effect on occasion some improvement in one direction, but that is usually found to be offset by some deterioration in another and the overall performance usually suffers.

The first type of equipment introduced was the G.L. I which was produced and supplied without having been submitted to the full range of trials and operational tests that are the normal procedure in peace conditions; this was, of course, due to the impending outbreak of war. The equipment had, therefore, more than the usual number of "bugs" to be found and eliminated, and the appearance of some of them was, naturally, made during operational use. Parallel with this difficulty the experience of the technical and maintenance staffs was very limited as also were their numbers. The aid of a number of scientists had to be enlisted as an *ad hoc* measure to act as "nurses" to these new and tender appliances, and to keep them functioning as effectively as possible.

The keenness of these scientists and of the Radar Is.F.C. and T.I.s allocated to A.A. units, achieved wonders but also involved a number of unofficial modifications. Most of these were, however, sorted out and some degree of uniform practice was attained which eventually led to the definition of officially approved modification.

This unorthodox procedure was accepted and endorsed by the G.S. as it was the only means of keeping the sets in effective action and of clearing up unforeseen troubles. It was realized, however, that this special case should not form a precedent for repetition with the more fully tested and proved equipment to be issued later. At the time of the introduction of the G.L. II type, particular attention was directed by the G.S. to this aspect, and while expressing appreciation of the work done in this unorthodox way, it specifically required all suggestions for modification and improvement to be submitted through the War Office directorate for official action to be taken to implement such modifications as might be approved and that local action should not be allowed without specific prior approval.

Radar Intelligence. One of the primary interests of our scientists, as well as of the Service operational staffs, was the nature and effectiveness of German radar. By interception and monitoring of the enemy radar transmissions from sites within reach of such appliances, it was possible to determine their working frequencies and other transmission details, and it was also possible to locate these stations with good accuracy. Further information could be gained by aerial photographic reconnaissance, but these methods could not expose the full details of the equipments; there was a distinct need for more detailed information to determine progress in development and the accuracy of performance of the German radar.

Towards the end of 1941 a novel type of set had been located at Bruneval, near the coast north-east of Le Havre, and the photographs taken from the air showed a large reflector, apparently parabolic, for its aerial system. Though it appeared too large for centimetric wave-length working—it was just at this time that we were entering the centimetric field—it was certainly a novelty. It was decided that parties of Airborne and Combined Operations formations should raid this station and dismantle such of the set as could be brought away. There were defence posts and a garrison protecting the site, and larger forces within reach at short notice, that would have to be dealt with or held off sufficiently long for the dismantling and removal of the radar parts and the withdrawal of the raiding parties. Time was an all-essential factor in the planning of this operation, but the feature with which this record is concerned is the radar aspect. The question was how to ensure that useful information could be obtained and how the parts of the equipment that were of the greatest importance to the scientists could be recognized and brought away.

It must be remembered that radar was a closed book to all but a comparatively small number of specialist personnel in the three Services and the fighting that would be needed to capture the set and get such bits and pieces of it safely away demanded highly trained troops—scientists or specialist technicians might be an added burden to those troops. There was also another reason for excluding scientific and technical radar experts, and that was that any personnel captured by the enemy would not be able to disclose information about our equipment as they would have no knowledge of it or its working.

This latter aspect produced something of a problem in how to instruct the raiding party and prepare them for the task of dismantling the set and selecting the most important components. A party of sappers of the 1st Airborne Division was detailed for the job and the C.R.E., Lieutenant-Colonel Henniker, got permission to consult the Deputy Director for Radar in the War Office. It was essential, of course, to maintain the greatest secrecy in regard to the contemplated raid and no one, except the minimum of individuals necessary for the planning, was to have any knowledge that such a raid was even contemplated. Brigadier Sayer, the D.D. for Radar, discussed the problem with Colonel Schonland of the Operational Research Group, who, apart from being a scientific soldier, intimately connected with radar, had facilities for unobtrusive instruction and demonstration that would be suitable for this purpose. It was arranged that an early type of G.L. I set should be used for explaining the important parts to be looked for, and that a mock-up set made up of various assemblies and an aerial system somewhat of the same nature as that of the German set, should be prepared. Henniker was then put in touch with Schonland and the sapper party received some general instruction and were shown how to take the sets to pieces, what to look for and how to recognize those parts that were of most importance. Only three visits for this instruction were needed, at the last of which a test was made on the mock-up set. It was so rapidly and effectively dismantled, unaided and without damage, that the remainder of the visit was, at the request of troops, given up to letting them put it all together again. Somewhat surprisingly they managed this, but they were most disappointed to find that it would not work—that was not their fault however, as the set had not been built to operate.

That this training had been useful was amply proved by the results in the raid itself at the end of February, 1942. An addition was actually made at the last minute to the dismantling party of a R.A.F. Flight Sergeant named Cox, a radar technician; he had volunteered for the job and had learnt how to use a parachute only a few days before the raid took place.

This dismantling party under Lieutenant Vernon certainly did their job and did it well; all essential parts were removed and all were embarked safely with the exception of one tender C.R. tube forming the presentation unit, which received damage. These bits and pieces with Cox's notes were most useful to the scientists and enabled them to determine practically all the information they required. To make quite sure that sufficient evidence was made available, the sapper party carefully removed a German radar technician and an operator found in the post, who were persuaded to accompany the party back to this country as prisoners—one of them talked quite usefully. This German set was a "Wurtzberg"—a 50 cm. wave-length air detection static equipment with a rotatable parabolic aerial reflector for Transmission and Reception.

The foregoing incident was not the only practical search for information on the details of German radar equipment, but it was the only one in which radar formed the object of a special operation. A special expedition across the Atlantic was made at short notice by some scientific personnel to retrieve what they could of the radar ranging gear from the *Graf Spee* before it should disappear in the mud of the River Plate. Full details of the aerial system were brought back but only one dipole was recovered in this case, as fire had destroyed the set itself, and the remainder could not be reached in the mud that had filled most of the ship.

Later, when land operations were in progress, radar stations were sometimes over-run before they had been destroyed by the enemy. In Sicily soon after the first landing a "Chimney" type Freya radar station was found abandoned, but unfortunately the enthusiasm of some sappers for demolition work had made its remains of little value to our technical observers by the time they reached it. Similarly, a little later in the U.S. area of operations, a new type of Fighter Direction radar set had been pretty well stripped of valves and other components before the technicians could examine it. These cases led to stricter orders on the subject and also to the pushing forward of technical observers with the leading troops when any such equipment was known to be in the vicinity. In this work the personnel of the Army Operational Research Group and specialist Army officers for technical information of all kinds of weapons and equipment, who were attached to formations, did most useful service. The latter in the North African, Sicilian and Italian campaigns, operated under the name of "Wheatsheaf" or more properly Weapons Technical Staff, Field Forces.

Further information of German radar was obtained from investigation of captured equipment. Arrangements between the United Kingdom and United States authorities were made for the distribution between them of captured weapons and particularly of radar sets and appliances. For the latter the first sample recovered was to be despatched to this country for scientific and technical examination and the second to the United States. Some information was obtained from these sources, but it was usually out of date, and of interest rather than of value, by the time the set or appliance reached the research establishments, though reports from the field observers who had access to such captured equipment before it was shipped were of some slight value as well as interest.

One other aspect of information on the effectiveness of the performance of German radar must be mentioned. This was the inclusion, in bomber aircraft crews or as passenger observers, of officers acquainted with radar fire control of A.A. guns and of the control of searchlights. These observers came mostly from A.A. Command and took part in several raids over Germany. Whether material value was obtained is somewhat doubtful in respect of the effect of German radar methods though some interesting reports on their observations were, however, received.

CHAPTER XXVIII. RADAR TRAINING

With the experimental development of radar for Army use showing promise of early useful employment and of important advances to come later, the War Office was faced in 1938 and 1939 with the problems of selection and training of personnel to operate and maintain this novel class of equipment. It was a completely new field of activity which had some technical relationship with signals radio communications and at the same time was aimed at fitting intimately into the artillery systems of anti-aircraft and coastal methods of fire direction and control. Though a small detachment of Royal Signals had been attached to assist at the Bawdsey Research Establishment, it was decided by the War Office that the primary responsibility for the use and operation of radar equipment should rest with the Royal Artillery. None of the Artillery Schools likely to be affected—the School of Anti-Aircraft Defence, the Coast Artillery School and the Searchlight School—had any facilities for this type of instruction, nor had they instructors with any knowledge of the subject. In the same way the Military College of Science, which was the establishment for higher technical and scientific training, had at that time but little knowledge of the subject and were not in a position to provide proper technical training for ordnance officers, artificers and mechanics for repair work, etc.

The initial problem of training, therefore, resolved itself into the means of instructing instructors for the Schools to enable them to start training personnel to operate the equipment and to study its uses. With the growing threat of war the need for getting training started was urgent and the needs of operational units and of technical ordnance repair and maintenance personnel had to be met in parallel with those of the basic operational training at the schools.

How these problems were tackled will be described briefly in the following paragraphs dealing with individual schools and establishments. Here it may be mentioned that the first start in training had to be made before any training equipment was available and, in fact, before the actual design of the first type of service equipment was complete—only a few experimental sets were in existence. That it managed to achieve what it did under the circumstances is remarkable.

Apart from the development of the training facilities and providing a nucleus of trained instructional staff, there was the question of the selection of personnel for all the different classes of radar work and their various degrees of training. The somewhat arbitrary selection from volunteers in the earliest days when numbers were very small, proved successful as judged by results. It was, however, necessary to replace that system, to deal with the increasing numbers needed, by more selective methods from the whole field of newly recruited personnel, male and female, and to allocate those selected to radar duties in parallel with approved volunteers from units. In this the Selection Committees, with their Psychiatrists to aid them, produced a high average of suitable individuals for those duties of the less technical nature and helped in the assessment of the qualifications of the higher grade duty.

Mention must be made of the value of the work initiated by Lord Hankey in tackling the long-range problem of providing adequately for the mechanic and artificer types. He, with his committee, instituted the scheme for instruction of boys intended for these grades, in civilian technical colleges before they had reached the enlistment or call-up ages. This produced a series of groups of young potential technicians with a basis of knowledge on which to build in the service schools. These boys on satisfactory completion of their technical college courses could choose to which Service they would prefer to go, for the scheme provided for radio and radar personnel for all three Services. There is no doubt that this scheme was of great value to the Services and the standard of knowledge at entry was of a high average which simplified and speeded up training after entry.

One further material point in the general consideration of the training problem must be mentioned and that is the decision to employ women, recruited into the A.T.S., for operational radar duties, or rather for H.A.A. fire control duties including radar. This was probably the first instance of women in any numbers being employed in Army units to assist in the actual handling and direction of weapons against the enemy. The nursing services had, of course, experienced the effect of enemy fire and domestic and administrative duties had been performed or assisted by women enrolled in the Service, but women had not been called upon before to play an active part in action against the enemy. Their employment on predictors, plotting, height and range-finding, radar and similar work with the A.A. ground defences was of great value in releasing men for the more active and offensive aspects of warfare.

In general, this type of work was well suited to the intelligence and aptitude of women who, on the average, were a little quicker to learn, though perhaps rather longer to attain the highest degree of accuracy. Perhaps it would be truer to say that, as a result of training, women were quicker to reach a good average of skill, but the proportion that achieved the highest grade of accuracy of performance was somewhat lower than with men. This was certainly the case with radar operation, though with experience in action the A.T.S. personnel really produced a standard of performance no lower than that of male operators. There was certainly no sign of unsteadiness under attack, and in the boring periods of searching without targets appearing, and uneventful watches, they seemed to have a greater facility than men to maintain their performance standard and not to let it be affected by uneventful monotony.

The numbers of women contemplated for radar and other fire control duties ran into large numbers, something between 50,000 and 60,000 were actually employed, and it will be appreciated that the training problem presented was by no means a small one.

School of Anti-Aircraft Artillery. This school developed during the war from the original peace-time school at Biggin Hill known as the School of Anti-Aircraft Defence. At Biggin Hill it had been beside the experimental establishment then known as the Air Defence Experimental Establishment, and each benefited from the association and contact with the other, as well as with that of the R.A.F. station. The war brought about removal and separation which, apart from the need for expansion of facilities and intensification of the output of each, was essential owing to the exposed position and the urgent need of the R.A.F. to extend their operational airfield. The move of the school to Norfolk had been contemplated for some time and steps had been taken towards implementing the decision, but work on the site selected at Langham had hardly commenced and it was never occupied. With one or two intermediate "perches" the school settled down at Manorbier with branches or wings for special subjects at different places which were eventually concentrated with the main school.

The branch that was formed to deal with radar is the one with which this book is mainly concerned; its formation and development will be described briefly.

Before the actual formation of a wireless wing for the school, a technical gunner officer—Major H. M. Paterson—was appointed to the War Office artillery directorate for radar purposes and was detached to the Bawdsey Research Station in June, 1938, to get fully into the radar picture; he and the officer in charge of the Signals detachment—Lieutenant Nolan—attended a course of instruction arranged by the Air Ministry at Bawdsey. Paterson on completion of the course, after an interruption due to the Munich scare, remained in constant touch with the development of Army radar; in addition he covered the maintenance and training aspects and the necessary arrangements to be made for them, until Capt. A. S. Milner, under D.M.T., relieved him of them.

In September, 1938, Major J. B. Hickman of the Royal Signals was seconded to Bawdsey to take over instruction of R.A. personnel in Radar; he first occupied himself in studying the subject as far as it had progressed by that time. Towards the end of that year arrangements had been made for a special instructors' course to be held at Bawdsey, before the formation of the Wireless Wing of the School, to deal with Army radar instruction, which was to be formed at Landguard Fort, Felixstowe.

This course started at the end of January, 1939, under the direction of Hickman with the aid of some of the Army "cell" working on development of equipment; Paterson gave instruction in A.A. gunnery and the use of the G.L. radar set, then in experimental form, that was to become the first equipment for the Army as the Mark I. The number taking the course was small, but among them was Major G. C. Gray, who became Second-in-Command to Hickman when the Wireless Wing was formed, and 4 or 5 other officers and 4 other ranks. These individuals on completion of their course became the first of the new class of Instructors in Radar; the officers became Instructors Fire Control (I.F.C.) and the other ranks, Assistant or Technical Instructors designated T.I.F.C., carrying the minimum rank of Staff-Serjeant.

The Wireless Wing of the school was established in Landguard Fort in March, 1939, with a staff of 1 Major (Hickman) as Chief Instructor, 3 officers as Instructors (I.F.C.) and 4 Assistants (T.I.), with an Adjutant and his staff of civilians. It was from this nucleus that the wing grew, by 1943, to a total of all ranks of over 200, including a considerable number of A.T.S. The latter were employed mainly on administrative, but some on technical duties; a maintenance and repair detachment of R.E.M.E. personnel was also included. In addition a number of I.s F.C. and T.I.s detached to the various practice camps, and to other wings of the school, were on its establishment.

The primary object of the courses was to train officers and N.C.O.s selected as potential instructors, not only for schools and their various wings, but the greater number of them, for formations and units in this country and overseas, including field forces. These courses were known as War Special Wireless courses and, with the introduction of new equipments, Refresher courses had to be introduced, to bring the earlier trainees up to date; lengthening of the W.S.W. courses was also necessary to compete with the number of types of equipment to be dealt with. Special courses were also introduced for a different type of trainee, namely, the N.C.O. in charge of operators of sets, and others for American officers, for Regimental officers, and for senior officers to give them a fuller appreciation of radar as an aid to their operations.

The growth in the output of trained personnel, in parallel with the development of radar equipment, is shown by the approximate totals of students dealt with in the early war years. The numbers were: 1940—130; 1941—280; 1943—380 plus 38 A.T.S.

The duration of W.S.W. courses rose from some eight weeks in 1939 to sixteen and a further six with the gunnery and searchlight wings in 1944.

Only two courses were held before the outbreak of war and the second was hardly completed when that day arrived; these two were "special Wireless Courses" but are referred to here as W.S.W. courses.

The first W.S.W. course assembled on May 1st, 1939, after some preliminary instruction at the M.C. of S., when the only equipment then available was one experimental prototype G.L. I set. The course was interrupted for a period of attachment to A.A. Command units pending return to Felixstowe in August, when two sets of the production type of G.L. I had become available. This course of 13 officers and 17 technical civilians (potential T.I.s), therefore overlapped the second course which had started at the beginning of July and consisted of 13 officers and 24 civilians, also potential T.I.s. The trainees were dispersed to their units, on 26th August, and no further entries could be accepted until the wing was moved to Watchet, previously a practice camp, as its early war-time home. The Wireless Wing continued there until it was moved later to Manorbier and concentrated with the rest of the S.A.A.A.

From its start at Watchet in September, 1939, it had included in its courses all the preliminary training in radar that had previously been done at the Military College of Science. This preliminary training was done, subsequently, starting in June, 1941, at technical colleges and at Southampton University College at which all students attended a 10 weeks' course before starting at Watchet. This assistance from these external training arrangements continued until September, 1944, when the Military College of Science re-assumed its function of initial and basic training for I.s F.C. and T.I.s F.C.

It was apparent in the early days of the training that, as these Instructors and Assistants found themselves largely responsible for the maintenance of radar equipment, there was a strong technical bias in the training. The necessity for this was reduced when R.E.M.E. took over this responsibility and as a result the instructors and their assistants concentrated more on instructional duties and on the essential role of the I.F.C. as an adviser to brigade, etc., commanders on the siting and tactical use of radar. These aspects took precedence over the more technical side of these courses during 1942, and was materially assisted by a re-arrangement of courses that ensured a period of attachment of all radar trainees to the gunnery wing.

The training in searchlight radar varied somewhat from the normal organization. Anti-aircraft searchlight training was carried out early in the war at the school established at Shrivenham. This was really a Searchlight Training Establishment, though linked to S.A.A.A. Later it was moved to Rhyl, where it became a specific part of the School as a detached wing. The Searchlight wing then became a somewhat curious exception to the general practice of the school, as training of searchlight operators and of selected personnel for radar control of searchlights was carried out in this wing. Instructors in Searchlights (I.S.) received their radar training in the normal W.S.W. courses and carried out the training at the Searchlight wing of S.L.C. operators as well as searchlight personnel. In all other cases, initial training of radar operators was carried out by Royal Artillery Training Establishments (R.A.T.E.).

Most of the officers who attended the first early course were associated with radar throughout the war and their names are closely linked with Army radar. They were selected from volunteers from all arms of the Service and they were the nucleus on which the operational use and effect of Army radar developed and expanded.

It is of some historical interest to note the names of these officer trainees at the first of the War Special Wireless courses. They were:—

Royal Artillery. Captain E. H. Cox, Lieutenants Hope, A. D. D. Tree, W. Heath; 2nd Lieutenant Deakin.

Royal Engineers. Lieutenant Jarrett.

Infantry. Major Curtiss, The Royal Fusiliers; Major Yates, Royal Scots Fusiliers; Lieutenant Northey, Cameronians; Lieutenant Briscoe, Leicestershires; Lieutenant Eden, Cheshires; Lieutenant C. M. Inigo-Jones, Bedfords.

R.A.S.C. Lieutenant Pearson.

All these officers were posted as Instructors, Fire Control, on completion of the course; the majority were appointed to Brigades in A.A. Command, but Tree was appointed to the B.E.F. and Heath and Deakin to Malta and Gibraltar respectively.

Captains A. E. G. Haig and R. R. Lindsay were Instructors to this course with Major G. C. Gray; the N.C.O. Assistant Instructors included S. M. Bell (School Serjeant-Major), Rushworth and Hall.

Of these early trainees some, after field experience in A.A. Command, held Staff appointments in the War Office or aided in directing development in the Ministry of Supply; others helped training in the Schools, while many justified their training and ability by developing the practical employment of radar in the defence of this country and overseas. Some took to the more technical aspects of modifications, authorized or otherwise, and of R.E.M.E. activities.

Many others could be mentioned but this is not the place to do so; Hickman, Paterson and Gray have been referred to as early founders of the Wireless Wing and they finished the war in appointments—Hickman in the Ministry controlling radar research and development with Paterson controlling the fire control radar and technical matters on D.G. of A. Staff, and Gray as Director of Radar in the War Office. The sound development of the S.A.A.A. and the value of its training was fully shown by the most effective results it produced; it undoubtedly made a material contribution to the efficiency of the Army's ground defences against air attack.

The Commandants of this school were successively, Brigadiers T. C. Newton, A. J.-R. M. Leslie, A. L. Pemberton, F. St. D. B. LeJeune and R. B. Peters.

Royal Artillery Training Establishments. An organization known as R.A.T.E. was brought into being to deal with the training of personnel for A.A. units and for unit training. Its activities dealt with all the varied requirements of A.A. units and separate regiments were established for intake and initial military training, for training of personnel in the different forms of operational duties for which they were to be allocated such as Heavy A.A., Light A.A., Searchlights, Driving, Radar, Fire Control instruments, etc. Separate initial training regiments were provided for A.T.S. personnel and were largely staffed by technically trained A.T.S. officers and auxiliaries.

In addition, R.A.T.E. had under their charge a number of A.A. practice camps at which units as a whole received unit training and carried out practice shoots and their team work could be assessed; A.A. Command in the same way owned and ran some practice camps and staffed them generally from their own resources. The training regiments and practice camps were no concern of S.A.A.A. except to the extent that it provided the specialist gunnery and radar instructional staff for them; except in a few cases, A.A. Command found their own. In this respect the School had some influence on gunnery and radar policy in the training.

R.A.T.E. were responsible for the training of all radar operators and the N.C.O.s or No. 1s of radar detachments and the supply to units of teams or individual trained personnel. In their early days the regiments concentrated solely upon the training of radar operators in the manipulation of the radar controls—little more than pure "knob turning"—but by degrees instruction extended to cover some general knowledge of the way in which the sets worked, elementary maintenance and the needs of the predictor, plotter or other instruments to which the output of their set was fed. As has been mentioned in the previous paragraphs the No. 1s of detachments were later given a higher degree of training at the Radar Wing of the school.

R.A.T.E. received the whole of the intake allocated to meet A.A. needs and gave them their preliminary training; they were responsible for selection for the various duties and training in the operational work required to perform those duties to an extent that would enable them to take their place in a unit and with experience to become fully operational and effective in the team work that depended so largely upon the radar equipment.

Major-General J. M. R. Harrison organized and controlled these establishments.

Coast Artillery School. The start towards the formation of a radar wing at the C.A.S. really dates from November, 1939, when Major F. A. Henslowe, R.A., and two B.S.M.s, R. Brennan and J. Mears, attended a war special wireless course (No. 6) at Watchet. On its completion Henslowe and Brennan were detached in February, 1940, to A.D.R.D.E. to get fully into the picture of the C.D./C.H.L. set then approaching its final development form. They then joined the wing at Watchet in July as Instructors for Coast Artillery and the wing thus had the dual role of A.A. and C.A. (or C.D. as it was then called) radar training of specialist personnel. The first C.D. radar course—No. II— was held at Watchet in September, 1940, and this really marked the birth of the C.A.S. Radar Wing.

At the C.A.S. itself, Major Henslowe was the first Chief Instructor in radar and later when he was appointed C.I.G., Major Liston-Foulis replaced him for a short time. The building-up of this wing into a very effective instructional organization was largely due to these two officers, but later officers also contributed to its success, notable among them being Major H. J. Dixon. Apart from these officers one other figure stood out as playing a leading part in the radar wing and its activities, S.M.T.I. R. Brennan, who remained with the wing until the end of the war. He carried out work of the greatest value, his influence on the trainees was remarkable, and he became more or less a legendary character with his success in carrying out "impossible" jobs and keeping equipment in action in spite of shortages of parts, breakdowns, removals and reconstructions.

The first course at the C.A.S. Landudno was held in October, 1940, for operators of C.D. radar sets, in parallel with the W.S.W. courses for instructors at the combined wing at Watchet; but in March, 1941, the equipment—such as it was—was removed to Llandudno and established there in conjunction with the new radar laboratory then under construction.

The first W.S.W. course held at the C.A.S. radar wing as a separate entity started in April, but with the incomplete laboratory and shortage of equipment and components, the course dragged on into August. The trainees, however, gained a variety of practical experience of radar equipment if not so much with its operational performance as they took part in the erection and installation of sets that were to be the basis of their practical instruction. At this time all installation, setting-up and maintenance of radar equipment was carried out by the personnel of the School, and it was not until the middle of 1942 that the responsibility was taken over by a R.E.M.E. detachment.

Shortage of equipment in the early days was a handicap to instruction, but by September, 1942, there was just sufficient for full training of classes singly. The permanent C.D./C.H.L. set was in action and the first—and only—pilot model of the C.A. No. 1, Mark I fire control set had been taken over on loan from the C.A.E.E. section established on the Great Orme alongside the C.A.S.; in addition, a certain amount of components and class-room equipment had been collected by various means. From this time both W.S.W. and Operators' courses began to run regularly; the former lasting for 19 weeks, of which the first 10 were spent on preliminary training at Technical Colleges, and the remainder on the practical radar and gunnery aspect.

By March, 1942, the establishment of the radar wing was 1 Major, Chief Instructor; 6 Majors or Captains I.F.C.; 8 T.I.s F.C. and a demonstration party of 6 N.C.O.s and 7 Operators; a maintenance detachment of 1 Armament Artificer (R.A.O.C.) and 2 Electricians; fire control was provided for but never materialized until the nucleus of a Radio Maintenance Detachment arrived in June.

Early in 1942, the last course for N.C.O.s-in-Charge of sets had been held and training of all operators of C.A. and C.D. sets from that time was carried out by the Coast Artillery Training Centre established at Plymouth. Up to this time some 320 students had been handled on "N.C.O.-in-Charge" courses and 840 odd on the junior O.F.C. courses. Actually one conversion course was held later for trained N.C.O.s-in-Charge to give instruction in the centimetric type of sets.

With the relaxation of pressure due to the transfer of responsibility for training of operators to C.A.T.C., and to the fact that the numbers of I.s F.C. and T.I.s F.C. needed for coast artillery were comparatively small, it was possible to ease the pace and to take single courses for these grades without overlapping. This also made it possible to run refresher courses to bring instructors up to date with the newer centimetric types of equipment, and more important still, to train them as instructors in gunnery and *vice versa*. This latter innovation started in February, 1942, and a considerable number of officers and warrant officers became qualified in both these aspects. This was a very sound and logical step with the great advantage that it brought radar as the primary means of C.A. fire control completely into the gunnery picture—gunnery and radar were interdependent.

In addition, further series of courses were introduced for unit officers and N.C.O.s and short courses of a somewhat higher standard for unit instructors; all of these helped towards a general understanding of the value and importance of the aid that radar could give to the coastal guns for effective operation.

Mention has already been made, in Part III, of the close liaison that existed between C.A.S. and the Dover defences which were the most active and effective in their operations, and there is no need to enlarge upon it here except to record that the C.A.S. and its radar wing fully appreciated the value of this operational opportunity.

There is one other point worthy of note and for which credit is due to the C.A.S. This is the Coast Artillery Radar Trainer, which was devised and brought into practical form entirely by the school—no other trainer existed and the capacity of the A.D.R.D.E. could not be diverted from its urgent operational commitments to design one. This trainer was originated by Major Dixon when the one and only C.A. No. 1, Mark I set had come to the end of its life and utility as an operational set in October, 1942. It was dismantled and its presentation unit was set up in a demonstration room of the school; from this it grew into the "Dixon Trainer" which provided target echoes and also those from shell splashes, so that operational training became available in class-room conditions. With further additions and accessories to permit of operation with all the communication and gunnery instruments, this device became known as "C.A.S. Series 2 Trainer"; it was eventually adopted by the War Office and approval was given for its production, in the limited numbers necessary, by R.E.M.E. Central Workshops. This school had evinced a full appreciation of the possibilities of radar for C.A. purposes and showed foresight in planning their training to deal with it effectively. There is no doubt that the good results produced are a tribute to the school staff under Brigadiers A. Court-Treat and C. Oliver who were successively the Commandants during the war period.

Coast Artillery Training Centre. The C.A.T.C. was established at Plymouth in conjunction with the defences of that important harbour; its object was to train all other ranks personnel in coast artillery duties and functions and to provide complete units, specialist teams of operators and individual trained gunners; with the advent of radar as a practical aid to C.A. operations it had to assume responsibility for radar operators' training.

In this, C.A.T.C. relieved C.A.S. of the training of radar operators at the beginning of 1942. Their initial radar work was the provision of trained operators for C.D./C.H.L. sets and 10 cm. C.D. sets to form Coast Observer Detachments to man the stations in the coastal chain. With the experience gained on these equipments these C.O.D.s provided a very useful supply of personnel, for retraining rapidly, to man the battery fire control sets for C.B. and C.D. batteries.

In contrast to H.A.A. radar it may be noted that no A.T.S. personnel were employed in the C.O.D.s nor on the C.A. sets; this was largely due to the exposed and isolated positions of some of the sets in the coastal chain and the intention, if not the full practice, of radar and visual range-taking being alternative duties of the same individuals.

Military College of Science. With their normal responsibility covering the higher academic and technical aspects of instruction in the principles and application of artillery weapons and their associated technical accessories, it was natural that the M.C. of S. should be one of the first to be brought into the radar picture. The scope of the training that the college provided covered the initial instruction in basic principles to form the ground work on which to build the more detailed training in the scientific and technical details of radar; it also provided training in maintenance and repair of individual types of equipment. The grades of personnel to be dealt with included technical officers of the Artillery and Ordnance—later R.E.M.E.—and the somewhat less technical officer instructors for schools, units and formations. In addition there were the highest grade technical W.O.s, the N.C.O.s artificers and mechanics to be trained in theory and in practice and to be given experience in fault finding, adjustment, maintenance, testing, calibration and collimation with the instruments and weapons to be served.

The wide scope and the varied grades of trainees presented a considerable problem when it is realized that the subject, radar, was not only novel but was continuously growing. That the College produced the good results it did is a tribute to the energy and foresight of the College staff.

It has been mentioned earlier in this chapter that the College undertook the preliminary stage of the training of officer and other rank candidates for the war special wireless courses, but this had to be given up on the outbreak of war to meet the urgent need for increasing the output of the artificer and mechanic classes. That part of the preliminary training was transferred to certain Technical Colleges and Universities, by special arrangement, which allowed the M.C. of S. to concentrate its radar instruction upon the higher technical and scientific needs of the Ordnance and later R.E.M.E. officers.

The move of the M.C. of S. from Woolwich to Bury near Manchester—with an eight months' interlude at Lydd, from September, 1939, and the expansion of facilities for the increasing numbers requiring training—did not make matters easy and the lack of radar equipment and components added materially to the difficulties; it at first limited the numbers of trained personnel that could be turned out. Even these limited numbers had to gain practical experience on completion of the College courses and this naturally meant that fully skilled maintenance and repair personnel were few and far between for some time.

Later the position improved with the training facilities and availability of equipment, components and sets; the improvement was also partly due to the start of the flow of "Boy Artificers" or young entry who had received their initial basic training in the technical colleges before joining the forces, which naturally relieved the College of part of the burden of initial training. The transfer in the summer of 1941 of the Electricians, Fire Control from the gunners to the R.A.O.C. as Radio Mechanics, also helped very materially, particularly as the majority of them had already been given instruction in R.A. units and A.A. Command schools and had gained some practical experience of maintenance and adjustments in the field.

In September, 1943, the M.C. of S. began to revert to its normal position of being the primary source of scientific and technical instruction for the Army. By then the pre-entry training of boys at the technical schools and colleges had become a normal feature of their preparation for the Services or industry. The College restarted the initial training of officer candidates for the I.F.C. special courses at the C.A.S. and followed that in 1944 by taking the S.A.A.A. course candidates also.

Criticism has been made at times that the M.C. of S. was too academic in its radar instruction and insufficiently practical, and there may be some small justification for this in those early days of the war period, when the stress and urgent need for trained and experienced technical personnel was great. The critics, however, do not seem to have appreciated the fact that there was not in existence at that time any one individual, let alone a number of individuals, who had practical experience of radar equipment and its needs, except for the few scientists who had developed and designed the early types, partly on an empirical basis. Further, there was a very limited supply of sets and components on which to instruct and to give practical experience. The M.C. of S. might have adopted *ad hoc* methods of providing rapidly an increased number of partly trained mechanics, and so-called artificers to be let loose on these tender and temperamental equipments.

Fortunately, they took a longer view and realized that developments in this new device were certain and had to be faced. The future requirements had to be provided for and that demanded a proper background of knowledge into which the details of new types and applications could be absorbed rapidly and easily.

Some considerable assistance, however, was obtained from firms engaged on radar production—notably the E.M.I. company, Messrs. B.T.H. and Cossors—as they accepted Army artificers and mechanics to work in their factories temporarily on the construction of radar sets. This gave them practical experience and knowledge of the detail make-up of the equipments, while they also received theoretical instruction as well. This was particularly effective in the case of the G.L. II set and was to a somewhat lesser extent, also, in the case of the G.L. III and other sets.

That the Military College of Science maintained its high standard of training and instruction in its radar activities and provided most effectively for a very wide variety of higher grade personnel, can be appreciated from the following selection from the special courses it held during the war.

In 1941 to 1943 it dealt with the conversion of over 650 Electricians, Fire Control, R.A. into Ordnance (R.E.M.E.) mechanics and artificers; the remainder were dealt with in 1943, by the R.E.M.E. schools.

By 1943 it had also passed out between 300 and 350 telecommunication officers—E.M.E. (Radio)—and had held 15 Courses (War Radar Courses) dealing with more than 300 American officers, by 1945.

Two special courses in 1943 for officers of the O.R.G. were held, and in 1944 and early 1945 special courses were held for officers for the Control Commission, totalling over 200.

From 1941 onwards, special War Advanced Courses on Fire Control Instruments, including radar, were continuous; they were of high-grade training for officers for technical appointments (not for I.s G.).

Over 50 officers from all three Services attended special inter-Service Advanced Radar courses during 1944 and early 1945; these courses were instituted in lieu of the proposed setting up of a Radar Staff College considered by the Radio Board, and proved very effective from the scientific as well as from the operational aspects.

All these involved radar in varying degrees of basic and instrumental application and that variety of instruction was of course paralleled by the wide variety of capacity of the different classes of trainees. That variety was extended by the revival of some of the instructional courses for initial training of I.s F.C. for T.I.s F.C. and even for artificers towards the end of the war. In them the College linked radar intimately with the gunnery aspect and thereby aided the elimination of the original idea of radar being an individual and isolated subject and an end in itself.

Throughout the war period Brigadier F. L. McNaughten remained as Commandant of the College, and to him must go some of the credit for its successful work.

Other Radar Training.

Mobile A.A. Training. The provision and selection of A.A. units for inclusion in 21 Army Group was largely controlled by Brigadier W. R.

Revell-Smith for units and individuals from A.A. Command, from R.A.T.C. and from ex-8th Army units. The School of Artillery, Larkhill, assisted in this training and accommodation of the courses; S.A.A.A. also assisted with I.s F.C. and T.I.s. The units were to be equipped with the British type G.L. III, Light Warning sets, S.L.C. mounted searchlights, and some Tactical Control and Warning sets—Gorgonzola—specially produced. The training was aimed mainly at movement, rapid tactical selection of sites and deployment for defence action including, incidentally, A/T action.

Some disturbance was caused in the normal defence arrangements of this country at times by the sudden appearance of "free-lance" batteries under training for field operations engaging enemy bomber raids—they were seldom able to link themselves into the chain of control of operations or the communications network.

School of Artillery. Towards the end of the war the S. of A. Larkhill was extending its multifarious Artillery training duties to include radar as an aid to operations in the field against ground targets. The sets, however, were not out of the experimental stage and had yet to be produced in a form suitable for use in the field. They were of use for training and for assessing their operational value and for deriving provisional ideas as to the methods of employment. A number of Field Artillery personnel were trained in their operation.

Trainers and Training Devices. A considerable number of training devices were produced of a variety of types—practically all of them being for A.A. operations. The devices ranged from the elaborate class-room trainers to small portable sets for "On Site" training of operators.

In all cases the provision of trainers, unfortunately, had to be later than that of the early deliveries of the equipments themselves. Available effort could not be diverted from the immediate needs of equipment development to meet the ever-present enemy air attacks. Many ingenious devices were improvised, and developed into valuable trainers, by Ratcliffe's band of scientists at Petersham, by A.A. Command enthusiastic radar instructors and others, which filled yawning gaps and aided instruction of operators.

The complication of design of a classroom trainer, if it was to be truly representative of actual set operation and to provide the means of recording and showing the faults of individual operators, is comparable in effort involved to the complete development of an accurate H.A.A. set. Some indication of the nature of the "on site" types of trainer has been given in Chapter XXII, but it is not necessary to describe the more elaborate types here. As an indication of the effort involved in producing these trainers the actual figures of the main types produced during the war were—Field Trainers, 4,074; Classroom Trainers, 42.

CHAPTER XXIX. A.A. COMMAND RADAR TRAINING

This is not the place in which to attempt to record the expansion of A.A. Command nor its full activities and achievements—that story must be sought in historical records of the Command. It is, however, appropriate to refer here to the action taken by the Command in providing for special training of operator and maintenance personnel for radar equipment and its adjuncts in the chain of fire control appliances.

A.A. Command was, of course, practically the sole user in the early days of Army radar and throughout the war had greater opportunities for accumulating experience than any other formation. It is no disparagement of radar personnel in other theatres of operations from which comments and reports were received, to say that the primary source of operational information for the guidance of new design requirements was A.A. Command. The later supply of equipment to the more distant theatres and the delays in receipt of reports due to distant and difficult communications, generally made them little more than confirmatory of the correctness of action already taken for improvement. A.A. Command was "on the door step" and immediately accessible to technical and scientific personnel as well as to those of the General Staff concerned with A.A. operations and appliances.

The first official introduction of radar to A.A. Command, as a new and developing device to aid A.A. ground defence, was made at a special conference held at Cambridge on 9th March, 1939. This conference was attended by the staffs of the two then existing A.A. divisions and by senior officers of units; in addition the War Office representation included M.O. 3 (Loch), M.G.O. 14 (Wrisberg and Paterson) and the R.E. and S. Board (Sayer and Colbeck) all of whom were intimately connected with the development of radar. The immediate possibilities of this new device were described and the production position of the earliest type as an aid to visual methods of fire control was explained.

From this discussion arose the question of special training of radar personnel—the first course for officers to qualify as instructors was just starting, but it was appreciated that training of both officer and other rank instructors would have to be expedited, and the selection and training of personnel, already serving with units, to be operators would have to be undertaken on a considerable scale. The A.A. divisions, or A.A. Command, as the combined formations became, at once undertook to provide instruction and training for at least a part of the number of operators needed from their own resources as soon as the first I.s F.C. and T.I.s F.C. to be allocated to them should have completed their radar course. It was in this way that instruction in radar operating started in the A.A. divisional schools that were established by the Command. As has been seen, the S.A.A.A. was already functioning with its Wireless Wing at Landguard in the training of the instructors, and R.A.T.E. was taking shape and was to include the training of radar operators from the new intakes for supplying new units and for completing existing units. The diversion of personnel already trained or partly trained for visual fire control duties could not be carried far without detriment to the efficiency of those duties, and the supply of suitable personnel from other duties requiring a lesser degree of intelligence and skill could not last for long.

After the early months the provision of operators from within their own personnel resources was gradually reduced, but A.A. Command found full occupation for the radar training facilities that they had established, in extended instruction and later, in the conversion of operators to man the newer designs of equipment that were supplied to replace the original types.

Those Command Schools did excellent work and materially helped R.A.T.E.'s normal contribution in this direction. It may be mentioned here that the introduction of S.L.C. for the direction of searchlights put a heavy burden on A.A. Command training facilities, as this equipment had to be introduced as a rush measure with little previous warning and at the same time methods had to be devised to make use of it in the most effective operational manner, which involved considerable operational experiment.

Another and a most important aspect of training was also helped very materially by A.A. Command, namely, instruction and provision for practical experience in repair and maintenance of this new class of equipment by three Divisional Workshop Company R.A.O.C. Schools. The normal organization for training of O.M.E.s, artificers and mechanics was the M.C. of S., but the supply of trained and experienced personnel was almost non-existent when the first supplies of G.L. I were issued to units; there were a few personnel trained in radar, but naturally their practical experience was extremely limited, if more than nil. The A.A. Divisional Workshop Companies R.A.O.C. included radio sections which soon had opportunities of gaining experience of maintenance in the field, and of repair in the workshops. They were, however, swamped with the growing amount of work and the added commitments of calibration and technical adjustment of the early G.L. sets which were, to say the least, tender, temperamental and tricky.

This difficult period eventually passed, but at the time special measures had to be taken to keep things going. Here General Pile, the G.O.C.-in-C. A.A. Command, with the assistance of Professor Blackett, his scientific adviser and observer, enlisted the help of the Ministry of Supply to provide a number of scientists to tackle this urgent need for care of these sets in operation. This action on his part had two definite and valuable effects—it started a new school for A.A. radar instruction and it provided a means, irregular or unconventional perhaps, but effective in its results, of tiding over this very difficult early period and keeping most of the equipment in action. A further and far-reaching effect also resulted in the formation of a group of scientific observers to assess the effect of actual operational use of equipment and to study the causes of errors in A.A. fire and how they could be reduced or eliminated.

A.A. Radio School. The difficulties experienced with the early radar sets and their maintenance in an efficient operating state had intensified by September, 1940, when Bedford's elevation attachment for the G.L. I was introduced. This system for providing for this radar aid to visual methods of engagements, a means of attempting action in unseen conditions has been described in Chapter VIII, page 47.

It was giving some success at a trial sites at Goff's Oak in the hands of Mr. Bedford's experts, but that success was not being repeated in the hands of troops on operational sites. The system required delicate adjustment and expert operation to give useful results, and on the advice of Professor Blackett arrangements were made by A.A. Command in September, 1940, to call in to their aid about eight or ten radar personnel from T.R.E. and elsewhere, to act as "Field Calibrators"—a temporary local arrangement without much organization, control or definite instruction.

At the beginning of October, J. A. Ratcliffe was called in to form an A.A. Radar School under A.A. Command to train civilians of suitable qualifications in looking after the G.L. sets on gun sites, and in particular to tackle the E/F attachments; though this was to some extent duplicating the work of the field calibrators, the latter were no concern of Ratcliffe's party.

Within a week of Ratcliffe's arrival the Command had requisitioned Petersham Hall. Instructional staff were collected from a variety of sources, including Shire from A.D.R.D.E., Lennox from Messrs. Cossors, Lieutenant Jones, an I.F.C. from A.A. Command and two staff-serjeants R.A.O.C. provided by the War Office, and some sets were allocated, two of which were set up in the Hall and two sited in Richmond Park. Recruitment of civilians for instruction was carried out by the Ministry of Supply, the first class being comprised of skilled radio personnel loaned from firms; they required only a short course on the particular type of set to fit them for the work. While this course was in progress, recruitment proceeded of volunteers from schoolmasters of mathematics and physics, who, with their good training background, were the main source of supply for succeeding courses. A later experiment with University professors of biology who had spent some years on biological research, also proved them to be very suitable. Steps had been taken at the beginning of 1941 to comb out from the Army, and to gather in some scientific men who were misemployed or rather whose capabilities were not being applied to the best advantage. A considerable number were thus transferred to the Petersham A.A. School for conversion to this radar work.

By June, 1941, this school was functioning regularly and turning out well-qualified personnel to deal with the radar sets on A.A. gun sites. The first ten or twelve had completed their short course and had been sent out to sites in the London area by the end of November, 1940; they were all experienced men from radio firms who did excellent work and filled a nasty gap. By the time the output of the school from the "schoolmaster" entries was running smoothly the former were needed again by their firms; with the increasing supply of trained personnel it was possible to release them.

With their first entry into practical gun site working some confusion arose between these school-trained men and the special radio "field calibrators" mentioned earlier. To clear the position and unify the arrangements, most of the original calibrators were returned to their establishment and the rest joined the course at Petersham to become part of Ratcliffe's organization.

This school at Petersham had been set up for the specific purpose of training civilians to assist in the effective use and maintenance of radar equipment in A.A. Command. On the satisfactory completion of their courses these civilian officers were sent out to gun sites, originally in the London area, but later to cover all gun sites in A.A. Command provided with G.L. sets. Though still civilians, they were generally well received by units under the arrangements made by General Pile, and the good work they themselves put into the job soon justified that reception.

The courses at the school varied from eight to ten weeks and dealt with the fundamentals of wireless and radar, the theory of the design and the practical use of the sets. Most trainees had opportunities of operating the sets in Richmond Park and of tracking enemy aircraft as there was plenty of air action over and about London on most nights. When sent out to units the duties of these radio officers as they were styled, were specifically to keep the equipment working in its designed form and not to initiate changes or modifications. If, however, in an emergency it was necessary to make some alteration to keep the set in effective action, it might be done, but had to be reported immediately.

Reports from these officers on their work were made to the Superintendent of the Petersham A.A. School and frequent meetings and discussions were a feature of the organization which permitted exchange of experience, consideration of suggested improvements and the bringing to light of difficulties and faults. Their actual work on the site consisted mainly of adjusting, rectifying small faults and, in particular, dealing with the elevation calibration; they also did a considerable amount of "crash" maintenance when the R.A.O.C. personnel could not be got to the site immediately.

They discovered trouble growing up from the use of braided feeders, due to corrosion, and did much to stabilize this trouble. Apart from their normal duties, these radio officers were of value in bringing to notice causes of faulty operation and failures of components, etc., and thereby aided the design of later models of equipment.

Furthermore they demonstrated the value of scientific observation, on the site, of the performance of the weapons, appliances and their crews. They began to fill the role of "scientific user"—as it was called by Ratcliffe; living on the gun sites, and with their scientific training and outlook, they were likely to notice and diagnose things going wrong more quickly than those whose main concern was the everyday stress of operational action. This aspect of the work of these civilian radio officers was, perhaps, the first real step towards the establishment of the Operational Research Groups that were formed shortly after.

This school started with the same difficulties as others in respect of equipment for instruction, but they were fortunate in having A.A. Command at their back to assist them; the War Office, also, did what was possible but could not starve the other schools to give them undue preference. A good deal of initiative was displayed in obtaining "bits and pieces" not only from A.A. Command resources, but from others less accessible to normal service personnel. A quotation from a note by Ratcliffe illustrates this:—

". . . a good series of fundamental experiments was got going by Mr. Shire, assisted by Mr. Baker and considerable stress was laid on experimenting with separate panels taken from the sets and displayed in the panel room.

At the start of the school when there was no equipment at all it was rather difficult to build up these experiments. Mr. Baker toured the junk shops of London accompanied by the Quartermaster-Serjeant. He would go into a junk shop looking like an ordinary civilian, select everything he wanted and then bring in the Q.M.S. to produce an A.A. Command voucher for the goods. The only authority quoted on this voucher was General Pile. Somehow this always seemed to produce what we required. No one ever knew (and apparently never cared) whether it actually got paid for in the end."

The War Office and the Ministry of Supply, as well as A.A. Command, had to adjust a good many similar commitments, but those somewhat irregular activities did bring with them the compensation of making effective and early results possible.

Though this school was started to serve A.A. Command and on its own initiative—and the early output was intended solely to help it through the difficult period—its potential further value was fully appreciated by the War Office. As the demands of the immediate emergency were met and Ordnance (and R.E.M.E.) personnel began to become available in increasing numbers, it was possible for the school to extend the scope of its instruction and to tackle the higher grade Ordnance and R.E.M.E. needs. It relinquished its purely parochial functions and covered wider Army fields which in fact embraced other radar activities in addition to A.A. applications. While it was put on a rather more regular basis it retained, fortunately, its close connection with A.A. Command.

Early in 1941 the War Office raised the question of bringing the radio officers produced by the Petersham School into the Service as technical officers instead of them continuing to serve on operational sites as civilians. Apart from that aspect there was the administrative and control side that had to be regularized if these Radio Officers were to continue to serve. They were being paid by the Ministry of Supply as members of their staff and, though little if any actual difficulty arose on this account, the Army could not really exercise control over them and their posting. It was eventually decided to commission those who were willing to continue serving, as radio maintenance officers or telecommunications maintenance officers as they were called later, in the R.E.M.E. —corresponding to the O.M.E.s (Wireless) of the R.A.O.C. who were being replaced by this new Corps.

This change was not much favoured by Ratcliffe who had maintained a high academic standard in the selection of his trainees—his limit on intake was to accept only men with first or second-class honours degrees in mathematics or physics, or with very good degrees and some research experience in biology. Ratcliffe was certainly justified in his views, at the start of this work, that such high standards were desirable, but as experience grew the nature of the work required of these specialist officers did not really support those views. He was naturally impressed by the need for highly qualified individuals capable of rapid absorption of specialist instruction, but he did not entirely visualize the improvements in equipment that were reducing that need and eliminating the faults and failings of the immature early types of equipment. He was, in fact, looking to a different kind of employment for those officers whom he visualized as "scientific users" or observers on operational sites to observe and locate faulty procedure in the whole train of operations for engaging targets and shooting them down.

In this view he was undoubtedly correct, but the "scientific user" could not be combined with the R.M.O. and his normal duties, and the use of civilians at operational sites was not practicable elsewhere than in this country—if still uninvaded. In his notes Ratcliffe stated "... I think the point of most of what I said was completely missed by several of the military people concerned." As a matter of fact, however, those responsible in the War Office and those concerned in the Ministry of Supply, fully appreciated his point of view when it was a matter of providing for scientific observation and assessment of the use of equipment and how improvement in operation could be effected. Provision was made for this in the formation of the Operational Research Group, an organization separate and distinct from that for maintenance, calibration, repair, etc. This group was mainly recruited on the basis which Ratcliffe had specified and their civilian status was maintained except in those cases where individuals were required to function in overseas operations, when they were put into uniform and given commissioned rank.

In the autumn of 1941, after having started the school and moulded it into an excellent establishment with a sound basis not only for instruction but also for effective post-graduate interchange of ideas and suggestions for improvement of Army radar, and having seen it achieve its primary objects, Ratcliffe returned to T.R.E., where he instituted similar courses for the R.A.F. and M.A.P.

The Army certainly owes a debt of gratitude to J. A. Ratcliffe for his work in establishing the Petersham school and directing its instruction. Those who passed through his hands and came under his energetic influence will endorse this comment as will also his successor, J. A. Harrison, who carried on his good work. All will agree that the results achieved in the early days with the limited facilities available, and the high standard that he initiated, were of great value to them as individuals as well as to the Army in its radar activities.

CHAPTER XXX. RADAR OPERATIONAL RESEARCH

Scientific study of the operation and effects of a weapon or device in action against the enemy is the primary object of Operational Research. From such study by independent personnel, a truer picture is usually obtainable than can be expected from those immediately engaged and concentrating upon their individual responsibilities during action. The independent observer has greater opportunities to see the whole picture and to notice where, how and why faults and errors may occur, provided that he is trained in scientific outlook and habit. Such observers are the doctors diagnosing troubles and following up the diagnosis with suggestions for remedial measures.

The old saying that "the proof of the pudding is in the eating" can be applied aptly to weapons and other appliances intended for particular operational effects against the enemy. In the case of the pudding it is of course assumed that it was designed, compounded, cooked and served solely for the operation of pleasant and nutritive eating, but it must also be remembered that the pudding is usually an accompaniment to other courses of a meal. If the operation of satisfactory eating has been achieved, the gourmand may ask for more, but possibly the gourmet, a more appreciative or ambitious eater, may suggest that the addition of a piquant sauce or other refinement would produce a more seductive taste that would add to his pleasure in eating. The proof of the pudding, therefore, depends largely upon the class of eater (or user) and perhaps also upon the urgency of the need to stave off the pangs of hunger so that immediate need may be satisfied by present adequacy in preference to a delayed ideal confection.

In the case of weapons or devices replacing the "pudding," the normal Service users must generally be the average "eater," for it is they who have to use the weapons in action rather than the highly skilled expert. With novel devices such as radar in its early days, it is desirable to raise the standard to be expected of the normal user in order to encourage a higher standard of training and to allow scope for improved performance that should result from experience. The scientific research, development and technical design staffs provide for this standard in their function as "chefs," "cooks," and "scullions"; experimental trials carried out by the design establishment and by Army specialists are necessary—a case of "trying it on the dog" or on the official "taster"—before the equipment can be approved for production and supply. The Ordnance Supply Service acting as "servers" then bring in the "pudding" on a lordly dish with the necessary forms, vouchers and suchlike trimmings, and the user, already primed by initial training, can get down to the operation of "eating his pudding."

The first proof of the "pudding" in operations probably results in some users complaining of "indigestion, of discomfort, and internal rumblings." Others are sure that their particular "pudding" was excellent but that it did not fit in with the other courses of the fire control "meal."

It is here that the "doctor," the independent scientific observer, must be called in with his "stethoscope" (or some other "scope") and other professional appliances to diagnose the faults and failures and to determine their origin and cause. When he has made a full check and found the trouble, he can prescribe suitable "medicines, remedial exercises or even surgical operations."

It was this function that Ratcliffe had in mind for his unofficial scientific users with the early radar equipment, but it was the Operational Research Group, formed to tackle the whole of the fire control problems and appliances for H.A.A. guns, including the radar sets, that became the specialist observers and advisers.

Of the civilian radio officers produced by the school at Petersham, Ratcliffe had retained a small number specially selected for scientific observation on sites during action. A short while before, Professor Blackett had set up a small group to study fire control problems and assess the suitability of the methods in use, excluding radar. These two parties were soon concentrated and combined—the Radar Group and Bayliss bringing the "Blackett circus" to Petersham. Here they were in close contact with the A.A. School and with practical gun site operation; this was aided by crews from gun sites functioning on equipment, in Richmond Park, on dummy runs by means of what was really the first synthetic trainer (developed by Mr. Bedford) which injected signals into the receiver of the set and correctly simulated attacking aircraft tracks.

The actual formation of these groups and their combination was spread over a period starting about September, 1940—the decision was actually taken at a meeting on 8th October, but the earliest members had already started work before that date. The self-adopted title of A.A. Command Research Group continued in use until March, 1941, when Blackett was transferred to Coastal Command, R.A.F.; it was reconstituted as a part of A.D.R.D.E. under the Ministry of Supply and its activities were extended to cover a wider field of radar. Thus the Ratcliffe research wing of the Petersham School, the Blackett "circus" under Bayliss and the A.A. Command Experimental Section became the A.D.R.D.E. Petersham Research Group in April, with official approval for its formation dated 1st July; but its title was amended to include "Operational" in September, when the A.D.R.D.E. (O.R.G.) was officially born.

The investigations carried out up to this time were various and largely exploratory; many concerned the elevation-finding attachment and its accuracy. They confirmed work previously carried out by A.D.R.D.E. that most of the factors affecting the accuracy of elevation finding, other than the slope of the surrounding ground, had negligible effect; but it showed that the setting up and calibration of Bedford's elevation attachment was a very delicate and critical operation, and that use in action or practice could and did upset the adjustments. This is in no way a detraction from Mr. Bedford's good work, but it is some justification of the decision by the G.S. to concentrate on the development of the A.D.R.D.E. design for the Mark II set. Other work of the group included the inception of the idea of employing recording vans on sites which came into widespread use later, while a beginning was also made with observation of enemy air tactics which radar tracking made possible, irrespective of weather conditions. This subject was of importance in determining the direction in which A.A. weapons and their aids should be developed.

The difficulties involved by applying radar information to mechanical predictors designed for visual methods were also studied and, as a result, some alterations made in training and operation methods; these demanded accuracy in preference to smoothness of output from the radar, and smoothing to be applied at the predictor. These and other matters were considered and dealt with and though some tended to duplicate work already done by A.D.R.D.E. they proved of value in bringing the Group into the practical picture.

On 1st August, 1941, Colonel B. N. J. Schonland was appointed Superintendent of this group which, though still closely associated with A.A. Command and the Radio School, became then a separate body. Later in the war the activities of the group extended to other fields of Army operations and it became a joint concern of the War Office (under the Scientific Adviser to the Army Council) and the Ministry of Supply; its radar activities continued to be the responsibility of two of its sections.

It would be invidious to mention the names of some of the individuals whose work materially assisted the development and the employment of radar, without referring to them all; it can be stated, however, that the work of this Group was most effective and valuable to the Army and especially so to the G.S. in assessing radar possibilities and new developments. Brigadier Schonland led the team most effectively and the members invariably put the team before the individual in their efforts and achievements.

As A.D.R.D.E.(O.R.G.), the work of the group continued on the radar and fire control problems, the assessment of fire effect and the recording of enemy tactics. Some of its earlier investigations rather dropped from under it with the introduction of the G.L. II equipment, designed for providing full fire control information; and the elimination of the elevation difficulties, by the provision of cams to convert the non-linear elevation scale to a linear form, had made possible the direct transmission of continuous elevation angle reading up to about 55 degrees.

There were, however, plenty of problems to be examined in connexion with radar feed to the predictor and the "wandering" of angular readings by the radar operators. The group also reviewed the possibility of raising the upper limit of 55 degrees for accurate elevation reading and a series of trials with altered heights of aerials was carried out in Windsor Park. The results of the trials of (1) a standard set, with normal height of aerial and manned by experts of C.A.E.E., and (2) a set using lowered aerials, manned by the O.R.G. personnel indicated that the normal set gave better accuracy of tracking, while the other had negligible advantage in maximum elevation angle for tracking. Though no change was made at that time, a compromise was effected at the end of 1941, and the standard aerial height was reduced to a mean position.

It is worth while noting, as reported by the O.R.G., that the *overall* performances attained in these trials,

". . . were never equalled by operational detachments under unseen conditions until the advent of auto-follow Radar and a fully automatic predictor . . . It is true that the Radar operators in the trial were largely drawn from research personnel, but *the Radar performance (by itself)* has been equalled by operational detachments . . .; the chief reason for the good overall performance of the fire control system was the high state of skill and training of the predictor detachments, who were all pre-war Territorials."

In so far as the radar set itself was concerned, it was apparent that it was adequate for the task for which it was designed and was capable of producing the results required with Service operators if fully and properly trained.

Quite a number of other results, ancillary to the main observations, emerged in these "Windsor" trials. Among them was confirmation of the value of photographic recording of the output dials of the radar and the predictor, so that careful study and comparison could be made without interfering with the operators in action. Eventually, the "Westex" Document Recording Camera was adopted and though its 16 mm. film required the use of binocular microscopes for reading, it was found perfectly adequate for the purpose of recording the eleven receiver dials and a stop-watch, simultaneously. These appliances were later set up in recording vans (to which incidentally the name "Westex" was applied by many people) and employed for recording performance in actual operations on site against the enemy. Detailed examination of the performance recorded could then be made and the origin of errors determined and assessed; these records also gave evidence of the actual courses and evasive tactics of the enemy aircraft.

Other major anti-aircraft radar trials undertaken or assisted by the Research Group included searchlight and S.L.C. layouts and the extent of mutual interference; recommendations for siting the G.L. "carpet" independent from gun sites, for tracking overland the movement and course of enemy attacks, to supplement the observations of the R.O.C. posts in conditions that limited their efforts; the large-scale trials of I.F.F. Mark III just before its introduction operationally, and recommendations on the limitation of interrogation and the need for directional discrimination. They assisted materially in the "Feeler" trials to determine the effect of close spacing of equipments of the United Kingdom and United States forces working together, in preparation for overseas operations, and they reinforced the "Window" trials at Earls Croome with close observation and detailed assessment of the effects of enemy use of Window in the raids of 1943–1944, and recommendations for reducing those effects.

They studied, operationally, each new type of A.A. equipment as it was introduced and carried out extensive siting and movement trials of G.L. III, and the different methods of "putting-on" including regular methods of self-searching which were adopted by 21 Army Group successfully in Northern Europe. The first set of the Canadian pattern G.L. III came under their consideration, in conjunction with the Canadian Forces; its performance—somewhat disappointing—was determined and assistance given in training the Canadian operators.

Apart from the A.A. aspects of radar, the O.R.G. were intimately concerned with the C.D. and C.A. developments—in fact a number of its members were practically employed solely on this side of Army radar. They reviewed the hastily selected sites and assessed the cover provided by the C.D./C.H.L. chain along the S. and S.E. coastline and were prominent in siting the extensions northward and westward. With the advent of the 10 cm. type of set they reassessed the more effective cover provided and were largely responsible for site selection. More important still, they devised means of determining that individual sets were working up to their proper standard performance—a matter that had not been tackled by the R.A.F. who were also employing this Naval type. These sets when working up to standard performance gave extended and reliable cover even on craft of low freeboard which was not the case with the C.D./C.H.L. type. Apart from this, with the means of verifying that they were giving the standard of performance, the O.R.G. personnel—Dr. Wilkes the two Varleys and Leck among them—devised a method of measuring the amplitude of the echo signals and by that means, of determining with reasonable accuracy the size or class of craft producing the echo at any range. This valuable information made a considerable difference to the effectiveness of the warning and tracking of hostile surface craft and permitted the nature of action to be taken to be determined early. Though it was not fully adopted when first put forward, really on account of the uncertainty as to the state of the performance of the sets, it was employed fully when the means of checking performance became available for the C.D. chain then in R.A.F. hands. These two developments by the O.R.G. were a major contribution to the effectiveness of radar surface and low aircraft detection, tracking and information, and of material aid also to C.A. operation.

The group extended its activities to investigate the use made of the information provided by these coastal sets, and assisted in the reorganization of the Naval plotting room arrangements and generally established an excellent understanding and co-operation with the Naval authorities concerned that flourished throughout the war.

With the R.A.F. (60 Group) manning the Coastal Chain of Stations, including the high-power stations with 200 ft. towers on the east coast, the work of the O.R.G. began to establish confidence in their methods. In particular, the proof they gave that the use of these sets, if properly up to standard performance, for aircraft tracking and detection was effective and accurate, encouraged the R.A.F. to adopt these methods of check. 60 Group soon brought in all supervisors of the stations for a special course of instruction on the subject and the two Varleys and Leck took on the check and adjustment of all stations along the east, south and west coasts as far as Hartland Point. The effect on operations was very striking in respect of the performance on aircraft and on shipping also. Perfectly good echoes were obtained at times from even single sea birds at ranges of 80,000 yards and over, and with their speeds of some 30 knots they were sometimes mistaken for E-boats, but the use of the system of size estimation by signal measurement enabled such "spurious" echoes to be recognized by the good radar operator.

The communications facilities had to be increased to deal with the increased reporting of tracks, and additional plotting had to be provided in the Naval plotting rooms to cope with the greater inflow of information. Whereas, in 1941, these 10 cm. sets were hard put to it to pass 5-minute plots on more than 6 tracks, by 1944 Ventnor station, for example, was able to keep continuity and plot on each track every five minutes for as many as 50 different shipping tracks, and to give size estimates, speeds and estimated numbers; using a separate P.P.I., the set was also tracking aircraft and passing their plots continuously at the same time.

The leaders of this sub-group of the O.R.G. were, successively, Dr. M. V. Wilkes, M. H. Lowson and S. R. Humby. In addition to the C.D. work referred to above, mention must be made of the C.A. activities, mainly at Dover. P. C. Varley, a Cambridge physicist commissioned in the R.E.M.E., practically lived with the various experimental and early model sets, provided for the very active defences at that station. Not only did he keep the sets in action almost single-handed, but he infused such keenness in the operators with his instruction and help that Dover's radar became a by-word for efficiency and reliability.

Another most essential activity undertaken by the O.R.G. was the investigation of jamming and interference. With the narrow separation of our southeast coast from enemy-occupied territory, it was there that land-based jamming was most to be feared and, as will be remembered, its tactical use to cover the escape up Channel of the German warships from Brest, affected most of our earlier $1\frac{1}{2}$ metre type equipments. A small station with a mobile van was set up in the area under the charge of J. S. Hey to watch for and investigate the nature, extent, and effect of enemy jamming when attempted. This station was linked with operational sets in the area and with T.R.E., who also maintained "J" watch. Sets experiencing trouble due to abnormal interference would be visited while it was in progress, if possible, and all reports were submitted in detail to Hey and his party for consideration and assessment before the official report of jamming was compiled.

This party would investigate on site and try various means of eliminating or reducing the effect and were able to compile elementary rules for operators to enable them to work through the interference whenever possible. At the same time they aided A.D.R.D.E. in devising fittings and other means for aiding operation in the presence of hostile jamming, and in practical trials of such devices.

Another major investigation was undertaken by the O.R.G.—mainly by those dealing with the C.D. radar aspect—which concerned fundamental effects of meteorological conditions on short-wave transmissions. On occasions it was found that radar echoes were received back from objects below and beyond the visual horizon, the first instance in which this deviation from the straight path was observed is mentioned in Chapter XV. Later, with the use of centimetric wave-lengths from coastal stations, occasional reports were received of abnormal long ranges having been read. There appeared to be a possibility of making use of this phenomenon, if its occurrence could be forecast, and, alternatively, it was most desirable to know when it was likely to happen to avoid misleading information being transmitted or the sets being thought to have gone wrong. Sir Edward Appleton established a sub-committee associated with the R.D.F. Applications Committee to investigate the problems of very short wave propagation, and at his request, the War Office called in the aid of the O.R.G. to investigate all cases of abnormal range observation and instructed all Army coast radar stations at home and abroad to submit reports with full details of weather, sea, set height, etc., conditions. The O.R.G. investigated the references to such abnormal working recorded in the log books of the stations and as they came in, analysed the reports submitted from home and overseas stations.

From the low-level site at Steamer Point, Christchurch, over a period of some ten days of fine weather in the summer of 1942, it was a common occurrence for the 10 cm. experimental set to receive strong echoes from the Cherbourg peninsular which indicated a considerable bending of the wave transmissions and reflections. Dover, on occasion, reported exceptional ranges on their sets sited about 400 feet above sea-level and complained of disturbance of normal actions in progress. Alexandria reported fishing boats well beyond the horizon as heavy warships; many other stations supplied other cases. All were analysed by O.R.G. and it became increasingly evident that height of site, and particularly meteor conditions, were primary causes of this phenomenon; a set at 700 feet above sea-level, for example, would not always conform to the performance of those at 400 feet or less. All the available information was furnished to Appleton's sub-committee and at the same time G. C. Varley tackled the question of forecasting the occasions on which anomalous propagation might be expected to occur. This he did in 1942, in conjunction with Flight-Lieutenant Hatcher, R.A.F., and some considerable success was obtained; the development of forecasting was, however, taken over by T.R.E. and the Meteorological Office, and forecasts were supplied from Dunstable. Throughout 1943 and 1944, complaints of inadequacy and inaccuracy were frequent from the chain stations and an analysis of log-book records showed that the forecasting was less successful than that produced by Hatcher some two years earlier.

When in 1944, 3 cm. sets were employed before and during the invasion period, the opportunity of duplicating sets at Dover and at Ventnor as a safety measure was used to have the sets in each pair sited at different heights, in order to note any differences in the effect of anomalous conditions. Little satisfactory evidence was, however, obtained owing to unsuitable meteorological conditions except that there appeared to be a definite variation in the effects on 10 cm. and on 3 cm. transmissions; the latter appeared to be more affected at lower levels than at higher sites. There was, however, insufficient evidence on which to base any final conclusions.

In connexion with this subject of anomalous propagation, it is of interest to note that ultra-short-wave radio communication is equally affected by similar meteorological conditions, which may be experienced more frequently in tropical areas. The Appleton sub-committee, through the R.D.F. Applications Committee, put forward the possibility of very long range—up to 400 miles—radar detection of surface craft in tropical areas, with fair regularity of occurrence during parts of each day, and enquired whether this possibility was worth while pursuing for operational purposes. The General Staff, after consultation with the Admiralty, replied that though the possibility was of scientific interest, no practical operational need could be visualized for it, and even if such long-range detection were effected no material action could be taken as a result. The pursuit of this possibility was, therefore, not encouraged as an operational requirement.

The A.O.R.G. made material contributions to the defence against the flying bomb attacks and in the detecting and tracking the V.2 stratosphere rockets. In the former their work on the 10 cm. coastal sets for early detection of these pilotless craft did not appear to be appreciated by the R.A.F. to the extent that it deserved, but their constant observation of the working of army radar equipments aiding the guns was of considerable value to A.A. Command. Their assessments of the value of the different appliances and weapons against these special targets enabled them to recommend changes in the dispositions of, and in operating, the different weapons. They also gave useful guides to the value of some of the improvised radar devices that had been applied to the Light A.A. guns and confirmed the value of automatic following for H.A.A. weapons and the complete chain of control from radar to fuze.

In the V.2 attacks they were largely responsible, in conjunction with A.A. Command, for the siting and disposition of the modified G.L. II sets, for detection and tracking of these missiles and particularly for the need of siting to obtain a broadside aspect of the rockets to get the best response signals. This was difficult in this country but improved when the Belgian coast was in our hands; they aided the extension of the lay-out into Belgium and Holland for the attacks on this country and also for those on the vital port of Antwerp and other centres.

When the O.R.G. became the Army Operational Research Group early in 1943, under the joint control of the War Office and the Ministry of Supply, it was no longer an appendage of A.D.R.D.E. The W.O. had a direct say in its employment, operationally, and extended its activities greatly in their scope to embrace all forms of operation; this is not the place in which to refer to their wider activities, but that they proved as effective and valuable as did their work on radar is undoubtedly true.

Their expansion carried them into the field of operations in and through the invasion of Normandy and all the operations in Northern Europe. Before this its members had participated in the campaigns in Northern Africa, Sicily and Italy, including Airborne operations in which Pike made full use of his opportunities. They accumulated a considerable amount of information on enemy radar and on the effects of our various weapons, in conjunction with the Military Wheatsheaf organization. They helped to carry this still further after the collapse of Germany, by special investigations, in conjunction with the Control Commission, of German equipment and of their research work and production methods.

Some of the main investigations of the Operational Research Group have been mentioned and there were many others on the radar side that they tackled. At least as important were the assessments, from the scientific and practical aspect, of new types of equipment and new devices, which were of material aid to the General Staff in forming radar policy for the Army. Naturally, many of these were post-design concerns, for the opportunity for Operational Research did not arise until equipment was in the hands of the troops and in action. Its primary function was the study of the overall effect of the equipment, the standard of operation achieved by the operators, the use of the information supplied and the effect upon the enemy.

As a body of independent observers, its most important activity was to observe operations in detail and to ask the right questions at the right moment. For success, much tact and a scientific outlook on which is imposed an appreciation of the practical aspects of operational work, are essential. The work requires access to the individual operator, to unit officers and officers of high rank and responsibilities, and to succeed in establishing the confidence of all these grades of service personnel in that work is not an easy matter.

In the case of the Army Operational Research Group under Schonland and later Johnson and its dealings with Army radar, there can be no question of the fact that they achieved very considerable success and served a most useful purpose that materially helped the development and employment of radar by the Army.

CHAPTER XXXI. SUPPLY, MAINTENANCE AND REPAIR

The record of the formation of the new Corps of Royal Electrical and Mechanical Engineers must be sought elsewhere, but some reference must be made here to their essential services in respect of Army radar. This novel device that grew so rapidly was of an intricate nature that was almost unknown to all but a very few scientific and technical personnel at the time that the first supplies were reaching operational units. It included many components and appliances previously unknown outside laboratories, and the equipments contained upwards of a hundred valves, thousands of radio components, several cathode ray tubes and complicated and delicate gearing and other mechanical aids. It presented new problems in training personnel of all grades, in devising the essential methods of test, in the technique of maintenance and in the development of new forms of testing apparatus. The provision of detailed instructional and technical pamphlets, as well as special means of store holding, parts lists and new methods of packaging for transport, shipping and handling had also to be initiated. The rates of replacement of individual valves and components had to be estimated or guessed, until practical experience grew sufficiently to provide reliable evidence of the quantities of spares it was necessary to hold.

It was no mean task that faced the Ordnance Engineering and Supply services.

The Ordnance Supply side was, of course, affected by this new form of radio equipment, but its organization was able to absorb it within its normal arrangements without major reorganization, though naturally expansion and some special provisions had to be made. Chief among the latter was the secrecy aspect of radar which involved special treatment for many components as well as for the equipments themselves. A special section of the Vocabulary of Army Ordnance Stores—Section Z—was used for these equipments, their components, test gear and other appliances, and special storage with restricted access, coverage of equipments in transit, guards for sets for delivery to units and similar measures were employed; they were, however, but extensions of the existing security arrangements.

The supply side, naturally, had to work in close liaison with the Ministry of Supply in connection with nomenclature, scales of provision and similar matters, and formed the official means of detailing the provision needed by the War Office for complete equipments, and for the supplies of components and spares either for accompanying the equipments or for filling stocks for continued maintenance. They translated the G.S. figures for equipment requirements into the complete form for the official Schedule of Requirements for submission to the Ministry. They were also the means of implementing the order of priority of issue of equipments laid down by the G.S.

The Engineering branch of the R.A.O.C. was faced with considerably greater problems, which were not merely in the nature of an expansion, but eventually involved a complete reorganization that resulted in the formation of the Telecommunications branch of the new corps, R.E.M.E. It was not, of course, only this new need for radar that caused the birth of this corps, but the radar needs reinforced the other electrical and mechanical needs of the Army that demanded concentration of effort in one Corps to meet the whole needs of the Army in the field or in static applications.

R.E.M.E. was formed in 1942 to take over responsibility for inspection, maintenance, modification and repair of the electrical and mechanical equipment of the Army. The special case of radar had been enquired into by a special committee, under Air Marshal Sir Philip Joubert de la Ferté, established in 1941 to examine the organization of A.A. Command, and the repair and maintenance arrangements.

It was this latter committee that gave a lead to the elimination of the odd *ad hoc* improvisations of the "field calibrator" and other unofficial or semi-official expedients used as a temporary means of keeping things going. It urged the absorption of the Ratcliffe "radio officers" into the R.A.O.C. as Radio Maintenance Officers. In addition, the Electricians Fire Control of R.A. units were transferred and were a welcome addition to the Telecommunications branch, and gave them opportunities for advancement in rank as tradesmen. This change, however, required that maintenance and repair should be effected by a continuous chain of echelons from the rear main workshops, through the field workshops, special test and check detachments right down to the daily maintenance on site, by a Corps other than the actual users. While this was undoubtedly necessary at the time, it was not in accordance with the general principle and practice of the Army that requires the unit to take responsibility for the condition of its own weapons and equipment and only to call upon a technical Corps for the 3rd or 4th echelon repair work, beyond their own facilities. As the war progressed, however, it was possible to give radar operators some increased knowledge of their equipments to enable them to undertake the more domestic daily maintenance tasks and to assist the R.E.M.E. artificers and mechanics in their tests and adjustments. On the other hand, it relieved the I.s F.C. and the T.I.s of some of their early activities and gave them better chances to effect the training of the radar crews—this was reflected also in the training at the S.A.A.A. where the tendency to the ultra-technical began to give place to the operational and training aspects.

This reorganization was effected immediately following the decision taken by the Army Council in April, 1941. With this new arrangement also went the use of the A.A. Radio School at Petersham for the training of R.A.O.C.(E) personnel of and for officer grades of the radio maintenance organization.

The basis of the R.E.M.E. repair and maintenance organization was the concentration of repairs at workshops established by the Workshop Companies. These workshop units included a number of radio maintenance sections each provided with its own transport, test gear, tools, etc., so that they could keep continuous contact with the units and their radio equipment in the field. They could carry out necessary repair and adjustment on site or replace defective components and remove them or damaged equipments to the "mother" workshop for repair which was beyond the scope of "on site" facilities. Each of these sections included specific sub-sections to undertake Installation of equipment; Repair (in workshops); Maintenance (on site); and general Servicing.

In addition, special detachments were provided for calibration and collimation of equipments in conjunction with the unit personnel; the equipment of these detachments varied with the nature of the radar equipment to be dealt with.

That the pre-war provision had been rendered quite inadequate by the rapid development of the early types of radar equipment became apparent before the outbreak of war. The number of O.M.E.s under training for radar duties in the special wireless course, at the M.C. of S., was only ten, and of armament artificers only slightly larger; further, the anticipated output from these courses was only ten each year. The students from the pre-war course only became available for posting in January, 1940, but steps had by then been taken to speed up the M.C. of S. courses and a number of schools were also being established, under A.A. Command arrangements, to provide for mechanics training in radar maintenance and repair. The original aim was to provide one school for each A.A. Division but that altered when the divisional organization was superseded by the Groups into which the Command was decentralized. The first of these schools for the 6th A.A. Division was established at the Repository, Woolwich, but in fact it served the whole command for some little time before the others had been fully established. It was attached to the 6th A.A. Divisional Workshop Company R.A.O.C. and moved into new quarters at Sidcup near that Company when others of the schools had started their training.

This provision began to make good the deficiencies in A.A. Command and continued to operate for the wider needs of overseas formations. A.A. Command being the major user of Army radar and using it continuously in action against the enemy, naturally provided plenty of practical experience for the Ordnance and R.E.M.E. personnel and though the conditions were more or less static, the experience gained of the repair and maintenance system enabled it to be fitted in well with the mobile formations of the field forces for which trained and experienced personnel were very necessary, for efficient maintenance in the field.

A final note here may be permitted to give some slight indication of the extent of the Ordnance and R.E.M.E. organization that was involved by radar alone. The number of major items of *test gear alone*, that had to be devised and produced to equip them for this work, ran into some 9,500 separate items, and the minor items certainly exceeded that number, if they did not more than double it.

When the conditions existing in 1940 are recalled, and the *ad hoc* arrangements for keeping things going, it is not surprising that the Chief Ordnance Officer at A.A. Command should have referred to things as "completely chaotic" —R.A. instructors and assistants with E.s F.C. were tackling maintenance, R.A.O.C. (if any) were attempting 2nd echelon work and repairs. "Special calibrators" and Ratcliffe's civilian "Radio Officers" and "Scientific Observers" were doing their bit, while oddments from A.D.R.D.E. staff, from C.I.E.M.S. and even from firms were running round helping where they might. Most were independent and one group often altered what a previous party had done a few hours before. However, these "doctors," "quacks" and others were gradually eliminated—they *had* kept things going somehow—and a real and effective organization grew up. The R.A.O.C. and its successor R.E.M.E. did an excellent job of work that contributed very materially to the success of Army radar.

For the W.S. side of the organization the quantities of the different types of radar equipment dealt with can be obtained approximately from the production total quoted in Appendix V. This, however, gives no idea of the total of the numerous components, valves, assemblies, etc., that had to be held for repair, maintenance and replacement, which would take the numbers into astronomical figures.

Taking one general class only, namely valves, some slight idea may be gained by the difficulty that arose in 1942–43, due to the serious deficiency in valve production in this country. The large variety of valves used in radio and radar equipment have varying working lives apart from breakages and an average figure for radar valves had been estimated at a requirement of six to eight valves a socket a year. A drastic reduction had to be made and for a time the Army radar figure was reduced to $2\frac{1}{2}$ a socket which, in fact, made the position very precarious for some time, and in this country where radar equipment was used continuously the equipment lived from hand to mouth. Army radio communications suffered similarly and so did the other two Services. Even with the cuts made, the yearly aggregate from production was estimated at only some 42 million valves, while the Service needs stood at just over 60 millions—not a pleasant position by any means. However, the production position gradually improved, and the balance between requirements and output was adjusted. Though few cases occurred of lack of valves putting equipment out of action, there were delays in replacements, and the valve shortage certainly limited the provision of new types of equipment.

CHAPTER XXXII COMMENTARY

Little comment is needed on the subject-matter of Chapter XXV except to stress the credit due to those Dominions that tackled radar development on their own initiative and to regret that the full liaison that was established during the war was not so effective before it and in its early days. The War Office kept Dominion representatives informed of progress and possibilities in radar and its operational aims and the Ministry of Supply provided them with periodical letters of information on technical and scientific aspects of the work of development.

If insufficient information was supplied from this end in the early days there was also a considerable reticence on the part of Australia in respect of its Sh.D. set until its limited production was in progress, and in the case of the Canadian G.L. III set, such reticence was carried still further with unfortunate results. The latter suffered from lack of adequate operational information and experience and from the snares of a more or less ideal trials ground—snares which we also experienced in some cases as, for example, with our G.L. II when it was found necessary later to "mat" the surround of the set for efficient action.

Some of the trouble was probably due to the inadequate representation of the scientific and technical aspects at the Dominions Military Headquarters in this country at that time. Later, such aspects were catered for and opportunity given of attendance at radar meetings in both the War Office and the Ministry of Supply.

In respect of liaison with the U.S.A. it will be appreciated that this had been established effectively even before the entry of that country into the war. Not only was this so on the military side, but the scientific and technical sides were also very closely in touch. If we in our need accepted their production aid, we saved them from the trudge through the wastes of the longer wave-length applications by putting before them the possibility of revolutionary technique by the development of the resonator magnetron.

Of the Russian liaison there is nothing to say beyond the fact that it was all give and no take on our part.

Chapter XXVI deals generally with the growth of G.S. direction of radar development and the background against which radar policy and priorities had to be determined. This is illustrated by the G.S. Policy Statements issued from time to time, and further detailed in the actual specifications of required performance, etc., issued to guide the work of the R. and D. establishment; of the latter, samples are included in Appendix IV.

In so far as radar is concerned the policy for development (and more so perhaps for production) is divided into an "acceptance" and a "direction" period—the latter might be limited towards the end of the war, when the supply of special new types of equipment for the Field Armies could not be produced in time, by what might be called the "frustration" period.

Reference is also made to the change from the "single authoritative voice" of the War Office to the dual-tongued direction that came in with the formation of the Ministry of Supply, such duality extends into the composition of the detailed specifications for equipment requirements and into the field of acceptance of new types for production as Service equipment. Practically, the difference was not of great moment in spite of its apparent division of responsibility, except in the case of representation of Army needs and urgency in the competition for production capacity.

In Chapter XXVII, a variety of subjects are mentioned, largely independent of one another but all having an influence on Army radar; the matter of inter-Service priorities, or rather the lack of any definite comparison of the needs of the three Services, is mentioned. This is strange in view of the comments in Chapter XXVI which led to the formation of R.P.E., and of the terms of reference of the Radio Board. Whether any indication of comparative priorities of Service operational need ever reached the R.P.E. or whether even the priorities stated by the G.S. and their urgency reached them is doubtful. The War Office had no official access to this body and its representation by the Ministry was at least third hand and, consequently, rather out of balance with the representation of the other two Services in the competition for production capacity.

Some brief mention is made of gaining intelligence of enemy radar—no comment is needed except to indicate that Army radar is really only on the fringe of such matters and less affected than the other Services. There is, however, one aspect not mentioned in this paragraph—but referred to in Chapter XXX—namely, enemy attacks on our equipment by jamming. For this a continuous watch was maintained as will be seen in the chapter dealing with the activities of the A.O.R.G.

Some comment is also desirable on the Time factor. Throughout this chapter Time has been cropping up frequently and the lack of information on it put the General Staff particularly in difficulties. It is a difficult matter to estimate time in development, impossible to indicate when research results will emerge and, with a novelty like radar, practically impossible for manufacturers to give reliable forecasts of how long it will take to get into production and the rate at which supply can be made. This lack of realistic Time information naturally affects planning ahead for particular operations and may affect the quantities of equipment to be ordered—particularly when further new developments are hatching out. While recognized as a very difficult matter, it is not easy to suggest any means of overcoming it, though some slight amelioration might have been possible had the production and development sides of the Ministry been in more intimate touch and perhaps, if the G.S. had had access direct to the Production authorities. Certainly things would have been better if the optimistic views expressed by some branches of the Ministry had been ignored.

Chapter XXVIII gives an outline of the training arrangements that affected radar and there are few points to which attention need be drawn. The chief matter that affected all training in the early days—apart from the general absence of knowledge of the subject—was the lack of special training equipment. The provision of Service pattern sets for instructional purposes was difficult enough in the urgency of the need for equipping our defences, and the diversion of development effort from improving the performance of that equipment limited very severely the design of special training sets and parts.

The schools and establishments had to improvise and a considerable amount of ingenuity and initiative was shown in mock-up trainers and other devices which served a very useful purpose till the standard training sets could be supplied. Even then, trainers for new types of equipment always lagged behind the equipment itself, though it became usual for the schools to get early supplies of such sets in parallel with operational units.

With its simpler problems and smaller number of trainees, the C.A.S. was able to link up the gunnery and radar sides at an earlier stage than was possible for the S.A.A.A. with its greater complication of appliances and larger numbers. From the middle of the war period a number of officers had been trained as combined I.s G. and I.s F.C. and it is possible that the separation of these two types may disappear in the future. With the S.A.A.A. the link-up of the two could only make a start in 1944, and its future would appear more doubtful though each class of instructor must gain an intimate knowledge of the other's line of business.

In their links with actual operations the C.A.S. established a close liaison with the Dover defences where the opportunity of observation of actions in progress was of considerable value to them, and at the same time proved the value of radar to Coastal Artillery—practical proof obtained from actual action. This with the aid of the Dover gunners enabled coast artillery methods to be developed and incorporated in the instruction at the school and in the standard operational text-books.

The liaison between the S.A.A.A. and A.A. Command and its more or less continuous operations against enemy attacks did not appear to be so effective, though on the radar side there was a fair degree of liaison.

The chapter on A.A. Command training—Chapter XXIX—needs little in the way of comment or stress, though a few points of interest may be mentioned.

First, it must be impressed that this account does not attempt to deal with all the operations and activities of A.A. Command which was always the major user of A.A. weapons and of radar. The Command did a great deal in adapting its methods to radar and in devising means for getting the best out of it in its youthful days. Most of the operational effect of radar during its different stages of development comes from A.A. Command and throughout the war that Command was a ready source for practical "user" information as to their real needs, which helped the G.S. direction of development.

Apart from that, two very material aids—the Petersham Radio School and the original Operational Research Group—were initiated by A.A. Command. The latter forms the subject of the following chapter, but the former is included and described in some detail in Chapter XXIX. Apart from stressing the valuable work done by the school while under the paternal care of the Command and also later, when it became more of a War Office concern, it may be mentioned that a serious proposition was put forward to convert it into an inter-service Radar Staff College. This was not proceeded with but the need for higher radar courses of instruction was met, not by creating a new organization, but by making use of the existing Military College of Science.

Chapter XXX deals with Operational Research. Organized operational research, as a means of determining the effectiveness of weapons and other equipment in actual use against the enemy, was a novelty introduced in this war, having started life purely as an associate of that other novelty, radar. Perhaps it would be better described as being introduced to observe the effect of radar-directed gunfire against aircraft which, naturally, involved the observation of all appliances, weapons and shells that combined to produce the burst in the right place and at the right time. It also involved close observation of enemy tactics and reactions. From this it spread, usefully, into other radar fields and still later covered practically all Army activities in war.

It should be remembered that the O.R.G. was concerned with the performance of individual equipment or appliances and with their combined performance including that of the human links in the combination. Those human links were not the scientists nor the expert technicians but the normal Service operators; and the performance of the operators and of the appliances with which they were concerned was that obtained in actual operation against the enemy and, perhaps, under the stress of his fire. The scientists and technicians can develop equipment of high performance and that equipment can be tested in trials with expert personnel to determine the performance of which it is instrumentally capable, but that is a different matter to its results in action in war.

There does not appear to be a real opportunity for operational research in peace time and it is doubtful if scientists could be retained for such work; possibly a nucleus might form part of, or be found from, the scientific staffs of the R. and D. Establishments that must necessarily be retained to keep Army equipment up to date.

There is no doubt that Army radar gained very considerable value from the work of Schonland and his group during the war; the General Staff, the directors of radar development and the R. and D. Establishment itself, all benefited from the results obtained by them and their assessments of new developments. The operational research organization was an innovation which was fully justified by the results it produced during the war.

The chapter on the Supply and Maintenance organization and its troubles and difficulties with the more or less sudden appearance of radar as a new Service equipment need not be embroidered. The complaint of the A.A. Command Chief Ordnance Officer of things being "completely chaotic" was no understatement and that state of things took a lot of clearing up. That the Ordnance Service carried on with meagre resources and few trained personnel, and eventually brought matters under control, was much to their credit.

R.E.M.E. soon proved themselves efficient and attained a high standard of radar from the technical aspect, nursed the early types through their teething troubles and continued their effective maintenance of the various forms of radar sets up to the end of the war.

PART VI

THE MINISTRY OF SUPPLY

CHAPTER XXXIII. HEADQUARTERS RADAR ORGANIZATION

The formation of the Ministry of Supply in 1939 naturally produced new problems of organization and subdivision of responsibilities between the War Office and the new Ministry that was to serve it in respect of the provision of weapons, equipment, clothing, and all other varied needs of an Army in training and as a fighting force in war.

The responsibilities of the Ministry were not, however, confined to Army needs and its services were not solely at the disposal of the War Office. It was charged with meeting the needs of the other two fighting Services in respect of a number of types of equipment and stores, and also many of the multifarious requirements of Civil Departments and of the civil population. Perhaps in some directions the War Office had the prior claim on its services, but the scope of its activities extended widely beyond the needs and concerns of the Army. It was only partially paralleled by the Ministry of Aircraft Production, which was set up some nine months later, in its relationship to the Air Ministry and the R.A.F.; the scope of M.A.P. was much more restricted and its activities were confined almost entirely to special R.A.F. needs. The Admiralty did not introduce similar arrangements and preferred to retain control of its provision organization in its own hands, though it did make use of the facilities available to it in the two new Supply Ministries for certain types and classes of equipment and stores.

It will be appreciated, therefore, that all three Services and their supply arrangements were differently organized. The Admiralty practically retained control in its own hands, the Air Ministry had M.A.P. to serve it almost entirely and reinforced its control in that Ministry, at any rate in respect of Radio and Radar, by having the "key" individuals holding appointments in M.A.P. and in the Air Ministry also. The War Office, on the other hand, was almost completely separated from the Ministry of Supply and that Ministry had many other functions besides serving Army needs. The War Office did, of course, provide a number of military personnel and technical directorates for the new Ministry, but though they could carry into it their experience of Army needs and could still act in an advisory capacity to the War Office, they could not represent fully the policy, needs and views of the General Staff.

These differences in organization were very marked in the radar field and were, to some extent, reflected in the effectiveness of direction of development and in the availability of production facilities; for the latter it was not, however, entirely a true reflection as the effect of operational priorities played a material part in their allocation.

In the case of the Ministry of Supply, there was a handicap added to radar provision for the Army which did not apply to its radio communications equipment. This was the continuance of the practice of ordering all Army radar through the Air Ministry or Ministry of Aircraft Production so that Army radar production remained a joint responsibility of the two Supply Ministries.

This dual responsibility for production of Army radar equipment increased the difficulties of the Ministry of Supply production branches, as well as those of the War Office who had no direct access to information as to the production time factor or of progress of urgently needed equipment, and had no means of representing directly the urgency of production needs.

It must be remembered, however, that control and co-ordination of radio and radar production capacity in this country was very necessary, owing to its inadequacy to meet all the demands of the Services. In this respect the combination of Army radar production with that for the R.A.F. was perhaps a necessity but, if that was so, it is difficult to understand why it was not applied equally to Naval radar requirements which never came completely into this arrangement.

Provision was, of course, the primary responsibility of the Ministry of Supply but in their case, as in that of the M.A.P., production carried with it research. The slogan at the time seems to have been—"Research must go hand in hand with Production"—and, like many slogans, it was sufficiently vague and ill-considered to permit of various interpretations. It linked two extremes—the purely scientific initiation of an idea with the final practical form—without taking into account the intermediate stages. These stages are all of concern to the military side—application of possibilities to meet a military need, experimental proof of adequacy of performance and development into suitable form for use as Service equipment—and are matters for the General Staff and its technical military advisers. They have to keep in mind that essential individual, the User—the ordinary war-time soldier—and the conditions in which he has to operate in action against the enemy; those considerations must always form the true criterion of suitability for any Army equipment. It is on that man that the effectiveness of the equipment, the fate of the scientist's efforts and the technician's work depend—he is apt to be forgotten in these slogans and shibboleths.

It is here that opinions vary as to the best organization for control of research, experiment and development; all parts of this chain involve combined efforts of teams of scientists, technicians, engineers, designers, etc., and with them the operational aspects must be ever present and the military user needs also.

There is no need here to discuss these different opinions, but the actual organization of the Ministry will be considered briefly in the following pages so that its effectiveness may be judged, in so far as radar is concerned, in the light of the results obtained.

Before leaving this general consideration of the radar aspect of the Ministry of Supply it cannot be said that the actual linking of research and production under their control was very effective. It may have been merely a slogan, but more probably, it was the considered and agreed opinion at the time that the whole chain of operations to devise and produce equipment should be controlled by the one Ministry. The delegation of part of radar production to M.A.P. did not conform to that principle, and within the Ministry itself there grew up an increasing gap between the research and development side and the production side, which eventually linked them only at the highest level; such action cannot by any stretch of imagination claim to adhere to that principle.

Organization of Radar Control. On the formation of the Ministry, Directorates of the War Office were transferred *en bloc* and continued to function for a time in the same way as they had done in the War Office. The D. of A.'s branch, M.G.O.14, immediately concerned with fire control, continued in being as A.4 and added A.5 for radar applied to fire control. The Mechanization directorate including its Deputy for Engineer and Signals Equipment who dealt with both radio and radar in development *and* in production, and the R.E. and S. Board who controlled development work in the experimental establishments, similarly continued for a short time. The Production branches, formerly M.G.O.11 and 13 under the D. of M., were brought in as E.S.1 and 2, E.S.3 being added later for Radar; they carried on their activities normally for a time though placing radar orders with or through M.A.P.

The Directorate of Scientific Research which had assumed responsibility for all the ex-W.D. scientific and technical personnel, and for the recruitment of all types and grades of staff for the experimental establishments, moved into the Ministry and initiated several important steps to aid the scientific advisory responsibilities of the Ministry.

The summer of 1940 brought changes in organization—a separate Directorate was formed under the Director of Engineer and Signals Equipment, with two Deputies for Technical Development and for Production respectively; the Director of Mechanization consequently dropped out of the radar picture. It was not long before the Engineering side also came under a separate Department and the Signals and Radar became separate branches E.S.2(T) and E.S.3(T)—the (T) being attached to distinguish them from the similarly initialled branches dealing with production. This eliminated the R.E. and S. Board as such and its C and B plus D Committees formed the new E.S. branches.

At the same time the Deputy, D.S.R. became Controller of Physical Research, with responsibility for fundamental work at the A.D.R.D.E.

For this period up to the end of 1940 there were therefore two masters of this Establishment, one concerned with fundamental research involving the scientific staff, and the other with the technical conversion of their results into the practical form of Service equipment. These spheres of activity naturally have no hard and fast dividing line, and dual control, as usual, was not very satisfactory and tended to slow up progress by delays in implementing decisions.

A further reorganization within the Ministry occurred about a year later, when in July, 1941, a Controller-General responsible to the Minister for all research and design work was appointed in parallel with the Controller-General of Munitions Production. This change was reflected at lower levels—the D.S.R. became Director-General of Scientific Research and Development, the C.P.R. expanded into Controller of Physical Research and Scientific Development and assumed complete control of A.D.R.D.E., where a scientific overlord or Chief Superintendent, Professor Cockcroft, had been appointed to that establishment. The Director of Signals Equipment—the Engineer side had by now departed elsewhere—became the Deputy Director-General of Signals Equipment as well as Controller of Signals (Communications) Equipment Development and was responsible in his two capacities to the Director-General of Mechanical Equipment for the former, and to C.G.R.D. through D.G.S.R.D., for the latter.

Duality of control of radar work still existed but at a higher level; it will be noticed that the link between development and production had now risen to Ministerial heights. At the Deputy Director-General level there was a link-up for Radio communications for a time, but it did not exist in respect of Radar.

Some nine months later, the responsibility for design of Army radar in all its stages was placed completely in the hands of C.P.R.S.D.; the E.S.3(T) branch was brought into the Scientific Research Directorate as S.R.11 under a civilian Deputy Director.

This change, apart from eliminating direct military control of the work of the A.D.R.D.E., had the unfortunate effect of cancelling the normal, even if at times nominal, responsibility of the Military Production side for engineering design. Though their experience was still available for advice, it was seldom called upon by the Establishment and it could not, without invitation, affect design or aid development in the early stages; by the time a design was nominally ripe for production, radical alterations could rarely be effected without delaying provision.

After this change of organization, the only official and regular contact between the design and production branches, other than occasional individual contacts, was the series of monthly "Release for Production" Meetings, at which all items under development for meeting W.O. requirements were reviewed. Later, some Progress Meetings at contractors' works, where development contracts were in hand, Monthly Review of Progress Meetings at A.D.R.D.E. and the D.G.S.R.D.'s. "Monthly Review of *Selected* items from the Army Radar development programme," were attended by the Production Directorate. At all but the last of these three meetings there was no representation of the War Office, and the last was not actually concerned with production though questions of that aspect were frequently raised by the War Office representative in search of information.

An addition of some importance was made in the autumn of 1943, when the post of S.T.C.O. was created to act for the D.G.Mech.E. to co-ordinate design and production of Signals equipment, including radar. Representing D.G.Mech.E. he had authority over the Signals Production Department, but in respect of research and development work under D.G.S.R.D., his position was not so definite though it was established at least by agreement. This appointment did at least tend to prevent any further deterioration in the contacts of production with development and was presumed to provide a means of linking G.S. policy to production effort. He became the M. of S. representative for Army needs on the Radio Production Executive, though he had no first-hand knowledge of the G.S. operational requirements and priorities, as had his colleagues on that body from the other two Service Supply Departments for the Naval and R.A.F. needs.

There was another Department in the Ministry outside the control of D.G.S.R.D. which had a material effect upon the development work for Army radar equipment. This was the Directorate of Artillery which subsequently became a Director-General's charge: its branch A.5 was very closely concerned with radar for fire control use or any other type of radar that affected it. It provided expert military advice on the instruments and appliances involved in the direction of artillery fire of all kinds and their needs. With H.A.A. fire as the highest priority operational requirement this branch was immediately concerned with radar, and Lieut.-Colonel Paterson, in charge of it, had been the first gunner initiated into the technique and possibilities of Radar.

This Technical Artillery Branch—advisory both upwards and downwards —was not easy to include in the chain of control. It had, necessarily, to be in very close touch and continuous contact with development from its earliest stages so that the essentials of performance and of the technical artillery details for using radar with existing equipment and appliances could be ensured. It was also the source of information and advice to the War Office on the technical aspects and had at its disposal a body of trained military personnel, in the form of the Coast and Anti-Aircraft Experimental Establishment, to test new designs in practical trials of their own or, in conjunction with A.D.R.D.E., to assess the actual attainable performance of new equipment or appliances.

Though this branch under the D.G. of A. provided the military mouthpiece for the technical artillery requirements and the detailed interpretation of accuracies, consistencies, etc., they were *not* the representatives of the General Staff on policy matters, nor could they "direct" the A.D.R.D.E. on matters of design of other radar equipment, as they were officially concerned only with the needs of fire control; they could not, therefore, advise officially on design for all forms of radar, though the G.S. frequently benefited from their contacts with development of those other types.

If the additional control provided by A.5 was not always understood by the S.R. Directorate, the liaison between the two was generally close and certainly grew more effective as experience was gained. The scientific side of A.D.R.D.E. at first seemed to regard A.5 as "a fifth wheel to the coach" of direction of their efforts, but confidence and co-operation were established, even if the official extent of A.5's authority was never entirely clear to the scientists.

The foregoing paragraphs give an outline—a somewhat complicated one but paralleled in that respect by the numerous changes in organization—of the development of control within the Ministry for dealing with Army radar needs up to the stage of putting new and approved designs into form for production as Service equipment.

The links with this organization from the War Office were naturally operated at different levels, the more formal and general matters being dealt with at the higher and the detail work at the Director's or perhaps the Director-General's levels.

In so far as Radar was concerned, G.S. Policy was in the earlier days transmitted from D.A.A. and C.D. (later D.R.A.) to D. of A. (later D.G. of A.), to D.D.G.S.E. and to C.P.R.S.D. From the winter of 1942-43, while this was continued, the more formal arrangement came into force whereby Radar needs were transmitted to the Ministry by the D.C.I.G.S. through the secretariat of the Organization and Weapons Policy Committee, and were also discussed at meetings of that Interdepartmental Committee held periodically at the War Office. This higher level indication of G.S. Policy requirements certainly placed the onus of distributing that information *to all concerned within the Ministry*, on the Ministry itself.

On the more detailed matters of development for Army equipment—and occasionally on research items in response to suggestions put forward by the Ministry, or otherwise brought to notice—transmission was direct to D.G. of A(A.5) and to C.P.R.S.D. from D.R.A. or D. Radar.

On the question of Production requirements the notification from the War Office emanated from the D.G.A.R. in the W.O. and radar was dealt with in the same way as any other weapon or Army appliance. The detailed schedules were submitted to the Ministry where they were dealt with and distributed, to the directorates concerned, by D.Stats on behalf of C.G.M.P. As has been seen, the details of requirements were submitted by the G.S. directorates and collated, with the necessary additions, by Q.A.E. (Ordnance), into the formal statements or schedules. At the same time it was normal for D.Radar, W.O. to notify D.G. of A(A.5), C.P.R.S.D. and D.D.S.E. in the Ministry, of the action being taken; this semi-official information tended to aid those concerned in making preliminary arrangements in anticipation of the formal and official requirements reaching them.

It will be apparent that the radar link-up of the two Departments was somewhat varied and variable—the organization did not permit of any single channel of communication from the W.O. to all those Directorates or Branches within the Ministry that were concerned with radar. At executive levels the W.O. was not linked to the Production side, and, on that of Development, communication was sometimes through D.G. of A. to C.P.R.S.D. and sometimes direct to the latter, according to the nature and application of the particular radar device in question. The arrangement was agreed that

". . . the channel of correspondence for all Radar matters affecting weapons is through D.G. of A. and the approval of such equipment is the joint responsibility of C.P.R.S.D. and D.G. of A. This is to ensure that the weapons aspect of Radar requirements is fully covered and that the Radar equipment developed will be in all ways in sympathy with the associated weapons."

The difficulty here, of course, lay in the precise interpretation of the term "radar matters affecting weapons" and the W.O. Radar Directorate undoubtedly, on occasion, disturbed the D.G. of A.'s branches by interpreting it differently to their understanding of it, and at times, perhaps, by sins of omission in endeavouring to save time or shorten the channel of communication.

It must be said, however, that at these levels, in both directions the liaison was effective and helpful and the co-operation of individuals largely overcame the difficulties of the official organization.

The co-operation between the W.O. Radar directorate and C.P.R.S.D. was also close; very considerable help was given by the informal arrangement made to permit of direct access for D. Radar to the Establishment so that constant touch could be kept with progress of development and the emergence of new possibilities. It also helped to bring the Establishment more directly into the picture of the policy and needs of the General Staff and the Army.

CHAPTER XXXIV. THE RADAR EXPERIMENTAL ESTABLISHMENT
(A.D.E.E.—A.D.R.D.E.—R.R.D.E.)

Some little time after the 1914–1918 war the Experimental Establishment dealing with acoustics and searchlights for A.A. work had moved to Biggin Hill, alongside the School of Anti-Aircraft Defence, and became known as the Air Defence Experimental Establishment to devise measures for aiding the detection and location of aircraft. Mention has been made of its pre-war activities in Chapter III and in Chapters V and VI has been described its entry into the Radar field. The detachment to the Air Ministry Research Establishment at Bawdsey, of some of its personnel formed an Army cell for adapting the new technique to aid ground defences to engage hostile targets effectively.

This and other establishments were controlled by the R.E. and S. Board which was therefore able to divert personnel and facilities from them to aid developments in radar. It was the A.D.E.E. that was mainly concerned with radar and that establishment, when concentrated at Christchurch early in 1940, became the Air Defence Research and Development Establishment, or A.D.R.D.E. as it has been referred to in this record; its name was, however, changed later in August, 1944, to Radar Research and Development Establishment.

During the twenty odd years of its existence under the control of the Board, a military superintendent was in charge of this establishment with a senior scientist to assist in directing and controlling the work of the scientific staff. It was transferred to the Ministry of Supply with the W.O. Technical Directorates and, after a period of about a year of dual control by the Board and the D.S.R., the Board ceased to exist as an organization in 1940. Civilian scientific control of the establishment then came into force in all respects, with C.P.R.S.D. and his S.R.11 branch at Headquarters, and a scientist as Head of the A.D.R.D.E.

Military direct control of the development of Army equipment thereby ceased and, as research had now been brought in as a specific function of the Establishment, it was perhaps inevitable though, to some extent at least, unfortunate.

It should be recalled that agreement at high level had provided that Radar research for all three Services should be the responsibility of M.A.P. (succeeding the Air Ministry in this respect), but some delegation of research was desirable on account of the individual problems of each of the three Services. Further, the construction of the new Establishment at Christchurch had been approved for *Development* work for Army equipment and its design and facilities had been provided on that basis. This conversion of the Establishment to include major research work had not, therefore, been fully catered for.

This increased concern for research cannot, however, be deprecated—it was needed as a prelude to advanced development; but this concentration in one Establishment did perhaps involve some competition between its research activities and the development of urgently needed equipment, since there was some difficulty in meeting the needs of both with the facilities available.

Apart from the inadequacy of the laboratory, workshop and drawing office, the staff itself was unbalanced in its composition: the engineering and design staff was not of sufficient size to compete rapidly and effectively with the development and practical design necessary to convert proved experimental sets into suitable production form and, at the same time, to compete with the needs of the research workers and their experimental sets for testing new ideas, devices or methods.

Before its demise, the R.E. and S. Board had continuously stressed the need for increasing the engineering—particularly the Radio engineering—component of the staff, its drawing office and design side. This was, however, never provided on an adequate scale and consequently its capacity to complete development up to the stage of turning it over to production remained the weakest part of the Establishment.

The distribution of the staff at its peak strength is shown by the following percentages in different classes.

(a) Staff for scientific research . . . . 30 per cent
    (excluding a proportion engaged mainly on engineering)
(b) Engineering and design, including drawing office and the
    proportion excluded from (a) . . . . . . 10 per cent
(c) Workshops staff, operatives and stores personnel . . 25 per cent
(d) Administrative staff . . . . 10 per cent
(e) Canteen, conservancy and miscellaneous . . . 25 per cent

These percentages are calculated on the peak figure of just under 1,000 to which the strength of the Establishment rose during the war period. These figures refer to civilian staff, except that a very small number of military officers are included: there were also a number of other military personnel attached to the Establishment from time to time, but their numbers never materially affected the proportions of the distribution between classes shown by the percentages given above.

The proportion of (b) to (a) is obviously inadequate for a *development* establishment alone and that of (b) plus (c) to (a) is similarly unbalanced for a *research and development* establishment.

With a new and vital subject like radar, it may well have been that the scientists, having to learn by experience the possibilities and new techniques for applying them, could not keep more than an equal number of "developers" fully occupied in the earliest days. In the later days with ripened experience and understanding, it would seem surprising if the output of the scientists could not fully occupy at least double their own numbers to get their ideas proved and translated into practical form for production.

However much of the final development for production may have been undertaken by contracts with manufacturing firms, there was always, necessarily, a material amount of development work and design needed to translate the experimental form into a fit state for the firm's engineering staff. In addition, close and continuous contact with the firm's development staff had to be maintained by experienced engineers from the Establishment to ensure that the military needs were fully met; this was a further but essential call upon the design staff of the Establishment.

That the engineering and design side of the Establishment did a large amount of very good practical work is not questioned. On occasion, as recorded in earlier Chapters, it provided from its own resources and energy, special equipment in small numbers to meet particular operational needs; but this side remained the weakest part of the Establishment owing to its inadequate strength. The drawing office capacity became a bottleneck, and resulted in urgently needed new types of equipment being delayed in starting production.

This trouble was intensified by the separation of the control of the establishment from the engineering design experience and contacts of the Ministry's Production Directorate and of the Inspectorate of Stores (see Chapter XXIII), though personal liaison was good.

This limitation on development to the production stage is indicated to some extent by the frequency with which major equipments were put into full-scale production during different periods of the war.

(a) In the period from mid-1939 to January, 1941, G.L. I and G.L. II were put into production as was also the C.D./C.H.L. set.

(b) From January, 1941, to April, 1942, the following equipments were put into production—the 1½ metre S.L.C. sets, the G.L. III, the 10 cm. C.D. types, the C.A. No. 1 and the L.W. set—all extensive programmes and in most cases involving several different types; by the end of 1942, the G.R. set for Light A.A. was ready for full production and a rush order for "Baby Maggie" was put into production, though it was not fully developed for long service.

(c) From the beginning of 1943 to the end of the war a number of new types had been proved experimentally, but *no more major equipments were put into full production in this period*—none had been sufficiently developed to reach that stage.

This does not, of course, mean that no development work had been completed during this last stage, but that no major equipments had become really ripe for full production. As a matter of fact, there was a considerable amount of development done in this period, but it was mainly concerned with modifications, anti-jamming appliances, trainers, test gear, and similar minor but very important items. There was one special form of the 3 cm. C.A. No. 1 Portable set, which required a lot of complicated design work, some few emergency type S.L.C. automatic-following sets and emergency auto follow G.L. Sets which were put into production, but they had not been completely developed as types for Service equipment.

Here again, however, the whole of the reduced production in this last period must not be attributed solely to the lack of development; some account must be taken of the shortage of components and the priorities of offensive equipment for the other two Services, which gave them claims on the limited production capacity ahead of that for more defensive types.

On the research and experimental side there is no doubt that the scientific staff of the Establishment did achieve excellent results. Those results led to the developments and advances in radar technique that have been recorded in the earlier parts of this record. In fact, this record is very largely made up of those achievements of the A.D.R.D.E. and the operational results obtained. It was the team work within the Establishment rather than individual efforts that made for effective results, and if the War Office and the Army had to regret that some of the more advanced applications of radar did not become available to the troops in time for use against the enemy, those scientists and technicians who made these advances possible have a like regret that their efforts could not be reflected in improved operational effect demonstrated by practical use in war.

Apart from the activities that have been dealt with, some others did not take practical form as Service equipment, but they did add materially to the experience and knowledge of radar as a whole and to the technique of applying it to Army uses. They had not ripened sufficiently by the time the war ended and a very brief mention of a few of them may be made.

The A.D.R.D.E. had taken Army radar from the 5 metre wave-lengths through the 10 cm.—"S Band"—and into the "X Band" around 3 cm. working, and practical forms of equipment in each had been devised. Investigations of still shorter wave-lengths in or approaching the millimetric zone were initiated by the A.D.R.D.E. Though the millimetric work was transferred to T.R.E. for a time, it reverted to the M. of S. Establishment later for them to pursue; practical trials were carried out, often in co-operation with the Naval and M.A.P. scientific representatives, and many of the performance possibilities, propagational problems, meteorological effects and false echo annoyances, were under investigation when the war ended.

Other lines of investigation and development were in connection with remote displays of radar information and with larger scale displays that would make possible easier access to radar information and would provide it, where most needed, in continuously up-to-date form. Techniques for combining very narrow beams with rapid zone scanning, for improved discrimination and definition, and other advances were being pursued at the time that the war ended. There were also a number of fundamental matters that were either sufficiently established or approaching the stage of full understanding to make them of practical use for future incorporation in equipment.

When the war broke out, the A.D.E.E. was in a disturbed condition. The "Bawdsey Cell" had been hurriedly moved to their new quarters at Christchurch where they were joined by the Biggin Hill staff in due course. The buildings at Christchurch were not complete and the state of the communicating roads will long be remembered. The new Superintendent, Dr. Black, joined two weeks after war started and had the unenviable task of trying to obtain a grip on all the activities of the Establishment and its needs, under this state of affairs.

At the same time, this scattered and moving Establishment had to accept and absorb the very valuable reinforcement of Professor Cockcroft's Group from the Cavendish Laboratories and other sources. It was by no means an easy time and it was a fine effort to get the work going so quickly in the discomforts and difficulties of partly finished buildings and lack of amenities, accommodation, and almost everything except mud.

By the beginning of the summer of 1940, the Establishment was working at full pressure and Cockcroft's crew had returned from their peregrinations in the North and had found their places in the team-work of the Establishment. They had brought to it new effort and new ideas, while they themselves were absorbing with advantage some of the practical experience of the old members of the teams. Colonel Sylvester Evans, who had largely organized the move from Biggin Hill, had succeeded Lieutenant-Colonel Costello as Commandant, and in 1942 it again fell to his lot to tackle the complicated removal of the whole Establishment, this time to Malvern. He carried it through with great skill and powers of organization which resulted in much less dislocation of work than could have been anticipated.

Cockcroft came in as Chief Superintendent, and continued as Head of the Establishment until he was required at the end of 1943 for other very special duties in Canada and the U.S.A. Black, occupied on special duties in America, did not return to the Establishment until after the war ended. Oatley, one of the new members of the A.D.R.D.E., carried on from Cockcroft and remained in charge until after the war ended.

The original Cockcroft party reverted shortly after the war to their University duties or joined Cockcroft in his new atomic establishment. Their departure left many gaps in the Establishment which, though much felt officially, were felt even more on the personal side in the break-up of teams and of close associations. They had become a very real and valuable part of the Establishment and, though enrolled under the Ministry, the Army appreciates the great assistance they gave in the application of radar to its purposes during the time they were serving in the Establishment.

Of the old team, Colonel Evans was transferred in 1943 to M. of S. Headquarters on administrative duties: Forshaw, Butement, and others also had mostly returned to S.R.D.E. or to the Ministry in that year. Of the original A.D.E.E. party, Young had acted in a variety of capacities in direction and control with the R.E. and S. Board, in S.R.11 and also in A.5; he returned to the Establishment at the end of the war. Pollard, after launching the G.L. III development with Messrs. B.T.H., took over charge of S.R.11 at the Ministry and rejoined the Establishment some time after the war. Colonel Raby, the prime mover in the development design work and in "crash" output by the A.D.R.D.E. workshops, officiated at Headquarters for a time before leaving to take charge of S.R.D.E. as Chief Superintendent, but his time there was interrupted for a period of special work in Germany in conjunction with the V.2 rockets. Other members, including Rothwell, also carried out very valuable investigations on German research, development and production with the Control Commission in Germany.

CHAPTER XXXV. EXPERIMENTAL AND TRIALS ARRANGEMENTS

Apart from the A.D.R.D.E. itself, there were a number of establishments or organizations that carried out trials of radar equipment—some were officially constituted and others of a less official nature were set up by formations. The former included the Coast and Anti-Aircraft Experimental Establishment (C.A.E.E.), and of the latter the Experimental and Trials Group set up by A.A. Command was the most prominent but 21 Army Group in the field also carried out a number of practical trials; the A.O.R.G. co-operated with all, in addition to its normal functions of observation of the performance of equipment in use against the enemy. There was also the technical military observation organization formed in the later part of the War to link D.G. of A. to the operational user of weapons in modern warfare; this was known as the Weapons Technical Staff with Field Formations (W.T.S.F.F.).

Very roughly these various bodies fitted into the scheme of things as follows:

(a) *Primary Stage.*—Initial trials of experimental types of set to determine the suitability of performance for development as Service equipment. This was the function of A.D.R.D.E., but was normally assisted by C.A.E.E.

(b) *Secondary Stage.*—Trials of equipment prototypes before full-scale production for modification or improvements to meet the specified standard of performance. This again was the responsibility of A.D.R.D.E. but was often assisted by C.A.E.E. and led to final acceptance for full production.

(c) The secondary stage was usually followed up by C.A.E.E. trials to determine the operational performance of the radar set and the associated equipment, in the hands of well-trained troops; sometimes A.O.R.G. co-operated in these trials.

(d) In parallel with (c), or as soon as possible, prototype sets were made available to the S.A.A.A. or to C.A.S.—under W.O. control—for their own trials which, though somewhat similar to those of C.A.E.E., were directed more to the consideration of the normal Service operators; they were needed for devising standard drills and methods of use——usually provisional at this early stage—for issue by the time the supply of production equipments reached units.

(e) *Final Stage.*—Observation and performance of the equipment in action and its limitations. A.O.R.G. and A.A. Command investigated operational performance in action and the effects on the enemy; the latter carried out experimental trials of their own to eliminate faults, to suggest modifications and to revise operational methods or plotting or prediction arrangements.

In parallel with these, C.A.E.E. would carry out more trials to investigate particular effects, such as those due to siting, and would join with A.D.R.D.E. in the proof of proposed modifications before they could be considered for official adoption. C.I.E.M.E. would also investigate proposed modifications and their effect, technically, with a view to defining the method of implementing those that were acceptable.

It must be realized that, in spite of the various organizations dealing with trials, modifications, etc., the A.D.R.D.E. was *the sole official authority* for radar equipment design and its members were, through the Ministry of Supply, the Technical Advisers of the General Staff on all such matters.

C.A.E.E.—This Establishment originated late in 1935 by the addition of an A.A. experimental section to personnel under the Fire Commander at Culver, investigating C.A. fire control and other instruments. In April, 1937, it became a separate establishment under the title of Coast and Anti-Aircraft Experimental Establishment, with a complement of 5 officers, 4 W.O.s and 66 other ranks, and a year later its Charter placed it under the Fire Control Sub-Committee of the R.A. Committee as part of the Ordnance Board.

After various trials abroad and at home with the new A.A. height-finder and the new Vickers predictor, as well as other instruments, it co-operated in 1939–40 with A.D.R.D.E. in radar trials—the first type of set investigated being the C.D./C.H.L.

A year later, this establishment came under the Ministry of Supply as an appendage of the D. of A. and was responsible for conducting trials of equipment under development and advising as to their acceptability for Army use from the technical artillery aspect.

In July, 1940, its Headquarters were moved to Deganwy, alongside the C.A.S. at Llandudno, where they were joined later by the Experimental Detachments of A.D.R.D.E. and T.R.E. Here Captain Ramsay of C.A.E.E. did a considerable amount of useful research on radar and formed a close link with A.D.R.D.E. Its A.A. Detachment after a time at Dunster and at Christchurch, moved to Woodyates, near Salisbury, in 1941–42, to co-operate with A.D.R.D.E. and later moved to Earls Croome in 1943, to keep in close touch with that Establishment then at Malvern and to share their trials ground. The establishment was increased in 1942 by the addition of 40 A.T.S. for kiné-theodolite and computing duties, and a year later it had grown to a total strength of some 200.

From its start with A.A. instruments, when the R.A. Experimental Officer at A.D.E.E., as it then was, was in charge of that side of their work, the C.A.E.E. was closely associated with A.D.R.D.E., but that link seems to have vanished with the end of the war, as this establishment reverted to War Office control and it became part of the Equipment Wing of S.A.A.A. as the Development Trials Sub-Wing.

This Establishment carried out a number of useful trials, some of which assisted in the design of equipment and others influenced siting and operational methods of use. Their first investigation was on the C.D./C.H.L. Set and proved of great value at the time and particularly so in their use of the Mobile Set for siting the Army component of the Anti-Invasion Chain of Coastal Stations. This was followed up by investigations of all the subsequent coastal types, the details of which need not be mentioned here. Their final verdict on the C.A. No. 1, Mark IV, the 3 cm. type, may be quoted as a matter of interest:

". . . is undoubtedly one of the finest pieces of Radar equipment produced by any nation during the war. Its excellent performance is combined with a high degree of reliability. . . . Basically this equipment is the complete answer to the problem of Coast Artillery Radar. . . ."

This opinion is endorsed by the independent comment of the Coast Artillery School after assisting in the initial trials of this set; that comment is as follows:

"This type of set . . . is undoubtedly the set of the future, and is a design in which A.D.R.D.E. seem to have hit the nail squarely on the head."

On the A.A. types, this establishment assisted A.D.R.D.E. in all the basic trials of G.L. II, III, III with A.D.R.D.E. type auto follow modification (which they assessed as equivalent in performance to the U.S. Type S.C.R. 584) and "Baby Maggie" but they were not able to complete their trials of the light auto-follow pattern of G.L. Most of these basic trials were followed up by their own trials of the whole system from radar to predictor output, involving all types of the latter, including the various electrical patterns. This class of trial was more their true business than that of the radar set alone and they really formed the link between the Development Establishment and the operational user and A.O.R.G.'s assessment of equipment in action against the enemy.

In time of peace, these further C.A.E.E. trials would ordinarily be factors in deciding on the adoption of a new type of equipment, but in war it was not possible to delay decisions for final and complete proof in all respects. As has been impressed earlier in this record, chances have to be taken on scientific and technical assessment and advice, rather than on complete trials and full facts, in view of the always present and pressing Time factor. For this advisory purpose, the C.A.E.E. provided a direct source of technical opinion to D.G. of A. and his staff for advising the G.S.

Some criticisms have been made of the pursuit of trials by C.A.E.E. after an equipment had been brought into the Service, but this seems to be unjustified. In no case does it appear that any new types of equipment in the early stages of consideration for adoption were prejudiced or delayed by trials of sets already in service. No trials that result in useful information or improved methods of operation are stale if the set remains in service and, moreover, in some cases those results may influence design of new types of associated equipment.

From the trials carried out by the Establishment, it was evident that the capacity of the equipment to produce the highest standard of performance specified had generally been attained. They also indicated that the operational performance achieved by units seldom approached that standard: the degree of skill of the operators was the limiting factor and not the capacity of the equipment. This points to the need for higher grade training which was not usually possible during the rush output of personnel necessary during the war; alternatively, it pointed to the need for elimination of manual operation in cases where high and consistent accuracy is required.

While the C.A.E.E. personnel cannot be classed as experts, they were of a high standard of training: in addition, their performance was obtained under trials conditions, rather than in action. They cannot therefore be considered as representative of the normal or average operators and their concern was primarily with the equipment itself and the whole chain of appliances from the radar to the gun and its overall performance. They might be considered as providing the practical stage of optimum Service performance for the scientist and, as such, giving the schools and training establishments a high target at which to aim for their trained output of Radar operators.

Schools and other trials arrangements.—The Schools under War Office control naturally had trials to carry out with each new type of equipment. These were necessary for bringing their instructional staffs fully into the picture of sets on which they had to instruct personnel under training and also for the staff devising the drills for use, the compiling of operational pamphlets or descriptive matter for guiding units who would receive the sets, and, as far as was possible, for defining the operational doctrine for their employment.

For this purpose the S.A.A.A. maintained a Trials wing that investigated in detail each type of radar set introduced, in order to determine for themselves its individual performance and limitations. These were followed up by trials in conjunction with predictors and "still" trials against air targets, with a system of recording, from which the effect of fire could be estimated. Active shoots would also follow with the chain of fire control instruments and the guns manned by the demonstration detachments from the Wing. The completeness of these trials developed gradually and did not come into full form till fairly late in the war when the necessary recording appliances and other instruments became available. C.A.S. similarly carried out their trials of the effectiveness of radar sets in conjunction with the Coastal methods of Fire Direction.

A.A. Command.—A.A. Command organized their own trials arrangements which made use of actually observed operational results, as well as of specific trials at their Trial Site 21, where a large number of investigations were carried out. As a result of these, many new devices, methods and proposed modifications, including some major radar modifications such as the means of converting the types of G.L. III to Auto Follow, were suggested, some being accepted and introduced officially. This was a case of "self help" in the emergency of continuous operations and was a valuable contribution to the practical aspect of A.A. operations. Naturally, however, it, too, duplicated much of the work and effort applied by the other organizations, though in the practical operational aspect A.A. Command undoubtedly led them with its experience.

Though perhaps unavoidable at the time, the apparent duplication of effort was wasteful and some of that waste could have been avoided had there been more effective co-operation between C.A.E.E. and S.A.A.A. and between S.A.A.A. and A.A. Command. There was common ground for meetings and interchange of views and results that could bridge some of the gaps, in the shape of the Petersham School colloquies, the periodical O.R.G. discussions and the War Office meetings of its Radio Executive Sub-Committee. It was the more direct contacts that appeared to be lacking.

There certainly was close co-operation between A.D.R.D.E., C.A.S., and C.A.E.E.; the Radar liaison between A.D.R.D.E. and A.A. Command was always close, in fact at times it tended to become embarrassing to the work of that establishment. The O.R.G. co-operated intimately with all its operational contacts and particularly so with its original foster parent A.A. Command, from whom it received full reciprocal assistance. Its liaison with the Coast Gunners at Dover, with Shore Naval organizations and with the R.A.F. was excellent, though Home Forces Headquarters in the early days (1941) were not very co-operative nor appreciative of its activities and assistance.

A.O.R.G. and W.T.S.F.F.—As has been seen in Chapter XXX the M. of S. initiated the O.R.G. and later shared control of its activities with the W.O.: the W.T.S.F.F. was purely a military organization but was under the direction of the D.G. of A. in the Ministry. Neither really formed part of the Trials organization and their true function was observation of the equipment in action. Early trials by A.O.R.G. may have appeared to duplicate some of the work of the A.D.R.D.E., but in fact they were really providing the technical background on which to base their observational work. Most of them were made in combination with C.A.E.E. or were delegated from A.D.R.D.E. but others, as in the case of C.A. sets, were combined with actual operations—carrying the observation and assessment role into the field of adjustments, alterations to improve practical performance and suggestions for modification —using and also proving the operational performance of experimental sets.

With field formations, they carried out their observation role and were often assisted by the Wheatsheaf organization for technical military observation of weapons and their associated equipment in the field. These two scientific and military technical parties with the field Armies were complementary to one another, not competitive nor overlapping; both achieved valuable results with realistic appreciation of the demands of modern warfare and of the practical needs of the user in those modern conditions.

Apart from the more or less static A.A. operations, the A.O.R.G. overseas activities were extended to the more mobile operations beginning with the North African campaign and operations in Sicily and Italy. Here also members of the Wheatsheaf organization were actively employed and though not primarily concerned with radar they were involved in its operation in the field as Fire Control Instruments and with the effect of the Radio Fuze against ground targets. The two organizations were consequently in fairly close contact in this aspect but they became even closer in endeavours to adapt existing equipment to aid in countering the Mortar menace.

In the Northern European campaign both organizations were increasingly represented and did very valuable work. Brigadier Cole as head of Wheatsheaf with 21 Army Group, landed in Normandy on D-plus 2-day with Johnson who had taken charge of the A.O.R.G. personnel for field operations when Brigadier Schonland took up the duties of Scientific Adviser to Headquarters of 21 Army Group; both these officers were able to call for selected individuals to reinforce them as and when they were required. Brigadier Cole took charge of the two groups for general administration, etc., but each carried out its duties under its own commander.

On the radar side much useful work was done and valuable reports were submitted. They assisted the Special Radar unit of 21 Army Group in operations and their reports were valuable in linking up with the experiences in Italy of 15 Army Group and C.M.F. Headquarters.

While both the O.R.G. and Wheatsheaf took part in observing radar operational performance, the latter were, if somewhat less concerned in the technical detail, of considerable value in the practical operational aspect; the close liaison between them was, therefore, a material factor in the assessment of the results and in pointers to future possibilities.

Radar was of course only one aspect of the interests of both these groups of scientific and technical military observers. Practically every weapon, vehicle and appliance came within their scope but this is not the place to record those activities. On radar matters both organizations provided that most necessary link between the designers of weapons and equipment and the practical use of them in the field. In addition they were, in their observation capacity, able to get a true picture from a rather detached point of view, of the conditions and effects of modern warfare.

CHAPTER XXXVI. RADAR PRODUCTION

A general idea of the changes in the organization of the Ministry of Supply in so far as Radar for the Army was concerned has been given in the preceding chapters. There are, however, some few details of the resulting arrangements on the Production side that should be mentioned here but the salient points that have already emerged may be summarized as follows:

(a) *Divided Responsibility.* The Ministry did not produce complete radar sets for the Army—the production of all radar parts and assemblies was delegated to the Ministry of Aircraft Production and, in some few cases, the complete sets were produced and assembled through that Ministry. Normally the Ministry of Supply retained in their own hands the production of the non-radar parts—cabins, structural and mechanical components, etc.—and the "free issue" Service components and accessories which they supplied to the M.A.P. contractors or provided for assembly under their own arrangements.

From the War Office aspect this division of responsibility prevented direct access for effective information on forecasts of supply and first-hand information of progress in production.

(b) *Separation of Production from Development.* Within the Ministry there was no official link between these interdependent stages; the gap between the two was only bridged at the highest level.

The War Office could not obtain reliable information on any radar equipment *as a whole* in all its aspects, from any executive level in the Ministry.

(c) *Lack of Development and Design Capacity.* The facilities at the R. and D. Establishment were inadequate to keep pace with the translation of experimental sets into a form suitable for equipment or to influence and direct such work in the hands of firms undertaking development contracts.

The War Office had no official say in acceptance of the final production design except to the extent that it conformed to their specified requirements; on technical performance details, acceptance was delegated to D.G. of A.'s branches concerned in so far as Fire Control was concerned.

The Production of radar equipment was at first dealt with in the Ministry by one of the two sub-Directorates for Signals Equipment under D.E.S.E. or D. Sigs. E, as he was called after the Engineer side had been moved to a separate department. Later in 1941, Major-General Archedeckne Butler became D.D.G.S.E. and served two masters, the D.G.Mech.E. for Production and D.G.S.R.D. for Research and Development of *Signals Radio*, but *not for Radar*, as D.G.S.R.D. controlled Radar R. and D. through C.P.R.S.D.

With the addition, in 1943, of the intermediate post of S.T.C.O., under D.G.Mech.E., the radio hierarchy may have been strengthened and perhaps simplified within the Ministry itself, but from the War Office aspect the position was still more complicated. The S.T.C.O., apparently, had only "permissive" contact with, but no control of the Radar R. and D. work and this appointment merely added to the difficulties of discovering among the "many cooks" a level at which reliable information on radar and its production could be obtained. There was also some doubt whether the priorities and urgency of needs stated to the Ministry, ever really penetrated to S.T.C.O. and the Production side. This was of particular concern to the War Office in view of the fact that the

D.D.G.S.E. was presumed to represent Army radar production needs on the Production Planning Committee of the Radio Board, and the S.T.C.O. similarly, on the Radio Production Executive where most of the allocation of capacity was decided.

The D.D.S.E. for Radar and Searchlights, Brigadier C. M. Simpson, had a difficult task, for his E.S.3 Production branches were separated from the R. and D. branch S.R.11, under C.P.R.S.D. In addition to tackling radar production within the Ministry he had to form the co-operative link with M.A.P. to whom responsibility for production of the radar parts had been delegated. His only regular official contact with radar development, and the same applied to the Inspectorate of Engineer and Signal Stores (I.E.S.S.), was the periodical "Release for Production" meetings held at the A.D.R.D.E., which reviewed the stage of development reached towards suitability for handing over to firms, or for final development by a firm, for production as Service equipment.

It may be noted that the War Office was not represented at these meetings—a strange arrangement as they were immediately concerned, from the planning point of view at least, with this key turning-point where Research and Development gave place to Production, where hopes and possibilities gave place to hard facts in the form of "ironmongery." Even information on this turning-point was seldom made available without it having to be "dug-out" and followed up by requests for time forecasts of supply. The responsibility for "Release for Production" lay jointly with C.P.R.S.D. and A.5—the latter only for the military user and technical Artillery aspects, when Fire Control radar was affected.

The link between the radar production side of the M. of S. and that of the M.A.P. was provided by the appointment to the Radio Production department of the latter Ministry, of an officer experienced in the inspection and production of Army radio equipment. Colonel A. W. Sproull held this post until November, 1940, when he was relieved by Lieut.-Colonel F. C. C. Bradshaw who became an Assistant Director of Radio Production; as such he was completely executive, and till 1942 he dealt with all R.A.F. radar production as well as that for the Army; by 1943 his responsibilities were confined to Army radar needs only.

It is of interest to note his view as an Army representative in a "foreign" organization, that within D.R.P.'s sphere no difference was made nor preference given in arranging for production for the Air Ministry or for the War Office —they were dealing with radar as a whole and not radar for any particular Service. They were, of course, affected by policy rulings of the Radio Board, or its Radio Production Executive, but where this M.A.P. directorate itself was concerned there was no bias in favour of any one Service.

In the early days of radar and its continuous rapid growth there were, of course, difficulties with the contracting firms and the supply of skilled personnel as well as with the supply of components. The firms seldom seem to have appreciated fully the extent of the work involved and often gave rather fantastic estimates of production times; this was perhaps particularly so in the case of Army equipment which demanded a high degree of mechanical accuracy not ordinarily needed for R.A.F. types. In consequence, delays in provision were constantly occurring and it fell to Bradshaw to convert those so-called forecasts into more practical facts when experience of actual production became available —often a year later.

The relations between the Production sides of the two Ministries were not always easy in the early days, partly on account of the different method or system of inspection employed by M.A.P. and partly to M.A.P.'s lack of appreciation of the accumulated experience of the ex-War Office Production and Inspection organization. Had more use been made of this experience in the selection of firms for high accuracy work and in discrimination between small firms and their methods of radio construction, it might have resulted in earlier and improved co-operation.

This link was also handicapped, in the early days, by some lack of co-operation on both sides; certainly D.D.S.E.(3) lacked information on production forecasts and A.D.R.P. did not receive the full assistance from E.S.(3) that was extended to him later. Matters improved considerably after the winter of 1941-42 and the link with the M. of S. became more effective; towards the end of the war A.D.R.P. was operating in the M. of S. at least as much as in the M.A.P., which helped materially in the liaison.

It must be recalled that the M. of S. had delegated to M.A.P. the responsibility for production of Army Radar and naturally the latter shouldered their responsibility and pursued their way as they thought best for both Services; there could be no question of requiring them to change their system of inspection nor of insisting upon the Army methods being applied specially to part of their work.

The Inspectorate of Engineer and Signals Stores which had been in existence for many years and dealt with a very wide variety of Army equipment became, during the war, the Inspectorate of Electrical and Mechanical Equipment. By the time that war broke out it had not established an adequate section to deal effectively with radar and had but few individuals sufficiently experienced in the special technique, though for radio generally it was amply staffed. By the time it might have been in a position to undertake full inspection of Army radar equipment under its own system, the M.A.P. arrangements were in full swing with A.I.D. carrying out inspection according to their normal practice.

Here it must be understood that the A.I.D. dealt with the inspection of Army equipment only to the extent of passing it for acceptance *ex-works*.

They could not, of course, carry on into the post-provision activities that fall to the Inspectorate in cataloguing, scaling spares and component replacements, post-production tests to establish the standard on which Technical Instructions and Descriptive Pamphlets were based, methods of incorporation of modifications, equipment records and other essential duties in connection with Army equipment during its Service life.

While in no way deprecating the methods of I.E.S.S. which had done so much to establish and maintain the very high standard of excellence of Army equipment, it must be said that the A.I.D. system of factory inspection appeared to be better suited to the immediate and urgent needs of war-time supply though, admittedly, they did not always ensure the same uniformity and high standard. It was not possible to change horses in the middle of the rapid war stream without involving disturbance and delays; the D.R.P. and the A.I.D. did what they could to permit access to equipment under manufacture which was helpful and was appreciated by the more senior and experienced members of I.E.S.S., but it gave rise to some confusion and friction in the firms by apparent duplication or contradiction of instructions by junior members who had not the wider view and understanding of their seniors.

I.E.S.S., or I.E.M.E. as it became, had originally some difficulty in maintaining contact with the development work in progress at A.D.R.D.E., but eventually this was overcome by having some of its personnel continuously attached to the establishment. This enabled them to foresee new types of equipment, to get early information of trials results and occasionally to advise on matters of design though, in fact, their advice was seldom solicited.

It may be that C.I.E.S.S. and his staff were handicapped by a lack of knowledge of the urgency of the G.S. requirements and the tendency to accept the "adequate" to meet the immediate need. It was a case of "pull devil, pull baker" for the G.S.—early provision or high standard of quality—and in many cases a short life only for the equipment was contemplated in view of technical development advances. Perhaps the G.S. were at fault in not specifically issuing guidance to C.I.E.S.S. on this aspect, but they had no direct access and their policy statements made this point of "adequacy" clear; it was also stressed at development meetings with emphasis placed upon the Time factor. Here, again, it seems doubtful if the G.S. views ever reached the I.E.S.S. or, if they did, they were not appreciated fully. The feeling certainly existed, and not in the War Office only, that the Inspectorate did not adapt itself to the conditions of war urgency and rapidly developing equipment employing this new technique.

Apart from the normal radar production through M.A.P., the D.D.S.E. for Radar Production, Brigadier C. M. Simpson, had to operate through other provision sources. It will be recalled that all the improved coast defence stations and the 10 cm. Coast Artillery equipments involved the use of Admiralty designed radar assemblies—the N.T. 271 and its successors—which had to be obtained independently of M.A.P. The Light Warning set and the early S.L.C. embodied Air Ministry assemblies, and numerous components, of course, had to be obtained from inter-Service sources. All this involved a very large amount of special work in co-ordinating supply to meet the provision of the structures, mechanical, electrical, etc., parts designed and produced by M. of S. contracts. These latter included the designs for such structures as the 200 foot C.D. towers and their erection, the small towers, turn-tables and rotational turning gear for the C.A. sets, for the C.D. sets and others, all of which were the responsibility of D.D.S.E.

There is no doubt that this work was carried out most effectively and the co-ordination of arrival of all parts from their different sources, their erection and assembly was a real achievement—it was rare if a forecast date of completion was not met for a C.D. or C.A. station to be ready for the radar installation and hand over for use.

This was also the case for the supplies of Canadian type G.L. III equipment and of the provision by the United States of a number of the S.C.R. 584 equipments—and their spares, etc.; but these involved little in the way of special components provision; the former, however, did demand a considerable amount of special provision for modifications, either from Canada or by this country.

The methods of production varied from the "Chinese copy" to the fully developed and proved design from complete production drawings. The first was seldom used and then only as a temporary or emergency means, while the latter would have been the normal method but could seldom be used in the stress of war urgency. Between these two there were a number of different forms of development contract work leading up to full production. These forms might involve initial development and proof of performance by the

Establishment and its translation into a form suitable to the production methods and practice of the selected manufacturing firm; alternatively they might place the onus on the firm for full development with varying degrees of advice or direction from the Establishment, on the basis of performance of a proved experimental model. In the former the liaison with the firm would be mainly at the Establishment, while for the latter the work would be almost entirely concentrated at the firms' works.

The selection of the method to be used was of course a matter for the Ministry to decide in conjunction with M.A.P. In most cases production by "hand-made" or "Model Shop" methods was involved, of a number of prototypes, to prove the production design before the full-scale production could be put into full swing. That initial production, however, could be made during the time for tooling up, collecting of materials and components, sub-contracting, etc., and on occasion provided some sets for test and for training before the proper equipment became available.

The success of any method depended very much on the class of firm selected and also upon the nature of the liaison by the Establishment. From an outside point of view—that is from the War Office aspect—this liaison seemed to be too much in the hands of the scientist, rather than the engineer. Delays in finalizing design, or by late alterations to improve performance, were reflected in increased delay in starting full production, but in some cases much of the delay was caused in the stage of test of the prototype set. While full proof of suitability was, of course, essential before full-scale production, the time taken to do this appeared excessive in many cases. This was due to what appears to be a general tendency of the scientist to "gild the lily" and to sheer off from finalizing a design; certainly in several cases modifications making for improvements were made, but they were made at the expense of time.

In some contracts in the earlier days it was possible to include in its terms a condition that after the first 200, or whatever number was considered suitable, some alterations or improvements could be incorporated, if necessary, and if fully proved by the time that stage had been reached; this, however, was seldom possible in the later stages of the war.

Mention has been made of the inadequacy of the design staff of the Establishment, but it must be realized that though first-class production design experience can complete design to a fully practical form, almost every manufacturer will require to convert it to some extent to suit his methods and tooling. This of itself made difficulties when a number of firms had to co-operate, or a large contract had to be divided among two or more groups of firms. This was not confined to firms in this country as was realized when the United States supplied us with a number of their S.C.R. 584 sets; there were two general patterns made by different groups and, in consequence, they were not entirely uniform and components not entirely interchangeable. Generally speaking we were fortunate in this respect and the production authorities managed to avoid this difficulty of lack of uniformity.

The use of the "Chinese copy" method was not encouraged but on occasion it was used for special emergency or "crash" production of small numbers of sets either for special purposes for very temporary operational need or to tide over a gap until normal production would provide the needs. Such methods were objectionable from the production point of view but demands by the G.S. for special urgent requirements grew with the progress of the war and, of course, aimed at exceptional priority for those special cases. Naturally this special emergency priority began to defeat its own ends in inter-Service competition as "crash" had to give place to "crash-crash" and absurdity could not be carried further.

Abnormal methods of production were employed in some special cases such as that of Baby Maggie and Gorgonzola, referred to earlier, where the A.D.R.D.E. workshops were enlisted to produce the goods in time for particular operations, which was far too short for normal methods. The M. of S. had also set up a Radio Production Unit—following the lead of the M.A.P.—for small scale emergency production, but radio had priority over radar on the limited capacity available. R.E.M.E. workshop units also contributed valuable aid in special cases, but mainly in assembly, as in the case of the early types of S.L.C., the Light Warning equipment and still later the auto follow centrimetric S.L.C., which was thereby enabled to get into action operationally in Northern Europe before the end of the war.

In Appendix VI will be found a chronological table or graph of the production of Army radar linked to its development and to the requirements of the General Staff. It indicates to some extent the hard fact that production involves a very considerable period of time and, naturally, it is a material factor in the result that equipment that was developing so rapidly was almost out of date before it was in full use by the troops in action. Though the user and the planner tended to be critical of the time lag between proof of performance and the output of the production stage—and at times, no doubt, expressed their feelings about production somewhat forcibly—neither the Production sides of the Ministries nor the firms concerned could overcome the hard facts. New ideas grow and follow one another rapidly in a new device like radar but the production capacity in this country though expanded and stretched to its limit, could not keep pace—material facts are more obstructive and unyielding than ideas. It was the frequency with which new ideas were evolved that outdated equipment so rapidly—but no one would wish to stay that progress and no one can justly blame those who strove to produce the goods for failing to keep provision in step with advances in technical performance.

CHAPTER XXXVII. COMMENTARY

The foregoing chapters of this Part have given an outline idea of the organization of the Ministry of Supply in so far as it was concerned with the development and provision of radar equipment for the Army. This record is not the place to discuss the organization for the other multifarious duties and responsibilities of the Ministry, but it is concerned with the effect of those other responsibilities on the output of Army Radar.

Those activities naturally widened the scope of the responsibilities and interests at the higher levels in the Ministry and, to that extent, made it impossible to represent at high levels the radar needs of the Army with the authoritative weight of concentrated interest and direct contact with urgent needs, as was possible on behalf of the R.A.F. by the M.A.P. representatives. It became apparent that this lack of full appreciation of the Army's operational needs and priorities added somewhat to the handicap under which Army radar already suffered, in comparison with that of the other two Services, on account of its lack of opportunities for truly offensive employment.

The differences in the organizations of the three Services and their respective supply arrangements have been mentioned in Chapter XXXIII. The Admiralty retained practically complete control of all aspects of radar concentrated in one organization, from the inception of a new technical idea or need to its ship-fitting and manning. The Air Ministry, nominally sharing responsibility with M.A.P., largely short-circuited duality of control by appointing the key individuals concerned to posts in both Ministries. The War Office, on the other hand, shared the responsibilities for radar with the Ministry of Supply, and though it expressed its policy requirements and priorities it could not represent them in the competition for production capacity. There was divided responsibility for Army radar at the Inter-Departmental stage though, in practice, the difficulties of such duality were sufficiently overcome to permit of reasonably smooth working and co-operation. The difficulties arose chiefly by reason of the lengthy channel of official communication and the "many cooks" involved in the preparation of the radar "consommé" in the Ministry without a Chief "Chef" responsible for getting them all working together.

Divided Responsibility. Within the Ministry itself the delegation of responsibility to M.A.P. for the production of Army radar may seem a strange proceeding, in view of the fact that the primary duty of the M. of S. was to produce the goods. The intention to concentrate radar production under one Ministry was an extension of the decision of the War Cabinet that research should be centralized for all the Services. This was accepted by the M. of S. at the end of 1939, when it was anticipated that the Admiralty would also conform to the arrangement and, though this did not actually happen, the M. of S. continued to honour their undertaking throughout the war, though at times the possibility of partial separation from M.A.P. for production was considered.

It is now apparent—wisdom after the event—that, at the time, the full implications were not appreciated nor were the complications involved in the M. of S. fully realized. From the point of view of the War Office this arrangement produced difficulties which might have been avoided had the Ministry retained full responsibility for production while using the M.A.P. facilities when desirable. This would have saved the split of responsibility and should have provided a recognized source from which the War Office could obtain information on production progress and forecasts.

This agreement for radar production did not necessarily refer to radar equipment as a whole but mainly concerned the radar parts and assemblies. Experience with the early Fire Control sets for Army use soon indicated, clearly, that the mechanical accuracy must be of a high degree if the value of the radar side of an equipment was to be made use of to its fullest capacity. This necessarily high accuracy of mechanical movement presented production problems beyond the scope of most radio manufacturers, and in fact the structural stability and mechanical accuracy of movement parts of Army radar assumed almost equal importance to that of the radar side. This aspect of design was increasingly taken into the hands of the M. of S. who also assumed most of the co-ordination of the assembly of the various parts to complete the equipment as a whole.

On the production of Army radar, therefore, dual control and divided responsibility was present. It also made its appearance in the direction and control of the Research and Development Establishment in the early days; here, however, it did not last long, as in 1941 single control was effected by the elimination of the Military side. Single control was achieved, but it was achieved at the expense of user experience of practical needs and conditions of use in action and, perhaps still more important, of the need to complete effective if not ideal designs for production and supply to the troops.

Segregation of Production. Further comment on divided responsibility need not be made, but a further handicap was created by that revision of organization in 1941. This went to the opposite extreme for it practically separated Production entirely from Development within the Ministry itself and provided no link at any executive level. From the point of view of the War Office, this was perhaps the worst feature of the radar organization in the Ministry. Forward planning was made impossible by the lack of any authority who was concerned with radar equipment as a whole and from whom reliable, realistic and up-to-date information could be obtained.

In the reorganization in 1940, a single authority, D.E.S.E. who later became D.Sigs.E., controlled both development and production of radio and radar. There, at executive level, was the necessary link and the single authority for the whole of the Ministry's concern with radar. This arrangement was, however, short-lived and the 1941–42 changes cut development of both radio and radar from his charge; the divorce of radar production from its development and, with it, the complete radar link to the War Office, then vanished. The why and wherefore of this unfortunate change cannot be determined—individual recollections or opinions from within and from outside the Ministry vary as to the reasons—but its effect soon became evident in the difficulties it produced; "unfortunate" is really too mild an adjective to apply to it.

The R. and D. Establishment. Some remarks are desirable on the establishment that produced the actual methods of applying radar to Army purposes —the A.D.E.E., A.D.R.D.E. or R.R.D.E. as it was called at different times during the war period. What that establishment achieved and the effects of its work have been dealt with in the earlier Parts of this record.

The first comment to be made is that the War Office and the Army as a whole have cause to pay to that establishment a grateful tribute for providing effective radar aids to its operations. That the results of its work were valuable, has been demonstrated and it may be said with truth that it made a material contribution to the Army's share in bringing the war to a successful conclusion.

Other comments and some criticism—of a minor nature in comparison with the foregoing general comment—that should be made are on points where delays or even failures were caused, which might have been avoided or reduced had the experience of the past been used to guide organization and reorganization of the Establishment and its work.

The first of these points is the lack of balance in the different classes of staff required in a research and development establishment of this nature—reference had been made to this in Chapter XXXIV. The inadequacy of the engineering and design side of the staff must be stressed as it was undoubtedly a cause of delay in translating new methods and devices into form suitable for production as Army equipment. This deficiency was recognized at the time of the expansion of the establishment in 1939, when, also, the possibilities of radar were growing rapidly and further expansion could be anticipated; this need was urged upon the Ministry but was never adequately met.

This weakness was certainly intensified by the official separation of the experienced production and inspection departments in the Ministry, from close co-operation with the development and design side of the Establishment. The mechanical design work for the high accuracy needs of the equipment remained as perhaps the least satisfactory aspect of the work throughout the war.

This lack of adequate technical staff for converting proved experimental sets into practical equipment form was apparent in cases of initial design work in the establishment and also in the guidance to firms undertaking development.

Inadequate Control. Some of this failing in guidance or directing development mentioned above was, undoubtedly, due to liaison with the firms concerned by members of the scientific, rather than the engineering, sides of the staff. While such access to firms was closely controlled while the establishment was under Military direction, it increased when that direction was replaced by civilian scientific control.

At the beginning of 1941 a procedure had been laid down that technical development personnel—scientific, engineering and design—from the establishment should be used for liaison with firms to supply them with technical guidance and instructions for the production of the prototype sets, but that on acceptance of those prototypes—modified as found necessary—the establishment was excluded from visiting the firm's work, unless specifically invited by the Production authorities to advise on technical matters arising during the course of manufacture.

By the end of that year when scientific control was in being, the only instruction in force was that "The Chief Superintendent shall be responsible for liaison with production firms" though responsibility really lay with the production side of the Ministry and M.A.P.

This was not interpreted effectively nor restricted to essential contacts with firms. The production authorities of both Ministries complained of the interference caused and of instructions being given to the firms direct—at times by junior scientists—without their knowledge. Attempts to introduce modifications in this way, without reference and without any idea of the effect on delivery dates, caused delays by disturbance of the planned work of production.

Really essential modifications from the operational aspect might be necessary occasionally, but should only be implemented with the approval of the General Staff after full information as to the effect on time of supply.

This lack of control and the resulting interference with production was a definite fault, probably due to the lack of appreciation of the practical aspect and the importance of the time factor in equipment provision.

Direction and Control of R. and D. Establishment. The last paragraph raises the question of the control and direction of the scientific and technical staffs—in fact the control of all the activities of an establishment charged with the duty of developing important new forms of equipment for Army use. The controversial question of whether control should be exercised by technical military officers or by civilian scientific personnel is discussed in Part VII. Here, attention may be drawn to the actual effect on Army radar provision caused by the change in 1941–42 which eliminated the Military in favour of the scientific.

When the Ministry of Supply was formed the existing organization—the R.E. and S. Board—controlling and directing this and other Experimental and Development establishments, was transferred with its establishments to the charge of the Ministry. It was split up shortly afterwards into its separate sections but the radio and radar activities were continued under Military direction, though scientific staffs and their research activities became the responsibility of the D.S.R. who dealt with them direct rather than through the Military directorate. This directorate continued, until 1941–42, to control experiment, development and design work of the Establishment as well as production; the last alone remained a military responsibility as the Establishment came under the Scientific Research directorate completely.

There is no doubt that the scientists did much excellent work in advancing radar performance and widening its field of useful employment, but it is also a fact that these advances were often partly discounted by delays. Some of the delays were attributable to what appears to be an inherent disinclination of the scientist to finalize a design or to accept a decision on the form a new device is to take as practical "ironmongery." There was also apparent a lack of enforcement of a decision once taken and the banning of further alterations and improvements to an accepted prototype design, though it must be said that this is *not* confined to scientists. The scientist's outlook tends to put the practical results emanating from his work and the Time factor, also, as secondary matters compared with the solution of the problems that are his chief concern; it is generally anathema to him to take a partial solution that can be developed rapidly rather than to await a full solution.

In war, the Time factor is a very material consideration and it is the function of an organization, charged with research and development, to provide the practical results and to do so in time for them to be of maximum value to the troops. Such practical outlook is, of course, not confined to the military representative, but with his knowledge of the operational circumstances he is the authority to make the decision as to what is worthwhile *vis-à-vis* Time and it is he who should have the power to enforce that decision. The decision may be taken by the G.S., but the enforcement of the "guillotine" cannot be exercised from outside the establishment. It is a case of the technical soldier and the scientist working together but one or the other must have the final say and, in the stress and pressure of war at least, it is or should be the function of the soldier.

Some comparison of the results achieved under the two alternative forms of control can be obtained from the tabular graph in Appendix VI. It will be seen that practically all the major radar equipments were put into production design form in the earlier period when military control was still in force. It has already been shown that the later period was more affected by lack of design capacity for evolving the practical forms of equipment, that production capacity was increasingly inadequate and that manufacturing firms were more concerned with fully planned production for large quantity supply than for small orders.

Those considerations as well as the over-riding priorities of offensive types of radar must be taken into account, but even so it must be said that practical results suffered more in the latter period from inadequate or indecisive control.

The Technical Artillery Side. The D.G. of A.'s department retained its military character throughout the war and kept its technical Artillery experience available to back its advice. It had fortunately, or perhaps it is more accurate to say, it had with foresight, provided specially for radar as an aid to gunners, by the appointment of Major Paterson, and so in the earliest days it managed to get right into the radar picture. On transfer to the Ministry it had recognized the growing importance of radar and had established a branch specifically to deal with the link up of this new device with its fire control methods and instruments. This branch contributed very materially to the development of radar to make H.A.A. fire effective even against unseen targets.

In retrospect—and occasionally wisdom after the event may be permitted —it seems a pity that greater use should not have been made of this department by making it the primary link between the Ministry and the War Office for *all radar* matters. As a military organization it could have represented the General Staff in the Ministry to the extent of controlling development and design, though on policy and quantitative requirements for supply it could not have initiated demands but it could have echoed the needs of the G.S. with an authoritative voice.

Alternatively, it might have been better if the D. of A. had taken back under his wing the Artillery development work of the section of the R.E. and S. Board concerned and the Establishment too; the activities of the A.D.E.E. at the time of transfer to the Ministry were entirely concerned with Artillery matters and had for many years been directed by D. of A. through the R.E.S.B. The experienced personnel of that section of the Board could have been absorbed as a branch or sub-directorate of the D. of A. equally as well as in the Signals Equipment directorate, and it would have been much more appropriately situated there. Whether the production side should also have been brought in is immaterial—there would have been little real difficulty in doing so—but, whether in or out of that directorate, the close links between the development and production sides that always existed under the Board's régime would have been maintained. The direction of the establishment would then have remained in military hands. This would have provided a short direct channel of communication and a single authority for transmitting all radar information, practically at first-hand, in both directions.

Production. From the War Office radar point of view the difficulties caused by divided responsibility and by the divorce of production from development were due to faulty organization, a view also held by many individuals within the Ministry itself. The latter expressed their views as follows: "As it was, at whatever level in the M. of S. chain—The Minister, C.G.M.P., D.G.Mech.E., D.D.G.S.E., D.D.S.E.(3), E.S.3—the War Office might approach (for information on production) on a pressing issue, the answer or promise they received contained an element, usually the most important part, of (at best) secondhand information relayed from M.A.P. and often in its earlier stages (of transit) garbled. Even when the practice of submitting M.A.P. reports *verbatim* was adopted, the War Office had officially no direct access to the responsible authority in M.A.P. . . . ."

Similarly after the reorganization that separated production from development and from policy for ultimate supply, their view was expressed as: "afterwards guidance to the General Staff on production possibilities was almost entirely obtained from or given by the design authority who quite frequently did not even consult the Production department before giving their advice."

In these conditions it is perhaps surprising that the radar policy of the General Staff did not fall into more serious errors. It is not, however, surprising that the War Office radar representatives complained so frequently of delays in supply and of completely misleading Time estimates which affected forward planning.

From the production side of the Ministry, with reference to the period up to April, 1942, comes the opinion that "It is suprising that with this system there was any achievement. In fact, taking into account the nature and complexity of the equipment and the technique, constantly changing and advancing, the achievement was certainly equal to or ahead of that in other (production) spheres." Not only can the War Office endorse that view but it can appreciate the very real efforts made by the Production side of the Ministry, that achieved the results in spite of difficulties and that those results were, for one reason or another, never equalled in the later period.

The severing of the official link within the Ministry, between production and development, certainly made things more difficult and had the effect of denying early knowledge of progress of development towards the production stage needed to earmark suitable capacity, etc. Personal contacts could not entirely overcome this handicap but they mitigated, somewhat, the delays caused by that lack of official information.

The organization for production of radar adopted by the Ministry of Supply is necessarily subject to much criticism, and in comparison with the Supply arrangements of the other two Services it could not compete with them effectively. Domestically radar was treated as an offshoot of Signals and the Signals production division was organized fundamentally to meet the requirements expressed by the Director of Signals, War Office, who was concerned with nothing but Signals. Many of the rulings and much of the procedure appropriate to Signals production were quite inappropriate to radar and its production problems. The psychological outlook had its effect; Signals had no interest in radar which was a gunner concern in the War Office and should have been dealt with in the Artillery department of the Ministry as suggested in Chapter XXXVII. Apart from that aspect it seems a pity that something on the lines of the Air Ministry/M.A.P. arrangements should not have been devised— it might have been possible had not production been segregated. The Controller of Communications Equipment, Sir R. Renwick, had a foot in both Air departments and had a staff of energetic and enterprising assistants to help him in keeping continuous contact with progress of development as well as of production. He was always up to date with practically first-hand information and that, with his undoubted ability and drive, was of great advantage to the R.A.F. In fairness it must be said that he tried to help the Army needs when possible, but they were, of course, competitors to those of the R.A.F. and were presumed to be fully represented by the M. of S.

A proposal for something of that sort to improve matters was put forward by the War Office at the beginning of 1944, but the Ministry did not accept it.

To close these comments it is pleasant to turn away from criticism and to mention a few outstanding matters for which the War Office can have nothing but thanks to accord to the Ministry.

The first of these is the formation by the Ministry of the Scientific Advisory Council and in particular, so far as this volume is concerned, its R.D.F. Applications Committee under the chairmanship of Sir Edward Appleton. This has been mentioned earlier but the value of its discussions, its advice on new possibilities and its welcome acceptance of the military members concerned with radar in their various capacities, was of great assistance. Though advisory, rather than executive, this committee probably had more influence upon the development of radar technique applied to Army purposes than any of the other boards and committees—and there were quite a number of them—that dealt with radar matters.

Acknowledgment is also made to the Ministry for the collection of those able scientists—and particularly for that strong team brought in to the A.D.R.D.E., under Professor J. D. Cockcroft, to work for the Army. Cockcroft himself was, of course, a most welcome addition and proved a tower of strength even if his peripatetic habits occasionally led him into unofficial by-ways. The rest of the team followed his lead and linked up with the pre-war staff of the establishment and became a real part of the teams working on the varied problems. It is hoped that they gained some benefit from their war-time association not only with the old staff but perhaps also with military personnel.

Finally, there is the formation of the Operational Research Group of Scientific Observers of equipment in action against the enemy. This was due to the initiative of the Ministry in response to the immediate radar needs of A.A. Command, but its activities were eventually extended into almost every field of weapon activity in the Army. It was really a new conception, born of the war on our doorstep or perhaps more correctly over our heads and its proved value here helped to clear away the difficulties of its extension to overseas operations. It resulted in a strengthening of the Army's appreciation of the help that scientists could give it and it confirmed the views of the General Staff that modern warfare requires the aid of scientists as well as of scientifically designed weapons and appliances.

PART VII

GENERAL COMMENTARY

CHAPTER XXXVIII. ORGANIZATION FOR RADAR PROVISION

The first four Parts of this volume have recorded the general development of Radar applied and adapted for Army purposes—how it was achieved and the effects of its use in action against the enemy. Parts V and VI have dealt respectively with the War Office aspects and with the problems, responsibilities and organization of the Ministry of Supply for the development and provision of radar for the Army. At the end of each Part some comments and criticisms on the matters dealt with have been included. Most of the comments draw attention to particular matters of organization and their effect on the equipment of the Army with up-to-date radar appliances.

Here in this last Part it is proposed to comment on more general aspects and matters of wider concern. In making them, there is no intention of trying to determine responsibility for faults or failures—it is, of course, obvious that there were errors, delays, disappointments and misjudgments, but it would have been surprising in the extreme had they not occurred in dealing with such a novel and rapidly developing technique. This is not the place to assign blame, nor to allocate praise to individuals or particular institutions; extraordinary developments were undoubtedly effected, as will have been appreciated by anyone who has studied the earlier parts of this record, and there were many most valuable achievements in bringing radar to the aid of the Army.

The aim here is to put forward some inferences from this story of Army Radar developments, so that the experiences from this special instance may perhaps serve some useful purpose in the future, in helping to guide planning and organization to deal with the development and provision of equipment based, similarly, upon novel scientific principles or the application of new techniques emerging from scientific research.

Mention has been made of the different methods and organizations adopted by the three fighting Services for their individual radar needs—they varied widely in their fundamentals and, naturally, were not all equally satisfactory in their results. From these different arrangements there must be some lesson to be learned or some experience to point a guiding finger to avoid the pitfalls of unsuitable organization in the future.

From this matter the particular arrangements for the link up between the War Office and the Ministry of Supply for radar development and provision naturally follow and, with the Ministry remaining in being as a peace-time rather than a war emergency concern, some general comments must be made.

With scientific control of radar work replacing military control within the Ministry and also in its Radar Research and Development Establishment during the war, some consideration of the most suitable form of direction and control is desirable and will be discussed in this Part.

There is no need to argue the case for scientific aid to the fighting services —that need has become a self-evident fact. It was a recognized, if limited, essential for peace-time progress, and the stress and urgency of war reinforced that recognition and demanded expansion of scientific aids and the bringing of scientists into intimate association with the actual operations of war. Experience with radar, almost a war-time development, can provide lessons and guidance for the future.

On one point in particular war experience definitely confirms the fact—and fact it is, though formerly perhaps there were doubts about it in some quarters—that scientists and Service officers can work together in the closest co-operation and understanding. Each can appreciate the other's outlook and value, and they can combine to bring scientific advances into practical use as aids to the efficiency of the fighting man.

Finally, a general review of Army radar as a whole and its effect from the point of view of the War Office, will be attempted. Perhaps here some "ifs and ands" and "might have beens" may be permitted, even though they arise from wisdom after the event.

Comparison of the Service Methods of Radar Provision. With any important new scientific technique such as radar, the one and only object in undertaking development, and perhaps research, by or on behalf of the Services, is the advantage to be gained in fighting efficiency. Whether that advantage is to be gained by more effective weapons, by aids to weapons, or by other appliances to provide essential operational information, it is the practical translation of that technique into equipment—the actual apparatus itself—that must be the first consideration. With this must go—also essentially a practical matter—the suitability of that equipment to perform the functions required of it in the hands of the Service user and the putting of it into those hands *in time to be of full value.* No other consideration, whether it be interest in the research work, the potential peace-time value or anything other than the essential war need, must hamper or delay the achievement of that practical result. The whole chain of work involved—research, experiment, trials, development, production and supply—must be applied with that specific object in view.

If that contention is accepted, it should be the foundation upon which the organization is designed for the direction and control of development and provision. At any rate, here it will be taken as a basis on which to compare the effectiveness of the different arrangements of the three Services for dealing with the radar provision to meet their individual needs.

R.N. The Admiralty assumed and retained full responsibility for all aspects of radar for Naval purposes; it did not share its responsibility even for production. It concentrated direction and control of radar—applied research, development, production, etc.—with radio communications under its Director, Signals Department, and that combination was repeated in the Admiralty experimental establishment (A.S.E.) with a Captain Superintendent in charge.

The D.S.D. received at first hand all information on operational requirements for radar and their priorities, and provided the higher operational staff with technical advice on radar possibilities and limitations, keeping them informed of the progress of development and provision to meet stated needs. On technical matters involved by the association of radar with weapons and other appliances, he was in direct contact with the Gunnery, Anti-Submarine, Naval Air, etc., authorities requiring radar aids. For scientific advice on new possibilities and advances emerging from research he had direct access to the Director of Scientific Research.

Being the executive head or centre for all matters concerning Naval radar, he could represent the Admiralty in all respects on inter-Service and Departmental Committees, as well as on such control and co-ordinating bodies as the Radio Board and its committees. His department was, moreover, linked to the A.S.E., which he directed and controlled through the Captain Superintendent; a direct link involving the minimum of time. The A.S.E. was provided with an excellent staff of scientists and technicians and was well equipped on the engineering side. At the establishment, development and production were closely connected; this was reinforced by enlisting the aid of suitable design and engineering firms to co-operate in development often at A.S.E. itself, into suitable production form and to undertake the production or to share it with A.S.E.

Some divergence from complete provision of all Naval radar occurred in the case of airborne needs, where development of equipment for the R.A.F. could be adopted or adapted for Naval aircraft; to a minor extent also some Army radar equipment and R.A.F. ground equipment were also adopted by the Navy.

The Admiralty also carried out research and development of valves and co-operated with firms in such work to provide for the needs of all three Services —a most valuable contribution.

The general impression of the Admiralty radar organization to an outside observer was that it was very effective. There was a concentration of direction, cohesion of effort, continuity of control throughout, from the expression of an operation requirement to ship fitting and actual use in action, and there was speed in achieving the practical results. As to the A.S.E. itself, perhaps a comment made by an entirely independent individual in another Service, who was closely associated with production of radar equipment for all three Services, may be permitted. This was that ". . . . in the A.S.E., the Navy seems to have 'something' that the other Services lack."

R.A.F. The Air Ministry, having "fathered" the initial development of radar for long-range detection and warning of air attack, had collected a special group of scientists at Bawdsey under Watson-Watt, and it was around this new research group or establishment (A.M.R.E.—later T.R.E.) that the organization for the direction and control of radar for the R.A.F. was moulded. Shortly before the outbreak of war Watson-Watt was brought into Head-quarters to a special appointment as Scientific Adviser on Telecommunications (S.A.T.) and he was succeeded as Superintendent at Bawdsey by A. P. Rowe, one of the scientific staff of D.S.R., Air Ministry. Before this the A.M. Signals Directorate took charge of radar with their Radio Communications responsibilities. S.A.T.'s responsibilities and duties tended, perhaps, to overlap those of D.Sigs., as he still had direct contact with the establishment and its work, as well as being in the operational requirements picture, if not largely initiating those requirements. He also covered a wider field beyond the A.M. limits in his advisory capacity. There was, therefore, some small degree of dual responsibility even at that early stage.

Later, with the formation of M.A.P., which took over the control of research and development at the establishment as well as radar production, the Air Ministry and M.A.P. shared responsibility for radar. The establishment retained its civilian scientific head and M.A.P. similarly directed its work, though the A.M. Signals Directorate had reasonable access to the establishment to keep in touch with developments and progress. Some considerable part of the difficulties of divided responsibility was reduced by Watson-Watt holding an appointment covering research and development in M.A.P. while also retaining his post at the A.M.; the same thing happened with the key post for production, in which Sir R. Renwick served both Ministries. Whether this arrangement can justly be called part of the designed organization is doubtful—it is not the sort of thing to be expected in a formal organization—but it was effective in its results.

There was also an unofficial and informal custom that contributed towards filling some of the gaps, or perhaps it would be better expressed as contributed towards mutual understanding between the scientists, the fighting personnel and the Service staffs and directors. This was the holding of periodical meetings at T.R.E., which were known as "Sunday Soviets" where free-for-all discussions on particular aspects of radar took place and juniors with scientific or technical ideas, or with practical fighting experience, could express themselves fairly freely in the presence of their seniors. This was, of course, no part of the official organization, but it served a useful purpose and ventilated many new ideas, views and needs.

Within M.A.P. production was linked with development by close contact with T.R.E. by production personnel of the Ministry and from firms and, in particular, by the general progressing of both development and production by Sir R. Renwick.

Operational and technical requirements for R.A.F. radar were represented effectively by D.G. Signals and his Radar Director, whose line of communication to the R. and D. Establishment was reasonably direct and speedy. This latter executive authority concentrated upon radar only, but though he could not control the development work officially he could influence it practically; he had access to first-hand information on production and supply and was well served in respect of such information and, generally, fully in the picture of all aspects of radar.

In his advisory capacity, Sir R. Watson-Watt covered an ever-widening field, and though he could give general direction to T.R.E., his wide interests did not permit of other than nominal control—T.R.E. really controlled itself and did so effectively in the hands of A. P. Rowe.

From an outside point of view the impression of the organization was that it was somewhat vaguely defined and was based more on individual personalities than on particular functions to be performed. The results, in practical form, served their purpose well, but there was, at least in the early "rush" days of defence needs growing apace, a tendency to save time at the expense of reliability and adequate design, but this improved materially in the later stages of the war.

T.R.E. was certainly effective, but it grew perhaps rather unwieldy in the spread of its activities. A tendency to individualism was apparent that brought in some duplication of development by the other Service establishments in preference to accepting their designs or adapting them. There was also a tendency towards "over-selling" new developments—each new device appeared to be almost a complete war-winner in itself—but that was mainly due to keenness and enthusiasm, which attributes in fact also resulted in the production of many remarkable achievements of great war value.

T.R.E. was, originally, the place at which research was to be concentrated on behalf of all three Services and though some research was delegated to A.S.E. and A.D.R.D.E., much useful research work was carried out at T.R.E. and, in particular, that establishment did excellent work in the early days on the application of centimetric wave-lengths and developing the new technique for their use. Though nominally this work was undertaken by an inter-establishment team, it was, in fact, the members of T.R.E. staff that carried the chief burden. They initiated the embryo forms of the first centimetric Naval type, the famous N.T. 271 set, and of the Army's G.L. III.

Army. The War Office started investigation, experiment and early development of radar for Army purposes through its existing and well-established organization, and continued with it until the Ministry of Supply was formed. This organization formed part of the M.G.O. Department and the executive work was in the hands of the R.E. and S. Board linked to one of the M.G.O. Directorates. This Directorate also controlled production for those matters for which it was responsible and the development work under the Board was closely associated with the production side. The appointment of a D.S.R. to the War Office brought in a minor degree of division of responsibility with his charge of the scientific staff and his higher advisory duties, but it produced no material difficulties and his tenure in the War Office was too short to affect the work materially.

With the separation of the M.G.O. Department from the General Staff on the formation of the Ministry of Supply, responsibility for radar was divided between the two Ministries. The G.S. stated its operational requirements and priorities, increasingly defined its policy for radar and indicated its technical and quantitative needs; while the M. of S. was responsible for research, development, design and production of equipment for the Army, in accordance with those defined needs.

After about a year from the outbreak of war, the existing organization, transferred from the W.O., was broken up. Some little time later, the military executive control of development was eliminated in favour of civilian scientific control, both in the Ministry itself and at the establishment; with this change went much of the military user representation and experience of practical equipment needs. More unfortunate still, the production side was entirely separated from development and no single executive individual or appointment had information on all aspects of radar provision and its progress towards supply. This position was complicated by the further division of responsibility with the delegation of part of radar equipment production to M.A.P.

Comments from the War Office point of view have already been made in Chapter XXXVII and need not be repeated here. The effectiveness of the organization involving both War Office and the Ministry of Supply suffered from the lengthy and tortuous line of transmission of information in both directions. In the Ministry it also suffered from "too many 'cooks having fingers in the pie" without much cohesion or co-operation, from lack of concentration of direction and control of the subject as a whole, and from the gradually widening gap between development and production. Many of the difficulties caused could have been mitigated—and particularly those within the Ministry itself—had the practical objective and the means to attain it been better appreciated. A balanced association of scientists and technical soldiers could have been effected, which would have extended from the G.S. policy and requirements, through research, development and production by the Ministry, and back again to the War Office at the supply stage with its training, maintenance, etc., responsibilities, right into the operational field. The existing organizations could have been so applied or adapted to provide for it; but this balance and continuity was lacking.

To summarize a comparison of these three systems employed for Service radar provision, it may be said that the Admiralty worked on the lines of concentration of responsibility and executive authority in one Service head, covering all aspects of radar provision. Under his direction, the experimental establishment was controlled by a Service Officer who concentrated his efforts on the attainment of the practical objective; it also linked its development work closely with production, supply and complete readiness of the equipment for action.

The Air Ministry and the War Office had necessarily to share their responsibilities with their respective Supply Ministries, which naturally involved some dispersion or duplication of effort and extended communication links. The Air Ministry suffered less than did the War Office by reason of the fact that M.A.P. was not involved in such a plethora of other concerns and interests as was the Ministry of Supply.

With this division of responsibility and functions, the A.M./M.A.P. set-up achieved many effective results, but did so more by defeating the split by using particular individuals in both Ministries than by any merits of the formal organization. The A.M. operational and technical authority had at least permissive access direct to the experimental establishment to keep in contact with progress, and in the A.M. itself was in close contact with both Controllers of Development and of Production, who led double lives or at least had dual existences. Scientific control of the establishment was retained to the end of the war with satisfactory results.

For the link-up of the W.O. and M. of S. the organization was, perhaps, insufficiently defined in so far as radar provision was concerned, or more probably the faults arose from the interpretation of its intentions. Army radar certainly suffered from the wide separation between the two Ministries and particularly from the separation within the Ministry of the different aspects of provision.

While the W.O. introduced a Director specially for radar duties as a whole, the Ministry provided no corresponding responsible authority with radar matters concentrated in his hands. The organization lacked cohesion and co-ordination, and even segregated production from development. Lacking a central authority in the Ministry it was difficult to ensure that G.S. policy and requirements reached all those immediately concerned and in reverse, to provide the War Office with complete information on progress and new possibilities. The transfer of technical directorates from the W.O. to provide departmental links was not made full use of by the M. of S., and in some cases they were even eliminated; some loss of practical experience and reduced appreciation of the Time factor resulted.

Though the chain of communications was lengthy, it was partly eased by unofficial agreement to periodic visits by D. Radar, War Office, to the establishment, but no such contact was available on the production side.

Considered from the practical, objective point of view, these comparisons point to the desirability of concentration of authority and responsibility at all stages of the work, and when primary responsibility must be shared interdepartmentally, to the need for an organization that brings and keeps the two Ministries in the closest association.

Then there arises the question of the detailed control of the experimental and development work itself; there is no question of the need for the association and close co-operation between the military and scientific sides. In the case of the Admiralty and the A.M./M.A.P., there is complete contrast, while for the W.O./M. of S. the military was replaced by scientific control during the period. It is doubtful if any definite lesson can be learned from these very limited reviews of the three systems, but some discussion on this subject, as far as Army equipment provision alone is concerned, will be found in a later chapter.

The contrast in practice between the three methods used by the Services may be, at least partly, accounted for by two factors. One is the build up of development, design, etc., around a nucleus already engaged upon basic research on a novel subject and the other is the expansion of an existing proved organization by increasing its research capacity.

The War Office and the Admiralty each had well-established experimental establishments and higher organizations capable of accepting more applied or objective research in a novel subject allied to more normal radio development, which already involved some research work. They consequently adopted the second of those methods though the War Office arrangements, taken over by the Ministry of Supply, were not quite so easily adjustable as their new experimental establishment had been designed for development primarily on the understanding that basic research would be centralized under the Air Ministry.

In the case of the Air Ministry—succeeded by the M.A.P. in this responsibility—the first method was employed, and a new establishment and separate organization was built up round the research nucleus. The Royal Aircraft Establishment with its wide and varied activities could not suitably absorb research work of such a vital nature nor apply sufficiently single-minded effort to it. This new arrangement grew from research as its initial concern and that research had to be carried on through and in conjuction with practical development of Service equipment.

This arrangement, with research as its starting-point, certainly suggests the need for scientific control and direction, but it also points to the need for military guidance and advice as to the possible operational value of results emerging from research and how they can usefully be applied. That initial predominance of research, however, wanes in comparison with increasing development of practical equipment and, really, both the methods come to a similarity with the urgent war need of ever greater performance of Service equipment. That practical objective is really the key factor in providing for control and direction.

Before leaving this matter of the different systems used by the three Services for their individual radar provision, it is desirable to mention that the concentration of all radar work for all the Services was suggested occasionally. It was, however, firmly rejected and each Service retained its own responsibility for development and design according to its particular requirements, conditions of use and limitations. There can be no question of the correctness of this decision—research of a basic nature can be centralized and perhaps production may be so treated, but the intermediate syages of application, development and design to meet operational conditions of use must remain a matter for the individual Service concerned. Those conditions and also the limitations they impose are different for each Service.

It is not generally realized that Army mobile radar has to withstand more hard wear and exposure than the radar equipment of either of the other two Services. Naval radar has an advantage in moving with its repair and maintenance workshops, but it is limited by a shortage of masts or other means of carrying its aerials without reducing the fighting efficiency of the ship. R.A.F. airborne radar has of course size and weight limitations and demands greater simplicity of operation, but it has shorter working hours and replacement can largely take the place of repair *in situ*. R.A.F. ground radar can "go large" on aerials but does not generally demand the high degree of accuracy required for Army or Naval fire control. These and many other material differences make it essential that the representatives of the particular users should control development for their own Services. Attempts at centralization of all this intermediate stage work would be quite unsuitable and impracticable. This was fully realized by the War Office and the Air Ministry when the separation of the "Army cell" from A.M.R.E. was agreed as necessary and the new Army establishment for development of equipment was initiated. The Admiralty, retaining their ordinary organization, never, of course, contemplated such a change.

CHAPTER XXXIX. THE WAR OFFICE AND THE MINISTRY OF SUPPLY

A letter to *The Times*, dated 19th July, 1946, raised questions concerning the design and production of technical instruments of war and pointed to the need for profiting from the experience gained during the war for guidance in the future. The two gentlemen over whose signatures this letter appears, had been two of the chairmen of sub-committees of the Select Committee on National Expenditure dealing with matters of Tank production.

This letter is in parts equally applicable to other weapons and devices as will be seen from the following extracts which may serve as a "peg on which to hang" some discussion on the link-up of the War Office and the Ministry in respect of Army Radar provision.

> (a) "We recognize that to bring about a perfect relation between the Service departments as users and manufacturing industry as producers of technical war stores is a task of extreme difficulty, and that the problem of how it can best be performed gives room for much legitimate controversy. Hitherto the Admiralty has been allowed to adopt one solution and the War Office and Air Ministry another.
>
> (b) As a result of the experience which we were privileged to have . . . we put questions such as the following: Did the arrangements between the War Office and the Ministry of Supply produce the best results which, given the limitations of human nature, could be achieved? Did our soldiers get the best weapons and equipment possible at the time when they needed them? Will the Ministry of Supply . . . be able to establish the right relations with the Service in future?"

The difficulty of the problem is fully recognized and the legitimacy of controversy is endorsed in so far as radar is concerned, but some discussion of the subject is most desirable as radar differed from tanks in that it was practically a wartime novelty starting from almost zero and, therefore, perhaps, exemplifying some vital future scientific development brought to light by impending war emergency.

The general answer to the first of these questions, if allowance is made for a further limitation, namely, the priority competition of the radar needs of the other two Services for the restricted production capacity available in this country, can, certainly, be that very good results were achieved and that many of them were in fact the best that could have been achieved *at the time of supply*.

The second question also must certainly be answered with a No—there was almost invariably a time lag between a proved and worthwhile advance and its appearance as equipment in the hands of the troops. That lag partly nullified the advance in performance and, where large numbers of sets were demanded, the later deliveries were almost invariably out-dated.

To the third of these questions the answer must lie in the future. This history has endeavoured to indicate certain points where improvements could be effected as a result of experience of the war-time relationship and also to suggest how some of the lapses might have been avoided. With the organization already in process of change and the M.A.P. already merged in the M. of S., an entirely new picture is forming and it is no concern of this record to discuss the new arrangements. This merger, however, does make it all the more important that the War Office—Ministry of Supply relationship should be of the best and closest, so that the Army needs are not swamped or submerged by those of the R.A.F. and possibly also of the Navy.

The first two questions should really have been considered as combined, and answered as one. With radar being an entirely new technique, with its Army application started only two or three years before the war, and continually developing to offer improved performance and fresh applications, there was at almost every stage a "best" though that temporary best was continually being bettered. It is, of course, true to say that "the best" as known at the end of the war—which did not actually reach the hands of the troops in action—is still not the last word. Throughout the development every worthwhile advance has had to be made by stages—by steps towards the ideal. Had not Time been such a controlling factor, as it must be in the urgency of war, no doubt some of these steps might have been passed over. As it was, each of these stages showed that the advances made by the scientists and technicians were reproduced in equipment that was capable of the full standard of operational performance aimed at, though the capacity of the average trained troops did not, generally, make it possible to reap the full advantage, at any rate in the H.A.A. application which was the highest priority Army requirement. With equipment ahead of the user in this way, the question of whether "the best" was available to the troops when they needed it does not really arise—they got better equipment than they could use to the full.

It is, therefore, only fair to the scientists and technicians to say that they provided "the best" radar equipment that was possible at the time when the troops needed it except that the final automatic stage of British radar, that would eliminate much of the faulty operation, did not reach the troops at the time they needed it most. For that, the delay caused by the time taken in the manufacture and supply of the equipment is partly responsible.

As has been seen, the scientific stage of radar work—research and experiment—was continually producing effective advances at a higher rate than that achievable in the stage of conversion of those advances into practical equipment form and in the production stage. In the former or development stage where scientist, technician and engineer combine as a team, there is necessarily a time period involved which is dependent for its length upon the complexity of the make-up of the set and upon the quality and, to some extent, the size of the engineer and design staff available. In the latter or production stage there is an unescapable period that must elapse between proof of the advanced performance in prototype equipment form and the supply to the troops of the new equipment. It was in this stage that the unescapable period was, unfortunately, often increased by delays in clearing faults, by introducing additions or alterations and by lack of concentration of effort—it was here, therefore, that there was scope for reduction of the time lag by the exercise of proper control.

Some of the causes of these delays have been mentioned in earlier chapters—they should have been avoidable if the organization within the Ministry had provided more effectively for the maintenance of the practical objective. These causes may be summarized as:—

(a) Lack of balance in the staff of A.D.R.D.E. and the inadequacy of the engineer and design sides.
(b) Segregation of production from development and design.
(c) Lack of firmness of control to avoid diversion of effort.
(d) Lack of a single authority for all aspects of Army radar.

To these may be added some for which the War Office must take responsibility, though in most cases their actions were partly, if not largely, based upon advice from M. of S. sources, unfortunately not always covering the complete picture. These were:—

(e) Insufficient information supplied to the Ministry as to the reason for urgent demands or the special operational situation and date to be met.
(f) Delay in taking a decision to go to production—a rare occurrence, though delays did occur in decisions reaching the executive sides of the Ministry and the Establishment, due to lengthy transit.
(g) Large numerical demands involving distant delivery dates for part of the supply.

Outside the two Ministries, there was also the centralized control of allocation of production capacity by the R.P.E. Here it is difficult to determine whether the time-lag on Army radar was adversely effected—it is true that the offensive priority needs of the other two Services had first consideration, but that could not be helped—except by the extra time involved in the wanderings of the stated requirements through many hands before reaching the R.P.E. It is very doubtful whether any material delay could be blamed on the R.P.E. itself and, even if it could, it would be more attributable to the inadequate representation of the Army case by the M. of S. member of the R.P.E.

Though all these points are referred to the Time factor they naturally had an effect on the relationship between the two Ministries. From this aspect the more important items on the M. of S. side, affecting this relationship adversely, were the lack of co-ordination of all the different stages of provision of Army radar and of centralization of responsibility in one authority; the other was the apparent lack of appreciation of the practical objective both in framing the organization and in implementing it.

The result was that the War Office was inadequately advised. The advice on new possibilities and advances in performance with assessments of their operational value, from the scientific and technical Artillery sides, were excellent. They were, however, never accompanied by realistic or even authoritative estimates as to production times and when supply could be expected to start. This inadequate information made planning very difficult and the War Office had to take chances in deciding on production of improved equipment and, at times, the failure of those optimistic estimates of the time involved made it necessary to embark on "rush" development and improvised production methods to meet special operational needs.

At times, from the War Office end, the information given to the Ministry, as to the special operational occasions requiring particular provision to be made, was perhaps inadequate. The Ministry grew accustomed to all requirements being urgent, and even though particular items were given priorities or over-riding importance officially by the War Office and stressed as such in personal contacts, the Ministry's executives would have been more impressed if they had been given an official "why, wherefore and when" to support the requirements. Here, of course, the security side covering pending operations was involved and the spread of information was restricted. Towards the end of the war some improvement in this was possible, as in the case of special provision for D-day needs, without disclosing time or place of the operations, and for the provision for the S.E.A.C. offensive operations where the transit time to that theatre provided ample cushioning to prevent disclosure of operational dates.

Excessive numerical demands were a doubtful factor—viewed in retrospect it is apparent that "excessive" is the right term to apply as the later supplies from production were generally out-dated by progress. At the time, however, the demands were always factual needs, being based upon the number of weapons, appliances or units that required radar aid, except in the last stages of the war when only a few sample sets were asked for to prove their operational possibilities. Furthermore, at the time the demands were made it was impossible for the War Office, and for the advisers in the Ministry also, to foresee with certainty what further advances would emerge within a year or two—the immediate need demanded a "bird in the hand" in preference to a finer couple at some indeterminate future date.

It must be remembered that the urgency of the immediate needs, with war over this country, did not make it possible to carry out such entirely complete trials as would be normal in peace conditions, before deciding on acceptance of an equipment and its production. Naturally, therefore, some snags were encountered—as, for example, the need for artificial surrounding surface for elevation finding with the G.L. II—which detracted from the value of the equipment to some extent when it was used by the troops. Such disappointments were due to chances that have to be taken in war and to the lower average efficiency of operators that war expansion involved. They were, however, rather increased by the over-optimistic opinions of the Establishment that the "bird" of the moment was the best type of Swan, though in the later "hatchings" from production it usually turned out to be the useful but less elegant Goose, and new Swans were already coming on the market.

The foregoing remarks may suggest that the relationship between the two Ministries was not very good—under the official organization it was not as good as it might have been, but there was, in fact, generally a very good liaison and co-operation at executive levels based largely upon individual association and personal contacts which helped materially to make the combination effective, though the production difficulties could not be overcome to the same extent as in the case of development.

Looking back on the earlier stages of the Ministry and its organization, it would appear that an opportunity was missed in the reorganizations in 1940 and 1941, when the Artillery directorate, transferred from the War Office, might have taken charge of the former executive radar section of the R.E. and S. Board and carried on the military direction of radar work. They could with advantage, also, have represented more directly the General Staff within the Ministry. This would have shortened the communication chain, could have retained the essential contacts with production and would have provided an effective executive link between the two Departments. The Artillery directorate would have become the intermediary between General Staff and Scientist and would at least have maintained the military influence, if not actual control, over the work of the establishment.

War-time needs differ very materially from those in peace and the organization covering a subject like radar must vary to suit the changed conditions. It appears that the Ministry has since tended towards more military direction for radar, with necessary scientific advice to aid that direction, and if that is so this reversion to the former practice is to be welcomed. Doubtless concentration solely on a subject like radar cannot be accepted in peace-time as economical, but that need not matter with the slower pace of events provided that the organization adopted allows for separation of subjects *as a whole* for war expansion without breaking up an established system.

With M.A.P. now combined with the M. of S., the latter's interests are extended still further, but Army radar tends to benefit from its production coming under a single Ministry. On the other hand it would be most undesirable from the War Office aspect if this new combination were to endeavour to provide for the development of Army radar by an establishment that was also charged with the development of R.A.F. radar—the need for individual development for their own uses by or for each of the Services has been stressed in the preceding chapter. It would be a real loss to the Army if the R.R.D.E. disappeared as a separate entity, but it would also be unfortunate if a close liaison were not maintained between it and T.R.E. The now combined Supply Ministries should be able to maintain both organizations at least in nucleus form in peace-time and so provide for expansion of both in emergency.

One final point must be mentioned and that is the need for keeping the military Radar staff allocated to the Ministry as up to date as possible in their experience of actual operations and the tactical requirements of a modern Army and the conditions in which radar has to be used. Quite apart from the interests of individuals and their Service careers, their period of employment in the Ministry should be limited in the same way as for those serving in the War Office. Whether technical or not, they cannot keep fully up to date with the military picture without personal contact with troops, their handling and their use of equipment. The organization of the link up of the War Office and the Ministry must provide for this and the responsibility for it rests with the War Office.

CHAPTER XL. SOLDIERS AND SCIENTISTS

There can be no doubt that the Army has very real need of the scientist to assist in devising new methods, new weapons, appliances and other aids if it is to wage war effectively in modern conditions. This fact was, fortunately, appreciated in the uneasy days after the 1914–1918 war and provision was made by the War Office for a nucleus W.D. Scientific Staff in certain of its experimental establishments. In the recent war that nucleus, experienced in the military problems and limitations, was the basis on which the expansion of scientific effort was effected in the case of radio and radar work. It was also the actual source from which the means of applying radar to Army uses were devised, and of the development of the earliest equipments so that they were put into the hands of the troops at the beginning of the war. The wide extension of scientific activities into many military spheres during the war produced valuable and even remarkable results, but none achieved more than did the application and use of radar.

This war certainly emphasized very strongly the value to the Army of scientific assistance and it also impressed the need for suitable direction and control of that effort if it was to be applied to the best advantage. In addition, with Time a key factor in war, it is obvious that a nucleus of scientific staff, experienced in the military needs, the conditions and limitations of operational use of weapons and equipment and the outlook of the soldier, must be maintained in peace so that scientific reinforcements without that experience may be grafted on to it in the emergency of war and guided rapidly into the military picture.

Scientific Advice. Shortly before the war, a Director of Scientific Research was appointed to the War Office, thus bringing that department into line with the Admiralty and Air Ministry; his tenure of that post was, however, short as he was transferred to the Ministry of Supply, on its formation, with other directorates. There he continued as Director of the scientific work and staff, but his wider advisory responsibilities to the Army Council being then less direct had to be taken over by a new appointment of Scientific Adviser in the War Office. This appointment was more appropriate because, having no executive or control of staff responsibilities, he was able to concentrate on the wider scientific aspects and to advise on new possibilities and their effects.

Within the Ministry of Supply, the D.S.R. with laudable foresight had taken steps to earmark strong scientific reinforcements for research and experimental work, including radar for the Army; this was a most valuable contribution to the scientific effort on behalf of the Army.

Direction and Control. Originally, the W.D. scientific staff had been controlled and directed towards the military objective requirements by technical military officers, through a military organization. During the early years of the war, though the military objectives of course remained, that form of direction was eliminated in favour of civilian scientific control both at Headquarters and in the establishment concerned with the actual work. It is not proposed to comment here upon the soundness of breaking up a tried and established organization and substituting for it a new system lacking much of the practical background and the contacts and links with the General Staff and users. It is desirable, however, to discuss some of the aspects of the association of soldiers and scientists collaborating in the development of vital new equipment such as radar for the Army. With it must also go some consideration of how best such association and collaboration can be directed.

As has been seen in Chapter XXXVIII, when the Services had charge of their own development, two out of the three adhered to Service or "military" direction and control, but with the introduction of the two Supply Ministries the odds were 2 to 1 for the civilian scientific direction. Perhaps this was influenced more by the civilian status of the Ministries than by appreciation of the practical objective needs—the results achieved, however, certainly do not indicate that the Navy suffered in respect of radar equipment provision under the Admiralty organization. Similarly for Army radar, military direction and control of the work did produce "the goods" effectively in the early days.

Direct comparison of the two methods is not practicable nor can results obtained under each be attributed solely to the form of control, but experience can give some guide as to which is the more satisfactory. The question is not one of Soldiers *versus* Scientists as, whatever the form of direction and control, the primary essential is the close collaboration and association of the two.

In this connexion it may be of interest to record the views of a scientist of proved research ability, based on his experience of several years working with technical soldiers in a W.D. experimental establishment and under the direction of a military organization. The following extracts are quoted from a note prepared by him after some twenty years of such work.

"On the controversial question of civilian Scientist versus Military technical control, I have the same views and have never hesitated to express them. The military User (representative) must obviously be in a position to dictate his requirements—at the same time drawing expert advice from the scientists as to how such could be met and to be given a clear picture of what is profitable and workable by trained troops. Scope would of course be given to investigate improvements resulting from a certain amount of research. The control of our own researches by the Board never deprived the establishment of investigations of a basic research nature when required and full latitude was given to the E.O.s (Experimental Officers) concerned even though they only bore indirectly on immediate requirements.

.   .   .   .

It occurs to me that you might like some specific illustrations of the way in which the Board, representing the "Soldier," originated, stimulated and encouraged research in fundamental problems ultimately leading to a military application and finally to military equipment. . . . That the very extensive development in the field of sound effected by the research work did not come into full general use was not due to misdirected research but to the discoveries of Radar and its practical application. The Board quickly reacted and gave similar support and direction and their scientists were given full latitude in the same way. The civilian staff with whom I was in contact felt the same degree of freedom to pursue possible advances in technique and again progress was encouraged. . . . I do not say that narrow-minded personnel on the military side might not have been capable of acting adversely on research matters on occasion, but the fact remains that we did not experience this—it might equally have happened under scientific control. At any rate we had the benefit of access to military operations—besides considerable experience in operations during the previous war—which I have always regarded as essential. In that way the capacity and limitations of the troops in using such gear as we could devise could be observed and would react in research and lead to modifications which a detached civilian would never have considered. . . . We were only a small establishment but I do not think that we were unrepresentative of a (combined) Military-Civilian Scientific organization whose object was to devise suitable and more effective aids to military operations."

The views quoted above coming from the scientific side may, perhaps, be supplemented by excerpts from some notes by an officer who had some years of experience in directing such work and who was closely associated with the scientists engaged upon it—the notes were included in a memorandum prepared early in the war.

"It is a complete fallacy to suggest that Soldiers and Scientists are as oil and water in being incapable of mixing to produce a useful result. My experience over a fair period of years convinces me that each can and usually does appreciate the outlook and ability of the other and that each has his part to play in the combined work aiming at a result of value to the Army. . . . The Soldier's outlook centres more upon the effective practical result and his knowledge must guide its suitability, while the Scientist has his interest primarily in the solution of the problems which make that result possible. The Soldier requires the advice of the Scientist as to the possibilities of meeting his needs and how they can be applied, while the Scientist requires from the Soldier full information of the objective in view, its nature and the performance needed. . . .

My experience also convinces me that there is real need for an intermediary between the Scientist and the General Staff to interpret the possibilities of applying scientific aids to improve Army Equipment—I am not referring here to the high level scientific advice on new possibilities or new methods that might be worthwhile investigating and such-like matters, but to the more executive work of actually applying results of research to meet military needs. That intermediary must be able to translate the nature and detailed requirements of Army needs in a manner acceptable to the scientists and in the reverse direction he must interpret the scientific advances and progress in terms of their military effects and possibilities to the G.S. Naturally he must have an understanding of the scientific aspect and be fully aware of the military picture and of the user conditions and limitations. This can in my opinion only be done adequately by a technical soldier in direct contact with the scientists and their work. . . . The Scientist cannot have the necessary intimate knowledge of the operational end of the work but a suitable Soldier can absorb the essential features of the scientific progress and achievements. I have no doubt that the only really satisfactory solution of the problem of direction and detailed control of such work—the combination of the efforts of Scientists, Technicians, Soldiers, Engineers and Designers—lies in executive military hands."

These two expressions of opinion, both based upon actual experience of combined working under military direction, are of interest, but without the view of the protagonists of scientific control the arguments are incomplete. No independent statement of the latter views are available in respect of Army radar development, but there is at least some indication of the effect in the comparison of equipment output under the alternative forms of control given in Chapters XXXIV and XXXVII of this book.

The experience with radar applied to military purposes must reinforce the experience gained in the development of other scientific advances and that combined experience, being based on actual practical results obtained, should not lightly be discounted by theoretical arguments. As stated in Chapter XXXVIII, the practical result must be the sole aim and object of development, and the key to the organization to effect that practical result is, surely, direction and control in the hands of the user representative with scientific advice immediately available to him.

Research. Before leaving this subject there is one consideration that affects the question of control; this is research and in particular research of a basic nature, which is not undertaken with a specific "military" object in view. Radar started under the auspices of the Air Ministry to determine whether the previously observed phenomena could be applied usefully to long-distance detection of aircraft. That investigation did, in fact, involve a considerable amount of basic research and later, research had to be continued in the endeavour to devise a technique for applying it to various other uses, such as the short-range accurate working for Army purposes. The research worker may well be required to carry his new possibility or technique through the experimental and trials stage and to follow it into the stage of practical development where he would be one of a team which included technicians, engineers and designers. There is much to be said for this continuity though it can be overdone, if pursued too far, or if the scientist attempts to decide or define the practical form that the equipment should take. That is the function of the engineering, technical and design members of the team and the control of the work at that stage should be in the hands of the Service or user representative. The scientist's place at this stage—and in the proof of prototype sets for production and supply—is to ensure that his new technique or advanced performance is not prejudiced by the make-up of the practical form.

When considerable research is involved, as appears to have been the case with some of the earlier R.A.F. needs, such continuity and follow-up was particularly desirable and its extent may well have justified a scientific head or controller of the establishment with Service advice to guide him as to the suitable practical form.

Where, however, research results become available from some other source, either outside or separated from development in an experimental establishment, and the work takes more the nature of applying those results, the practical objective would best be provided for by Service or user representative control advised by the scientist.

It is not really possible to define any hard-and-fast line of division between the primarily scientific stage and that of the engineer and designer and no arbitrary decision can apply to all cases of combined working. Even if, as in the case of Army radar, the practical aim and the time factor in war point definitely to the need for military direction and control of development and supply, it is not intended to imply that R.A.F. radar was wrongly controlled—each case must be judged individually—but there did appear to be a tendency towards the end of the war for a change towards the more practical side taking over control of R.A.F. radar development.

To sum up: this problem of direction and control and how best to effect it is a complicated one, and each case must be considered individually. The experience with Army radar certainly confirms the previous experience gained in a variety of scientific work for the Army, that direction without control of the actual work is not effective. It also points directly to the need *in war* for both to be exercised by the military or user representative with scientific assistance immediately available to him. Decision and firmness—even ruthlessness—is needed to overcome the emergency of Time; that is more likely to be an attribute of the soldier than of the research scientist. The scientific urge is always towards the ideal while the soldier under the practical pressure of war must often demand the "worthwhile" rather than the best as more readily achievable rapidly. Temporarily that scientific urge may have to be curbed to prevent the "best" denying the "good," even though partial solutions may be anathema to the scientist. The scientific energies may have to be diverted to aid the completion of the practical form to get it into production and that is usually irksome to the scientist. The habit of the scientist, so often referred to during the war, in regard to radar, by such phrases as "scientists will never finalize" has some background of fact in the frequent attempts to make additions, improvements and modifications which delayed the clearing of designs and often affected production-time. It is here that the Time factor in war demands most decisive control of the work to be exercised.

There is, perhaps, justification for scientific direction and control of such work in the amount of research involved, but that cannot justify scientific control of the practical aspects of development, design and production. If research and development are combined in one establishment—and there are some advantages in it—it is a matter of balancing research against the more practical aspect of producing effective and timely results.

The general conclusion is that in war Military or Service direction and control is the effective answer while in peace, without such urgency of time, a scientific head may in some cases be desirable if an entirely new technique or other novel possibility is concerned; even then the practical aspect should be fully provided for by practical Service control of development.

Operational Research. One of the most valuable and effective associations of scientist and soldiers really owes its origin to the early difficulties experienced with radar in actual operations against the enemy in defence of this country.

This association started on the initiative of the G.O.C.-in-C. A.A. Command and Professor Blackett, his Scientific Adviser materially supported by J. A. Ratcliffe and the Ministry of Supply. It soon developed into the Operational Research Group under Brigadier Schonland, a soldier and a scientist. It was originally formed to observe radar and its effects in H.A.A. actions but soon expanded to cover all aspects of fire control appliances in combination and also entered the field of coastal radar; later, it covered all Army radar uses with extensions into Naval and R.A.F. ground radar and their plotting and control arrangements.

Their Army radar activities have been described in general terms and the results of their work were of considerable value. Its scope was extended to cover observation of a wide variety of other military activities, weapons, appliances and effects on troops in the field in all the later campaigns and theatres of operations. It produced valuable results, but apart from that main aspect of its work it achieved something that should prove fruitful in the future. Undoubtedly these scientists obtained a practical insight into the conditions of fighting and the needs of the troops, tactically and technically, and, with their closer association with the troops of all ranks, they gained appreciation of their side of the picture. With their gain in understanding they left the troops with the impression that scientists were not necessarily wild and woolly nuisances, but capable of helping them in action.

With the proved success of this organization, the link-up of scientists and soldiers in this form should undoubtedly be revived again when a similar emergency arises. It must be a case of revival for, with no actions in peace time, there can be no fully effective work done by operational research, but its value should not be overlooked when war comes.

This precedent shows that the most important function of such an organization is to observe operations and to ask the right questions. For this the best grounding is general research experience which teaches a scientific approach to tackling any problem. Technical matters can be picked up quickly by individuals of that type without previous experience as was amply proved by the success of biologists who soon fitted into the radar picture and tackled radar repair, servicing and adjustment with only a few weeks' instruction. The younger students from University or other research centres are not always suitable, as tact and experience are most necessary to avoid rubbing the soldiers up the wrong way during operations and to gain the confidence of men operating the equipment under observation. The role of detached observer needs tact and attempts to "throw one's weight about" seldom achieve results of value.

If this is appreciated the key to revival is selection of the individuals as good mixers as well as scientists.

In this country these observational duties could be carried out by scientists in their civilian capacity, but where ground fighting is occurring military status is necessary. The civilian often had the advantage here of being "rankless" which enabled him to discuss matters with all ranks and grades—operators in the ranks actually using the equipment were more natural and communicative —and at important meetings views and opinions would be valued as those of a scientist and not of a person of a certain rank.

G. C. Varley who did such good work with coastal radar puts this well in his notes on Operational Research, thus:—

"This kind of operational research was a composite study of the performance of an instrument, the training of operators, and the use to which the information (from the particular type of radar) was put. It required close personal touch with the operators, and operational experience for the experimental officer (the O.R.G. member), so that he could fully appreciate the operator's difficulties. It also required the status necessary to discuss problems of training and policy on equal terms with those officers responsible for it. For these duties civilian status was quite satisfactory, and was perhaps better than uniform for inter-service work."

As to the actual direction and control of the work of such a group, the experience gained suggests that a scientist should be in charge—reliance cannot be placed upon repeating the good fortune that produced Schonland with his dual ability as soldier and research scientist—but he will require the close assistance of a suitable military counterpart.

Finally a few words must be said of the association, on high-level committees and boards, of scientists of repute and Service officers, which was so fruitful in its results in aiding the Services in their radar planning and, incidentally, benefited each in their understanding and appreciation of the other. Co-operation was close and discussion of problems and policy to govern radar and its application to war needs was free and open. While the Service representatives obtained much value, help and interest from these contacts, it is also true to say that the scientists were interested in the Service outlook on the operational problems to be solved by the application of radar and in their approach from the practical side of those problems. Radar was, of course, of considerable interest in itself to scientists of all grades and many contributed to the discussions on its application. Among them were Sir Henry Tizard, Sir Edward Appleton, Lord Cherwell, Sir Robert Watson-Watt, the late Professor Fowler, C. S. Wright, J. D. Cockcroft, Blackett and many others in or attached to the Supply Ministries and their experimental establishments. Indeed there was no lack of high-level advice available to the Service representatives—in fact, it was sometimes rather confusing as views and opinions varied on occasion, as is proverbial in the case of doctors. However, in general the Service representatives were sufficiently appreciative of the possibilities put to them, and aware of their practical problems and operational needs, to weigh up and benefit from that advice.

That this association was remarkable is evidenced by the outside opinions of Dr. Karl Compton and his associates, when his Radio Mission from the U.S.A. visited this country. They were surprised and much impressed by the close link-up between the Services and the scientists in this country and it was noticeable later when individual American scientists came over to discuss special problems—such as the Radio Proximity Fuze—how they approached Service officers concerned directly, with full anticipation of getting the detailed needs clearly defined and good appreciation of the scientific and technical proposals and limitations that they raised.

If the war produced many devices of value to Army operations, it is doubtful if any exceeded in value that of the real linking of soldiers and scientists and their understanding of one another's problems and outlook; that association and understanding will surely survive for some time at least.

CHAPTER XLI. GENERAL REVIEW

This record of the development and provision of Army radar up to the end of the war must now be brought to an end. It has covered most of the salient points, some of the side issues and given, at least, an indication of what was achieved. It is not the concern of this volume to consider the future of Army radar nor to prophesy in respect of the extent to which it may serve the Army with the changes in weapons and methods of warfare that the future may bring. Radar is no longer a novelty, but it has yet to reach the ultimate limits of its possible uses and applications; it may still have an important part to play, but that is a matter that the future alone can determine. It is, however, certain that if it is to play such a part, radar development will have to provide more specific protection and precautions against disturbance and jamming by enemy countermeasures—it may also have to cope with improved screening of targets, with possible reduced reflecting surfaces and with speeds and rates far greater than were encountered in the war that has just passed.

Post Factum Views. To some extent, perhaps, this record gives a rather depressing story in looking back upon the six or seven years of growth and development; though an attempt has been made to describe the facts, achievements and effects as known at the time, it may be that wisdom after the event has crept in to colour the picture rather too drably. It is true that high hopes were entertained with the incorporation of each major advance in equipment, but they were seldom completely realized in use in action. Similarly, some of the later advances and possibilities of new applications, like those offering chances of radar aids against ground targets, did not materialize in practical form in time for use against the enemy.

Naturally disappointment was caused and some feeling of frustration to those responsible for providing the troops with the best possible equipment. That there were some errors in direction and in execution of development and some undesirable diversion of effort is true, but even when reviewed at the end of the war period they are found to be remarkably few in number.

It is also true that there were delays that could have been avoided by better organization and more effective control; in the main they occurred in the stage of preparation for production. All classes of the Ministry of Supply's staff were involved—the scientists with delays in clearing approved types of production, the engineer and design side with its weakness in high grade mechanical work and inadequate numbers, the production staff with restricted access to current development and resultant inability to influence design and prepare for production.

All this really centres upon the absence of a single authoritative head in the Ministry to deal with all aspects of radar and the consequent lack of drive and of a firm grip on all the practical and material work towards the supply of the equipment. Complaint was made at times of delay by the War Office in decision to adopt a new advanced type but, where it may have occurred, it was mainly due to the difficulty of obtaining adequate information from the Ministry, particularly realistic estimates of time for supply. In the later years of the war the War Office decisions were generally taken well ahead of the Ministry's stage of practical development of equipment form.

There is no need to pursue this aspect further as it has been discussed in detail in the earlier chapters, nor is there need to apportion blame or praise between the two departments. Let it be said that in spite of the faults, failings and disappointments—such as they were—remarkable results were achieved and that fact cannot be questioned or disputed. In spite of divided responsibility between the two departments and in spite of the inadequate organization referred to, the personnel concerned effected very good co-operation and their combined efforts overcame many of the difficulties that faced them.

Army radar development was successful and contributed its share to the defeat of the enemy—that it might have been still more successful is also true, but that is so only on subsequent review with knowledge after the event. Some individuals may be able to point to particular errors or lapses and say, "I thought so at the time"—a few may even have said so at the time—but there was no one individual, aware of all the needs and conditions, advised by the various authorities in the Ministry on the different aspects of provision, who had the responsibility of deciding the action to be taken.

In embarking on new equipment supply that decision had to be taken on the most complete information available at the time and, where the contributory facts or proofs were not complete, that information had to be supplemented by the best ascertainable probabilities as assessed by the scientists, the technical military advisers and the production side. Chances have to be taken in war, and the odds had to be balanced with the need and with the Time factor, so far as it was assessable.

Looking back, perhaps the most unfortunate case was that of over-ordering by the War Office of the G.L. III British type of 10 cm. set, which had the effect of putting back the introduction of the auto following type for H.A.A. fire control. Here, the delays in finally clearing the design of the prototype sets, and the delayed start of production, nullified the estimate—or perhaps the over-optimistic guess—of the time involved in manufacture and supply. Had a more realistic time figure been available, the total supply requirement might well have been reduced and scientific effort and technical aid could have been concentrated earlier on the automatic design and experiment without interfering with the early supply of the G.L. III. That, however, is a "might-have-been" —at the time auto-following was only in embryo and little practical work on it had been done, though its possible suitability had been discussed in November, 1940.

Might-Have-Beens. Having raised the matter of "might-have-beens" in the previous paragraph, it may well be pursued here to refer to a few points that stand out in the earlier work of the scientific and technical sides of radar development and provision. There are four of these points worthy of mention, which, had fortune or facilities been a little kinder, would have contributed materially to earlier supply of advanced equipment.

The first is the earlier development of an electric or electronic predictor for H.A.A.; this would have been better suited to accept the output data provided by the radar set than was the mechanical predictor in use. The desirability of developing such a predictor was represented in December, 1936, but all available effort was then concentrated on the new Vickers pattern and on the provision of Sperry predictors. The electric type did not appear in action until some seven years later, when some of the American B.T.L. predictors were made available and some British experimental patterns were being tried.

The second case is that of the "beam" set on a very short wave-length with which experiments were in progress in 1937. It was on this type of very narrow beam working that Dr. Paris permitted himself to forecast the probable future form of accurate set for Army use. Owing to lack of sufficient staff for the Army cell at Bawdsey at that time, this experimental work had to be curtailed. Had it been possible to carry on those experiments, even though low power working only was then possible, valuable experience would have been obtained in accurate angular measurement and the means of effecting it continuously. This would have materially speeded up the development of the G.L. III when the resonator magnetron made high power working on centimetric wave-lengths a practical proposition.

The next of these points is that of the difficulty of solving, practically, the problem of measurement of elevation angles and of doing so continuously for the G.L. II set. An earlier solution of this problem would have been a saving grace and would have permitted a more effective approach to the needs of fire control in unseen conditions. However, the scientists cannot be blamed for the delay and they did devise a system that made use of the local ground reflection for comparison with the direct reflected ray, which was ingenious and could be operated with reasonable accuracy with skill and discrimination.

This particular device provides a good example of one of the difficulties of rapid development in war to meet pressing needs. Time does not permit of complete and extended trials and chances have to be taken; in this case the "snag" that arose was the necessity for providing each set with a level mat surround to provide a good reflecting surface if accuracy was to be obtained. This imposed an unfortunate limitation on the set which in itself was of excellent design—no other radar equipment in any of the Services improved upon it in reliability and general design, and few equalled it.

The last of the four cases is of a rather different nature; it is the spoiling of the design of the Canadian pattern of centrimetric G.L. III by lack of a little co-operation and liaison. It was a good set, but it could have been much better had use been made of the experience gained in this country both as to performance needs and user or operational requirements. It might well have saved the duplication of effort expended in producing the British and Canadian types and a uniform design might have been developed for production in both countries, while much British effort could have been applied to the next stage of advance in the auto following field.

Security. There are still some loose threads that should be woven into the general tapestry picture or otherwise tidied up, but only a few of them are of sufficient importance or interest to be dealt with here.

Perhaps the most important of these is the security aspect and the essential provisions made for reducing the chances of information on this novel subject and its uses from reaching the enemy; these protective measures not only covered radar as a whole but were also applied to specially important valves and components.

It will have been appreciated from the earlier chapters of this record that the importance of radar, as a novel and most effective aid to air defence, was such as to demand the highest degree of secrecy in its development and application. These restrictions, naturally, were a handicap in some respects in developing suitable equipment, in bringing it into operational use and in impressing its actual and potential value on the higher staffs. There is, however, no doubt that the restrictive measures achieved their object and the limitations they imposed were well worth while, for as a result the Germans remained for some vital period without real appreciation of its value and they were never able to catch up with the development made in this country; it was only their failures that proved to them the tactical advantages radar had given us.

In the early days when few individuals were in the picture and only three manufacturing firms of repute were concerned, the security control could be maintained comparatively easily, but with the expansion for war, the issue of equipment to troops and the training of operators and of repair and maintenance personnel, the chances of leakage naturally increased. It must be said, however, as a tribute to all the various individuals inside and outside the Services who were in any way concerned with radar, that remarkably little information of any material value leaked out. In so far as the Army was concerned, the security aspect was maintained most satisfactorily by all ranks even when large quantities of equipment had been issued and used in action.

The limitations imposed by secrecy did, of course, tend to reduce the understanding of the value of radar in the early days and the equipment was often looked upon as "a mystery box of tricks" that was the concern only of those strange beings the "specialist electrical and wireless mongers." It took time to establish radar as a valuable aid to A.A. gun operations, an achievement, of course, made more difficult by the lack of training and experience of the operators and the consequent strange target indications and fire directions they occasionally produced. Strange rumours also circulated about the unpleasant effects produced on operators, or others in close contact with the sets, supposed to be due to some strange rays emitted. Unit officers as well as other ranks were shy of it at the time—they had "come into the Army to fight: not to be a blanky electrician."

These prejudices and fears soon dwindled with experience and radar became more and more relied upon, particularly as improved equipment was made available. A.A. Command, as the primary user of radar, was foremost in developing the use of this equipment and in making it an integral part of the direction and control of fire in H.A.A. operation, and combined intimately with the R.A.F. for its radar controlled searchlights to aid night-fighter operations.

With the revolutionary development of the resonator magnetron and its application to various purposes, new security problems arose. This major advance in radar technique had to be denied to the enemy for as long as possible and special precautions had to be enforced to cover all stages of development, manufacture, incorporation in equipment and use. Here the security object was not radar itself, for our use of it was by that time well known to the Germans, but it was a particular valve development, the key item, that made our equipment so much in advance of anything that the enemy could produce, that had to be protected. It was not possible to make certain that the enemy could not detect the fact that we were employing the ultra-short wave-lengths of the centimetric band, though it was in some cases possible to do something to disguise that fact for a short time. The primary security consideration was to prevent his acquisition of samples of this valve from which he could develop them for himself. Special precautions had therefore to be taken to ensure that sets, or at least the valve itself, should not fall into his hands.

Similar restrictive measures were applied when the still shorter wave-lengths were brought into use, and here it was possible in some cases to cover up 3 cm. working by ensuring that its transmissions were always duplicated by a 10 cm, set, but that was not possible for all R.A.F. working. The Army was, of course, the least affected by these measures as it was only in special cases that they were sufficiently in contact with the enemy.

Generally speaking all major advances in radar technique and performance were held until they could be used in quantity to obtain the maximum effect—they were not disclosed nor frittered away in "penny packets." They were held subject to War Cabinet decision for supporting particularly important operations and once used in that way the advantage was pressed home by continuous use.

The result of these security measures was, generally, satisfactory and if they did not deny all information to the enemy they certainly denied it for such a time that he was unable to profit materially from it. As our offensive action took increasing precedence over the defensive in the approach to the culminating phases of the war, the importance of the security aspect gave place to the need to concentrate every improvement and advance to add to the effect of our offensive.

"*Window.*" The use of "Window" against the enemy with the probability or almost certainty that he would retaliate in kind, presented another type of security question. Here again, the decision as to whether and when we should employ it rested with the Chiefs-of-Staff advice to the War Cabinet. Our defensive radar equipment was known to be liable to very considerable interference and dislocation by Window properly used; R.A.F. ground equipment as well as the Army searchlight radar and some types of warning sets were likely to be adversely effected. When the expected retaliation came our defences came through with very fair success—they were, however, vulnerable to this form of screening and disturbance if it was applied with the maximum efficiency but the German effort never reached that standard.

Part of the vulnerability of our equipment was due to the fact that a number of types of equipment were all operating within a fairly narrow waveband so that all were liable to be affected by one size of Window. The R.A.F. low-flying warning C.H.L., the Army local warning A.A./G.C.I. and the L.W. sets and both the G.C.I. and the S.L.C. searchlight sets all operated in the $1\frac{1}{2}$ metre group and were covered by a band width only 17 M/cs wide. This was perhaps a fault in the inter-service direction of development, or rather may now appear to have been so. At the time, however, the need for sets to meet these operational requirements was urgent and they had to be crowded into the then available wave-band—centimetric working was not available when these types were urgently needed. The danger had been realized from the first but here again offensive aids had to take precedence over the defensive. Rather than a fault in direction, it was a chance that had to be taken, and it was taken with open eyes.

H.A.A. Radar. Another loose thread is that which links radar to the weapon itself; this thread is not so much a matter of radar but of the other essential links in the chain of operations and appliances that directs, controls and effects the fire of the guns. It must be understood that radar and its development was not alone the cause of the great advances made in the effect of H.A.A. fire. Radar was only one part of this directing chain to produce the effective result, but its importance in that chain increased with its improving performance until it eventually became the primary concern. It could not, however, produce its results without the intermediary aids of the transmission gear, the predictor, the automatic loader, the fuze setter or the proximity fuze and, above all, the trained personnel. Development and improvement in all of these items contributed to the final effective result. The stage reached by the end of the war—though not completely provided in time from British sources unfortunately—was the complete direct chain, almost entirely automatic in operation, from the radar selection of the target to the bursting of the shells within lethal distance of the aircraft. Automatic following radar provided continuous information of the "present" position of the target, transmitted electrically direct and automatically to the electric predictor which rapidly produced continuously the "future" position for engagement, according to the time of flight of the shells, and controlled the pointing of the gun, loaded automatically and fired similarly at the correct moment so that the shells, coming within effective distance of the target, would burst of their own accord when at the right position in relation to the target, and this could be effected at the maximum effective range of the gun. The automatic operation enabled considerable reductions to be made in the man and woman-power formerly required but increased the number that required higher technical skill.

Finally, to close this record let us turn to the salient points in the development of radar and its application to Army purposes; the opening chapter has mentioned briefly what radar did for the Navy and the R.A.F. and this volume has recorded details of the development for the Army and indicated some if its effects on operations.

After the primary achievement of Sir Robert Watson-Watt and his team in devising the means of distant detection of aircraft and warning of approaching air attack, the W.D. scientific and technical team, known as the Army Cell, at the Bawdsey Research Station, adapted the long range technique to provide the means of meeting the Army's need for accurate short range location of aircraft, and applied it also to the detection and tracking of surface craft.

The development of increasingly effective means of directing or controlling H.A.A. fire, which was the highest priority Army radar requirement, eventually reached the stage in which the engagement of targets in unseen conditions became more effective than visual control in the best visibility conditions.

Similarly, the accuracy of tracking and locating hostile surface vessels at long range, converted the more or less impotent coastal guns into active and effective defensive, and in some cases offensive, weapons in all conditions of darkness or bad visibility. The accuracy obtainable by radar aids was greater than that of visual methods and, in fact, outmatched that of the guns themselves.

Radar converted the A.A. searchlight from almost futility in the early war days to an effective aid to the interception of night bombers to supplement the R.A.F.'s Ground Control of Interception.

For aiding the Field Armies radar was under development for observation and engagement of hostile ground targets but was too late to be used for this purpose in the field; other devices and possibilities of useful aids were also in hand when hostilities ceased.

There remains that important device, the Radio Proximity Fuze, which was a most valuable and effective device against aircraft and against ground troops, but unfortunately the British production pattern failed to emerge before the end of the war.

On the technical aspect, the scientists of the Ministry of Supply and its establishments contributed to some of the outstanding advances in radar technique. The most important of these advances was the high power centimetric wave-length working, made possible by the development of the Resonator or Cavity Magnetron valve and the components and devices allied with it, which revolutionized radar technique and made so many things possible. It opened the way to a variety of applications not previously possible and put into the hands of the personnel of all three fighting Services appliances that differed so completely from the original types of equipment in which the wonders of radar were first presented to them, that it was difficult for them to appreciate that the latest equipments operated on the same basic technique.

This history, which has endeavoured to describe the growth of Army radar and what it achieved up to the end of the war, may now be closed with a sincere tribute to all those, of whatever grade, or rank, who contributed to its provision or to its effective use in operation against the enemy. The Army has cause to be grateful to them for making this new device available and increasingly effective.

APPENDIX I

Details of the War Department Scientific and Technical personnel engaged upon the initial Investigations and Experiments leading to the development of Army Radar.

The names recorded below are those of the members of the W.D. Scientific and Technical Staffs of the Air Defence and the Signals Experimental Establishments—and a few specially recruited—who formed the Army Cell attached to the Air Ministry Research Establishment at Bawdsey. Under the general guidance of Mr.—later Sir Robert—Watson-Watt they adapted the long-range technique developed for the Air Ministry to the short-range and high-accuracy needs of Army A.A. and Coastal weapons and developed the first Army R.D.F. (Radar) equipments.

Dr. E. T. Paris. A Principal Scientific Officer (P.S.O.) from the A.D.E.E. selected to make the initial investigations of the possibilities of R.D.F. for Army use; later in charge of the work of the Army Cell from October, 1936, until appointed Deputy to the D.S.R., War Office in 1938. Later Controller of Physical Research and Scientific Development in the M. of S.

H. W. Forshaw. A P.S.O. from S.E.E. who took over charge of the work in succession to Dr. Paris in September, 1938, and remained in charge until he returned to the S.R.D.E. in 1943.

P. E. Pollard and H. S. Young. Scientific Officers from A.D.E.E. later promoted to P.S.O. They were the original team leaders and contributed valuable ideas and suggestions—Pollard chiefly on radar fundamentals and Young on operational aspects. Pollard later was in charge of the S.R. II branch at M. of S. headquarters and Young in various technical appointments including S.R. II and A.5 branch of the Artillery directorate of the Ministry; both returned to the R.R.D.E. at the end of the war or shortly afterwards.

C. S. Slow. Joined the Army Cell at Bawdsey in 1937 as a Junior S.O., having been recruited from D.S.I.R.; promoted S.O. in 1938.

G. H. Barker, D. H. Priest and J. Dollin. Detached from A.D.E.E. in 1936 and joined the Cell as Assistants II and III.

W. T. Laite and D. A. Kerridge. Detached as Laboratory Assistants from A.D.E.E. in 1936.

E. J. Gamage. Not technically concerned but joined the Cell at Bawdsey from A.D.E.E. in 1936 as Motor Driver with a car to serve the Army Cell, from its formation.

Later additions to the Cell from A.D.E.E. included *F. S. Lager* a Technical Officer, *F. W. Eastes, H. P. Jarvis, D. N. Tyrer, C. F. Neild,* and *H. R. Whitfield*—all Assistants II and III—and six more Laboratory Assistants.

During 1938, the following joined the Cell from the S.E.E.:—

W. S. Butement. A Senior Scientific Officer later promoted P.S.O., who contributed a number of effective new ideas of a technical nature that materially aided development of equipment; subsequently reverted to special Signals work at M. of S. Headquarters.

E. Coop, S.O., *L. Tweedale, D. R. Chick,* and *G. W. Higgins,* all three J.S.O.s, and *L. A. Love*, T.O., joined the Cell from S.E.E. during 1938, as did also *W. A. Creeth* and *A. E. Padgett* (for a short time) who were Draughtsmen.

Further postings to this Cell from the A.D.E.E. included *Friend, Holman* and *Wettel*, but by the time they were made they were no longer W.D. personnel as the Ministry of Supply had taken over all the W.D. scientific and technical staffs.

Apart from these scientific, technical, etc., personnel there are two military officers who were intimately associated with this group and with the direction of its work—both had a considerable influence on the early development and their names deserve mention here.

They are Colonel C. E. Colbeck, the Radar member of the R.E. and S. Board, and Major H. M. Paterson of the Technical Artillery branch of the War Office. The former dropped out of the picture after seeing the G.L. II well launched, but the latter continued to be increasingly associated with Radar development throughout the war.

APPENDIX II

Proposal—of the nature of Radar—submitted in January, 1931, by Messrs. W. A. S. Butement and P. E. Pollard, of the Signals Experimental Establishment, for record in the Inventions Book of the Royal Engineer Board.

This proposal has been referred to in Chapter IV of this book and is quoted here as a matter of interest.

It was recorded as P. 1235 in the Inventions Book and the matter was dealt with in War Office file 84/General/5827 and R. E. Board record number C. 974, later transferred to B/2509/S.R.4.

As mentioned in Chapter IV, it was submitted to the Admiralty for consideration and in view of the subsequent development of Radar as now known, and particularly of the revolutionary effect caused by the high power transmissions on very short wave-lengths of the Resonator Magnetron, it is of interest to note that D.S.R. Admiralty qualified his opinion that the method of obtaining range would be difficult to apply practically by stating—"The outlook might well be modified if it were found possible to produce powerful sources and detectors of waves of the order of millimetres in length."

Following this proposal there is included a memorandum from the two scientists concerned, prepared in late December, 1945. As both of them were very intimately in the Army Radar picture and contributed materially to its development, their remarks are of interest.

OUTLINE INVENTION PROPOSAL

COASTAL DEFENCE APPARATUS

Apparatus to locate ships from the coast or other ships, under any conditions of visibility, or weather.

This apparatus depends on the reflection of Ultra Short Radio waves by conducting objects, e.g. a ship.

It will determine the range and traverse (i.e. the exact position) of the object practically instantaneously.

One station only is required and in one position.

Alternatively several stations may be employed and locations obtained by cross-bearings, as is usual in direction-finding practice.

The apparatus is reasonably certain to operate over a definite range, the magnitude of which is yet to be determined experimentally.

An ultra short-wave transmitter (of wave-length say 50 cms.) and a corresponding receiver, either or both having beam aerial systems, which may be rotated, are supplied with high tension derived from a medium frequency oscillator (frequency of say 50,000 cycles) in such a manner that when the transmitter is radiating the receiver is inoperative and vice-versa. Any other means of ensuring that the receiver is unaffected by its local transmitter may be employed.

The medium frequency oscillator may be itself modulated at a low frequency (say 1,000 cycles) so that an acoustic note may be obtained in the phones of the receiver if required.

On rotating the moving system no signals will be received until the beam is reflected by some conducting object. Thus the bearing of the object is directly determined.

The signal takes a definite time to travel from the transmitter to the reflecting object, and back to the receiver; which time gives a measure of the distance of the object from the apparatus.

One method of measuring this time is as follows. If the time taken by the signal to perform this journey be a multiple of the period of the medium frequency oscillator, then the reflected signal will arrive when the receiver is inoperative; and no signal will be observed. If the frequency of the medium frequency oscillator is varied the signal in the receiver will pass through a series of maxima and minima. By measuring the frequencies at which any two successive maxima or minima occur a measure of the distance can be obtained directly.

It will be observed that as the high tension supply to the receiver is periodically discontinuous it will operate on the super-regenerative principle, which is desirable, in fact almost essential, for sensitive reception on ultra-short wavelengths.

In addition low frequency amplification may be provided, sharply tuned to the low frequency modulation of the medium frequency oscillator. In this way low frequency amplification may be employed on a super-regenerative receiver resulting in increased sensitivity and freedom from interference. It must be pointed out that the low decrement of such a low frequency amplifier is in no way detrimental to the success of the apparatus.

A vibration galvanometer tuned to the low frequency or other means may be used to give visual or other indication of the maxima or minima.

It may be found desirable to provide for variation of the frequency of the ultra-short wave transmitter and receiver so that better reflection may be obtained. For example, if on the ship whose position is to be found there is a metal object of some definite length, it may be desirable that a multiple of half the wave-length of the ultra-short wave transmitter shall be equal to this length.

Preliminary work is necessary to measure the magnitude of the reflected wave under these conditions and hence the useful range of the apparatus.

Signed—W. A. S. Butement.
P. E. Pollard.

Jan. 26th, 1931.
S.E.E.
Woolwich Common.

Extract from a
Memorandum on Work carried out on "Radar" by Messrs. W. A. S. Butement and P. E. Pollard in 1931

1. HISTORICAL. It is not possible after so long a lapse of time to apportion credit for various points specifically to one or other of us but as the work was done by both of us in close collaboration it should be considered a joint effort.

As a result of discussions between ourselves we wrote a memorandum dated 26th January, 1931, proposing the use of radio for locating ships.

This memorandum was the first as far as we know to propose the use of a method of range measurement which may be described as the electrical analogue of Fizea's method for measuring the velocity of light.

We were allowed to carry out experiments on a small scale in our own time....

... We proposed to use short waves, about 50 cms., this being the shortest wave-length we could generate at that time.

2. CIRCUIT DETAILS. We tried various kinds of valves ranging from V.24, and its dull emitter equivalent, up to 250 watt valves. We found that nearly as much power could be obtained from a V. 24 as from larger valves, one of the limiting factors being the temperature of the grid, which we ran at a bright red heat. After considerable tests, an experimental type of A.T. 40 with "top connected" grid and anode was found to be the most satisfactory. It was also found that only bright emitter valves were suitable for use in the Barkhausen-Kurz circuit.

Transmitter was a simple B.K. oscillator with the aerial situated at the focus of a cylindrical parabolic mirror about 4 ft. wide and 18 in. deep.

This transmitter was then used as the nucleus of a receiver. We proposed to quench this B.K. oscillator using a separate valve oscillating on a medium frequency, but found that quenching could be effected merely by adding in the anode or grid circuits of the B.K. oscillator circuit tuned to the medium frequency....

We arranged to modulate the quenched receiver at 1,000 C/S approximately and a low frequency amplifier to enhance the received signal. The quenched B.K. receiver oscillator gave sufficient radiation to act as transmitter for preliminary experiments in detecting echoes from various targets.

3. EXPERIMENTAL RESULTS. We used a sheet of metal about 5 ft. × 2 ft. as a target and observed that the reading of the millimeter in the output circuit varied as the sheet was moved. We then put long leads with chokes on the headphones, so that the man carrying the sheet could listen to the variation of signal strength as he moved. Definite maxima were observed every half wave-length. The limit of space available to us was about 100 yds. at which distance a marked signal was obtained. Signals were also obtained from masts, etc., about the Establishment and we recollect receiving a good signal from a mast about 100 yards away.

Looking back on this work in the light of our present knowledge of Radar, we feel confident that our experiments, if we had ... used a bigger aerial would have shown that we could detect a destroyer at a distance of from $\frac{1}{2}$ to 1 mile.

Signed—W. A. S. Butement.
P. E. Pollard.

Comment. To the non-scientific reader it is obvious that the experimental work at that time was severely limited by the lack of power output and that lack reduced the range capacity below effective operational needs. Development in that direction might have brought it into the practical sphere but whether the method of range measurement would have proved practicable for long ranges is a matter upon which only a technical expert could form an opinion.

It would appear, however, that this outline of a method for using the reflected rays from a target was actually Radar in embryo. Perhaps the term Pulsed in reference to the transmission is not quite justified, but it certainly provided for frequently Interrupted transmission. The proposal contains the elements of combined T and R working and of concentration of the transmission in a narrow beam; its presentation seems to have taken the form of the Meter Display that was used in some forms of Radar sets.

It is unfortunate that this investigation could not have been pursued at that time.

APPENDIX III

WAR OFFICE RADAR STAFF

On the formation of the Directorate of Anti-Aircraft and Coast Defence under Major-General K. Loch, a small section of the branch A.A. 1(*d*) was formed in 1940, to deal with R.D.F. (Radar) and Searchlights; this consisted of Major A. A. Eden, who had been on the first I.F.C. Course of Landguard, as G.S.O.2 with Captain A. J. Fisher, G.S.O.3, for R.D.F. duties, and Captain Roberts, G.S.O.3 with Captain Jacobs, G.S.O.3 for Searchlights.

In December, 1940, Brigadier A. P. Sayer filled the new appointment of Deputy Director of Anti-Aircraft and Coast Defence specially for R.D.F. policy and direction of development, though searchlights and other weapons duties were included in his responsibilities.

In September, 1941, Captain E. W. Clarke succeeded Captain Fisher when the latter was transferred to A.5 branch, Ministry of Supply. Two additional appointments in that year for C.A. and C.D., R.D.F. (radar) were approved and were filled by Major A. H. Ayscough as a G.S.O.2 and Captain F. Grant as G.S.O.3; at the same time Major Smith as a G.S.O.2 replaced Captains Jacobs and Roberts for searchlight duties. In July of that year Major Eden was posted to the British Army Staff in Washington for radar duties as a G.S.O.1 and was succeeded in A.A.1 branch by Lieut.-Colonel F. W. Baston as a G.S.O.1; in addition, Major D. Waldock from R.E.M.E. filled the technical G.S.O.2 radar post.

On the C.A. and C.D. radar side Captain Grant, on promotion, was replaced by Captain H. Dearns for a short time; then Captain C. V. Lucas who was classified as an I.F.C. and also as an I.G. for C.A., filled this G.S.O.3 post.

In April, 1943, Junior Commander L. W. M. Clarke, A.T.S., who was classified as an I.F.C., filled a new G.S.O.3 radar post.

In September, 1943, Major R. W. B. Gatehouse relieved Major Waldock who, with Lieut.-Colonel Fisher, joined the British Army Staff in Washington and relieved Lieut.-Colonel Eden. Eden returned to the first grade radar post at the War Office in October, 1943—Major Blair from A.A. Command having been lent temporarily to bridge the gap as Lieut.-Colonel Baston had been posted to A.A. Command.

In 1944, Lieut.-Colonel Eden was appointed to India for a special appointment for all radar duties—policy and instructional. About the same time a second G.S.O.1 appointment was approved for the War Office Radar Directorate and these two appointments were filled by Lieut.-Colonels J. P. G. Lewis and the Hon. J. W. Fremantle. Majors R. D. H. Phayre and N. B. Cork joined as G.S.O.2s, while Major Dicks relieved Major Smith for searchlight duties.

Early in 1944, Brigadier Sayer became Director of Radar, but remained under the Director of Royal Artillery; at the end of that year he was relieved by Brigadier G. C. Gray—one of the original officers introduced to R.D.F. and with experience of the use of radar in action.

Late in 1945, reductions of the staff of the Radar Directorate were effected and it was separated from the Directorate of Royal Artillery, coming under the Director of Weapons Development.

APPENDIX IV

SAMPLE SPECIFICATIONS

HEAVY A.A. FIRE CONTROL SERIES

A few samples of the Specifications for Army radar equipment requirements issued to guide the development work of A.D.R.D.E. are included in this Appendix. As the H.A.A. needs had priority over all other Army uses of radar, a series of specifications for the H.A.A. fire control sets is given to show not only the growth of detail included and the improvement in performance required, but also the use made of new developments of components, valves, etc., that made these improvements in performance possible.

The other samples given are individual selections from other classes of radar equipment and show the latest forms aimed at during the closing stages of the war.

A.

A.A. NO. 1, MARK II
(G.L. II)
G.S. SPECIFICATION (AMPLIFIED)

1. **Performance.** The equipment is to be capable of the following performance.

(a) *Early Warning.* To detect and locate by continuous measurement the range, bearing and elevation of aircraft whose "echo" is similar in strength to that of the Blenheim Bomber.

The minimum range for detection and location to be 20,000 yards with an angle of sight of 6° and 30,000 with an angle of sight of 15°.

   Range: accuracy ± 200 yards; consistency 200 yards.
   Bearing: accuracy ± 1 degree; consistency 1 degree.
   Elevation (from 10° to 55°): accuracy ± 1 degree; consistency 1 degree.

(b) *Fire Control.* To determine and transmit continuously the range, bearing and elevation (measured from the Receiver) between 2,000 and 14,000 yards and from 6° to 65° angle of elevation.

   Range: accuracy ± 25 yards; consistency 25 yards.
   Bearing: accuracy ± 30 minutes; consistency 30 minutes.
   Elevation (from 10° to 55°): accuracy ± 30 minutes; consistency 30 minutes.

The transmission of range, bearing and elevation is to be sufficiently smooth to allow of satisfactory rate balancing with the predictor in use.

2. **Bearing and Elevation Rates.** The equipment is to be capable of measuring the data required up to a maximum bearing rate of 10° per second and an elevation rate of 5° per second.

3. **Radio and Pulse Frequencies and Pulse Width.** The equipment is to be capable of working at any radio frequency between 54 and 85 megacycles.

The pulse frequency is to be capable of variation between 1,200 and 1,500 cycles. The pulse width is not to exceed 2 micro-seconds.

4. **Weight and Mobility.** The axle load of the equipment is not to be

greater than nor the mobility worse than that of the 3·7" mobile H.A.A. Gun. The dimensions of trailers and cabling must conform to Ministry of Transport regulations.

5. **Power Supply.** A suitable generator will form part of the equipment but the set should be able to work off supply mains (230 volts, 50 cycles, A.C.) if voltage and frequency can be stabilized to 2 % and 5 % respectively.

6. **Transmission of Data.** Transmission of range, bearing and elevation will be by magslip transmission, the shaft values of the high and low speed elements being as follows:

Range, one turn 2,000 yards and 36,000 yards; bearing, one turn 10° and 360°; elevation, one turn 10° and 180°.

Means of conversion of the value of the high-speed bearing elements from 10° to 20° per turn is required.

7. **Displacement Correction.** Provision of space and suitable shaft drives in the Receiver is to be made for the addition of a displacement corrector.

8. **Personnel.** The equipment is to be capable of being worked by a range operator, a bearing operator, an elevation operator, and an operator for generator and transmitter, and an N.C.O. in charge.

9. **Safety of Operators.** The operators are to be adequately protected against electric shocks and against damage from breakage of C.R. tubes. Interlocking devices are to be fitted to prevent access to high tension compartments without switching off the power supply.

Note. This specification was based upon trials results which had shown that the range performance should cover the operational requirements of warning and the acceptable minimum for engagement by the guns, and that the accuracy of angular measurement required was at least approachable. The specification in fact called for greater accuracy *and* consistency than had actually been achieved in the trials; this was to some extent a spur to urge on the designers but also provided for some give and take in the acceptability of the performance achieved by production sets as compared with that of the experimental sets.

B.
G.S. SPECIFICATION FOR G.L. III (PROVISIONAL)
16TH NOVEMBER, 1940.

To combine a G.L. Mk. I or II set for early warning with a V.H.F. set (wavelength 10 cms. or below) for Fire Control.

Pick up for early warning 30,000 yds., for Fire Control 22,000 yds.

Accurate range measurement required from 2,000 to 17,000 yds., though a maximum of 14,000 yds. would be accepted.

Beam width 14° desirable; 10° minimum acceptable. Elevation from 10° to 90° for following, 10° to 70° for Fire Control.

C.
OUTLINE G.S. SPECIFICATION FOR R.D.F., A.A. No. 3, MARK II
(G.L. III)

1. The R.D.F. equipment to be suitable for use in a wide variety of climatic conditions, including tropical. . . .

2. The ultimate requirement is the provision of sufficiently accurate

information for the fire control of heavy A.A. guns to enable them to engage successfully unseen hostile aircraft within their effective range limits.

3. To enable the guns and fire control instruments to be in action in sufficient time, adequate early warning of approach of hostile targets is necessary. Provision for this may be included in the accurate R.D.F. set or may be made by means of a separate set as most convenient from the technical aspect.

4. . . . .

5. The number of personnel for manning to be reduced to the minimum essential for accurate operation.

6. The conditions within the cabin or emplacement to provide for adequate comfort for the operators to permit of consistent good operation. . . . Anti-gas protection to be on the basis of individual protection (respirator, etc.). . . . Adequate provision for ventilation and for heating to be made both for operation and for drying out the electrical components and assemblies.

7. The arrangement and accessibility of the R.D.F. parts of the equipment to be such that maintenance and replacement can be effected under cover from the weather. . . . .

8. . . . .

Note. The amplified specification which translated these requirements (C) into practical details for the designers is given below; this was prepared by the technical Fire Control branch of the Ministry under the D.G. of A. and accepted by D.A.A. & C.D. War Office.

D.

(G.L. III)

AMPLIFIED G.S. SPECIFICATION

SEPTEMBER, 1941

1. The G.L. III will be a fire control equipment. It will operate in conjunction with a G.L. Mark II or other device which will provide local early warning and the necessary information to direct the Mark III beam on to the target.

2. **Frequency.** Each equipment will be capable of operating at one frequency in the band 2,700–3,000 Mc/s.

3. **Performance.** Equipment is to be capable of the following performance . . . .

(a) Maximum range 26,000 yards (for an aircraft whose echo is similar in strength to that of the Blenheim Bomber).

(b) Minimum range 1,000 yards (2,000 yards acceptable).

(c) To determine and transmit continuously the range, bearing and elevation subject to the rate limitations of para. 4.

Range accuracy $\pm$ 25 yards, consistency 25 yards.

Bearing accuracy $\pm$ 10 minutes, consistency 10 minutes.

Elevation accuracy (10° to 70°) — 10 minutes, consistency 10 minutes.

These figures for accuracy refer to the transmitted data and for normal conditions (less than 30 ft./sec. wind).

(d) The transmission of range, bearing, and elevation is to be sufficiently smooth to allow of satisfactory rate balancing with the predictor in use.

(e) The equipment must be capable of movement in elevation from 5° to 90° for following the target through the whole of this elevation range.

(f) For a small number of equipments a maximum range of 33,000 yards will be required. To obtain this deviation from standard design will be permissible.

(g) To provide for (f) and other contingencies, the range-finding part of the equipment should provide accurate range measurement and transmission to 36,000 yards.

4. **Bearing and Elevation Rates.** The equipment is to be capable of measuring the data required up to a maximum bearing rate of 8° per second and an elevation rate of 5° per second.

5. **Pulse width.** Not greater than 1 microsecond; maximum time for pulse build-up 0·2 microsecond.

6. **Width of beam.** Not greater than 10° and not less than 6°.

7. **I.F.F.** Not required. To be provided on early warning part of the G.L. station . . . .

8. **Personnel.** The equipment is to be capable of being worked by the following operators.

One each for Range, Elevation, Bearing and a Radio Mechanic or Specialist.

9. **Weight and Mobility.** The axle load of the equipment is not to be greater than, nor the mobility worse than that of the 3·7" mobile H.A.A. Gun.

10. **Power Supply.** . . . as before . . . .

11. **Transmission of Data.** . . . as before . . . .

12. **Safety of Operators.** The operators are to be adequately protected against electric shocks. Interlocking devices are to be fitted to prevent access to high tension compartments without switching off the power supply.

13. **Gas Proofing** is not required.

14. **Shipment.** For shipment the equipment should conform to the following maximum overall dimensions.

Height, 11' 4"; Length, 21' 0"; Width, 7' 9".

Parts liable to damage should be capable of being dismantled for shipment.

15. **Time of Warming up.** Should not exceed 10 minutes.

16. . . . .

17. . . . .

Note.—To complete the series of Fire Control A.A. radar equipments, extracts from the specification of the last form developed during the war are given; this was the light automatic following type which unfortunately did not actually get into action against the enemy.

E.
D.G. OF A.'s AMPLIFIED G.S. SPECIFICATION
RADAR A.A. NO. 3, MK. 7
12TH OCTOBER, 1944

1. **Function.** The equipment shall be an automatic following mobile Radar set for Hy. A.A. fire control. There shall be automatic following in bearing and elevation. Range shall be followed optionally by automatic or by manual aided-laying control. The equipment shall also be suitable for use as a target indication set for use with fire control Radars A.A. No. 3 Mks. 1, 2, 4 and 7.

2. **Frequency.** S. Band (10 cm.).

3. **Performance.** For an aircraft whose echo is similar in strength to that of a Beaufighter. . . .

(a) *Range.* An echo should be visible on the display system and such that the set can be "put on" and follow automatically at 35,000 yards. When used for target indication not less than 80 % of standard targets shall be detected at 40,000 yards desirable, 35,000 yards acceptable range.

The minimum desirable range is 500 yards, but 1,000 yards is acceptable.

Note. Range scales and transmission are to be provided to 36,000 yards but range correlation for I.F.F. shall be to 50,000 yards.

(b) *Average error.*

Range: 35 yds. or $\frac{1}{2}$ %, whichever is the greater.

Bearing: 8 × secant of angle of sight, mins. of angle.

Elevation: 8 mins. of angle.

Note (i) The angular accuracies to be obtained between angles of sight of 8° and 75° at rates up to 8°/sec. Between 75° and 85° angle of sight and between rates of 8° — nx 16°/sec., the error figures may be doubled.

(ii) Outside the range required for accurate prediction (24,000 yds.) the range accuracy need only be 1 %.

(iii) The figures for average error are to be maintained in wind velocities below 40 m.p.h.; reduced performances will be accepted between 40 and 60 m.p.h.

(c) *Quality of Output data.* This output data shall be acceptable by all Service predictors with which this equipment will be used (Nos. 1, 4, 9, 10 or 11) and the Transmitter Convertor, Rectangular Co-ordinate Mk. I.

4. **Slewing.** The equipment shall be capable of being slewed without excessive overshooting, 180° in azimuth in 7 seconds and 60° in elevation in 4 seconds.

5. **Putting-on Target.**

(a) *Self-scanning.* The set shall be able to scan at least 20 r.p.m. in azimuth and 15° in elevation in steps of 3°.

The elevation scan shall be adjustable about any mean angle and may be stopped at will at any angle. The resultant display shall be upon a P.P.I. giving a paint from a given target not less frequently than once in 15 seconds.

(b) *External data.* It shall be possible to "put on" to a selected target by data supplied by Magslip from an external source and to follow this magslip data automatically or with over-riding manual control. The sector values of magslip required are as follows:—

Range 16,000 yards per turn; Bearing, 360° per turn,

Elevation, 180° per turn.

(c) *Conical scan.* A conical scan of $\pm 2\frac{1}{2}°$ in amplitude at 1 revolution per second shall be provided. The mean position shall be under the control of the operator.

(d) The set shall be able to supply target indication data to other fire control Radars where used in that role.

6. **Discrimination.** It shall be possible to discriminate between similar targets separated by the following amounts:—

Range: 200 yds. desirable, 400 yds acceptable. Angle 2° desirable, 4° acceptable.

7. **I.F.F.** I.F.F. Mk. III shall be provided with discrimination in range and bearing. Provision shall be made for easy and positive correlation between targets echo and I.F.F. response.

Control of bearing movement of the I.F.F. aerials shall be independent of the scanning of the Radar aerial system. The provision of a separate light structure to carry the I.F.F. aerials and associated units is acceptable. It is desirable that the units shall be readily removable for installing in a remote display and control unit (see para. 24).

8. **Personnel.** Provision will be made for two operators, one to work the set, the other to plot, operate the I.F.F., etc. A simple writing table should be provided for the latter operator. The design shall be such that a Radio Mechanic will not normally be required during starting and stopping the set. It should be possible for a third person to be in the cabin for such purposes as supervision of training and inspection of operation. A simple folding seat will be adequate for the latter person.

9. **Mobility.**
(a) The equipment shall be mounted upon a trailer the mobility of which should not be less than that of the 3·7″ Mk. III Hy. A.A. Gun. . . .
(b) It should be possible to tow the set in the normal manner from standard landing craft. . . .
(c) The equipment shall be able to travel through 5 feet of sea water with 1 foot 9 inches of lop for periods up to 15 minutes without affecting immediate subsequent action or permanent damage. Temporary sealing arrangements are permissible but as far as possible the conditions should be met in the basic design.

10. **Weight.** The weight of the equipment including the trailer shall not exceed five tons.

11. **Dimensions.** The equipment shall not exceed the following overall dimensions:—
Height: 11′ 0″; Length: 15′ 0″; Width: 7′ 6″.

12. **Power Supply.** The equipment shall operate from a 230 volt, 50 cycle, 3 phase A.C. power supply with voltage and frequency regulation of 5%. The maximum load is not to exceed 12 KVA.

13. **Electrical range/height convertor.** An electrical range/height convertor will be built into the equipment, the mechanical dials of which should be visible to both operators.

14. **Transmission of Data.** (i) Transmission of slant range, bearing, elevation, height and ground range shall be by 3″ magslip transmitters. (ii) Either height, slant range or ground range may be required at any one time, and a switch shall be provided to select the desired quantity. (iii) Slant range shall be available on a separate outlet in addition to (ii).

15. **Safety of operators.** The operators shall be adequately protected against injury particularly by the high-speed slewing of the aerial system or electrical shock.

16. **Time into operation.** With four men the set (excluding erection of I.F.F. aerial) should be capable of being brought into action in 10 minutes if in a dry condition. If special drying out is required then the set should be in action in 30 minutes.

17. **Time to warm up.** The set being dry, it shall not require more than 2 minutes to warm up.

18. **Blast.** The equipment shall be tested against the effect of blast when placed 25 yds. from the pivot of a 3·7″ Mk. III Hy. A.A. gun fired at Q.E. 10° and bearing difference 10°.

19. **Arctic and tropical conditions.**
(i) The equipment will be required to operate satisfactorily under either arctic or tropical conditions of wind, temperature, humidity and dust. It should withstand without damage temperatures of: Minimum − 50° F. desirable, − 20° F. acceptable; Maximum + 160° F. The range of ambient

temperatures for operation is: Minimum − 40° F. desirable, − 20° F. acceptable; Maximum + 135° F. The set shall be able to operate in conditions of 95 % relative humidity up to 100° F.

(ii) In the event of difficulty being encountered with any components being suitable for both tropical and arctic conditions, relaxation will be in favour of the tropical condition. Limited special preparation for arctic conditions, such as change of lubricants, will be acceptable.

(iii) The ventilation of the equipment racks and the operators' space may be treated separately and either heating or refrigerating units for the operators' compartment may be issued and used as required.

20. **Interference.** All reasonable precautions shall be taken to prevent interference to or by other telecommunications equipment and to minimize the effect of enemy jamming. It shall be possible to operate two equipments of this type, one for target indication and the other for fire control, with a separation between 50 and 100 yds. A locking cable between the two will be acceptable.

21. **Collimation.** A telescope shall be provided for orientation and lining up with other fire control instruments within $\pm$ 2 minutes . . . .

22. **Overlapping echoes.** Means of locking the rates shall be provided to aid the operator to follow when echoes overlap.

23. **Ballistic correction.** Ballistic correction between $+$ 20 % and . . . . shall be provided upon the range. The accuracy of setting this correction shall be commensurate with the accuracy of the equipment.

24. **Remote control.** Provision shall be made in the design for remote control and display from a separate unit installed in the Command Post from which the functions of target selection, identification and indication shall be performed. Switches and cable connectors shall be provided in the main Radar to enable the remote unit to be connected when required without modification of the main Radar. It is desirable that the I.F.F. units in the main Radar may be removed for installation when required in the remote control unit.

25. **Test gear and maintenance.** The set shall be designed for easy maintenance. Components likely to be renewed in the field shall be readily accessible and all chassis to be designed for easy replacement.

. . . .

26. **Essential Spares.** All essential spares are to be carried in the equipment.

27. **Levelling.**

(i) A non-binding jacking system shall be used to enable the equipment to be levelled to 2 minutes of arc. . . . They should support the set rigidly.

(ii) Levelling bubbles are to be fitted upon the elevation assembly.

28. **Telephones.** Provision shall be made for telephone communication over two external lines and also to enable an operator on the roof looking through the telescope to communicate with an operator inside the set. It is desirable that the telephone circuits should be incorporated in the design and switching facilities provided for each operator to speak on either line at will. Lamp signalling and power ringing is desirable.

29. **Armour.** It is desirable but not essential that the operators should be protected from small arms fire and shell splinters.

30. **Service and durability.** The equipment should be capable of 2,000 hours' running between major overhauls. It may normally have to operate

for 12 hours per day, but should be capable of 23 hours' operation per day without rapid deterioration.

F.
INDIVIDUAL SAMPLES FOR OTHER TYPES OF EQUIPMENT
G.S. SPECIFICATION FOR S.L.C. 9X
A.A. NO. 2 MK. IX

1. **Role.** A Radar equipment working on a centimetric wave-length for locating aircraft and for directing a S.L. beam continuously on to a selected target.

As at present envisaged, this equipment may be provided on a limited scale for deployment in conjunction with existing S.L.C. Locators, thereby providing an alternative system of operation in the event of jamming on one of the S.L.C. frequencies.

2. **Mounting.** To be mounted directly on a Standard Projector A.A. 150 cm.

3. **Control.** Movement of the Projector to be through Control Gear which must provide, at the discretion of the operator, the following forms of control—(i) Automatic scanning. (ii) Laying by hand operated controls. (iii) Laying by the auto following unit.

Provision also to be made for hand control from a visual directing pillar.

4. **Scanning Speed.** Elevation $12°$ per second. Bearing $2°$ per second. Arc covered: Elevation $35°$ (Aerial System Movement $= 30°$)
Bearing $60°$ (,, ,, ,, $= 50°$)
Centre and extent of scan to be adjustable.

5. **Frequency alternatives.** 3,060–3,000 Mc/s (9·8–10·0 cms.)
or
3,120–3,060 Mc/s (9·6–9·8 cms.)

6. **Pulse Width.** 2 microsecs.
7. **Beam Width.** Static, to 6 dB down $7°$; Split $3°$.
8. **Performance.**
   (a) Range. Maximum for tracking 20,000 yards; Minimum 2,000 feet.
   (b) Angular accuracy $\pm \frac{1}{2}°$ down to $5°$ elevation; Bearing $\pm \frac{1}{2}°$.
9. **Warming up period.** Not to exceed 2 minutes.
10. **I.F.F.** I.F.F. Mk. III Interrogation units to be provided.
11. **Personnel.** One operator for Signal Selector Unit.
12. **Power Supply.** Nominal 80 V. D.C.; equipment must cater for fluctuation from 65 V. to 90 V. (continuous rating) and for peak of 120 V.
13. **Telephones.** Two telephone circuits to be provided.
14. **Transport and Mobility.** As for existing 150 cm. Projector F.S.
15. **Weight and Shipment.** As for existing 150 cm. Projector F.S.
16. **Special Operating Conditions.** To be suitable for use in arctic or tropical conditions. Attention is directed to the necessity for adequate weatherproofing.
17. **Co-ordination.** Optical Sight for co-ordination of radio and light axis to be provided.
18. . . . .
19. **Maintenance.** As far as possible assembly in sub-units to facilitate replacement in the Field is desirable; all parts requiring regular maintenance or check must be easily accessible.

G.

D.G. OF A. AMPLIFIED G.S. SPECIFICATION

C.A. NO. 1 MK. V

SEPTEMBER, 1944

1. **Function.** A portable Coast Artillery Radar Fire Control Equipment to operate with medium Coast Artillery Guns.

The fire control system will include a Computor which will provide correction for travel of target, spotting observations and displacements between C.A. set and Battery Pivot and will convert range to Q.E.

The equipment will also be required to act as a range-finder for a No. 17 Director.

2. **Range Performance.**

(a) . . . At an aerial height of 100 ft. above sea level the set should determine and transmit continuously accurate range within the limits:—

M.T.B.s 2,000 yds. to 17,000 yds.; Destroyers and larger vessels up to 30,000 yds.

(b) Location of fall of shot relative to the target or to the point of lay should be achieved with the 6 in. C.A. Gun to 25,000 yards.

(c) It is desirable that the equipment should be capable of working alternatively in conjunction with guns of larger calibre to a maximum range of 45,000 yds. with observation of 15 in. fall of shot to 42,000 yds.

(d) . . . Ability to indicate targets to 65,000 yds. is desirable to enable the equipment to be used in an emergency early warning role.

3. **Accuracy.** Within the limits of paragraph 2, provided the rates of change of bearing and of range do not exceed 1° per second and 30 yds. per second respectively, the overall average errors should not exceed: Bearing: 5 minutes; Range: 25 yds.

This performance should be obtained provided the shell splash is not within 50 yds. plus and 1 degree of angle right or left of the target.

4. **Bearing Control.** (a) Direct lay permitting a steady rate of following is required. In changing target the bearing should be capable of movement at 10° per second. (b) . . . . (c) Mechanical indication of bearing should be provided. (d) . . . . (e) . . . . (f) Provided the primary functions of the equipment are not prejudiced, it is desirable that provision should be made for a bearing drive suitable for the later addition of a remote P.P.I. type display.

5. **Range Control.** (a) Direct lay permitting a steady rate of manual following up to 30 yds. per second is required. . . .

(b), (c), (d) . . . .

6. **Display.**

(a) A display is required allowing fall of shot to be accurately observed within the limits ± 1,000 yds. and 3° right and left of the point of lay. A suitable high resolution display is required for the bearing and range operators.

(b) A coarse range display, 0–60,000 yards convenient to both bearing and range operators, is required.

(c) In addition to those at the set, remote fall of shot and coarse range displays which can be displaced up to 100 yds. should be provided for installation at the B.O.P.

(d) The provision of a normal "A" type display is desirable, utilizing the coarse range tube if practicable.

7. **Width of Beam.**
(a) In azimuth the beam width should be as narrow as possible, but the zero to zero width should not be greater than 2°.
(b) In elevation, the spread should be sufficient to ensure that targets at minimum range are not invisible from a 400-ft. site.

8. **Pulse Width.** The received pulse width should not exceed 0·2 microsecond.

9. **Frequency.** The wave-length will be 3·2 c.m. $+$ 1 %.

10. **Recurrence Frequency.**
(a) Recurrence frequency should be approximately 2,000 pulses per second.
(b) Some measure of control of the recurrence frequency is desirable to enable ambiguity of very long range signals to be resolved.

11. **Transmission of Data.**
(a) Continuous transmission of bearing and range by magslip is required. . . .
(b) . . . .
(c) Transmission of fall of shot data relative to the target will be by telephone or by reading off the remote display.

12. **Use with No. 16 Director.** Means should be provided to enable the equipment to be laid continuously on the same target as the Director.

13. **Datuming.** Means should be provided for checking and correcting range and bearing indications against suitable internal and external datums. A suitable rigidly mounted optical sight with means for collimating the Radar with line of sight should be provided.

14. **General Design.**
(a) The equipment should be suitable for erection on ground with up to 5° cross slope and be provided with adequate means of levelling. Means should be provided for securing the structure without recourse to concrete or other special foundations, against winds of velocities up to 70 m.p.h.
(b) . . . .
(c) Weather cover for the equipment and operators is required. A structure with suitably braced canvas covering, would be acceptable.

15. **Packaging.**
(a) The equipment should break down into package form. Unit packages should be capable of being carried under tropical conditions by not more than four men; their weight should not exceed 200 lbs.
(b) For simplicity of transport to the theatre of war, the packages should be grouped in convenient cases weighing about one ton.
(c) The equipments should be suitable for beach landing in either packaged or cased form.
(d) Packages should be fully waterproofed and should withstand, without damage, immersion in sea water for one hour. They should be suitable for re-packing a number of times locally on site to the same waterproof specifications.

16. . . . .

17. **Robustness.**
(a) In packaged or cased form the equipment should withstand without damage dockyard, beach landing, and cross-country handling. . . .
(b) In operating form it should withstand the blast at 50 yds. to the flank of the 6 in. Coast Artillery Gun.

18. **Time into Action.** The equipment should be capable of being erected and prepared for action within eight hours of landing.

19. **Preparation for Operating.** The set should be capable of operating

and giving the required performance in a period after switching on not exceeding ten minutes.

20. **Climatic Conditions.**

(a) The equipment should be capable of working continuously for long periods under temperate and tropical conditions of temperature, humidity, rain, spores, insects, dust and wind. . . .

(b) It should be capable of being subjected without damage to extreme temperatures: Minimum — 50° F. desirable, — 10° F. acceptable. Maximum + 160° F.

(c) Range of ambient temperature for operation: — 20° F. to + 140° F.

(d) The equipment should be capable of operating with the performance required in this specification in wind velocities up to 50 m.p.h. and should still be capable of working, with reduced accuracy if necessary, in wind velocities up to 70 m.p.h.; it should withstand wind velocities up to 100 m.p.h.

21. **Number of operators.** One operator will be required for bearing and one for range following. A third operator will observe fall of shot indications. . . .

22. **I.F.F.** I.F.F. is required but need not be integral with the C.A. set. . . .

23. . . . .

24. **Power Supply.** A suitable generator should be provided with the equipment and should be capable of breaking down into manhandleable loads.

25. . . . .

26. **Maintenance.** The design should allow for maintenance and calibration being effected as simply as possible and a minimum of skilled attention should be required.

Component assemblies should be capable of individual replacement on site, and repair or reconditioning at base should be aimed at.

27. . . . .

H.

GENERAL STAFF OUTLINE SPECIFICATION

FIELD ARMY CONTROL OF FIRE (FALL OF SHOT) RADAR EQUIPMENT

RADAR FA NO. 1 (EMERGENCY TYPE)

JULY, 1944

1. This equipment is required to assist control of fire of Field and Medium Artillery by correction of fire from observation of shell ground bursts in relation to the target or to a witness point, in conditions of darkness or bad visibility. It may also be employed when conditions permit to observe targets and to track moving vehicles with a view to accurate engagement. The equipment must be capable of good cross-country performance for use in forward areas. . . . It may be required to operate in conjunction with Radar FA No. 2, using the latter as a warning set for engagement of moving targets, or independently.

2. **Accuracy.** The set should be capable of locating the fall of shot relative to the target or a witness point, with adequate accuracy for destructive engagement of targets.

3. **Siting.** Siting restrictions should be reduced to the minimum to allow for the greatest possible tactical freedom; limitations imposed by a visual line of sight to the target area are accepted.

4. **Range.** Ground bursts should if possible be located up to the full range of the British 25 pdr., 4·5″ and 5·5″ guns. Should the full range be

unattainable reduced ranges would be accepted, but the following are most desirable: 25 pdr. 7,000 yds.; Medium guns 14,000 yds.

The possibility of obtaining location at greater ranges of ground bursts from the 155 mm. and 8″ (U.S.) guns should be examined.

5. **Coverage.** Without moving the vehicle, the equipment should be capable of sweeping through an arc of not less than 120° in bearing, and should cover an angle of 5° from the horizontal. A coarse display should be provided to cover the full range of the equipment, and a fine display covering an area of 4° in bearing and 4,000 yards in range.

6. **Selectivity.** The equipment should have a high degree of discrimination in bearing and range. It must have the highest attainable power of resolution to reduce ground clutter and permit recognition of actual targets.

7. **General design.**

(a) The vehicle in which the set is installed should be of the type of the International Half-track M.14. The vehicle and the set must be capable of being waterproofed up to the normal standard. The equipment should be as low and inconspicuous as possible consistent with the performance required of it.

(b) The power unit of the vehicle with its existing power take-off may be used to drive the generator for the Radar units and aerial turning gear; the generator should be mounted on the vehicle and a suitable clutch and gearing provided. An independent power unit would, however, be acceptable provided it can be carried in the vehicle and run on standard R.A.S.C. petrol.

(c) The detachment required to man the equipment should not exceed 3, including a driver-operator. They must be able to operate the set under cover from weather, either in the vehicle or under side shelters.

(d) Provision should be made for a No. 19 or 22 W/T set in the vehicle.

(e) Time into action from arrival on site should not exceed 5 minutes; provision for rapid and easy orientation, with a visual telescope, is required. Warming-up time should not exceed 5 minutes. The equipment should be capable of rapid withdrawal in emergency.

(f) The equipment should be fully tropicalized, and separate provision should be made for incorporating adequate air conditioning and cooling.

(g) Easy access to parts and components for maintenance and replacement should be provided for in the design; it must be robust enough to allow of operation in the field for considerable periods with little skilled attention.

(h) So far as is possible the equipment should be designed to resist enemy jamming counter action.

APPENDIX V

PROVISION OF MAJOR RADAR EQUIPMENT

RADAR H.A.A. FIRE CONTROL

Class	Type	Duty	Wave-length	Provision	From To	Remarks
A.A. No. 1 Mark I	G.L. I	Local warning and aid to Visual control; modified to embryo, unseen Fire control.	5 m.	410A	Aug. 1939 April 1941	Modifications and addition of E/F attachment started Aug. 1940. Type replaced by G.L. II.
Mark II	G.L. II	Local warning and unseen Fire Control.	5 m.	1679	June 1940 Aug. 1943	First type designed for "unseen." 204 supplied to U.S.S.R.
A.A No. 3 Mark I	G.L. III A.P.F.	Unseen Fire Control.	10 cm.	667	Nov. 1942 Feb. 1945	Canadian type—600 supplied for British Army, 67 for Canadian forces.
Mark II	G.L. III	Unseen Fire Control.	10 cm.	876	Dec. 1942 April 1945	British type—900 order increased to over 2,000 but later reduced. 50 supplied for U.S.S.R.
Mark III	Baby Maggie	Emergency Fire Control.	1¼ m.	176	Sept. 1943 Mar. 1945	200 approx. ordered—small reduction later. 50 to U.S.S.R.
Mark IV	Auto-follow	Emergency Auto Fire Control and prototype for Mark VII	10 cm.	(50) (Ordered)	Early 1946 et seq.	50 emergency order and for development of full Service pattern, Mark VII.
Mark VII	Auto-follow	Fully designed Auto-follow Fire Control.	10 cm.	—	—	326 ordered—no deliveries by end of war and order cut.

RADAR LOCAL WARNING

A.A. No. 4					
Mark I	Z.P.I. G.L. III(C)	Local warning and "putting on," A.P.F.	1¼ m.	as for A.P.F.	Nov. 1942 Feb. 1945.	Part of G.L. III(C)—not satisfactory.
Marks II and III	Light warning	Local warning and "putting on," G.L. III	1¼ m.	933	1943 and '44	Inter-Service design—total order 2,000 approx. 50 supplied to U.S.S.R.
Mark V	Gorgonzola	Warning Tactical Control, "putting on."	10 cm.	22	May and June	Special provision by A.D.R.D.E. for 21 Army Group, Normandy operations.
Mark VI	M.Z.P.I.	Warning and Tactical Control.	10 cm.	(150) (Ordered)	End of 1945 et seq.	No deliveries by end of war.

RADAR SEARCHLIGHT CONTROL

A.A. No. 2					
Marks I and II	S.L.C.	Direction and control of A.A. Searchlights; emergency types.	1¼ m.	100	Sept. 1940 Feb. 1941	24 trials models by A.D.R.D.E. and 76 by firm with minor improvements.
Marks III to VII	S.L.C.	Service equipment design.	1¼ m.	8,796	April 1941 Dec. 1943	Includes 100 prototype models for improved pattern.
Mark VIII	S.L.C.	Emergency Auto-follow type and prototype for Mark IX.	10 cm.	50	Sept. 1944 Feb. 1945	Emergency type and for development of Mark IX.
Mark IX	S.L.C.	Service Auto-follow design.	10 cm.	(300) (Ordered)	June 1946 et seq.	No deliveries by end of war; order placed for 1,000 but later reduced to 300.

APPENDIX V—continued

PROVISION OF MAJOR RADAR EQUIPMENT—continued

Class	Type	Duty	Wave-length	Provision	From To	Remarks
C.D. No. 1		RADAR COAST DEFENCE				
Marks I to III	CD/CHL	Anti-invasion, Surface craft tracking, Convoy, protection.	1½ m.	120	Dec. 1940 Sept. 1941	Permanent structure stations; replaced by longer range, centimetric types.
Mark IV	Mobile	Long Range cover and Tracking of surface craft.	10 cm.	62	12 emergency sets, July 1941–Mar. '42 50 May to Aug. 1942	Incorporating N.T. 271 parts.
Marks V and VI	Gibson Box	Long Range cover and Tracking of surface craft.	10 cm.	205	Sept. 1942 Feb. 1944	Transportable; operated in container or transferred to structure as Mark VI.
Mark VI	Tower	Long Range cover and Tracking of surface craft and low aircraft.	10 cm.	13	Sept. 1942 July 1943	200-ft. tower stations.
		RADAR COASTAL ARTILLERY FIRE CONTROL				
C.A. No. 1						
Mark I	—	Battery Fire Control.	1½ m.	nil	—	
Marks II and III	—	Battery Fire Control.	10 cm.	99	Aug. 1942 June 1945	Cancelled and modified as Mark II.

C.A. No. 2 Mark I	Fire Command.	10 cm.	(60)	Included in provision for C.D. No.1, Marks IV, V and VI.	As for C.D. No. 1, Marks V and VI, but L. 17 unit added.
C.A. No. 1 Mark IV	Charlie	Battery fire control and Fall-of-Shot observation.	3 cm.	6	A.D.R.D.E. provision Mar. to May 1944.	Complete Battery fire direction and fire correction set.

Notes

(1) In addition, the U.S. provided 135 plus 165 (on loan) of their pattern S.C.R. 584 Auto Fire Control sets that became A.A. No. 1, Mark V; a supply of 30 of their S.C.R. 545 in replacement of some 75 of the loaned 584 sets was arranged but subsequently cancelled.

(2) All C.D. No. 1, Marks V and VI, C.A. No. 1 Marks II and III, and C.A. No. 2, Mark I modified to medium power working, C.D. No. 1, Mark VI (Tower) Stations modified to high power working.

(3) A special form of C.A. No. 1, Mark IV, classed as Mark V, was put into production, but subsequently diverted to other uses.

(4) Three emergency patterns of F.A. equipment were put into production, but subsequently cancelled owing to delayed deliveries and end of the war emergency.

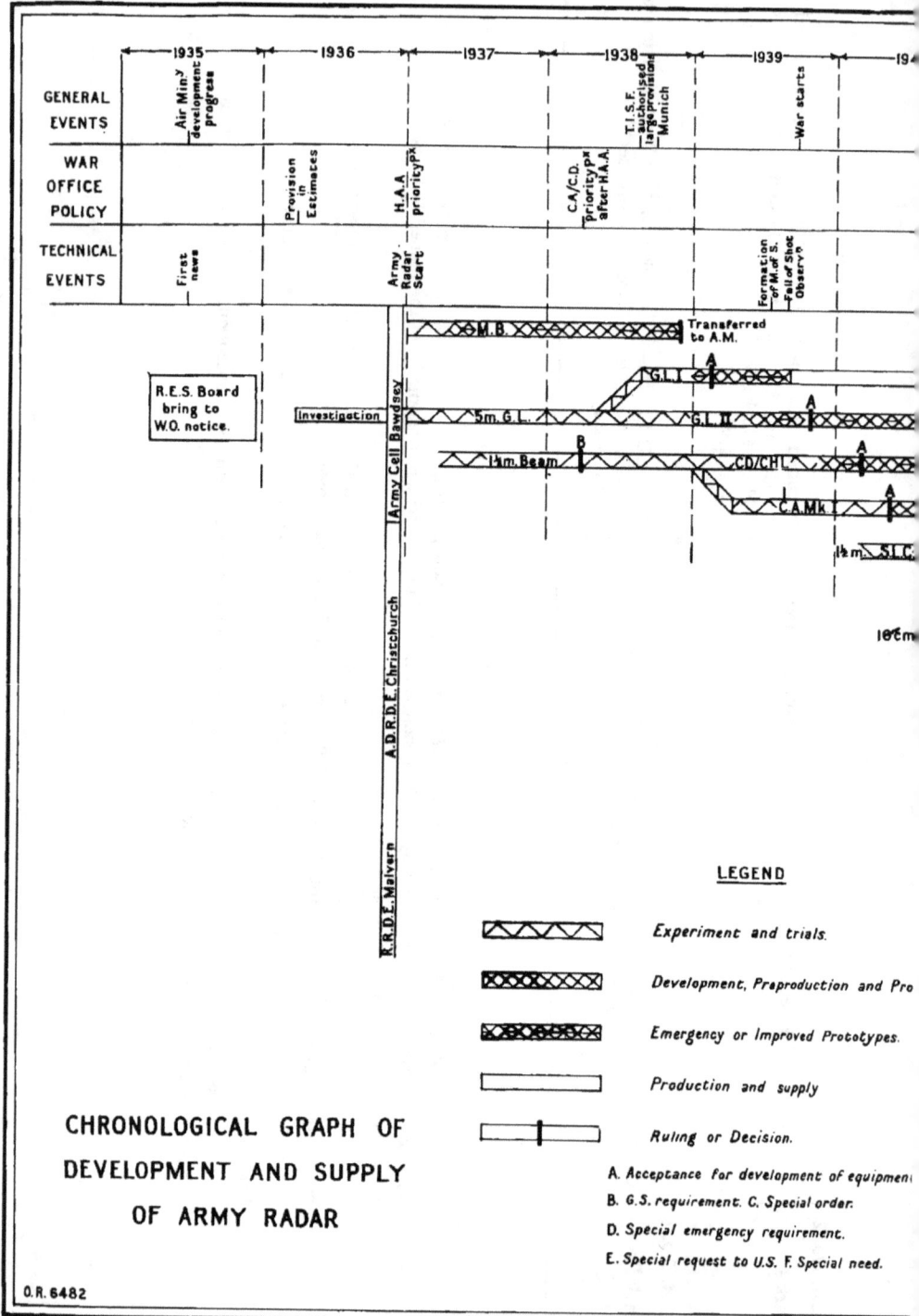

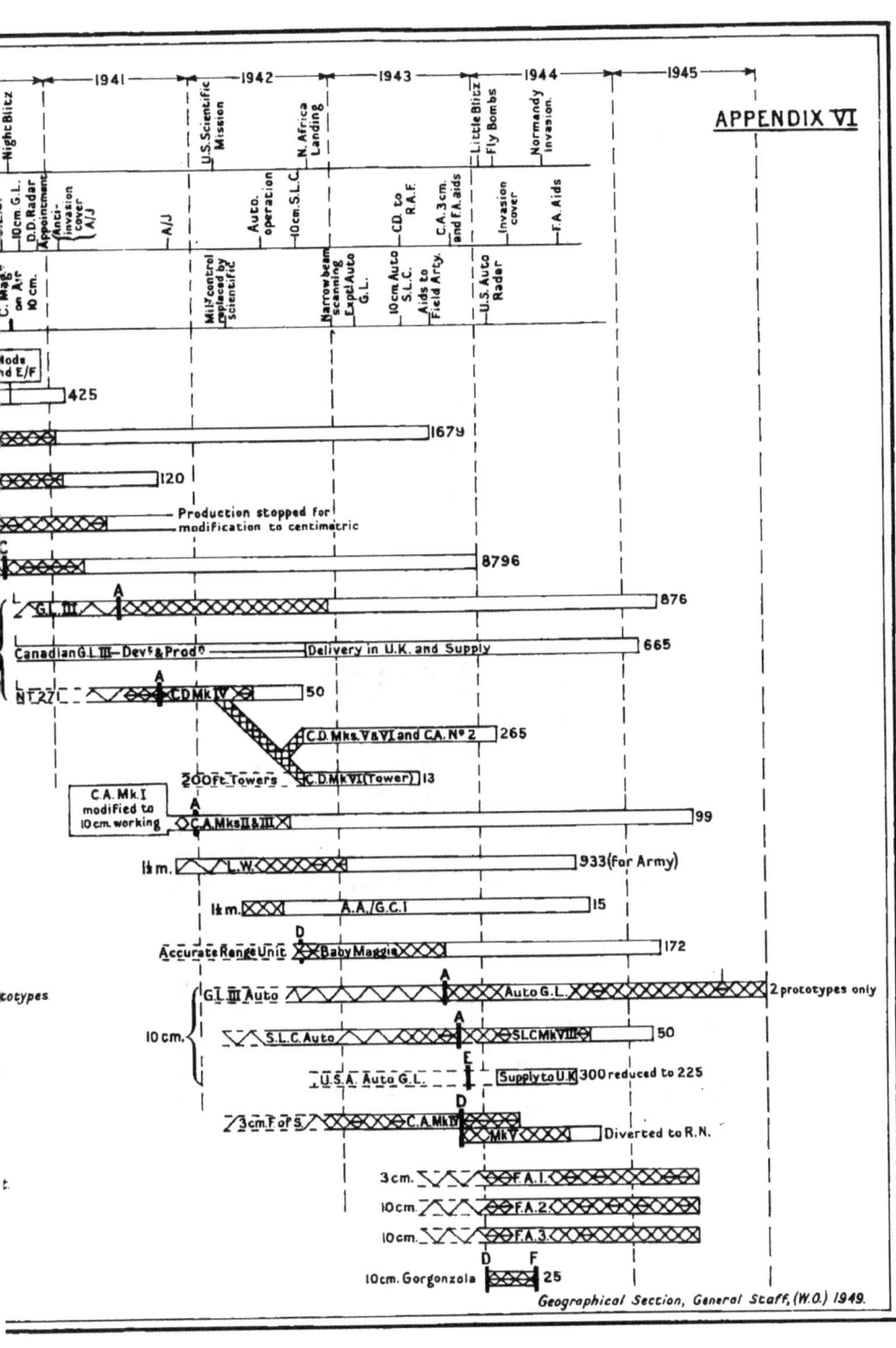

APPENDIX VII

Illustration 1.

G.L. II—A.A. No. 1, Mark II—Receiver Unit

A.T.S. Operators checking and adjusting the aerials—fixed to the rotatable Receiver cabin ready for action. The accurate position of the different sets of aerials is essential for accurate operation of the set. The wheels of the trailer cabin have been removed and the frame has been levelled by the jacks on a firm base in this case; a level wire-mesh "mat" surrounding the set can just be distinguished in the photo—some of the supporting pickets can be seen to the left of the cabin.

Illustration 2

G.L. III—A.A. No. 3, Mark II—Aerials

This aerial system may be compared with that shown in Photo No. 1 to gain some appreciation of the effect of using centimetric wave-lengths. The aerials can rotate above the cabin roof and be moved in elevation from the horizontal to the zenith, without movement of the cabin itself. In the case of this set separate aerials were used for Transmission and for Reception—the small dipole at the focus of the paraboloid reflector in each case is protected by a perspex cover, and that for the Receiver is rotated rapidly inside the cover to give double echo switched beam readings for accurate angular measurement in bearing and in elevation—by echo matching (see Photo No. 16.)

The N.C.O. Operator in charge is seen checking the "lining up" of the Radar beam with the visual by means of a special telescope fixed to the frame of the aerial system.

Illustration 3

G.L. III—Operators in action inside cabin

The senior operator in charge is seen on the right with two display tubes in front of her. She detects incoming targets on the Coarse (upper) Range tube and selects the target to be engaged, by means of a strobe; this automatically brings the echo signal from that target only on to the Fine Range tube enabling her to follow it accurately in Range. At the same time it brings the double echo signals on to the Bearing tube and the Elevation tube which are facing the centre and left operators. These operators, by matching the two echoes on each of their tubes, provide the essential angular measurements. Each of these actions on the Range, Bearing and Elevation tubes automatically transmits the information continuously to the Predictor. See Photos 4, 15 and 16.

Illustration 4

G.L. III—Range Tubes

This photo gives a close-up view of the Coarse Range tube and the Fine Range tube can just be seen below it. The Time Base and a number of Target echoes can be seen and the range scale is clearly visible. It is on the display of these targets that the one to be engaged is selected and strobing the particular echo brings that one echo signal on to the Fine Range tube and on to the Bearing and Elevation tubes also, so that it can be followed accurately in all three senses without disturbance by other echo signals. See also Photo No. 3.

Illustration 5

G.L. Auto—A.A. No. 3, Mark IV

This photo shows the external appearance of the Automatic following G.L. set that was produced at the end of the war and was to form the prototype for the fully developed pattern of Service equipment, the Mark VII.

    This set was small in comparison to the Mark III and little more than one-third of its weight: only one operator was required. It was fully automatic in following the selected target in range as well as in bearing and elevation, but when necessary manual operation could help it on the selector tube through trouble, or could control following in Range. It will be noted that it has a single Aerial and Reflector for both Transmission and Reception which effected a reduction in the mass to be moved in following the target.

    This Mark IV model was the first set designed specifically for complete Automatic Following in all three senses.

Illustration 6

1½ m. S.L.C.—A.A. No. 2

This photo is representative of the various forms—Marks I to VII—of Radar direction of Searchlights; it shows a standard Searchlight 90 cm. Projector on which the S.L.C. is fixed directly.

The Long-Arm visual means of control of the projector is retained and can be seen to the right of the projector. On the barrel of the projector can be seen the two pairs of Receiving aerials—(Yagi) for "split" readings of bearing and elevation; a framework, also fixed to the back of the barrel, carries two aerials—the longer one on the right is the Transmission aerial while the other is for I.F.F. The three operators —one for selection of target and the others for the angular following—are accommodated at the rear with their display tubes, and are carried round with the "U"-arms and turntable of the projector—they are free from elevation movement of the barrel. Echo matching is not involved but the spot of light on the angular measurement tubes has to be kept on the central cross-wire.

Illustration 7

10 cm. Auto S.L.C.—A.A. No. 2, Mark VIII

Automatic Following (or officially, Aiming) was applied only to the standard 150 cm. Searchlight projector which had largely replaced the 90 cm. type. In this photo it will be apparent that 10 cm. working has materially refined the design and the "Christmas Tree" effect in Photo No. 6 has disappeared.

The Yagi aerial on the left is for I.F.F. and the Radar aerial is in the tube in the middle of the paraboloid reflector on the right; both are fixed to the trunnions of the barrel of the projector and move with it. The axes of the Radar and the I.F.F. beams are maintained carefully lined up with the axis of the searchlight beam.

One Radar operator only is required for the selection of the target and strobing the particular echo to bring the automatic angular following mechanism into action. He is accommodated in a water-proof curtained cover with the Selector tube behind one of the "U"-arms, and is carried round with the turntable—the cover can be seen in the photo below the aerial reflector.

The Mark VIII pattern shown was produced as an emergency type and also to act as a prototype for the fully designed and strengthened Mark IX for full Service equipment.

Illustration 8

1½ m. Light Warning—A.A. No. 4

A general purpose, Inter-Service type of Radar set; the vehicle pattern as shown was the form in which it was most generally used.

The aerial system projecting through the roof of the light van is rotatable by power or hand drive; it consists of an upper and a lower pair of Yagi aerials—in the photo the aerials are looking forward. The aerials are dismounted for travel and carried on the roof—holding-down attachments can be seen in the photo.

A P.P.I. and a Range tube display are provided inside the cabin as well as room for the operator and for plotting and reporting.

For Army use this equipment was applied to warning of aircraft approach for Light A.A. units and for local warning and "putting on" centimetric type G.L. sets.

Illustration 9

Gorgonzola—10 cm. set—A.A. No. 4, Mark V

This set was an emergency provision for the Normandy landing force. The Trailer cabin was originally for the G.L. II Receiver, and in it were accommodated the high power 10 cm. N.T. 277 Radar assemblies, provided with power and hand rotation. The aerial system can be seen on the roof through which it was fed by wave-guide.

Immediately above the roof can be seen the "cheese" type reflector and the projecting wave guide with its widened orifice at the centre of the cheese. Above the cheese is a wire mesh reflector for the I.F.F. aerial which can be seen projecting forward.

This set had good warning range and could be used with reasonable effect also as a tactical control set.

Illustration 10

Coastal Artillery Fire Direction—C.A. No. 1

This photo shows the standard pattern of Radar station for the control or direction of fire of Counter Battery and Close Defence guns. It is a 10 cm. Radar set with separate Transmission and Reception aerials and reflectors fed by wave-guides, carried on a small tower above the operating room to which is also attached a small office and the power supply chamber. Rotation of the aerial system is effected by power drive, but movement can alternatively be manually controlled. Continuous rotation is not usually required and the normal movement through any desired arc up to 360 degrees is arranged so that under power, the direction of movement is automatically reversed at the arc limits. No movement in elevation is provided.

Illustration 11

C.A. No. 1, Mark III on Tower

In cases where the height of site above sea-level is insufficient for range, the C.A. No. 1 set is raised on a 60 ft. tower as shown in this photo. The power supply remains on the ground and only the essential operating compartment is at the head of the tower.

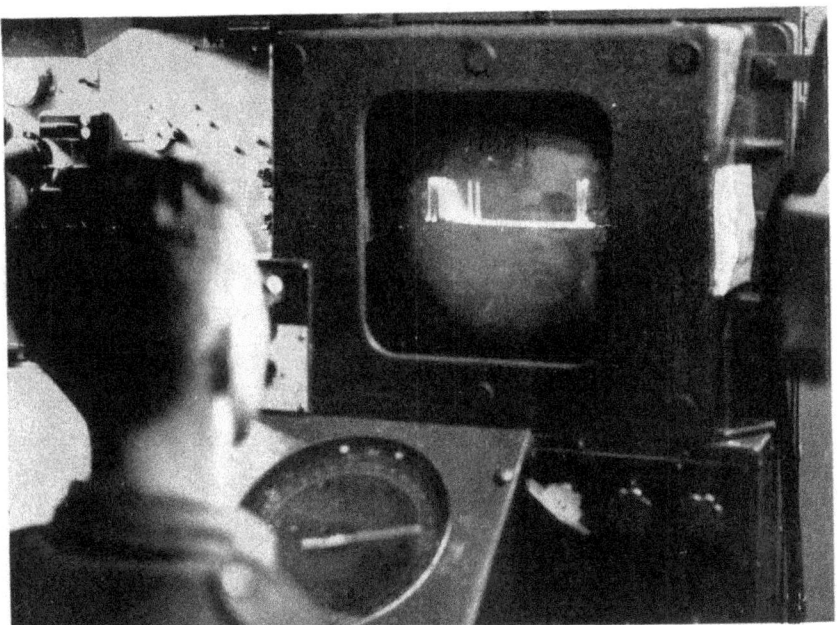

Illustration 12

C.A. No. 1—Internal

This photo shows the Bearing tube of the set in front of one of the two operators; the main Selector and Range tube display is to the left and does not appear in this picture. The Bearing operator controls the movement of the aerials and the dial below the tube gives him the true bearing of the target he is engaging.

In this case double echoes from two targets can be seen; that on the left appears to be the selected target and the operator has the echo signals accurately balanced in amplitude and therefore he is providing the true and accurate bearing of the target. The other pair of echoes on the right of the display are not balanced—if that target had to be followed the aerials would have to be moved in a counter-clockwise direction to balance the echoes.

Illustration 13

L.A.A., G.R. set—A.A. No. 6

The Radar component of the Predictor in this equipment provides accurate Range only, as an aid to visual direction, through the predictor, of fire for the Light A.A. (Bofors) gun seen in the foreground.

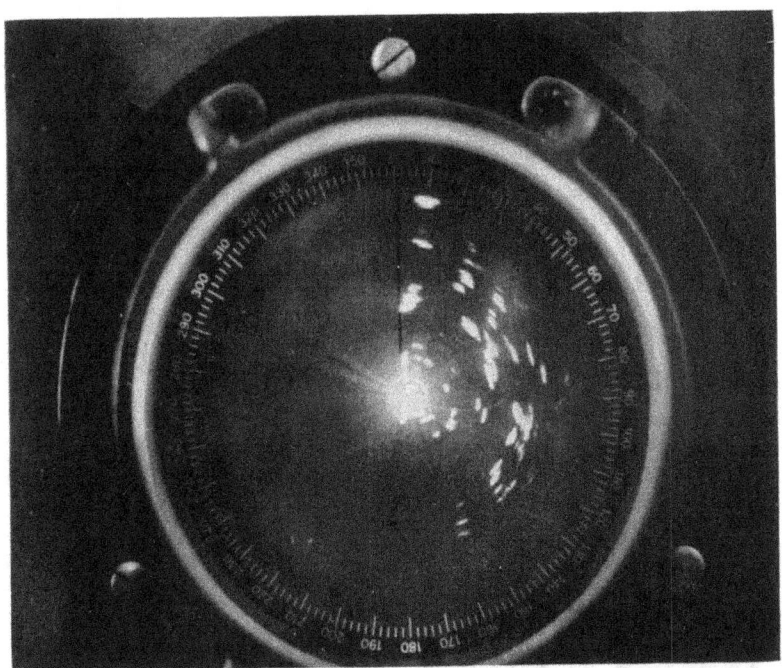

Illustration 14
P.P.I. Display

This photo is of the Plan Position Indicator type of display that has been shown diagrammatically in Figure 5. The dial is graduated circumferentially in degrees and can be set to conform to the compass bearings of the particular site at which the set is in action.

The radial Time Base rotates continuously—it can just be distinguished about the 300 degree mark. As it rotates any echo-producing object causes a "paint" to be made on the screen and a number of these appear in the photo. With a target moving in any direction its echo will be painted each time the Time Base sweeps over it. In the picture several of the paints indicate moving targets—others such as those close in to the centre (i.e. at fairly short range) do not show movement and are presumably due to some structure, ground surface, or other fixed object.

RANGE MEASUREMENT

(A) Coarse Range tube showing single target echo brightened by strobe patch

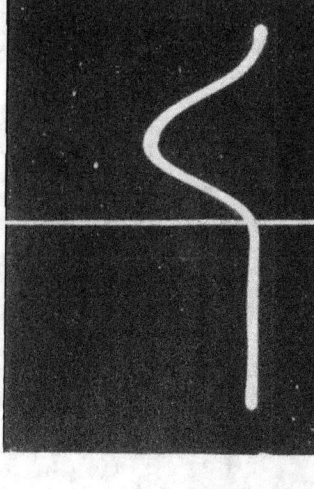

(B) Fine Range tube, showing target echo on the crosswire

Illustration 15

Type A Display

This photo shows the appearance of a break on a Horizontal Time Base —in this case that of a Coarse Range tube as in the G.L. III set. This target echo has been strobed and appears on the Fine Range tube for accurate range reading and following. In the second picture the break is enlarged to permit of greater accuracy in centering the commencement of the break on the cross-wire. See also the diagram in Figure 3 and Illustration No. 4.

BEARING MEASUREMENT

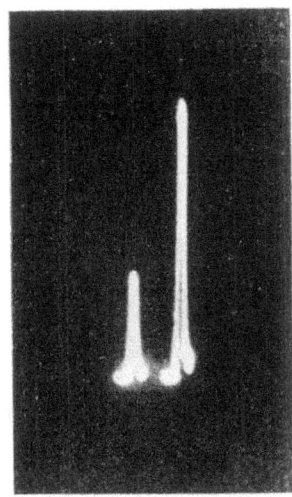

(A) Off Target 1¼° counter clockwise

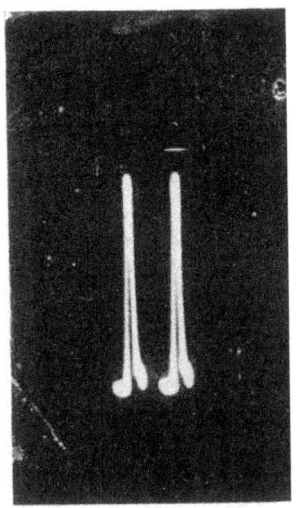

(B) On target

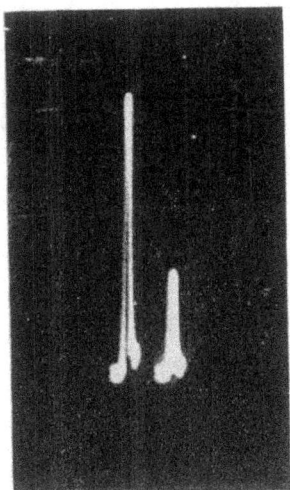

(C) Off target 1¼° clockwise

Illustration 16

Echo Matching

For increased accuracy of angular measurement the comparison of a pair of echo signals obtained by Beam switching is used. In this photo the appearance of the signals on a Bearing tube is shown and it indicates the direction of movement necessary to bring them into balance, thereby permitting continuous following of the target. When out of balance there is a phase difference between the signals—see Appendix VIII, Figure 8.

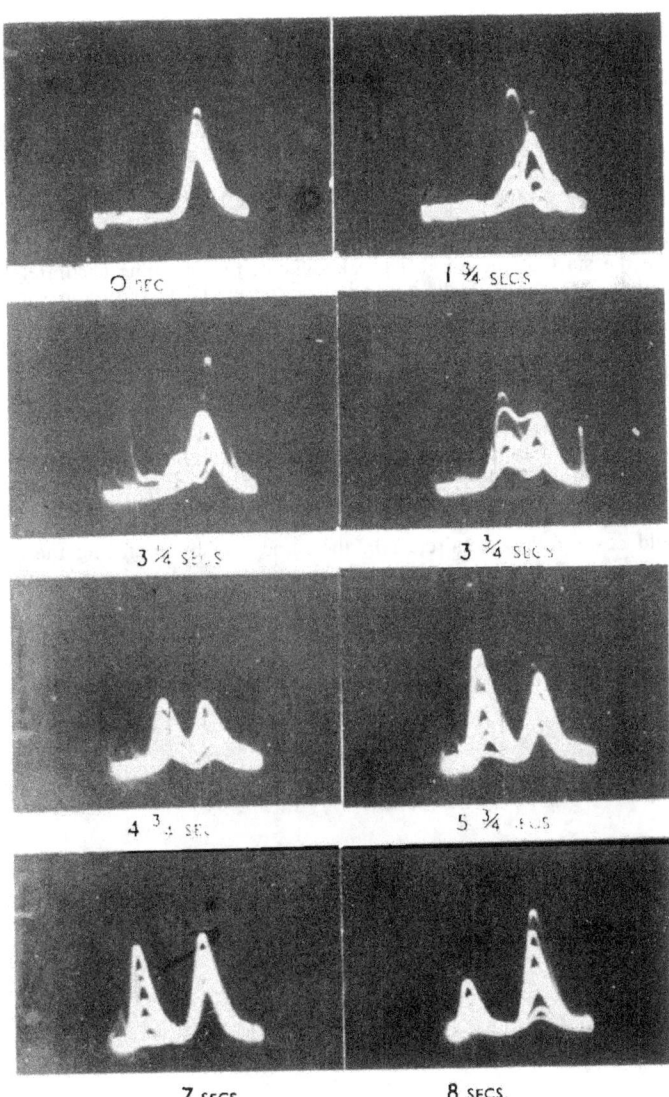

Fine Range Tube—A.A. No. 3, Mk. II, G.L. Mk. IIIB
Target sowing one bundle of Window

Illustration 17
Window

This photo shows the effect of dropping a single packet of Window material from an aircraft. The size of the strips of Window is appropriate to the wave-length of the observing set and the quantity of strips in the packet is designed to give an echo signal equivalent to that from the aircraft.

The break on the Time Base appearing on a Fine Range tube is shown at short intervals from the time of dropping the packet. It can be seen that the packet has opened up and produced a sufficient confusion to make the start of the aircraft break difficult to determine accurately, in less than 2 seconds. This confusing of the actual start of the wanted echo continues until the travel of the aircraft separates its echo sufficiently from that of the slower moving Window material. The fluttering of the Window echo can be seen and it is apparent that no real attempt at accurate reading of the aircraft break becomes possible for 6 or 7 seconds.

Though it is possible to recognize the tip of the aircraft echo gradually moving to the right relative to the Window echo, it is the actual start of the break that has to be used for accurate measurement. If the aircraft continued to eject packets of Window at intervals of some 10 seconds it could provide for itself cover or confusion on the Radar screen. Similarly, it could provide an infected area persisting for some time which would cover following aircraft in the same way by confusing the echo display.

APPENDIX VIII

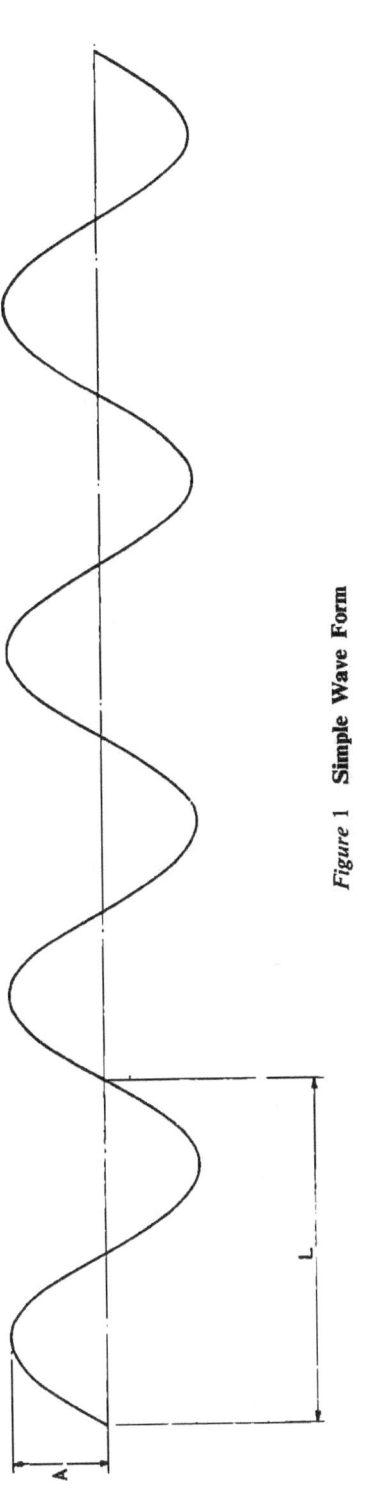

Figure 1 **Simple Wave Form**

NOTES

(i) "A" is the amplitude of the wave-form. "L" is the wave-length i.e. one complete cycle.

(ii) The frequency of the wave-form is the number of complete cycles repeated each second, expressed in Megacycles per second—Mc/s—for Radar wavelengths, in Kilocycles per second—Kc/s—for normal Broadcast Radio, or in cycles per second for ordinary A.C. electric lighting supply.

A megacycle is 1,000,000 cycles.

A kilocycle is 1,000 cycles.

(iii) The relation between wave-length and frequency in describing any wave transmission is:—
Wave-length = frequency = speed of travel of radio waves, i.e. 300,000,000 meters per second (or 186,000 miles a second).

Examples:

(a) A 5 meter wave-length = a frequency of $\dfrac{300,000,000}{5}$ c/s = 60 Mc/s

(b) A 10 cm. wave-length = a frequency of $\dfrac{300,000,000}{1/10}$ cycles a second = 3,000 Mc/s.

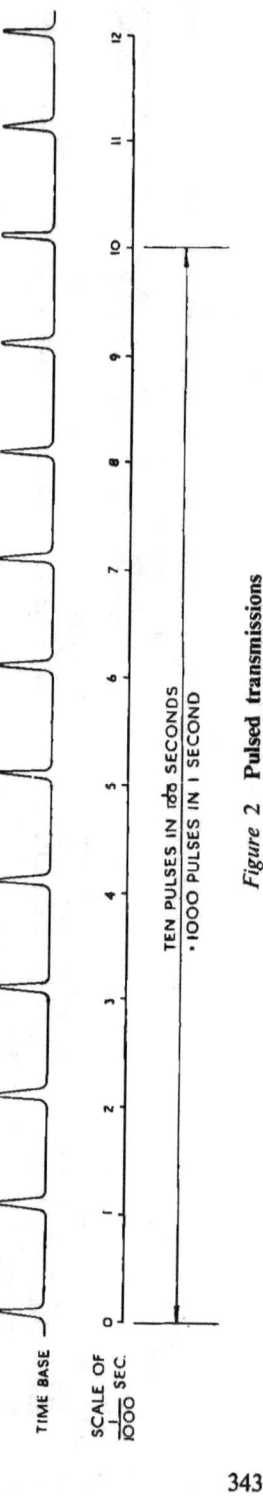

Figure 2 **Pulsed transmissions**

NOTES

(i) The diagram represents a Pulsed Transmission, each Pulse being indicated as a "blip" rising from a horizontal line of Time Base.

(ii) The Pulse Duration is the length of time during which a Pulse is transmitted; this is followed by a Blank or No Transmission period.

(iii) The Pulse Recurrence Frequency is the number of Pulses, each separated by similar Blank periods, that are emitted in 1 second.

(iv) If the Pulse duration is $\frac{1}{1,000,000}$ second and the Pulse Recurrence Frequency is 1,000 a second, the length of the Pulse in space is 300 metres and the length from Pulse to Pulse is 300,000 metres, leaving a Blank space of rather less than 299,700 metres with no transmission; this space is clear for the Return Echo Signals from Targets to be received.

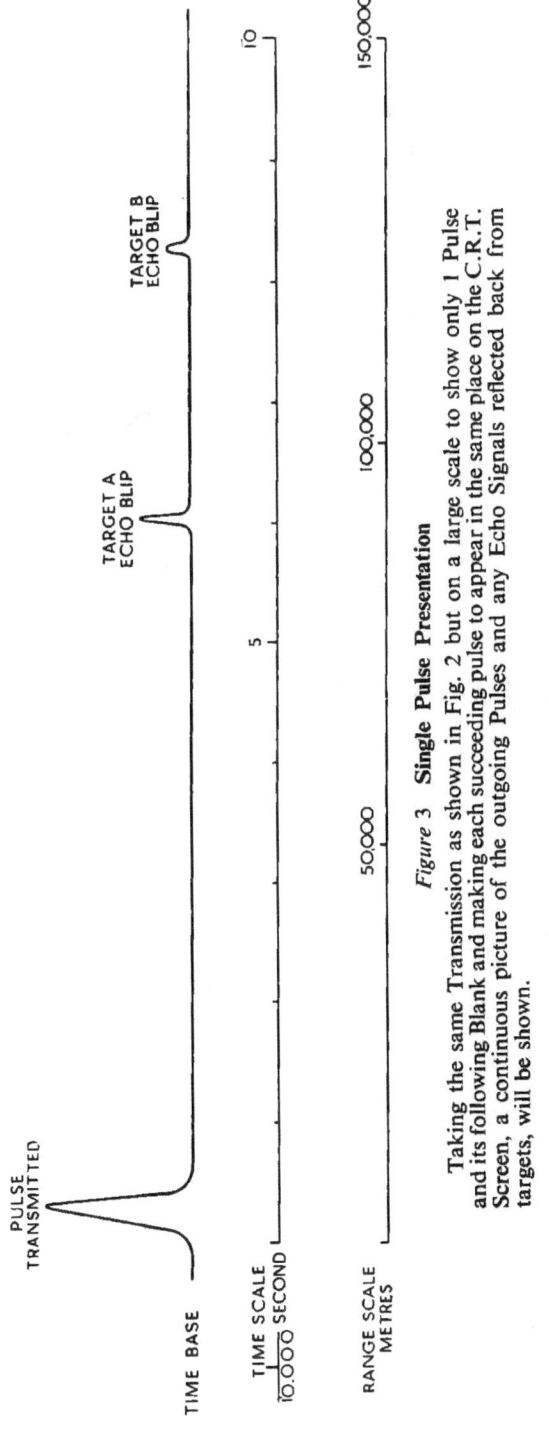

Figure 3 **Single Pulse Presentation**

Taking the same Transmission as shown in Fig. 2 but on a large scale to show only 1 Pulse and its following Blank and making each succeeding pulse to appear in the same place on the C.R.T. Screen, a continuous picture of the outgoing Pulses and any Echo Signals reflected back from targets, will be shown.

NOTES

(i) The Range measurement to a Target blip is one half of the apparent Time distance from the start of the transmitted pulse, as the wave has to travel out and the reflected wave has to return over the same distance.

Target A reads a Range of about 90,000 metres;
Target B reads a Range of about 123,000 metres.

(ii) This form of presentation is the Horizontal Time Base that is used for Range Measurement, Target Selection or Detection for Early Warning. It is the normal form for A.A. Fire Control and for Searchlight Control.

(iii) See also Appendix VII, Photos 4 and 15.

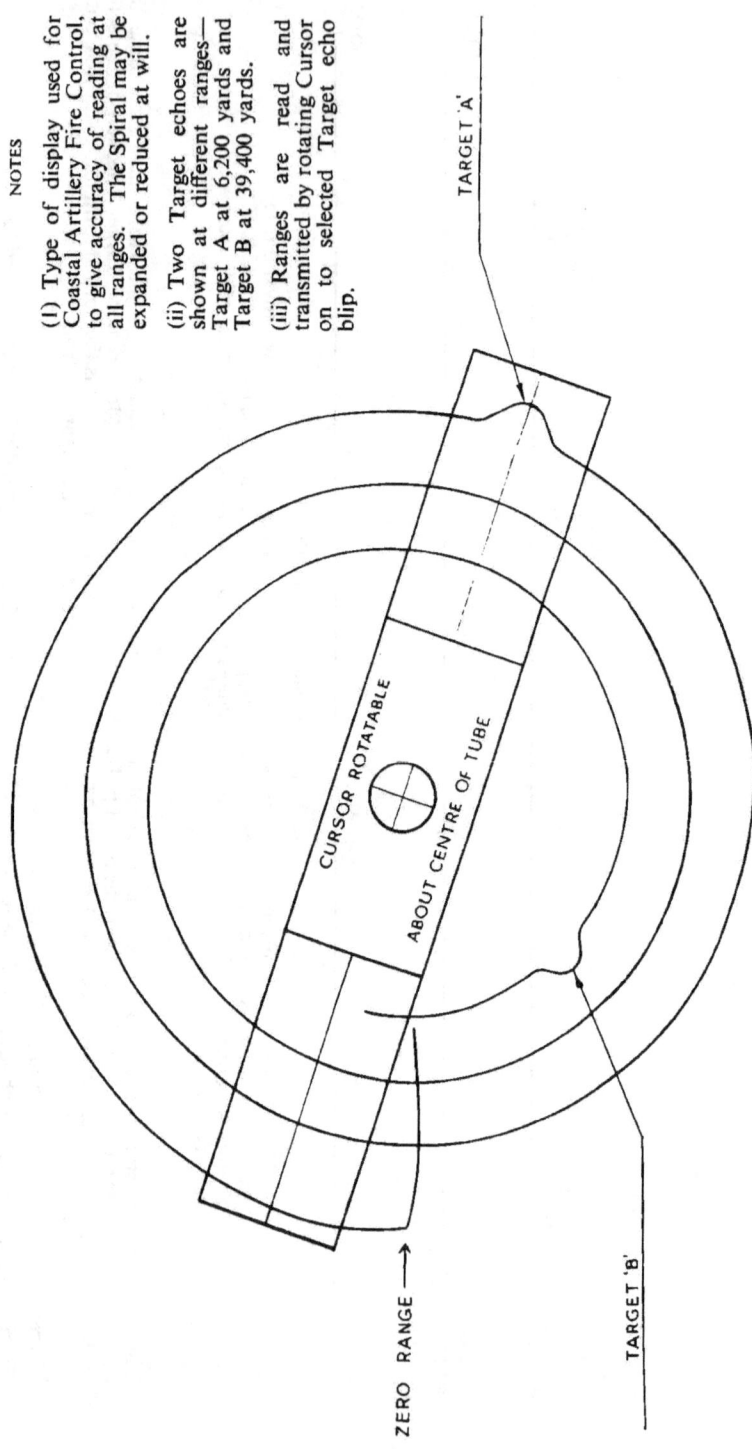

Figure 4 C.R.T. Presentation Picture with Spiral (and Expanding) Time Base

NOTES

(i) Type of display used for Coastal Artillery Fire Control, to give accuracy of reading at all ranges. The Spiral may be expanded or reduced at will.

(ii) Two Target echoes are shown at different ranges—Target A at 6,200 yards and Target B at 39,400 yards.

(iii) Ranges are read and transmitted by rotating Cursor on to selected Target echo blip.

Figure 5
**C.R.T. Presentation of
Plan Position Indicator (P.P.I.)**
of which the Time Base is radial and rotates continuously

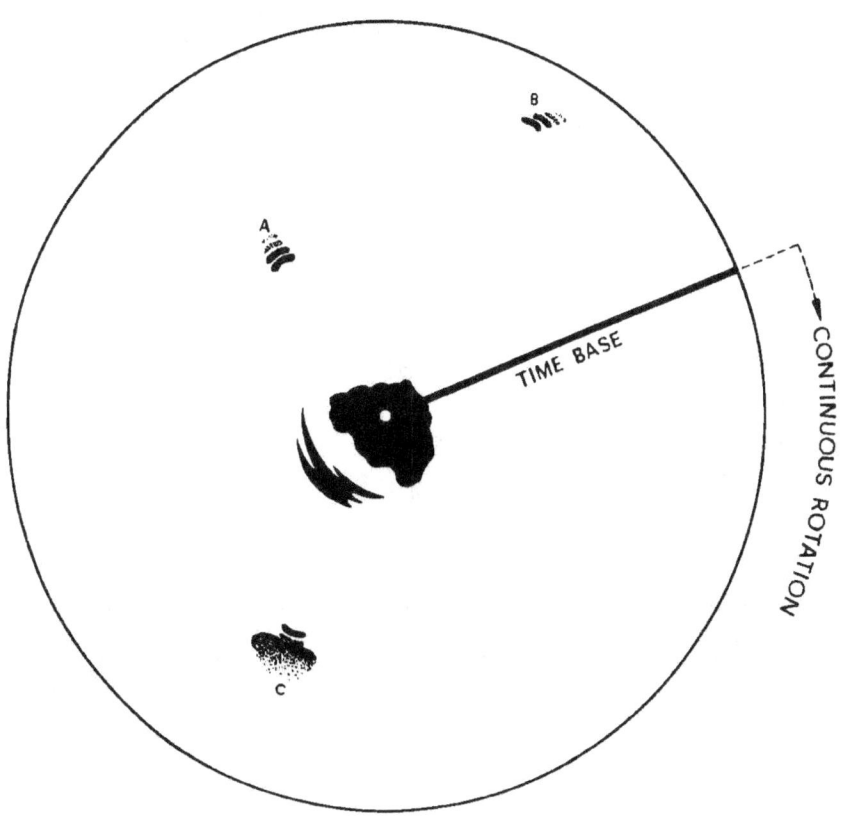

NOTES

(i) Type of display to show Plan Position of all aircraft or objects producing echo signals within a range of 50 miles from the Radar set.

(ii) As the Time Base sweeps round all target echoes are "painted" on the Tube screen and persist for some time; succeeding sweeps of the Time Base make additional "paints" so that after several sweeps the direction of movement can be determined by joining the centres of each "Paint." The range of any Target is measured along the Time Base radially outward from the centre.

Target A is shown as a Direct Approacher at a range of 24 miles.

Target B is shown as moving W.S.W. from its first pick-up position 48 miles N.N.E. of Radar set.

Target C is referred to separately in Chapter 21.

(iii) The centre dark mass represents local ground clutter and the mass to the S.W. represents clutter from high hills about 12 miles distant from the set.

(iv) A Bearing or Azimuth ring scale is provided around the C.R.T. screen (*not* shown in the diagram) to enable the Bearing at any echo signal to be read.

(v) See also Appendix VII, Photo No. 14.

Figure 6
Gridded Presentation of C.A. Fall of Shot

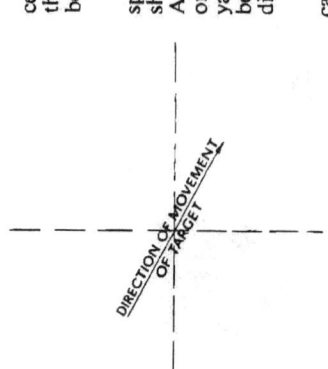

NOTE

This form of C.R.T. presentation was first used for the 3 cm. Coastal Artillery Set that became C.A. No. 1, Mark IV.

The target echo is kept centred on the cross wires and thereby transmits range and bearing continuously.

Echoes from the shell splashes of a 3-gun salvo are shown giving a "straddle." Any shell splash, surface craft, or other object within 1,000 yards in range and 3° in bearing will appear on the display.

The position of the echoes can be related direct to that of the target vessel echo and corrections can be made as may be necessary to bring fire on to the target.

See also Chapter XVII.

Figure 7 **Gridded Presentation for Field Artillery Use**

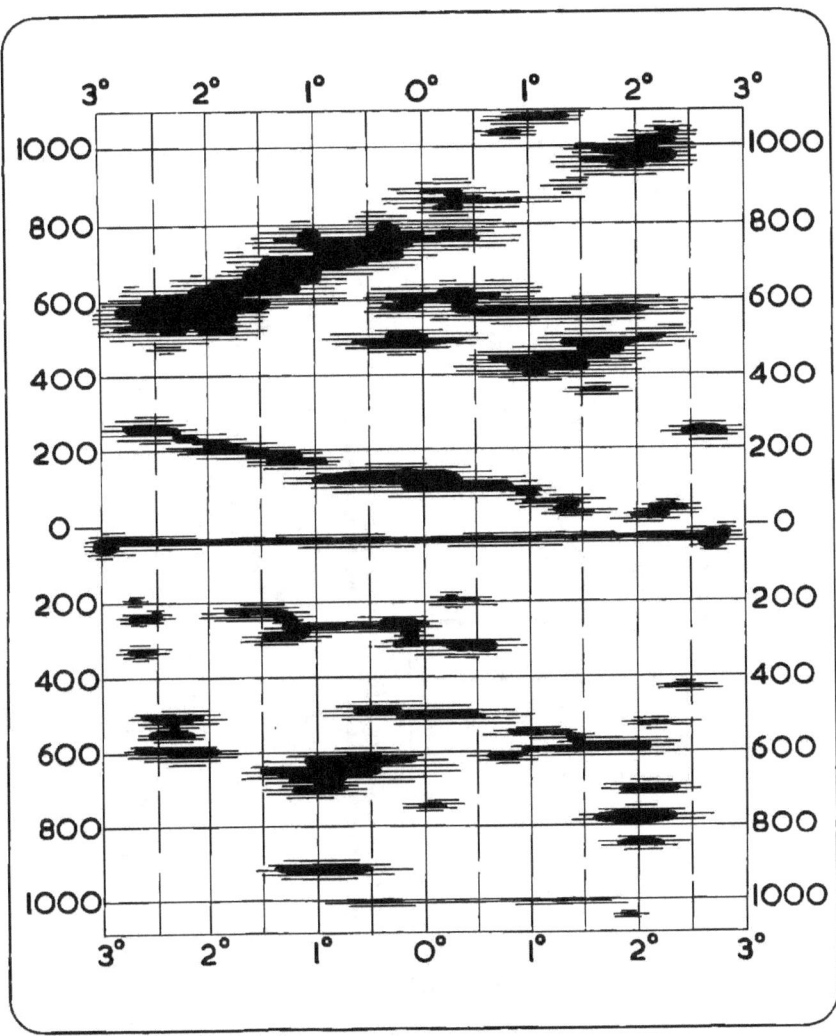

NOTES

(i) Special form of C.R.T. presentation to permit of centering the grid on a selected point or object on the ground and measuring the position of a ground burst shell in relation to that point or object.

(ii) The dark patches shown in the diagram represent ground reflections or clutter from particular slopes or objects; the Radar set used has the power of discriminating between various degrees of intensity of clutter.

(iii) A Tank may give an intense reflection that can be differential from ground clutter and could be engaged by bringing its echo on to the central cross lines of the grid. This is similar to the use against Ships illustrated in Figure 6.

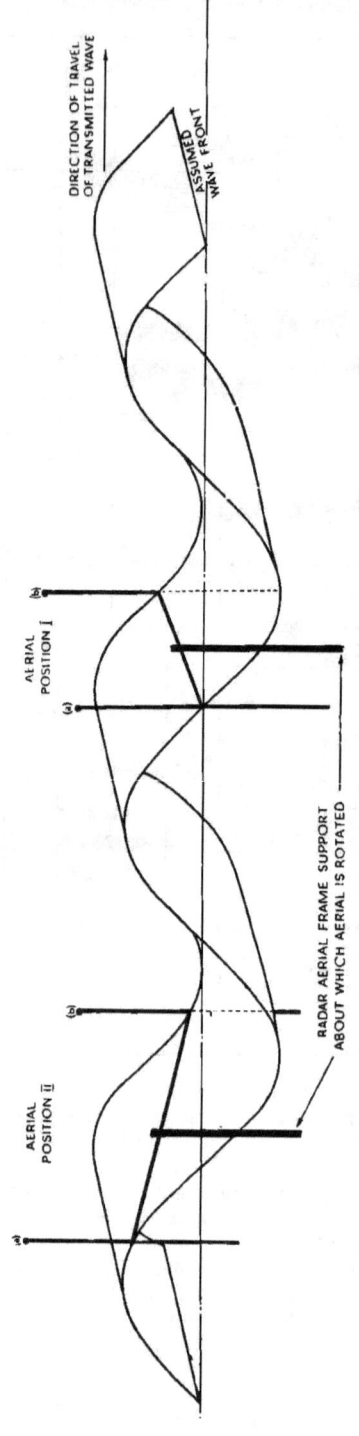

Figure 8 Diagram of an imaginary Strip of a wave of transmission showing the wave meeting a rotatable Aerial Frame with two vertical dipoles

NOTES

(i) In position I the two vertical dipoles are "in phase" in that they are both intersecting the *same part* of the wave-form.

(ii) In position II the aerial frame has been rotated slightly clockwise and dipole (*a*) receives a particular part of the wave earlier than dipole (*b*); the two are therefore *not* in phase and there is a minute fraction of time between them in receiving the same part of the transmitted wave.

The diagram suggests a phase difference at about 60° or 1/6 of a complete wave cycle; in the case of a 10 cm. wave-length or 3,000 Mc/s frequency transmission this difference would

be, in time $\dfrac{1}{6 \times 3{,}000 \times 1{,}000{,}000}$ or $\dfrac{1}{18{,}000{,}000{,}000}$ of a second.

349

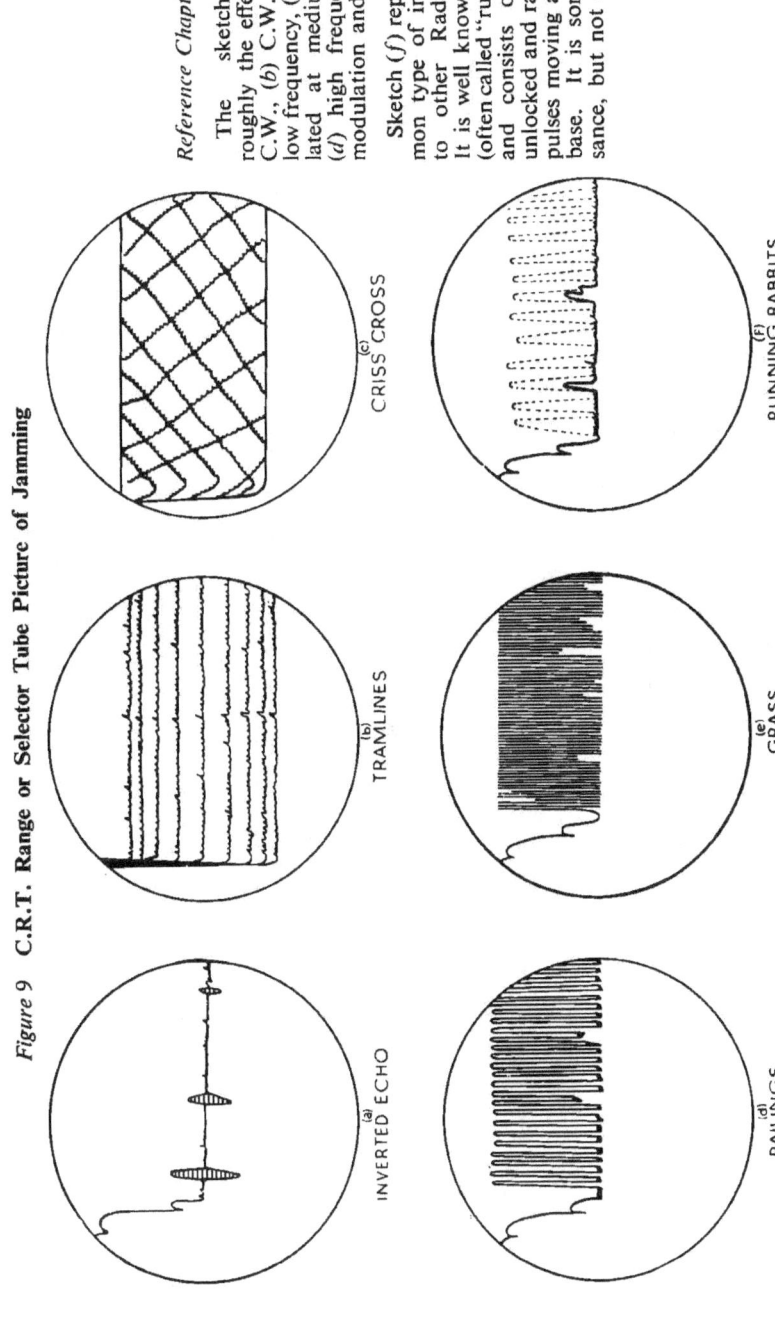

Figure 9 C.R.T. Range or Selector Tube Picture of Jamming

Reference Chapter XXI.

The sketches represent roughly the effect of (*a*) pure C.W., (*b*) C.W. modulated at low frequency, (*c*) C.W. modulated at medium frequency, (*d*) high frequency or pulse modulation and (*e*) "noise."

Sketch (*f*) represents a common type of interference due to other Radar equipment. It is well known to operators (often called "running rabbits", and consists of a series of unlocked and rather ghost-like pulses moving along the time-base. It is sometimes a nuisance, but not serious.

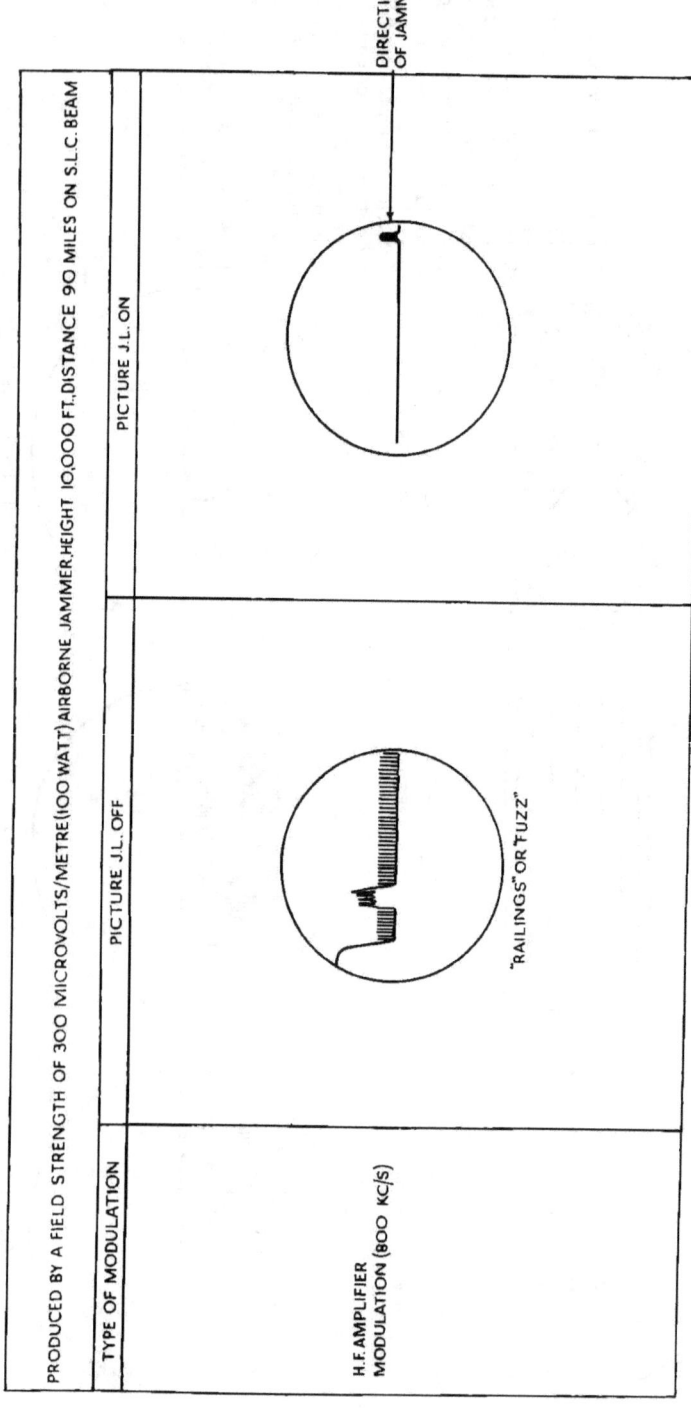

Figure 10 **An Example of S.L.C. Selector Tube Picture of Jamming**
Reference Chapter XXI.

SOUTH EASTERN COASTAL RADAR CHAIN.

BEACH APPROACH COVERAGE OF CD/CHL CHAIN. - 1941.

DOTTED ARCS SHOW RANGE LIMITS.

AREAS OF WAVE CLUTTER LIABLE TO OBSCURE ECHOES FROM LANDING CRAFT SHOWN.

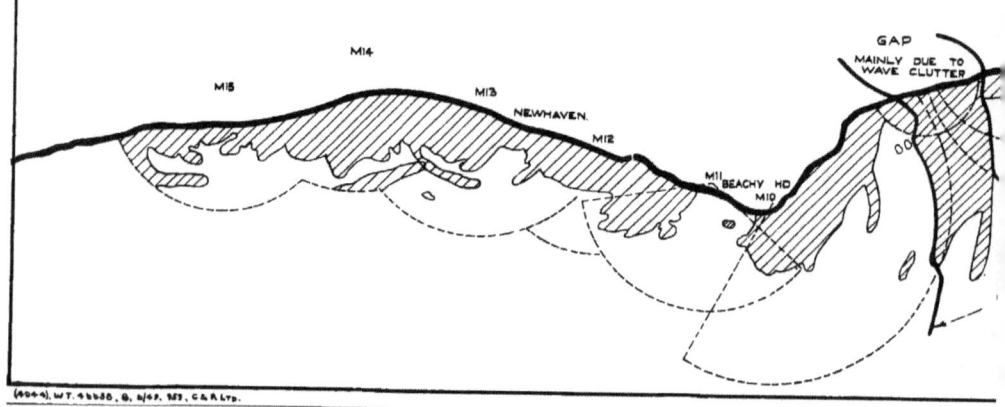

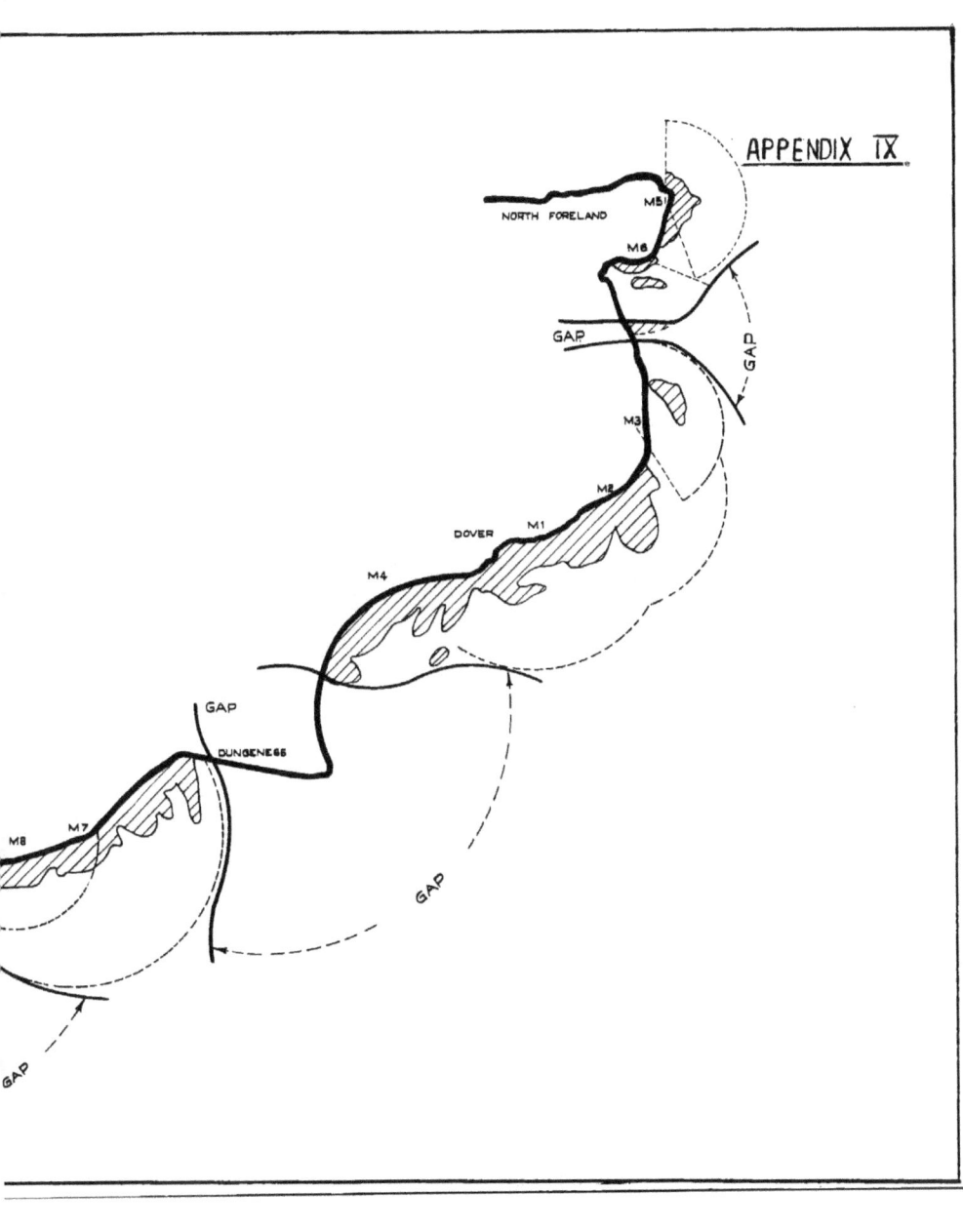

RESTRICTED

Printed under the authority of His Majesty's Stationery Office
By Unwin Brothers Limited, Woking and London

Bk. 4975. Wt. 46638. 8/50. U.B.L. G428.

SECOND WORLD WAR
BRITISH DIVISIONAL HISTORIES

All Written Shortly After The Cessation Of Hostilities

Authoritative and scholarly they are essential to any serious study of the Second World War

THE FOURTH DIVISION 1939 to 1945

The British Fourth Division was engaged in World War Two from beginning to end. It was part of the BEF in 1939, left France from Dunkirk in 1940, moved to Tunisia and fought throughout the campaign in Africa. It then moved to Italy fighting all the way up the Italian mainland to Forli and Faenza before being sent off to Greece to aid the civil power during the Greek Civil War. It was an honourable division which through the fortunes of war did not take part in the great adventure in Normandy, being thereby consigned to the relative background in the military history of the Second World War. Such divisions are unjustly given less attention than those which were chosen for Overlord, but their histories are none the less of great importance. This history is one of those narratives. The book is illustrated with a number of photographs and a good set of maps.

SB 9781474536646

HB 9781474536943

THE FIFTH BRITISH DIVISION 1939-1945

The story of the Fifth British Division 1939-1945 begins with the division in the BEF in France in 1940 which it joined from reserve division status. It returned to the UK and underwent training before taking part in the Madagascar operation. Then it went to India and Persia before moving to the Middle East Theatre in 1943 where it took part in the conquest of Sicily before moving into Italy. It fought through much of the Italian Campaign before finishing the war in Lubeck, having made the final move to France and then Germany shortly before the end of the war.

SB 9781783316083

HB 9781783316649

TAURUS PURSUANT
A HISTORY OF 11TH ARMOURED DIVISION

11th Armoured Division is widely recognised as one of the best British armoured divisions in the Second World War, earning its spurs in all of the most famous actions of the North West European campaign and commanded by the desert legend Pip Roberts. Originally printed in occupied Germany soon after WW2 had finished, this is an excellent Divisional History, with good, clear colour maps and a well written narrative. A Roll of Honour by regiment (Name, Date and Place) completes this fine history.

SB 9781783315611
HB 9781783316663

43RD WESSEX DIVISION AT WAR 1944-1945

This is the story of the 43rd Division from its arrival in France during Operation Overlord in June 1944 through to the end of the war with Germany. It relates how the division fought and where, and is illustrated with 21 maps. The division was engaged on the River Odon, and at Hill 112, then in the Seine crossing, the attempted relief at Arnhem, at Groesbeek, in Operation Blackcock and the advance to Goch and Xanten. It also took part in the Battle of the Rhineland and in Operations Plunder and Varsity and made its final move to capture Bremen in 1945. A very readable and an important Divisional History.

SB 9781783316076
HB 9781783316571

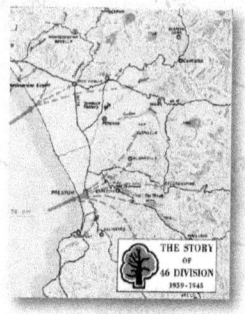

THE STORY OF 46 DIVISION, 1939-1945

Although not one of the D-Day Divisions, like many other formations, it was fundamental to the success of the broad plans for the direction of the war. The fighting in North Africa and Italy is detailed. Good photos, coloured maps, rolls of commands, staff, awards, and an Order of Battle complete this very good contemporary Infantry Divisional that is scarce in its original 1948 printing.

SB 9781783316335
HB 9781783316564

THE PATH OF THE 50TH

THE STORY OF THE 50TH (NORTHUMBERLAND) DIVISION IN THE SECOND WORLD WAR 1939-1945

This is a very valuable history of the 50th (Northumberland) Division in the Second World War. The division fought in France, North Africa, Sicily, and took part in the D-Day landings, finally ending the war in Holland. illustrated with photographs and maps.

SB 9781783316090
HB 9781783316632

THE HISTORY OF THE 51ST HIGHLAND DIVISION 1939-1945

The 51st Highland Division fought and lost in France in 1940, was reborn, and fought and won in the North African desert, Sicily and finally in North Western Europe from D-Day to the end of the war. As a division the men earned the respect of friend and foe alike, and this is their story. Amply illustrated with 36 photographs, 18 maps and battle plans (many coloured) that help the reader to follow the course of the conflict. A good index (persons, units and place names) and a statistical battle casualties list complete this good WW2 Divisional History.

SB 9781474536660
HB 9781474536950

MOUNTAIN AND FLOOD
THE HISTORY OF 52ND (LOWLAND) DIVISION

The 52nd Lowland Division was one of very few "special" divisions of infantry, in that it was trained for mountain warfare, although it spent much time after D-Day locked in battle on the flat lands of the North European coastal plain. This history of the division starts before the war in England, and goes on to describe operations in France in 1940. For four years they then trained and waited, before forming part of 21st Army group, and fighting the Germans in France, Holland and Germany. As with all good divisional histories, it is the story of men in battle that counts, and this volume is no exception.

SB 9781783316069
HB 9781783316588

THE STORY OF THE 79TH ARMOURED DIVISION OCTOBER 1942 - JUNE 1945

A magnificent and fully illustrated official history of Britain's 79th Armoured Division - the specialised unit which developed and operated 'Hobart's Funnies', the adapted tanks which carried out a range of tasks on D-Day and after ranging from mine clearance to bridge laying. Follows the unit from its formation to victory in Europe.

SB 9781783310395
HB 9781783316731

www.naval-military-press.com

The Naval & Military Press offer specialist books and ground breaking CD-ROMs for the serious student of conflict. Our hand picked range of books covers the whole spectrum of military history with titles on uniforms, battles, official and regimental histories, specialist works containing medal rolls and casualties lists as well as titles for genealogists, medal collectors and researchers.

The innovative approach we have to military bookselling and our commitment to publishing have made us Britain's leading independent military bookseller.

www.naval-military-press.com

www.ingramcontent.com/pod-product-compliance
Lightning Source LLC
Chambersburg PA
CBHW071358300426
44114CB00016B/2098